Reading, 'Riting, and Reconstruction

The Education
of Freedmen
in the South,
1861–1870

Robert C. Morris

The University of Chicago Press
Chicago and London

The University of Chicago Press, Chicago 60637
The University of Chicago Press, Ltd., London

88 87 86 85 84 83 82 81   5 4 3 2 1

ROBERT C. MORRIS is assistant professor of
history and education and head of special
collections, Teachers College, Columbia
University

LIBRARY OF CONGRESS CATALOGING IN PUBLICATION DATA

Morris, Robert Charles, 1942–
  Reading, 'riting, and reconstruction.

  Bibliography: p.
  Includes index.
  1. Afro-Americans—Education—History.
2. Freedmen—Education—History. 3. Reconstruction. I. Title.
LC2801.M64   371.97'96073   80–25370
ISBN 0–226–53928–8

To Darlene, my wife, and
John Hope Franklin, my teacher

Contents

Preface   ix

Acknowledgments   xiii

1 An Army of Civilization   1

2 Yankee Schoolmarm   54

3 The Black Teacher   85

4 The Southern White Teacher   131

5 Educational Objectives and Philosophy   149

6 Reading, 'Riting, and Reconstruction:
  The Content of Instruction in
  Freedmen's Schools   174

7 Political and Social Issues   213

Notes   251

Bibliography   305

Index   331

Preface

  Like most aspects of Reconstruction, the Northern-based effort to educate Southern blacks has long been a subject steeped in emotion and controversy. Depending on one's point of view, the program was either a necessary crusade for reform or an instance of harmful interference in another region's affairs, a benevolent endeavor or a calculated move to control Negro votes. Freedmen's educators were either courageous heroes or reckless, meddlesome fools, beloved Yankee schoolmarms or hated "nigger teachers." From the 1860s on, the topic has hardly lent itself to dispassionate analysis.

  In *Reading, 'Riting, and Reconstruction* I have undertaken to present a comprehensive picture of this controversial school experiment from its beginnings during the early part of the Civil War through 1870, the final year of educational activities under the Freedmen's Bureau. Over this period more than fifty religious and secular organizations participated in Southern Negro education, establishing schools and colleges, providing teachers, and, after the creation of the bureau in 1865, working with that federal agency to coordinate operations covering seventeen states and the District of Columbia. Toward the end of the 1860s aid societies had several hundred Northern white teachers in the field along with black instructors from both sides of the Mason-Dixon line and a relatively small number of Southern whites. Receiving an average salary of $20 to $50 a month, educators supported by the societies often took on responsibilities outside of the classroom, acting as missionaries, social workers, dispensers of charity, labor superintendents, legal advisers, and even politicians. As an instructor from upstate New York aptly described her activities in the South, "I preach & teach & civilize & reconstruct generally!"[1]

  Writers sympathetic to the freedmen's school enterprise have emphasized its idealism and devotion to principle. Using a bit of poetic license, the noted black scholar W. E. B. DuBois compared it to the religious crusades of the Middle Ages. The "crusade of the New England schoolma'am," DuBois wrote in 1901, "seemed to our age far more quixotic than the quest of St. Louis seemed to his. Behind the mists of ruin and rapine waved the calico dresses of women who dared, and after the hoarse mouthings of the field guns rang the rhythm of the alphabet."[2] To DuBois and others who have dealt with freedmen's education these instructors were genuine nineteenth-century heroes.

Less sympathetic historians like Henry L. Swint and George R. Bentley, on the other hand, have focused their attention on the Northern educator's supposed disregard for the feelings of the South's white majority. According to this interpretation, Southern opposition was in large part an understandable reaction against "the Bureau schools' advocacy of the ideas of 'social equality,' of remaking the South in the image of New England, and of converting the freedmen into Republican voters." In his 1941 monograph *The Northern Teacher in the South*, Swint contended: "The Southerner did not fear the education of the Negro—he feared Negro education in the hands of the typical 'Yankee teacher,' under the program of education advanced by the Radical legislatures."

Though divided in their sympathies, these admirers and critics of Northern efforts seem to agree in their perception of the school program as an idealistic movement substantially influenced or even dominated by abolitionists. For the most part participants are assumed to have been committed to essentially egalitarian objectives in the area of civil and political rights. While by no means rejecting this interpretation entirely, the present study attempts a more balanced appraisal by showing the extent to which idealism and lofty goals were tempered by pragmatism and an awareness of the need for sectional accommodation. As in the ante-bellum period, the underlying philosophy of black education was moderate in tone, stressing order and a kind of gradualism—the idea that prejudice and discrimination would diminish as Negroes rose on the "scale of civilization." Through careful examination of educators' statements, class lessons, and textbooks prepared specifically for freedmen it is possible to obtain a fairly good idea of what these reformers wanted students to learn not only in the academic sphere but with regard to the vital issues of Reconstruction. It is also possible on a broader scale to follow the changing attitudes of this important reform element from the early Civil War years to the end of the nineteenth century. Such a survey yields valuable insights into the factors contributing to the rather precipitant retreat from Reconstruction in the 1870s.

Black education was a cooperative venture involving the Freedmen's Bureau, benevolent societies, and a corps of teachers that by July 1870 numbered over 3,500. Bureau and society officials set the overall policy, but individual instructors played an important role in determining how policies were implemented at the local level. I have consequently devoted considerable attention to the backgrounds, social and racial attitudes, and politics of those who actually conducted the classes from elementary school through college. In completing this study, I have attempted to shed light on a specific aspect of nineteenth-century reform and to explain the motivation, attitudes, objectives, and policies of those persons engaged in educating freedmen during the Civil War and Reconstruction. To some degree I have linked black education in this period to what came before and what followed, outlining in brief a course of development from the ante-bellum years to the early 1900s. With more and more pieces of the jigsaw puzzle falling into place, it is to be hoped that we will soon have a detailed study of Negro public and private education in the United States.

Acknowledgments

Although not realizing it at the time, I began this book during my first week of graduate study at the University of Chicago when, with the assistance of Professor Richard J. Storr, I selected a research topic for Louis Gottschalk's introductory course in historical method. Having previously devoted considerable attention to black education while an undergraduate, I chose to write a paper on sectional bias in textbooks used in Freedmen's Bureau schools. Such was the beginning of a prolonged and intense investigation, which in time grew from several seminar papers to a master's essay, a dissertation, a reprint series (*Freedmen's Schools and Textbooks: Black Education in the South, 1861–1870*), and the present work. In the course of these projects I profited greatly from valuable suggestions made by professors Storr, Daniel J. Boorstin, Walter Johnson, Mark M. Krug, Arthur Mann, Richard C. Wade, and especially John Hope Franklin, who unselfishly shared his time and ideas throughout the long gestation period of this publication. Without imposing his interpretations, he helped me to refine and strengthen my own even in those areas where we disagreed. The list of historians who have provided insights in their particular areas of expertise also includes Lawrence A. Cremin, Richard B. Drake, William Gillette, Louis R. Harlan, Clifton H. Johnson, William S. McFeely, August Meier, and Joel Williamson.

Over the years many people have graciously tolerated my endless discussions of freedmen's education and either offered opinions or asked the kinds of questions that stimulated further thought and research. Of special importance in this respect are Prof. William Dabney of the University of New Mexico, my former students at the University of Maryland and the Newark campus of Rutgers University; colleagues and students at Teachers College, Columbia University; my close friends William

T. Kerr of the New Jersey State Library and Don C. Skemer of the New Jersey Historical Society; my wife Darlene; Mr. and Mrs. Clarence E. Heimbaugh; and my parents—Mr. and Mrs. Chester O. Morris. A word of thanks is also due to Lynda M. Trooskin, who quickly and efficiently turned a patchwork final draft into a neatly typed book manuscript.

I gladly acknowledge the assistance provided by archivists and librarians at the many repositories mentioned in this book's footnotes and bibliography. Those individuals most closely associated with my research are: Elaine C. Everly of the National Archives; Clifton Johnson, director of the American Missionary Association's Amistad Research Center; Sophy H. Cornwell, special collections librarian at Lincoln University; Judith A. Schiff, chief research archivist in the Manuscripts and Archives Division of Yale University Library; Donald A. Sinclair, curator of special collections at Rutgers University Library; Kenneth C. Cramer, archivist of Dartmouth College; Arthur M. Byers, Jr., alumni secretary of Princeton Theological Seminary; and Joyce Ann Tracy, the American Antiquarian Society's curator of newspapers and serials.

In the AMS Press reprint series *Freedmen's Schools and Textbooks* I have collected and introduced as many of the textbooks prepared for the former slaves as possible along with the semi-annual reports of Freedmen's Bureau General Superintendent of Education John W. Alvord. With the kind permission of AMS Press I have included material from my introductions to these volumes in *Reading, 'Riting, and Reconstruction*. Moreover, John Hopper, editor-in-chief for AMS, supplied photographs from the series for use in this monograph. Two other photographs are from the S. Willard Saxton Papers in the Yale University Library and are published with the permission of that institution.

Reading, 'Riting, and Reconstruction is dedicated to two people who have supported this scholarly venture from its inception. Darlene K. Morris not only has shared in the lonely, sometimes painful, process of research and writing, but she has been an astute editor and at times a near collaborator in the production of this study. Although sharing a preoccupied husband with hundreds of freedmen's schoolmarms cannot have been easy, she never ceased encouraging my labors, and I welcome this opportunity to express my deep appreciation.

John Hope Franklin has been equally encouraging as a teacher, constructive critic, and friend. I can think of no higher compliment to an educator than to say that I learned a great deal from him and continue to do so. He and scores of other talented teachers have contributed more to my education than they will ever know.

1 An Army of Civilization

The school established near Fortress Monroe, Virginia on 17 September 1861 was as significant as it was unassuming. Conducted in a front room on the first floor of the teacher's small house and initially consisting of only about half a dozen black students, the classes nevertheless represented the beginning of an educational program which would soon encompass seventeen states and the District of Columbia.[1]

Maintained by Mary Peake, a light-skinned free Negro, in cooperation with the American Missionary Association, this school on the Peninsula emerged at a time when thousands of runaway slaves sought protection in Union-held territory under the provisions of a military ruling labeling them "contraband of war." By the end of September, between fifty and sixty of these "contrabands" were receiving instruction from Mrs. Peake in a curriculum that combined basic academic exercises with liberal doses of religious training. Like her sponsors in the American Missionary Association, she "felt that the teachings of the week-day school ought to be largely preparatory to the rehearsals of the Sabbath school,"[2] a feeling which translated into prayers and hymn-singing in the classroom.

The author of an 1874 history of the American Missionary Association saw irony both in the location of the school and in the color of its teacher. After pointedly noting the proximity of the building to a large seminary that once educated "the proud daughters of the South," he observed that the initial day-school for freedmen stood "on the coast where, two hundred and forty-one years before, the first slave-ship entered the line of the American Continent." Shifting the emphasis to Mrs. Peake, whose father was white, he ended the discussion with an assurance that this woman, the representative of both races, "though by the bitter logic of slavery classed with the oppressed, will be remembered ages hence, as the teacher of the first colored school in the slave States that had legal authority and the protection of the national guns."[3]

Mary Peake succumbed to tuberculosis less than six months after teaching her first class of contrabands, but the American Missionary Association continued its educational involvement in Virginia under the direction of Charles B. Wilder, a member of the AMA executive committee and Gen. John Wool's superintendent of Negroes in the southeastern corner of the state. During the first two years of the war, the Association opened schools at several locations in the Peninsular region, including Hampton, Norfolk, Newport News, Yorktown, Mill Creek, Portsmouth, and Suffolk. In addition, the AMA as early as January 1862 began sending a few missionaries and teachers to join the "Port Royal Experiment" on the South Carolina Sea Islands.[4] At the time of the annual meeting in October, two employees were active on the Islands and thirteen in the vicinity of Fortress Monroe. Although the numbers were not large, they presaged a significant change in priorities for an organization that before 1861 had employed only 8 teachers out of a total of 263 home missionaries.[5]

By the early stages of the Port Royal venture, however, the AMA was no longer alone in offering instruction to Southern blacks. On 8 January 1862 Rev. Dr. Solomon Peck of Boston opened a contraband school in Beaufort, South Carolina, and over the next few months three aid societies sprang up in the North to help meet the physical and educational needs of freedmen. The stimulus for creating the first of these new societies came from Edward L. Pierce, a Massachusetts lawyer commissioned by Treasury Secretary Salmon P. Chase to investigate conditions at Port Royal and make recommendations on how best to organize blacks for cotton planting under government supervision. Pierce, who earlier had served as Gen. Benjamin Butler's superintendent of contraband labor at Fortress Monroe, wrote to the abolitionist assistant pastor of Boston's Old South Church shortly after arriving in the Islands. Conditions were "strange and chaotic," he advised Rev. Jacob Manning, and blacks might well become hopelessly demoralized if measures were not taken "to make them industrious, orderly, and sober." What was needed, according to the young Treasury Department agent, was a corps of freedmen's teachers of "talent and enthusiasm . . . regulated by good understanding."[6]

Manning published the letter in the *Boston Transcript* on 27 January 1862 and helped arrange the first of two meetings leading to the formation of a body to implement Pierce's recommendation. Organized under a constitution adopted on February 7, the Boston Educational Commission took as its objective "the industrial, social, intellectual, moral, and religious improvement of persons released from slavery in the course of the war for the Union." Prominent among the officers of the commission were ministers, businessmen, philanthropists, and such well-known abolitionists as John A. Andrew, Henry Ingersoll Bowditch, George B. Emerson, Dr. Samuel Cabot, and Edward Everett Hale.[7] Governor Andrew was chosen president, and the post of secretary went to Edward Atkinson, a Boston cotton-manufacturing agent who saw in the Islands a potential proving ground for economic theories positing the superiority of free over slave labor.[8]

The commission and the American Missionary Association were products of two conflicting abolitionist traditions. From its inception in 1846 until the beginning of the Civil War, the New York-based AMA had tended toward the evangelical wing of the movement, fashioning a program which combined Christian anti-slavery activity with evangelism, colportage, and a limited amount of educational work in Indiana, Ohio, and Kentucky. The religious orientation of these few ante-bellum schools was pronounced, and teachers were often expected to double as ministers. Extending this approach into the war years, the association sought to employ freedmen's educators with a "missionary spirit" from among the ranks of the "orthodox" or evangelical denominations. Unitarianism, Rationalism, Universalism, and the more liberal philosophies simply had no place in an organization increasingly dominated by Congregationalists. The Boston Educational Commission, on the other hand, was strongly influenced by the secular reformism of the Garrisonians and by the very ethical and religious tenets which the American Missionary Association rejected. In direct contrast to the AMA, the commission envisioned a freedmen's school program that was nonsectarian as well as nonevangelical.[9]

The Boston Educational Commission was soon followed by two more societies, founded 22 February and 5 March 1862. The earlier organization—the National Freedmen's Relief Association—was an outgrowth of efforts by AMA officials Lewis Tappan and George Whipple to involve New York City reformers in the Sea Islands enterprise. In cooperation with Rev. Mansfield French, who visited Port Royal at their behest, the veteran abolitionists put together a relief society that would also promote "civilization and christianity" among the freedmen by teaching order, industry, economy, self-reliance, and self-respect.[10] Two weeks later a public meeting in Philadelphia established the Port Royal Relief Committee. Launched by Garrisonian abolitionist James Miller McKim and supported by wealthy manufacturers like Stephen Colwell and Matthias W. Baldwin, the committee dedicated itself to teaching Southern blacks "the rudimentary arts of civilized life" and instructing them in "the elements of an English education and the simple truths of the Bible divested as much as possible of all sectarian bias." The group would change its name to the Pennsylvania Freedmen's Relief Association in July.[11]

A plan devised for the Treasury Department by Edward Pierce and approved by Secretary Chase called on freedmen's aid leaders to send supplies, teachers, and plantation superintendents to the Sea Islands. After a careful selection process taking nearly a month, the Boston and New York societies dispatched the first boatload of forty-one men and twelve women from New York harbor on 3 March 1862. The contingent comprised abolitionists, underground railroad agents, "socialists," Unitarians, freethinkers, and members of evangelical denominations. There were recent graduates of Harvard, Yale, Brown, and Andover, professors and teachers, engineers, an architect, and the wife of a United States senator—all bound for Port Royal as "evangels of civilization."[12]

Among the evangels were several who would participate in the educational effort. William Channing Gannett was a Harvard Divinity School graduate and the son of Unitarian leader Ezra Stiles Gannett. A Garrisonian abolitionist struggling with the issue of pacifism, the younger Gannett found in the Port Royal Experiment a suitable alternative to military service.[13] Samuel Phillips was a medical student, a devout Episcopalian, and a nephew of the noted abolitionist Wendell Phillips. According to Pierce's description, he "had good business-capacity, was humane, yet not misled by sentiment."[14] Secretary Chase's friend John C. Zachos was an experienced educator from Ohio. Born of Greek parents in

Constantinople, he was a graduate of Kenyon College and had studied at the Medical School of Miami University in Oxford, Ohio. In the 1850s he was associate principal of the Cooper Female Seminary at Dayton, principal of the Grammar School at Antioch College, and the author of a number of textbooks on reading and speaking.[15] On the female side, Ellen Winsor was young but said to be "admirably fitted by character and experience" for the task before her.[16] Representing the National Freedmen's Relief Association, Rev. Isaac W. Brinckerhoff was a Baptist clergyman, a former employee of the American Tract Society, and a future author of educational pamphlets for freedmen. Forty years old when he obtained his commission from the Relief Association, Brinckerhoff left behind a wife and five children.[17]

The passengers aboard the steamer *Atlantic* reached the Islands on March 6 and within two weeks received their assignments from Edward Pierce, who as a special Treasury Department agent had full responsibility for appointing teachers and superintendents. Taking up residence in houses abandoned by the planters, they and later arrivals commenced the difficult process of building an educational program in an unsettled environment. Progress at first was slow. Many instructors came for a brief time, and upon its expiration or for other reasons, returned home, leaving their classes to be disbanded. During the spring and summer of 1862 not more than a dozen schools were in operation, and these were repeatedly interrupted by the heat and by the necessity of assigning some teachers to act as superintendents. Those who tried to combine educational and supervisory functions often found themselves devoting the larger portion of their working hours to relief activities and various aspects of plantation management—labor supervision, discipline, "accounts, pay-rolls, rations to be measured exactly, complaints to hear and satisfy, authority to exert."[18] This emphasis on practical considerations was pervasive enough to prompt one future teacher to confide in her diary: "The danger now seems to be—not that we shall be called enthusiasts, abolitionists, philanthropists, but cotton agents, negro-drivers, oppressors."[19]

At the outset at least, education had to take a back seat to more pressing economic and social matters. "The instruction most needed by the blacks was not in the knowledge of school books," according to the Boston Educational Commission's Committee on Teachers, "but in that which should lead them to appreciate the advantages of civilized life, to relinquish many of the habits and customs of slavery, and to learn the duties and responsibilities of free men." Schools were established on many plantations, "and were highly prized and eagerly attended by old and young," the committee announced in its first annual report, "yet the time and attention required for those offices more strictly belonging to a superintendent left but little opportunity for school-teaching."[20] Within the Boston commission, the influence of Edward Atkinson and Edward Philbrick guaranteed that economic considerations would take priority over school matters. Like the federal agents administering the government's labor system, these two leading proponents of the free-labor thesis were primarily concerned with getting Negroes back to work on the plantations. For Atkinson and Philbrick, the Port Royal Experiment represented a unique opportunity to refute Southern arguments concerning the adverse effects of emancipation by demonstrating that freedmen could raise cotton more efficiently than could slaves.[21]

Cotton production and relief activities became focal points of the Port Royal enterprise, influencing everything from teacher availability to school hours and stimulating controversy over reform priorities. At times the women from the North were even "borrowed and driven to the different plantations to talk to and appease the eager anxiety" of discontented black laborers.[22] Teachers, moreover, usually had to schedule their classes for two or three hours in the afternoon, leaving mornings "for the children to work in the field or perform other service in which they could be useful." When available, classes for adults met in the late afternoon or evening.[23]

With so few Northern instructors teaching in 1862, freedmen had to take up some of the slack by opening schools on their own or assisting in those maintained by the aid societies. When refugees were brought to Saint Helena village from Edisto Island, for example, two freedmen who could read and write educated one hundred and fifty of the children as best they could for five months until Northern teachers were provided. Another black instructor in the village—a woman named Hettie—taught several of her students their letters and words of one syllable before enrolling them in classes held at the Central Baptist Church. Having received only rudimentary instruction from her master's daughter before the war, Hettie transferred the more advanced pupils because "she could carry them no farther." Using these and other examples, Edward Pierce described the situation by noting: "A few freedmen who had picked up an imperfect knowledge of reading, have assisted our teachers, though a want of proper training materially detracts from their usefulness in this respect."[24]

It was not until the fall of 1862 that freedmen's education began to take shape on the Islands, but by the end of the year an estimated 1,727 children were attending classes on Port Royal, Saint Helena, and Ladies islands alone.[25] Between January and September 1863 this total increased to the point where there were more than thirty schools in the area conducted by as many as forty or forty-five instructors representing the American Missionary Association and the three societies in Boston, New York, and Philadelphia. On an average the institutions had a combined attendance of about two thousand students, most of whom were between the ages of eight and twelve.[26]

First-hand accounts by teachers and interested observers add vitality to these statistics by describing the day-to-day operation of individual schools during a period when freedmen's education progressed from simple instruction in the alphabet to more advanced lessons in standard academic subjects. The extent of the progress was suggested by Edward Pierce in an *Atlantic Monthly* article published fifteen months after he relinquished control of the Port Royal Experiment to Gen. Rufus Saxton and the War Department. Basing his generalizations on a return visit extending from 25 March to 10 May 1863, Pierce observed:

> The advanced classes were reading simple stories and didactic passages in the ordinary school-books, as Hillard's Second Primary Reader, Willson's Second Reader, and others of similar grade. Those who had enjoyed a briefer period of instruction were reading short sentences or learning the alphabet. In several of the schools a class was engaged on an elementary lesson in arithmetic, geography, or writing.[27]

To these conventional exercises were added oral lessons developed by the teachers themselves, lessons dealing with the war, politics, slavery, black heroes, abolitionism, and other topics of immediate concern. Ellen Winsor, when drilling a small group of boys and girls "in some dates and facts which have had to do with our history," used the following set of questions and answers:

> *Where were slaves first brought to this country?*
> Virginia.
> *When?*
> 1620.
> *Who brought them?*
> Dutchmen.
> *Who came the same year to Plymouth, Massachusetts?*
> Pilgrims.
> *Did they bring slaves?*
> No.

A teacher in Beaufort used the same format with her students:

> *What country do you live in?*
> United States.
> *What state?*
> South Carolina.
> *What island?*
> Port Royal.
> *What town?*
> Beaufort.
> *Who is your Governor?*
> General Saxton.
> *Who is your President?*
> Abraham Lincoln.
> *What has he done for you?*
> He's freed us.[28]

These exchanges were obviously rehearsed. When students had not been prepared beforehand, the results were less predictable. Charlotte Forten, a cultured young Negro woman representing the Pennsylvania Freedmen's Relief Association, once asked her pupils what their ears were for. One bright-eyed little girl answered promptly "To put rings in." When a second teacher, Mrs. Hannah Hunn, asked some of them the same question, they said "To put cotton in." Another day Miss Forten had been telling the class about metals and, specifically, how they were dug from the ground. Afterward, in review, she asked "Where is iron obtained from?" "From the ground" was the prompt reply. "And gold?" "From the sky!" shouted a little boy.[29]

Industrial schools such as the one in Beaufort offered a more "practical" form of instruction. When examined by Pierce early in 1863, the Beaufort institution met two afternoons a week and was conducted by a lady from New York along with a dozen female assistants. On the day of Pierce's visit there were present "one hundred and thirteen girls from six to twenty years of age, all plying the needle, some with pieces of patchwork, and others with aprons, pillowcases, or handkerchiefs."[30]

Inevitably the antislavery crusade affected the nature of instruction in the schools. The song "John Brown's Body" was a favorite on the Islands, and abolitionist educators like Miss Forten and Laura Towne tried to impart their enthusiasm to the students. Converted to Garrisonian-style reformism in Philadelphia by the Unitarian minister William Henry Furness, Miss Towne had come south to do antislavery work and was critical of Northerners at Port Royal who kept abolitionism "in the background."[31] Miss Forten, the scion of a Philadelphia family that produced several prominent black abolitionists, had been a part of the movement since her days as a student and teacher in Salem, Massachusetts. Her description of two classes which met in the winter of 1862 make it abundantly clear that she and Laura Towne incorporated antislavery lessons in the curriculum. Discussing a class on November 10, she wrote:

> We taught—or rather commenced teaching the children "John Brown," which they entered into eagerly. I felt to the full significance of that song being sung here in S[outh] C[arolina] by little negro children, by those whom he—the glorious old man—died to save. Miss T[owne] told them about him.

On November 13 Miss Forten talked to her pupils about a second hero of the abolitionist movement—"the noble Toussaint [L'Ouverture]." "It is well they sh'ld know what one of their own color c'ld do for his race," she declared. "I long to inspire them with courage and ambition (of a noble sort,) and high purpose."[32]

Knowing that blacks living in relative isolation on the Sea Islands were regarded as among the most backward anywhere,

educators watched the progress of their students with great interest. Many instructors were pleasantly surprised, some enthusiastically reporting that the rate of advancement had been "more
rapid than in any schools they had ever before taught."[33] William
Allen, a teacher employed by Edward Philbrick in 1863 and 1864,
kept a running record of his impressions.[34] Shortly before assuming his responsibilities at Coffin Point, this Harvard-educated
classical scholar visited a class taught by one of his future colleagues. Though admitting his seven years as associate principal
of the English and Classical School in West Newton, Massachusetts had given him little experience with students "in the *a
b c*'s," Allen thought the children "seemed as bright as white
children of the same age." In his own schools he soon encountered pupils who did not understand what they read and others
whose vocabularies were "so small and their ideas so little developed," that it was hard to converse with them. But he also had
students who were "really very intelligent" and understood
"very well." After seven months on the job, Allen was still willing to say: "As far as I have carried my scholars, I do not think
that there is any inferiority to white children."[35]

In making these encouraging statements, Allen and most other
teachers took into account the effects of generations of slavery on
the students. "Of course there are some stupid ones," Charlotte
Forten allowed, "but these are the minority."

> The majority learn with wonderful rapidity. . . . It is wonderful
> how a people who have been so long crushed to the earth, so
> imbruted as these have been . . . can have so great a desire for
> knowledge, and such a capability for attaining it. One cannot
> believe that the haughty Anglo-Saxon race, after centuries of
> such an experience as these people have had, would be very
> much superior to them.

Directly challenging claims of innate racial inferiority, Miss Forten berated those "who, North as well as South, taunt the colored
race with inferiority while they themselves use every means in
their power to crush and degrade them, denying them every right
and privilege, closing against them every avenue of elevation and
improvement."[36]

No one was certain exactly how slavery and discrimination
would affect the race in the long run, but William Gannett in 1865

pointedly cited evidence indicating that in some Northern schools for Negroes black scholars began to fall behind their white counterparts after the age of twelve. Noting the experience at Port Royal was insufficient to test the hypothesis suggested by this evidence, Gannett nevertheless concluded "it is more than probable that the untrained mind of generations will reveal its weakness just where the higher faculties begin to come into exercise."[37]

Gannett's speculation on this sensitive topic appeared in the July 1865 *North American Review* in an article coauthored by Edward Everett Hale. Devoting three pages to school-related matters, the authors undertook to correct "very exaggerated" notions as to "the extent of education already accomplished" at Port Royal. "Perhaps," they surmised, "[teachers], for want of material to form definite reports, were obliged to make general statements at first, and may have colored them too warmly."

Gannett and Hale presented what they thought was a truer picture of the situation at the end of the Civil War. Commencing with a discussion of the freedmen's "intellect," the two men claimed that only the "mental faculties . . . in close connection with the outward senses" were well developed. Blacks had keen powers of observation and remarkable memories. But whereas they apprehended and held detached facts easily, they were slow to comprehend them in connection—were "deficient in the more ideal operations, which require reflection and reasoning." The authors, however, did hold out hope for the future. They noted that the minds of Negroes on the Sea Islands were by no means inactive, nor did their "ignorance appear dulness." At the moment the more sophisticated faculties existed in a dormant state, waiting to be developed. Three years of instruction were obviously insufficient to bring about this major transformation, but it was to the children in the schools that one might "fairly look for evidence of greater mental ability than that exhibited by their parents."[38]

Although the Negro's mental abilities were widely disputed by those familiar with the school program, several teachers confirmed the article's basic description of freedmen's education on the Islands in 1865:

The higher classes have gone through the multiplication table, and in many schools the cardinal operations of arithmetic, with a little geography and history, have been introduced. None can read with perfect confidence, few without frequent hesitation. The majority of the scholars are young children still in their First or Second Primer. In writing and spelling for the length of time spent, the relative advancement has been greater than in reading.

Summing up the results of three years of educational work in one sentence, Gannett and Hale accurately concluded: "With children more ignorant at first than our most neglected street-wanderers, and amid all the difficulties which beset any new undertaking in so unsettled a place and time, the progress thus described is at least satisfactory to those engaged in the work."[39]

During the three years reviewed by Gannett and Hale the freedmen's education movement grew to the point where by the end of 1865 there were schools in all eleven Confederate states plus Maryland, the District of Columbia, Kentucky, Kansas, and Missouri. The number of supporting organizations kept pace. The early central societies branched out into the smaller cities and towns of the North, organizing locals and auxiliaries, while major new associations appeared in New York, Brooklyn, Philadelphia, Cincinnati, Chicago, Baltimore, and Washington, D.C. Negro education in the South received an added boost from the United States Army. Not only did black troops learn to read and write in several of the colored regiments, but commanders and their appointees made provision for educating freedmen in the Mississippi Valley, North Carolina, Virginia, and the Department of the Gulf.[40]

Various attempts to coordinate the operations of a growing number of nondenominational associations resulted late in 1865 in the formation of the American Freedmen's Aid Commission, a loose coalition of societies from the Northeast and Midwest. When announcing its affiliation with the AFAC, the Boston organization, at that time known as the New England Freedmen's Aid Society, expressed its hope that this combination would "simplify, amplify, and energize the great work of elevating the freedman; harmonize the action of all the instrumentalities employed for that end; purify each and all from even the suspicion of sectarianism or partisanship; appeal more strongly to the respect and support of benevolent people both at home and abroad;

command greater influence with the Government, and meet with less opposition at the South, than any one of the societies composing it.''[41]

The ever-recurring issue of religion, however, divided the commission into two factions, which would eventually split apart. The three eastern societies at Boston, New York, and Philadelphia adhered to an essentially secular philosophy of education, while the Western Freedmen's Aid Commission in Cincinnati and the Northwestern Freedmen's Aid Commission in Chicago employed only members of evangelical churches as teachers.[42]

Fragmentation was no less a factor among the sectarian societies. The Congregationalist, Wesleyan Methodist, Free-Will Baptist, and Dutch Reformed churches generally worked through the American Missionary Association, but many others developed their own educational agencies. The most important of these denominational organizations were the American Baptist Home Missionary Society, the General Assembly's Committee on Freedmen of the Presbyterian Church, and the Freedmen's Aid Society of the Methodist Episcopal Church.[43]

Standing somewhere between the secular and religious societies, Quakers were especially active in the freedmen's education movement. Philadelphia Friends participated in the formation of the Pennsylvania Freedmen's Relief Association and established two major Quaker societies with rather imposing names: (1) The Friends' Association of Philadelphia and its Vicinity for the Relief of Colored Freedmen, and (2) The Friends' Association for the Aid and Elevation of the Freedmen. The New England yearly meeting also supported black education by conducting day and evening schools in Washington, D.C.[44]

Not all educational agencies were controlled by whites. The African Methodist Episcopal Church carried on mission and Sunday school work from 1864 to 1868. And the African Civilization Society, which had been founded in 1858 to promote American Negro missionary settlement in Africa, reconstituted itself during the Civil War as a freedmen's aid society. In the words of one of its executive officers, the society was "an organization of pious and educated Colored people . . . who believe, and always have believed that the black man of education can best instruct, direct and elevate his race." Built around the premise that the black man was a "better leader and teacher among his own people than the white man," the African Civilization Society employed only Negro instructors in its schools. Controlled by prominent black clergymen, many of whom were abolitionists, the society commenced in 1864 with schools in the District of Columbia, Virginia, and Maryland and over the next four years extended its educational activities into the Carolinas, Georgia, Mississippi, and Louisiana.[45]

Although Gen. Rufus Saxton had lent some support to the educational effort at Port Royal, the military's first systematic school program was set in motion in November 1862 when Department of the Tennessee Commander Ulysses S. Grant appointed John Eaton as his superintendent of contrabands. It was Eaton's duty to take charge of all unemployed slaves living within Union lines around Grand Junction. He was to relocate the Negroes in special contraband camps and "organize them into working parties in saving cotton, as pioneers on railroads and steamboats, and in any way where their service can be made available."[46]

The rationale for the program was more practical than humanitarian. Grant was no abolitionist, and, like many of his fellow officers, he felt that large numbers of idle blacks in and around the army camps disrupted military operations. The federal government's encouragement of the utilization of freedmen as laborers after the passage of the second Confiscation Act, however, precluded the option of refusing protection to the thousands of refugees living along the Tennessee-Mississippi border. Grant thus tried to fabricate a system that would remove them from the army camps, raise money for the government, and make the blacks at least partially self-supporting.[47]

The man Grant chose to oversee the program was a Dartmouth graduate, a former superintendent of city schools in Toledo, an ordained minister, and most recently chaplain of the Twenty-Seventh Ohio Infantry. Critical of those he considered demagogues on both sides of the slavery issue, Eaton had written to a Northern newspaper in October 1861: "A pro-slavery fanatic in Missouri is twin brother to an antislavery fanatic in Ohio."[48]

Between November 1862 and March 1865, John Eaton ran a Freedmen's Department, which eventually grew to include not only Tennessee, but Mississippi, Kentucky, Arkansas, and parts of Louisiana. Although primarily concerned with relief and labor matters, he also cooperated with various aid societies in extending the benefits of freedmen's education into the Mississippi Valley. Limited at first to advising the societies with regard to the distribution of teachers and the location of schools, Eaton on 29 September 1863 received authorization from Adjutant General Lorenzo Thomas to furnish instructors with rations, living quarters, and transportation. The superintendent's authority was further enhanced in early October when he accepted an appointment as colonel of the Ninth Louisiana Native Guards (later the Sixty-Third United States Colored Infantry).[49]

These tentative moves toward centralization were not enough. Friction among the societies, duplication of effort, and the failure of speculators to maintain schools on plantations leased from the government led the adjutant general to place education in the department under Eaton's control. Intended to prevent "confusion and embarrassment," Thomas's order of 26 September 1864 specified that "the General Superintendent of Freedmen will designate officers, subject to his orders, as Superintendents of Colored Schools, through whom he will arrange the location of all schools, teachers, and the occupation of houses, and other details pertaining to the Education of Freedmen."[50]

In carrying out Thomas's order, Eaton set up headquarters in Memphis and appointed school superintendents and assistants for the various districts. Four of the seven original appointees were ministers. Rev. L. H. Cobb, superintendent of the Memphis district, had been a classmate of Eaton's at Dartmouth. Arkansas Superintendent Joel Grant was chaplain of the Twelfth Illinois Infantry. And at Vicksburg, James A. Hawley and his assistant, Charles W. Buckley, were both chaplains of black regiments. Buckley, who was a graduate of Beloit College, had taught school for a year before preparing for the ministry at Union Theological Seminary. C. S. Crossman, Hawley's assistant stationed in Natchez, was formerly a teacher in Toledo, Ohio. The two remaining appointees were J. L. Roberts at Columbus, Kentucky and William F. Allen, who had left his school on the South Carolina Sea Islands to become the Western Sanitary Commission's agent in Helena, Arkansas. Eaton had definite reasons for selecting Allen. As Allen recorded in his diary, the colonel "expressed himself much pleased at having got a Harvard graduate and practical teacher for Helena—it was his desire to get a strong New

England influence, and the Memphis superintendent, Mr. Cobb, is also a Dartmouth man...." After a delay of several months, Eaton named Chaplain Joseph Warren as general superintendent of colored schools throughout the department. A "very scholarly and capable man," Dr. Warren for fifteen years had been a missionary among the people of North Hindustan.[51]

The location of teachers from the freedmen's aid societies was to be determined by consultation between the school superintendent and each society's agent, "but the school hours, the text-books, and matters of school organization and discipline were put entirely in the hands of the superintendents." Unable to assess property taxes to support the system, school officials collected a tuition fee from parents who could afford it. The fee, Eaton later asserted, "did much toward rendering the schools self-supporting, and also toward developing a sense of dignity and responsibility in the Negro." The monthly rate generally varied from twenty-five cents to a dollar and a quarter a student, the amount depending on the ability of the parents to meet the expense. Industrial schools carried the self-help concept one step further by training female students to make garments for dependent fugitives with material sent from the North and to adapt second-hand soldiers' clothing donated by the Medical Department. In performing these needed services, black women and girls would also learn "to labor effectively for their families."[52]

Most of the freedmen's teachers in Eaton's department were white Northerners sent by the American Missionary Association, the Western Freedmen's Aid Commission, the Society of Friends, the United Presbyterian Church, and other such groups. There were, however, a number of native black teachers both in the towns, and on the plantations, many of which were considered too dangerous for Yankee schoolmarms.[53]

As for the students, conditions in the Mississippi Valley made it extremely difficult to obtain reliable information concerning their numbers and progress. The black population "was migratory and changeable; the children were irregular in attendance; the great variety of books made classification often impossible." Nevertheless, Eaton and Dr. Warren felt safe in saying early in 1865 that thousands had been taught to read the simpler schoolbooks, and hundreds were able to read well. Many had learned to write and had begun studies in arithmetic and geography. Putting the best possible light on the situation, Eaton's report for 1864 stated:

> The seeds of knowledge have been sown. The extraordinary eagerness of the people for instruction has been encouraged. They are not now human brutes, whom it would be safe to re-enslave. Irregular, cramped, partial, rudimentary, as their education has been, it has unfitted them for being chattels.[54]

As at Port Royal, educators in the Freedmen's Department went beyond mere academic evaluations to make judgments relating to the overall question of racial abilities. Observing colored troops in Memphis on his way to Helena, William Allen naturally compared them to blacks on the Sea Islands. There was "a much higher grade of intelligence" among the soldiers around Memphis, Allen asserted, but he stopped short of saying "better *natural* abilities," for that he "couldn't judge."[55] In the 1864 general superintendent's report, Colonel Eaton included a synopsis of responses to a questionnaire which included three questions specifically on the "aptitude" of Negro students. The respondents were Dr. Warren; District Superintendents Hawley, Grant, and Cobb; American Missionary Association representative Rev. S. G. Wright; and J. C. R. Faris, the Reformed Presbyterian Church's agent at Natchez. Clearly meant to convey a favorable impression, the published extracts nevertheless reveal the pervasiveness of the idea that blacks might be deficient in some of the higher "faculties." The questionnaire began:

> 1. What can you say of the aptitude of the colored people to receive instruction?
> All answer: They receive instruction very readily.
> Mr. Wright: Used to think them inferior; but two years' experience convinces me that they are equal to whites with equal advantages.
> Three answer: They have great aptness for language, music and the imitative arts.
> Messrs. Hawley and Warren: Perhaps they will prove deficient in logic and the mathematics.
>
> 2. Compare the mixed and unmixed races in this respect?
> Messrs. Hawley and Wright: The mixed are generally superior; but have had greater advantages.

Messrs. Faris and Cobb: Think the black superior to mixed.
Messrs. Grant and Warren: Can see no difference.

3. Have you been disappointed or otherwise in the results of your endeavors to improve and elevate this people?

Messrs. Hawley, Warren, Cobb and Faris: No: the results are better than we had thought slavery had prepared them to exhibit.

Mr. Grant: No: I never believed the pro-slavery argument, that the negro is incapable of intellectual culture.

Mr. Wright: The whole work, so far, is a success.[56]

The report from freedmen's schools under Eaton's jurisdiction for the quarter ending 31 March 1865 showed a total of 51 schools and 105 teachers in Memphis, Vicksburg, Natchez, Helena, Vidalia, Little Rock, Pine Bluff, President's Island, Davis Bend, and camps around Vicksburg. Teachers reported an enrollment of 7,360 pupils and an average attendance of 4,667. These statistics excluded the city of Columbus, Kentucky and a number of smaller points, but they give an idea of the magnitude of an undertaking that Eaton would later claim was "the most important and probably the most permanent result of the military effort to secure justice and well-being to the Negro."[57]

In the Department of North Carolina educational pioneers encountered a problem that Eaton did not have to face—opposition from a military governor who considered freedmen's schools potentially harmful to the Unionist cause. The governor—Edward Stanly—was a native North Carolinian who had been a powerful Whig politician, a state legislator, and United States congressman. Moving to San Francisco after failing to gain reelection to Congress in 1853, he had supported John C. Frémont as the least of three evils in the 1856 presidential contest. And, though still a slaveholder in 1857, he had run unsuccessfully for governor of California on the Republican ticket. Stanly blamed North Carolina's secession on Democratic deception of the people and made known his willingness to undertake the task of reclaiming the state for the Union. Much to his surprise, President Lincoln accepted his offer in May 1862, naming him military governor with the rank of brigadier general.[58]

Shortly after assuming his post, Governor Stanly received a visit from Vincent Colyer, a United States Christian Commission agent who had acted as Gen. Ambrose Burnside's superintendent of the poor around Roanoke Island before taking on similar duties at New Bern. Having initiated freedmen's schools in both locations, the artist from New York City informed Stanly of relief and educational activities at New Bern and asked for his opinions. According to Stanly's account of the conversation:

> I approved all he had done in feeding and clothing the destitute white and black, but told him I had been sent to restore the old order of things. I thought his negro school, if approved by me, would do harm to the Union cause. . . . Another reason I urged was, that by one of the cruel necessities of slavery the laws of North Carolina forbade slaves to be taught to read and write, and I would be most unsuccessful in my efforts if I encouraged the violation of her laws.

The governor subsequently asserted he had no intention of interfering with the schools, but that giving his approbation would enable "secession-traitors to excite prejudice" against him.[59]

Colyer remembered the meeting differently, reporting that Stanly said he would have to enforce the state's antiliteracy statute if called upon for a decision in the freedmen's school matter. In either case, the result was the same—Colyer closed the school and soon afterwards travelled to Washington, where he presented his case to Sen. Charles Sumner. Incensed by the superintendent's story, Sumner "without delay" located President Lincoln at the War Department. The senator from Massachusetts "related what had occurred, when the President, with an impatience which Mr. Sumner never encountered from him on any other occasion, exclaimed, 'Do you take me for a School-Committee-man?' " Sumner promptly retorted: "Not at all: I take you for President of the United States; and I come with a case of wrong, in attending to which your predecessor, George Washington, if alive, might add to his renown."[60]

After an amicable but inconclusive discussion with Lincoln, Sumner brought the matter before the Senate on June 2. The same day, the House adopted a resolution introduced by Rep. John Hickman inquiring of the president: "Whether . . . Edward Stanly had interfered to prevent the education of children, white or black, . . . and if so, by what authority, if any."[61]

In the flurry of paperwork that resulted from these congressional actions, the school matter was settled to no one's real satisfaction. Stanly told the War Department he had given no intimation of any intention to "enforce" the antiliteracy law; Departmental Commander Burnside defended the governor's actions; President Lincoln refused to issue a reprimand; and Colyer reopened his school sometime in June.[62]

With neither the military governor nor the commanding general providing much support, freedmen's education in the state was largely left to chaplains like James Means and Horace James. Not until the consolidation of the Departments of Virginia and North Carolina under Maj. Gen. John G. Foster did things take a turn for the better. Assuming command in July 1863, Foster placed Chaplain James in charge of Negro affairs in the district of North Carolina. James made education one of his top priorities, and his "first inquiries and correspondence had reference to the opening of day schools for the Freedmen, to be taught by cultured females from the North." The first of these schools opened its doors on July 23. By the end of the year the number of pupils in all such schools was approximately 1,500.[63]

General Foster's successor, Benjamin Butler, continued the policy of lending military support to the educational endeavor. In his order establishing a well-organized system for helping the freedmen, Butler directed his men to assist those who had come into the department "for the charitable purpose of giving to the negroes secular and religious instructions." Issued on 5 December 1863, the general order specified "that every officer and soldier shall treat all such persons with the utmost respect; shall aid them by all proper means in their laudable avocations; and that transportation be furnished them whenever it may be necessary in pursuit of their business." The aid societies furnished teachers and supplies, while the government was to provide quarters, fuel, and rations.

Butler appointed a general superintendent of Negro affairs—Lt. Col. J. Burnham Kinsman—and three district superintendents: Capt. Charles Wilder for that section of the department north of the James River, Capt. Orlando Brown for the area of Virginia below the river, and Horace James for North Carolina. When the counties of Northampton and Accomack in Virginia and Saint Marys in Maryland were added to the department, a fourth district was created with Dr. C. S. Henry as its superintendent.[64]

Official returns prepared by these superintendents were admittedly incomplete, but they constitute the most reliable statistical source of information on educational progress in the department. Converted to tabular form, the returns show that by the end of March 1864 there were at least 97 teachers and approximately 6,000 students in the 3 districts where schools had been established:

Table 1   Students and Teachers in the Department of
Virginia and North Carolina, 1864

	Students	Teachers	
1st district (north of the James River)	794	11	
2d district (south of the James River)	2,355	41	
			36 white
			5 "colored"
3d district (North Carolina)	2,781	45	
			41 white
			4 "colored"
Total	5,930	97	

Most of these students were black, but some provision was also made for loyal white children, as in North Carolina, where Captain James listed four white schools and two native white teachers.[65]

Butler's superintendents measured the impact of the schools through a special census that included statistics on literacy. Complete as of 1 February 1864, the census recorded that in the original three districts 4,983 of the 14,463 Negroes surveyed could read, a proportion of about 10 percent. In the First District there were 654 able to read (6 percent); in the Second 2,098 (10 percent); and in the Third 2,231 (13 percent). The Fourth District, which as yet had no schools within its jurisdiction, suffered by comparison, reporting only 62 readers out of a black population of 14,463, a rate of less than one-half of one percent. This contrast and the overall figures seemed to indicate the schools established between 1861 and 1864 were having a meaningful effect, even though the results were obviously influenced by the inclusion in the census of free blacks and slaves who had received some education before the war.[66]

By the beginning of June 1865 official reports listed 36 teachers and 3,000 students in North Carolina and 74 teachers and 3,224 students in eastern Virginia. Horace James and many others were encouraged but not ready to rest on these laurels. In concluding his tenure as district superintendent of Negro affairs, James wrote:

> *The first want of the negroes is instruction by devoted and cultured teachers.* . . . The tyranny under which they have been ground was nursed by ignorance. Upon intelligent people it would have been powerless. Send out teachers then, and especially female teachers. Let them follow in the track of every conquering army. Let them swarm over the savannas of the South. Bring hither the surplus of females in New England, greatly increased by the bereavements of war, for here it can essentially contribute to the national wealth and honor. No more beautiful resolution of a difficult and delicate social dilemma can be conceived of.[67]

While James was calling for more Yankee schoolmarms, the Board of Education for Freedmen in the Department of the Gulf was following its own unique policy—"that of employing, not exclusively, but mainly, Southern women as teachers." "They understand the negro," the board chairman explained in justifying this controversial practice. "They have a competent knowledge of the people. Their Southern origin and education fit them to combat the prejudices of their former friends and associates against negro education." Consequently, 130 of the 162 instructors employed by the board in December 1864 were "of Southern origin," the remaining 32 coming "from the West and North."[68]

The board and its policy were extensions of a program mandated by Department Commander Nathaniel Banks in 1863. Receiving reports of the freedmen's strong desire for schools and aware of President Lincoln's opinion that any reconstruction plan in Louisiana should include education for young blacks, Banks on August 29 had appointed a three-man committee "to regulate the enrollment, recruiting, employment, and education of persons of color."[69] In October the officers on the enrollment committee selected Lt. William B. Stickney as superintendent of schools for colored people in New Orleans. A "practical teacher after the best model," Stickney took over a few schools already in existence and established others "on the New England system." The first instructors he employed were local white women who had applied for positions soon after the plan was announced. These ladies reportedly lacked the "drill" given by Northern normal schools, but they were readily available, and the superintendent was willing to work with them to correct any deficiencies. By the beginning of 1864 there were 1,800 pupils in eight schools under Stickney's supervision, including one directed by Pelleman M. Williams, an experienced Northern black teacher who had studied at Dartmouth College in the early 1840s.[70]

When the American Missionary Association stepped up its own school program in Louisiana, the Enrollment Commission and General Banks promised assistance, specifically authorizing rations and housing for AMA teachers in New Orleans, Baton Rouge, Donaldsonville, and on plantations in the more remote areas. Military authorities were not always able to deliver on these promises, but their aid did permit an expansion of educational efforts outside of the limited region administered by Lieutenant Stickney.

To facilitate still further expansion on a more systematic basis, Banks modified the existing educational arrangement when he issued his famous General Order Number 23 on February 3. Best known for its labor regulations, the order also directed that the parishes be divided into police and school districts and that "provision . . . be made for the establishment of a sufficient number of schools, one at least for each of the . . . districts, for the instruction of colored children under twelve years of age."[71] A second, more specific, order on March 22 created a board of education with the following powers and duties:

1. To establish schools in every school district defined by the parish Provost Marshals.
2. To acquire tracts of land for educational purposes.
3. To erect schoolhouses on these tracts.
4. To select and employ "proper teachers for said schools, as far as practicable from the loyal inhabitants of Louisiana, with power to require their attendance for the purpose of instruc-

tion in their duties, one week at least at a Normal School, to
be conducted by the Board."

5. To purchase the necessary books and supplies.

6. To regulate the course of study, discipline, and hours of
instruction for children on weekdays and adults on Sundays;
to require such returns and reports from their teachers "as
they may deem necessary to secure uniformity, thoroughness
and efficiency in said schools."

7. To assess and levy a school tax on real and personal
property.

The board, consisting of three members, was to cooperate, as far
as practicable, with Lieutenant Stickney, who had recently been
elected superintendent of public education. The three original
appointees to the board were Col. Henry N. Frisbie of the
Twenty-Second Infantry, Corps d'Afrique; Lt. Edwin Miller
Wheelock, Fourth Infantry, Corps d'Afrique; and Isaac Hubbs,
the American Missionary Association agent in New Orleans.
Frisbie was soon replaced by B. Rush Plumly, a Philadelphia abolitionist who had served on the Enrollment Commission. Banks
appointed Plumly chairman of the board, while Wheelock became
secretary. A Unitarian minister from Dover, New Hampshire and
a "John Brown abolitionist," Wheelock had gained experience in
freedmen's education as the Enrollment Commission's inspector
of schools.[72]

In designing the system, Banks and his advisors clearly took
into account the realities of reconstruction politics. The former
governor of Massachusetts was primarily concerned with
stabilizing the labor situation and building enough Unionist support to allow Louisiana to resume normal relations with the federal government. The architects of the system tailored it to fit
these overall objectives, continuing to employ native white
teachers and repeatedly emphasizing the economic advantages of
freedmen's education. As stated in General Order Number 38,
Banks was undertaking to provide "for the rudimental instruction
of the freedmen of this Department, placing within their reach the
elements of knowledge which give intelligence and value to
labor." Equally practical subordinates argued that the availability
of schools made for more contented, more productive black
workers. "Educate the children," a provost marshal exhorted,

"let their influence be felt at home and free labor will prove an entire success."[73]

Putting the plan into operation was predictably difficult. Some rural parishes were simply unsafe or at least extremely inhospitable to freedmen's educators. So great was the problem of obtaining suitable living quarters in these areas that Banks issued a circular letter threatening to remove black laborers from the plantations of those who refused to board freedmen's teachers. He advised parish provost marshals against asking any family to provide accommodations where circumstances made it "greatly inconvenient," but added "I desire you to notify all persons interested, that it is indispensible to the cultivation of the soil, that schools for colored children shall be maintained. The policy of the Government demands this, and nothing will be allowed to interfere with its success."[74]

A change in policy regarding schoolhouses contributed to a further deterioration in relations with white residents of the state. Considering the expense and the probability of change in school districts, the board decided to appropriate existing buildings rather than constructing new ones. In a move bound to antagonize local property owners, it directed provost marshals to seize and turn over to the board all buildings designated by its agents.[75]

Provost marshals frequently showed a reluctance to enforce these policy decisions or to assist teachers in their districts, a fact of military life which deeply disturbed Board Chairman Plumly. "Where the parish Provost Marshal is indifferent or opposed to negro education," Plumly complained in his annual report for 1864, "the annoyance and even peril of the teachers, is often great, from the remains of that class from which slave drivers and negro hunters sprang." Plumly gave several examples to illustrate his point. The first concerned an instructor in a parish some distance from New Orleans who claimed she could get no aid from the marshal despite her dire circumstances—"Nothing to eat but strong pork and sour bread. Insulted for being a 'nigger teacher.' Can't buy anything on credit, and have'nt a cent of money. The school shed has no floor, and the rains sweep clean across it, through the places where the windows should be." Still, the officer refused to help, saying he did not "believe in nigger teachers—did'nt 'list to help them." A second example concerned a woman who blamed the provost marshal in her district for allowing Union soldiers to harass her school, specifically citing one officer's practice of letting his dogs loose after supper ''to bite the night-scholars.'' In Thibodaux a night-school instructor's repeated complaints about vandalism and rock throwing failed to bring relief or protection. According to Plumly's account, Gen. Robert A. Cameron ''kindly and promptly sent a guard, on one or two occasions; but as the detection and arrest of the cowardly assailants depends upon the disposition and vigilance of the parish Provost Marshal, the outrages continue.''[76]

The report asserted that before his resignation in the summer of 1864 Provost Marshal-General James Bowen had dealt with uncooperative parish marshals by overruling their decisions or removing them. Bowen's successor, however, allegedly showed less concern for freedmen's education. Had the board received from the provost marshal's office ''a continuance of the active interest in these schools manifested by General Bowen during his incumbency,'' Plumly predicted ''we should have had, at this time, at least three thousand additional pupils.''[77]

The board of education probably underestimated the difficulty of affording military protection to teachers in rural areas, just as it certainly underestimated the problems involved in collecting a school tax from reluctant native whites. Forced to depend on government loans until it finally levied the tax early in 1865, the board even then was able to take in only a small percentage of the revenue needed to support the schools.[78]

Internal dissension added to the board's problems. Early in May 1864 a disagreement developed over the question of who should control the schools maintained by the American Missionary Association. While AMA representative Isaac Hubbs was in New York, Plumly and Wheelock proposed that the board take complete responsibility for the schools, replacing association teachers with its own appointees. This was later modified to allow the AMA to retain and support its teachers under the supervision of the board. Finally, a compromise was worked out whereby the board agreed to assume responsibility for teachers' salaries, rations, and housing. Later in the year Secretary Wheelock wrote association officials that there was no need to send more Northern instructors since General Banks had settled on the policy of employing ''mainly southern teachers.''[79]

At about the same time, charges of corruption and immoral behavior leveled against Hubbs resulted in his being dismissed from the board and expelled from the department. Hubbs, who denied the allegations, saw his dismissal as part of a "vigorous persecution" of the AMA and its interests. Whether guilty or innocent, he departed under a cloud of suspicion. Banks did not name a replacement, choosing instead to leave his two military employees in charge of the system.[80]

Many of the AMA instructors now paid by the board considered its educational policies too Southern and too secular. "My assistant teachers, with one exception are not of the right stamp for this work," one principal wrote to AMA Secretary George Whipple. "The 'Board of Education' is not very particular in the selection of teachers."

> To be a *professedly* loyal Louisianian appears to be about the only necessary qualification. I fear that very few have any real desire for the Education of the colored people, and a still smaller number have any care for the spiritual welfare of their pupils.

John C. Tucker in New Orleans claimed that almost anyone could procure a teaching position. Myra Buxton wrote from Thibodaux that she was not satisfied with the operations of the board. While conceding they had accomplished "much good," she thought "they would have done *very much more* had they been actuated by higher and holier motives."[81]

Plumly and Wheelock willingly defended not only the educational policies but Banks's entire labor program. Reacting to charges that Banks had in effect instituted a form of black "serfdom," both men justified the system as a necessary expedient. "*I think the policy . . . has been dictated by profound wisdom,*" Wheelock opined in a letter published in the *Liberator*. "Considering the peculiar population here, the mixture of elements, the pro-slavery tone of much of our army, and the hesitating policy of the central Government in 1862, *a better system could not have been devised.*"[82]

Designed to eliminate "vagrancy" in the department, the orders issued on 29 January 1863 and 3 February 1864 required unemployed black males to negotiate contracts with local planters (preferably their old masters), or to labor on public works without pay. Freedmen were permitted to choose their employers, but once the agreement was made, they were to be held to the contract for one year. Specific provisions encouraged planters to keep families together whenever possible and prohibited flogging and all "cruel or unusual punishments." Other sections of the labor orders provided for schools, medical treatment, a freedmen's bank, small plots of land for workers, and a wage scale based on ability. Laborers, however, were not allowed to leave the plantations without a pass, and military authorities took responsibility for enforcing on freedmen "all the conditions of continuous and faithful service, respectful deportment, correct discipline, and perfect subordination." Indolence, insolence, disobedience of orders, and crime were punished by forfeiture of pay and by such punishments as were provided for similar offenses under army regulations.[83]

Enforced by officers who were often unsympathetic to freedmen, the labor order of 3 February 1864 encountered vehement opposition from critics who denounced Banks as a "born slave-driver" and his system as tantamount to slavery.[84] Expressing an opinion held by many abolitionists and nonabolitionists alike, Wendell Phillips complained the program denied blacks every element of citizenship and freedom. Phillips claimed he was more willing to accept "the bullet from ... Jeff Davis than ... serfdom from General Banks."[85] In New Orleans, treasury agent George S. Denison wrote to Secretary Chase that "slave labor" had been restored under Banks, "and local police regulations regarding slaves, enforced and executed by New England bayonets with all becoming severity."[86] The *New Orleans Tribune*, an organ of Louisiana's ante-bellum Negro elite, came to the same conclusion after the 1864 growing season. Initially praising what they thought were temporary controls, the editors in the fall began criticizing the economic exploitation of freedmen by "greedy adventurers." Before the end of the year the *Tribune* was comparing Banks's system to the state's old slave code. "If we except the lash," an article asserted on December 8, "one is unable to perceive any material difference between the two sets of regulations."[87]

Plumly and Wheelock dismissed these indictments as grossly exaggerated. Experienced in both the educational and labor aspects of the program, the two abolitionists wrote several letters to William Lloyd Garrison's *Liberator* defending the embattled policies. Plumly, who claimed Banks had consulted him on every order affecting the social and political status of Negroes, cast doubt on the motives of the critics, charging that many were inclined to disapprove anything the general did in the department. Major Plumly appealed for a more objective appraisal of the results and predicted "if our friend Wendell Phillips would go with me over this 'Delta,' where everything is as formative as the soil beneath our feet—meeting at every turn the tremendous 'facts' of the time and place—we should hear no more from him of 'Serfdom'."[88] Wheelock, formerly a deputy superintendent of labor under Banks, credited the commander with remedying some of the worst abuses in the system—mistreatment of workers, imprisonment of freedmen without due process of law, corruption and tyranny on the part of provost marshals. As far as Wheelock was concerned, Banks's reconstruction policies had been largely vindicated by early 1865. In a letter to Garrison published in the March 3 issue of the *Liberator*, he painted a romantic picture of the results:

> Now these people are quiet and thrifty laborers, *doing better as to wages than farm hands at the North.* . . . They have redress for their grievances, pay for their services, and schools for their children. . . . They stand as equals of any before the law; they are enrolled into the militia with the whites, and their testimony is received in courts of justice. . . . They are moving, and that not tardily, on the straight line to the goal of all their rights.

Borrowing a sentence from another of his published letters, the school board secretary wrote that "education followed in the footsteps of Liberty." "The success of Major Plumly," he boasted, "has been a wonder even to the most hopeful of his friends."

> In the face of every obstacle, the good work has gone on, until ninety-eight schools, amply supplied with school furniture, and the best text-books of the North, have been established; with an attendance of upwards of eleven thousand pupils, and with night schools and Sunday schools . . . dispensing instruction to twenty-two hundred laboring adults.

Wheelock enthusiastically projected that at the end of another twelve months there would be "more white men than black men in Louisiana, unable to read and write!"[89]

Along with Banks himself, the two school board members succeeded in influencing the views of Garrison but failed to sway
Wendell Phillips and many others who continued to oppose what
they thought was a "middle course between acknowledgement
and denial of the negro's manhood." These opponents were dismayed that abolitionist leaders like Garrison and Gerrit Smith
would defend the "apprenticeship system" proposed by General
Banks and President Lincoln. "We say now, as ever," Elizabeth
Cady Stanton wrote to Susan B. Anthony, "Give us immediately
unconditional emancipation, and let there be no reconstruction
except on the broadest basis of justice and equality."[90]

Plumly and Wheelock met less resistance from fellow abolitionists when they concentrated on defending the actions and
accomplishments of the board of education, which in the nine
months between March and December 1864 had increased the
number of government day-schools from 7 to 95. When the board
took over from the Enrollment Commission in late March,
schools were confined to New Orleans, and there were only 23
teachers, with an average attendance of 1,422 pupils. Depending
heavily on its native white instructors, the board during the remainder of the year extended educational work into all 15
parishes controlled by Union forces. The December report
showed schools for black children in 95 of the 174 school districts
established under Banks's General Order Number 23. These
schools were staffed with 162 teachers, and the number of students enrolled was 9,571 or approximately 60 percent of the children in the department between the ages of five and twelve. The
average daily attendance was 7,052. In addition, over 2,000 adults
received instruction in night and Sunday schools under the auspices of the board. Of the pupils in attendance in December there
were:

3883	writing on slates.
1108	writing in copy books.
283	studying Grammar.
1338	studying Geography.
1223	studying Practical Arithmetic.
4628	studying Mental Arithmetic.
7623	Reading.
8301	Spelling.
2103	learning the Alphabet.

Secretary Wheelock reported that students were "rapidly demonstrating the capacity of the African to receive our civilization." According to information supplied by teachers, many children were reading in first readers after eight weeks of classes and were "solving with facility problems in the primary rules of arithmetic." As early as September 1864 some students had advanced to the third and fourth readers and had acquired a knowledge of fractions, long division, and the multiplication table. "They are quick-witted," the board's annual report said of the black pupils, "excelling in those branches that exercise the perceptive and imitative powers, and the memory, while they are slower in arithmetic, and in studies that tax the reasoning power—probably from a hereditary dormancy of those faculties under the long night and cruel weight of slavery."[91]

The authors of the report claimed such advances had brought about a change in racial attitudes. Perhaps indulging in a bit of wishful thinking, they observed that an "almost immediate and marked influence of these schools is seen upon the white people in the lessening prejudice, and in the reluctant admission of the African's ability to learn, and his consequent fitness for places in the world, from which we have hitherto excluded him."[92]

The optimism expressed in published accounts, however, was not always warranted. Intense local opposition persisted, regardless of whether Yankees or native whites taught in the schools, and predictions that Louisiana's reconstruction government would soon enfranchise educated blacks proved ill-founded. The constitutional convention of 1864 sidestepped the sensitive issue by limiting voting rights to white males while empowering the legislature "to pass laws extending suffrage to such other persons, citizens of the United States, as by military service, by taxation, . . . or by intellectual fitness, may be deemed entitled thereto." Never acted upon by the legislature elected under the new constitution, this provision was the closest the state government came to authorizing even a limited form of Negro suffrage during presidential Reconstruction.[93]

Far from gaining general acceptance among white residents, teachers often suffered ostracism, scorn, intimidation, and various other forms of abuse. In outlying districts schools were in constant danger from Confederate raiders, recalcitrant planters, and unsympathetic Union soldiers. The withdrawal of federal troops from a given area frequently led the affected teachers to suspend operations or move to a safer location. Yet, in spite of these obstacles, the educational system continued to grow so that by the end of July 1865 the board of education was overseeing 121 schools with a total student population numbering about 14,000 children and 5,000 adults, more than 1,000 of whom were soldiers.[94]

The establishment of a freedmen's bureau within the War Department during the early part of 1865 perpetuated the military's involvement in Southern black education. Formally designated the Bureau of Refugees, Freedmen and Abandoned Lands, this federal agency was the culmination of more than three years of lobbying by abolitionists and others who believed the government had a responsibility to help the former slaves until they were able to take care of themselves.

Many of those calling for the creation of such a bureau between 1861 and 1865 specified that freedmen's education should be one of its chief concerns. "With an act of emancipation, let there be a new Executive Bureau established," Rev. William J. Potter sermonized in July 1861, "with a new Cabinet officer, whose duties shall be to care for and protect, and educate these four millions of new born freedmen."[95] The Massachusetts Anti-Slavery Society followed suit at the end of January 1863, endorsing the idea of an agency "for the special purpose of guarding the rights and interests of the liberated bondmen, providing them with land and labor, and giving them a fair chance to develop their faculties and powers through the necessary educational instrumentalities."[96] On June 30 the three-man American Freedmen's Inquiry Commission added substance to these generalizations in its preliminary report. Created by the War Department on 16 March 1863, the commission had been authorized to investigate the condition of freedmen within Union lines, and "to report what measures will best contribute to their protection and improvement, so that they may defend and support themselves."[97] Basing the preliminary report on questionnaires and their own investigations, Commissioners Robert Dale Owen, James McKaye, and Samuel Gridley Howe outlined a plan that included a freedmen's bureau and government support for black education. As described in the report, financial assistance to schools in the South would be a temporary expedient, supplementing the efforts of Northern aid societies until the institutions became self-supporting. When necessary, the government would pay teachers' salaries and provide them with transportation.[98]

Four of the societies took their case to the president himself in November 1863, and, at his suggestion, drafted a memorial for submission to Congress. Dated December 1, the memorial was signed by representatives of the New England Freedmen's Aid Society, the National Freedmen's Relief Association of New York, the Pennsylvania Freedmen's Relief Association, and the Western Freedman's Aid Committee in Cincinnati. It was clear to these men that the task was "too large for anything short of government authority, government resources, and government ubiquity to deal with." They had no doubts about the aptitude of slaves for freedom "under any fair circumstances." "We have found the freedman easy to manage, beyond even our best hopes," the memorial proclaimed, "willing and able to learn as a pupil; docile, patient, affectionate, grateful, and although with a great tribal range of intellect from nearly infantile to nearly or quite the best white intelligence, yet with an average mental capacity above the ordinary estimates of it." In order to guarantee that blacks were given the chance to develop this potential, the representatives asked Lincoln to recommend to Congress the immediate creation of a bureau of emancipation.[99]

Lincoln sent the memorial to Congress on December 17, three days after the introduction of a freedmen's bureau bill by Rep. Thomas D. Eliot of Massachusetts. A sponsor of what became the second Confiscation Act in 1862, this Radical Republican had introduced a bureau bill in the Thirty-seventh Congress, but the measure had died in committee. The new bill provided for an agency in the War Department to take charge of freedmen's affairs. Under the administration of a commissioner and assistant commissioners, the bureau was to develop regulations for the treatment and superintendence of freedmen, to protect them in their rights, to set up special courts, and to settle blacks on confiscated or abandoned property. Eliot's bill, with slight changes, passed the House on 1 March 1864 by a slim majority of two votes but then bogged down for nearly a year when the Senate accepted Charles Sumner's amendment to locate the agency in the Treasury Department. Senator Sumner favored the treasury because it oversaw the administration of confiscated lands, and he gave in only when Congress agreed to transfer this responsibility to the War Department. Finally, on 3 March 1865, both houses passed the bill, and President Lincoln signed it into law.[100]

The act established a bureau to operate until one year after the end of the war. It was charged with "the supervision and management of all abandoned lands, and the control of all subjects relating to refugees and freedmen," under rules and regulations prescribed by the bureau commissioner and approved by the president. The chief executive was to appoint this commissioner and up to ten assistant commissioners with the advice and consent of the Senate. Any military officer could be assigned to duty as assistant commissioner without increase of pay or allowances, and the secretary of war received authorization to "direct such issues of provisions, clothing, and fuel, as he may deem needful for the immediate and temporary shelter and supply of destitute and suffering refugees and freedmen." One of the most important sections of the new legislation permitted the distribution of abandoned property, but, surprisingly, nothing was said about education.[101]

Fortunately for the schools, the man chosen as bureau commissioner was a believer in government-aided industrial and academic training for freedmen. As early as January 1857 Oliver Otis Howard had linked education and emancipation in a letter written during his first visit to the South. On his way to Fort Brooke in Tampa, Florida the newly commissioned army officer had observed what he thought were amicable relations between masters and slaves and wrote his mother that the blacks were not yet ready to be enfranchised. "They had better be cared for as they are now in this place," Howard opined, "than turned loose on the world, with all their simplicity & improvident habits without a proper education."[102] As commander of the Army of the Tennessee in Sherman's devastating March to the Sea, the future bureau commissioner had observed freedmen's education on the Sea Islands firsthand and was impressed with what he saw. On 19 January 1865 he visited five of these schools, where he "found the children sparkling with intelligence, the teachers noble women who had devoted their strength to this work."

> One school bears the look of our best New England schools;
> the order, the reading, the arithmetic, and the singing strike
> you with wonder. The "America" and "Rally Round the Flag,

Boys,'' ring out with such heart and harmony as to imbue you with enthusiasm. You can't help saying, That is not the stuff of which to make slaves.

In the classes run by Elizabeth Botume and another Massachusetts teacher, Major General Howard adjudged the students "quite as well advanced as white children of the same age."[103]

Though apparently not Lincoln's first choice for the commissionership, this "Christian soldier" from Maine was a logical selection to head the bureau. Howard had some experience with freedmen's affairs, and, while neither an active abolitionist nor a prominent Radical, was supported by Secretary of War Stanton, Rev. Henry Ward Beecher, and Gen. Rufus Saxton. Congress's failure to appropriate funds for the agency virtually guaranteed that its head would be supervising a staff consisting mainly of military personnel. The pious young general had sufficient rank for this purpose and was less controversial than someone like Benjamin Butler or Nathaniel Banks. Freedmen's aid officials were impressed with his humanity and Christian character. Lincoln barely knew the prospective commissioner, but, according to Stanton, the president was ready to make the appointment at the time of his assassination. Accepting this assurance from the secretary, Andrew Johnson assigned Howard to duty on 12 May 1865. The magazine of the National Freedmen's Relief Association applauded the selection of "so good and capable a man as Maj. Gen. O. O. Howard," and a comparable journal of the New England Freedmen's Aid Society simply stated that "a better appointment could not have been made."[104]

The morning Howard accepted his new post Secretary Stanton handed him a large, oblong bushel basket filled with letters and documents and said with a smile: "Here, general, *here's your Bureau!*" Almost literally taking the bureau in hand, the enthusiastic new commissioner established headquarters at the corner of Nineteenth and I streets in Washington in a house of a prominent senator who had joined the Confederacy. Upon entering the discharge of his duties Howard separated the agency into four divisions: one of government-controlled lands, one of records, one of financial affairs, and the fourth a medical department. Education fell under the records division, which embraced "official acts of the Commissioner touching labor, schools, quartermaster and commissary supplies."[105] Before the year was out,

Howard and his assistant commissioners selected bureau educational superintendents for the various states, and John Watson Alvord was designated chief inspector of schools and finances. Each superintendent was "to work as much as possible with State officers who may have had school matters in charge, and to take cognizance of all that was being done to educate refugees and freedmen, secure protection to schools and teachers, promote method and efficiency, and to correspond with the benevolent agencies which were supplying his field."[106]

The educational and moral condition of blacks would not be forgotten, Howard assured aid society leaders in his first important circular. "The utmost facility will be afforded to benevolent and religious organizations and State authorities in the maintenance of good schools (for refugees and freedmen) until a system of free schools can be supported by the recognized local governments." Lacking funds for direct financial aid to the societies, he made do with what he had at his disposal, turning over for school use confiscated property and government buildings no longer needed for military purposes; providing transportation for teachers, books, and school furniture; and supplying quarters and rations to teachers and superintendents while they were on duty.[107]

As inspector of schools and finances and later as general superintendent of schools, Rev. John W. Alvord would set the tone for the new endeavor. A veteran abolitionist, Alvord had developed his reform philosophy over a period of nearly three decades, beginning with his student days at Oneida Institute, Lane Theological Seminary, and Oberlin College. While pursuing his advanced studies in the 1830s, the future Freedmen's Bureau official taught in a Negro school in Cincinnati and acted as an American Anti-Slavery Society agent.[108] Like many of his fellow agents, he came under the influence of Charles Grandison Finney, a dominant figure in the religious revival that swept through the western states after 1824. Particularly important in shaping Alvord's reform philosophy was Finney's approach to the slavery question. The fiery evangelist took a decided stand on the issue but preferred not to "make it a hobby, or divert the attention of the people from the work of converting souls."[109] Finney, in fact, openly criticized the antislavery movement, claiming abolitionist attacks on slaveholders were made more in the spirit of anger than of love. Such attacks, he cautioned, would only alienate the

South and ultimately would precipitate a civil war. The only reasonable alternative was to make abolition "an appendage of a general revival in religion." In short, the antislavery crusade would have to become a missionary movement to save "the bewildered Southern brethren in the Lord" from their "state of desperation."[110]

Alvord adopted the same basic philosophy. He too believed that church involvement in the abolitionist movement was absolutely essential at a time when the entire nation was "breaking loose from the bonds of brotherhood and the restraints of laws." Abolition efforts should be imbued with more of the spirit of God and of prayer. This approach would win to the antislavery cause "those parts of the church (by no means contemptible in piety or moral worth) who are either timid, or stubborn, or else afraid of ultraism." "It sometimes seems to me," Alvord wrote to Theodore Weld in 1836, "that a *few words* ad[d]ressed to the warm heart of the convert or to a broken down church will do as much for the slaves as *many words* when poured out upon the flinty rock. . . . I believe . . . that nothing will make the slaveholder unclench his grasp but the horrors of Hellfire."[111]

Alvord maintained his ties with evangelical abolitionism throughout the remainder of the ante-bellum period, serving in turn as pastor of Congregational churches in Winsted, Connecticut and South Boston, Massachusetts and as secretary of the Boston branch of the American Tract Society. During the Civil War he gained firsthand knowledge of freedmen's affairs while representing the tract society as a missionary and colporteur among Union troops in the South. More to the point, it was during this time that he launched his career in freedmen's education by helping Negroes in Savannah, Georgia establish their own school system, complete with an exclusively black board of trustees and teaching staff. This missionary work soon attracted the attention of Commissioner Howard, and in September 1865 Alvord was appointed inspector of schools.[112]

One year later the inspector advanced to general superintendent of schools, a position he occupied for the duration of the War Department educational program. During his five-year tenure, between thirty and forty men acted as superintendents in the eleven Confederate states. Turnover was fairly high, with a majority of the states having three or more superintendents from October 1865 to December 1870. Most were drawn from the ranks of army officers, chaplains, and ministers, and several had been engaged in freedmen's education during the war. Rev. Dr. Joseph Warren moved from his post as general superintendent of colored schools in the Department of the Tennessee to that of chief Freedmen's Bureau educational officer for Mississippi, while the department's assistant superintendent at Vicksburg, Rev. Charles W. Buckley, became state superintendent of bureau schools in Alabama.[113] Edwin M. Wheelock left Louisiana for Texas, where he served two terms as superintendent between 1866 and 1868.[114] Two more chaplains from black regiments— H. H. Moore and Ralza Morse Manly—were assigned respectively to Florida and Virginia. Both men were Methodist ministers, as were John F. Ogden in Tennessee and R. D. Harper, Buckley's replacement in Alabama.[115]

Manly, Henry Roberts Pease, and Edmund Asa Ware were all experienced educators. Manly, who held both a bachelor of arts and a master's degree from Wesleyan University in Connecticut, had been principal of a grammar school in Randolph, Vermont, a teacher at the Newbury Seminary, principal of the Troy Conference Academy at Poultney and of the New Hampshire Conference Seminary in Northfield, New Hampshire.[116] Captain Pease had received a normal-school education and taught for eleven years before entering the legal profession in 1859. This native of Connecticut during Reconstruction would serve as school superintendent first in Louisiana and then in Mississippi.[117] Georgia's two-time superintendent, Rev. E. A. Ware, had spent two years teaching at the Norwich Free Academy after graduating from Yale in 1863 and in 1865 had assisted in the establishment of schools at Nashville, Tennessee. He moved to Georgia in 1866 to administer the American Missionary Association's Atlanta educational district.[118]

Alvord's old position as general inspector of schools went to John Mercer Langston, one of the few Negroes selected for a top-level post in the education division. Chief Justice Salmon P. Chase recommended the eloquent abolitionist from Ohio, and Howard made the appointment in April 1867. Destined for a distinguished educational and diplomatic career, Langston had already amassed impressive credentials as an attorney, antislavery lecturer, local officeholder, recruiter of colored troops, and civil rights advocate. A graduate of the collegiate and theological departments at Oberlin College, this light-skinned son of a deceased Virginia planter had broken through racial barriers in a number of areas—gaining admission to the Ohio bar in 1854, winning election as clerk of Brownhelm Township in 1855, and serving on Oberlin's city council and board of education in the 1860s.[119] Howard and Alvord moved quickly to counteract the impression that the new inspector was being sent South to campaign for the Republican party. They encouraged him to instruct freedmen in the rights and responsibilities of citizens but cautioned against interference in partisan politics. Time would demonstrate the difficulty of distinguishing between the two functions.[120]

Considering the Army's ambiguous reputation with regard to racial matters, it comes as no surprise that Howard's military-minded assistant commissioners appointed few, if any, state superintendents who might be considered extremists. The commissioner himself discouraged the selection of James Redpath, the British-born militant responsible for organizing the Charleston public school system. Understandably concerned about the precarious position of the new agency under a Southern president, Howard deemed Redpath "the very worst man" to put in charge of bureau schools in South Carolina. Assistant Commissioner Rufus Saxton concurred and passed over this outspoken John Brown biographer in favor of Reuben Tomlinson, a less provocative Quaker abolitionist from Pennsylvania who had managed freedmen's affairs on Saint Helena Island for nearly three years prior to his appointment in October 1865.[121]

A bank clerk before the war, Tomlinson was one of a handful of abolitionist superintendents employed by the bureau between 1865 and 1870. Also included on this list were Pease, Wheelock, and William Colby, the government's educational officer for Arkansas.[122] Wheelock in particular had attracted national attention as a result of his impassioned ante-bellum sermons inveighing against Southern slavery and Northern racial discrimination. In his most famous published address, the Unitarian minister had firmly defended John Brown's raid on Harper's Ferry, generalizing that never in history "was a tyrant race known to loosen its grasp of the victim's throat, save by the pressure of force" and arguing against those "mistaken friends of the slave" who believed American bondsmen could achieve freedom only through "purely moral and peaceable means." Putting these non-Garrisonian principles into practice, the Harvard-trained clergyman had enlisted as a private in the Fifteenth New Hampshire Infantry shortly after Lincoln issued his preliminary Emancipation Proclamation.[123]

In choosing his assistant commissioners, O. O. Howard generally sought "those who had been long in the work—men who had been successful and who were earnest in securing the rights of the freedmen." When compelled "to go beyond this class," he took those whom he "knew to be men of integrity and with Christian hearts."[124] Secretary Stanton and others involved in the selection process introduced politics into the equation, and the result was a heterogeneous group of appointees representing a wide variety of viewpoints on racial and sectional issues. These men in turn appointed educational superintendents who ran the gamut from radical to conservative, from steadfast Yankee to accommodationist, from abolitionist to paternalistic Southerner.

The range of this diversity was most clearly demonstrated in the designation of Rev. E. B. Duncan as superintendent for Florida. A longtime domestic missionary and former Union Army chaplain, this Southern white minister also headed the state's public school system.[125] Making little attempt to conceal his sectional biases, Duncan quickly alienated even those bureau officials who advocated relatively lenient Reconstruction policies. Georgia's director of education G. L. Eberhart had only to read Duncan's first school report before deciding to call for his ouster. His report was, in Eberhart's estimation, "a disgrace to the State he represents and his appointment as Supt. in the Bureau, a reproach to the A[ssistant] Com[missioner] who gave him the appointment." With some justification Eberhart in December 1866 charged that his counterpart to the south had ignored Northern educational efforts and Northern teachers, "altho' they did *all* the work *worthy* of notice last year."[126] According to Duncan's interpretation, Southern whites had been the best missionaries the world ever knew. Receiving "this black race from English and New England ships as barbarians," he elaborated, "we have brought them to the social and religious status which they at present enjoy."

We have no reason to hate the black man, he has done nobly. It has been by his strong arm that we possess our wealth, while on the other hand, the white man has ever been his

friend, protector, and provider. . . . We are under the strongest
obligations to help him in his present condition, with that assistance he needs in counsel, and otherwise, to make him
what he should be; we did so in slavery times, we should do it
more in times of freedom.[127]

It was this mixture of sectionalism and paternalism that eventually led to Duncan's dismissal from his bureau position after less
than a year of service. On 10 May 1867 he was replaced by
C. Thurston Chase, a general agent for the American Freedmen's
Union Commission. One questionable account claimed the
Southern minister had lost the superintendency because he refused to distribute a speech by Thaddeus Stevens advocating the
confiscation of Confederate property as a means of paying the
war debt.[128]

Not that Northerners like Eberhart were themselves oblivious
to Southern attitudes and biases. "We must be governed in this
work by great prudence," the Georgia superintendent generalized
in 1866, "and, so far as we possibly can without any com-
pr[om]ise of principle, or conflict with truth, be controlled by
policy and expediency." Since men were largely the product of
their circumstances and education, Eberhart contended "we can
not therefore expect to excite any thing but ill feelings and dis-
respect among the white people here, if we run too far beyond
what they deem the limits of prudence and propriety."[129]

In this instance the Georgia superintendent was reacting to the
behavior of a female teacher who had angered local citizens by
doing and saying "very unnecessary things" on the public
streets. Eberhart described the situation in a confidential letter to
an American Missionary Association official stating: "For a white
Northern lady here to kiss a colored child is very *imprudent* to say
the least of it, and, in reply to an insulting remark made by a white
person, to say that the negroes are as good as that white person, is
entirely unnecessary."[130]

Bureau leaders from the commissioner on down were especially anxious to counteract allegations that teachers openly
practiced "social equality," a breach of Southern racial etiquette
that Howard considered one of the chief causes of local resistance.[131] Denials were frequent and clearly stated in forums as
prominent as Alvord's published semiannual reports. Typical was
an account provided by Mississippi Superintendent Joseph War-

ren, who worked to refute charges against educators of "unbecoming social intimacy with the colored people." Because of these innuendos, Warren carefully watched the conduct of teachers, and it gave him pleasure to say that no body of young people whom he had ever known had shown conduct more exemplary and discreet. "I have not known a single case of association with the people on the ground of social equality," he informed the general superintendent in his report for the first half of 1866. "Families have been visited in the proper work of the mission, but beyond this, I think no occasion has been given for even prejudice to find fault."[132]

Wholehearted acceptance of racial intermingling was far from unanimous among high-ranking school officials, and even the most egalitarian recognized the danger of flouting Southern mores. Violence and schoolhouse burnings were too frequent to be ignored, compelling compromise from moderates and radicals alike. James Redpath himself found it necessary to bend before the winds of expediency while employed as superintendent of public instruction for Charleston. Redpath has been described as "an energetic reformer—always seething with ardor, in some cause or other, scornful of compromise."[133] Yet it was he who developed the half-measure allowing blacks and whites to attend some of the same schools but dividing the races into separate classrooms. As the passionate reformer indicated in a report published in the *Freedmen's Record*, he was quite satisfied with this partial triumph:

> I am obliged to have separate rooms, and white teachers for the white children,—but all our friends here regard it as a great victory to our cause, to have succeeded in getting the two classes into the same building.... [I]t is a great step toward destroying the prejudice against the colored people. All the colored people are delighted at this arrangement.[134]

Other educators were still more tentative in their commitment to implementing full racial equality in the post-war setting.

In his capacity as the bureau's inspector of schools and finances for freedmen, John W. Alvord left Washington on 6 October 1865 to observe educational conditions in all the Southern states below Tennessee and east of the Mississippi River. Touring nine states and obtaining information on six others from bureau personnel, Alvord submitted a detailed report of his findings to Commissioner Howard in early January 1866. The results of this survey of fifteen states and the District of Columbia were encouraging— 90,589 students, 740 schools, and 1,314 teachers. Most of the instructors were Northerners, but in several states Southern whites had accepted positions in the schools, a promising sign for a program so dependent on local support, or at least toleration. Some provision was also being made for the small number of white children attending either freedmen's schools or those institutions maintained by the American Union Commission, an organization devoting much of its attention to educating the sons and daughters of professed Unionists.[135]

Alvord's statistics (see table 2) give a good idea of the relative growth of freedmen's education in the various localities during and just after the war:

Table 2   Freedmen's Bureau Educational Statistics, 1865

	Schools	Teachers	Students
Va.	90	195	12,898
N.C.	86	119	8,506
S.C.	48	76	10,000
Ga.	69	69	3,603
Fla.	30	19	1,900
Ala. (southern part)	2	15	817
Miss.	34	68	4,310
La.	150	265	19,000
Tex.	16	10	1,041
Ky., Tenn., northern Ala.	75	264	14,768
Mo., Kans., Ark.	39	51	3,444
D.C.	45	100	5,191

The superintendent noted the importance of Negroes both as sponsors of schools and as teachers. In Georgia forty-three of the sixty-nine teachers were black, whereas the ratio in South Carolina was twenty-four out of a total of seventy-six.[136]

By the time Alvord submitted his second semiannual report on 1 July 1866 the field of freedmen's education was largely dominated by two organizations—the secular American Freedmen's Union Commission and the evangelical American Missionary Association. Methodists, Presbyterians, Baptists, and African Methodists maintained their own independent societies, but most aid groups aligned themselves with one of the two competing coalitions.

The younger organization—the AFUC—was a product of several mergers culminating in a partnership between the American Freedmen's Aid Commission and the American Union Commission. Initially included under this umbrella were: the National Freedmen's Relief Association of New York, New England Freedmen's Aid Society, Pennsylvania Freedmen's Relief Association, Baltimore Association for the Moral and Educational Improvement of the Colored People, Western Freedmen's Aid Commission, and Northwestern Freedmen's Aid Commission.[137] From the start the AFUC philosophy and commitment to educating whites as well as blacks stirred some internal controversy. William Lloyd Garrison and other early opponents of the merger argued that incorporating the American Union Commission's policy of financing schools for loyalists would divert funds intended for blacks. In a meeting held to consider the consolidation plan, Garrison "said the 'Union Commission' was formed for the Southern whites, and *his* first duty was to the freedmen."[138] Hannah E. Stevenson, formerly secretary of the New England society's committee on teachers, was so incensed she refused to transfer her membership to the AFUC. She claimed those contributing to the American Union Commission "would scorn to give their wealth to the negro." Though the agency professed to aid both races, Stevenson cited her own experiences in Richmond, where the commission allegedly "helped 10 whites at least to one black, & . . . established a large number of schools there & elsewhere, to which no negro has ever been admitted."[139] These same issues split the Pennsylvania association, forcing J. Miller McKim to ask some of his abolitionist coadjutors if poor whites were not also victims of slavery. "Shall we," he inquired, "denounce President Johnson & his Congressional confreres for not legislating and administering the Government without respect to color, and yet ourselves . . . minister *with* regard to color?"[140] Likewise, McKim called the western societies "retrograde" when they joined the opposition to a merger. "Let the unreconstructed demand class legislation," he chided, "the true friends of freedom will consent to no distinction of classes either in political, religious or humanitarian legislation."[141] With relatively few individual defections, the auxiliary societies eventually accepted the pro-merger position and by May 1866 ratified a constitution for the American Freedmen's Union Commission stipulating that services would be provided without distinction of race or color. It was a short-term victory, however, as the Cincinnati branch switched to the more compatible American Missionary Association in 1866, followed by the Cleveland branch in 1867 and the Chicago branch in 1868.[142]

Throughout its three years of operation this nondenominational society maintained a central office in New York City with branch offices in other parts of the country. American Union Commission Secretary Lyman Abbott became the general executive officer for the AFUC, while most other principal officials were carryovers from the American Freedmen's Aid Commission. James Miller McKim was selected as corresponding secretary, George Cabot Ward as treasurer, and Francis George Shaw as the first chairman of an executive committee made up of representatives from New York and the regional branches.[143]

Abbott's duties as general secretary were specified in the executive committee's minutes and bylaws:

> The General Secretary of the Commission shall be its general Executive officer; all reports of Branches, Agents, or Agencies, shall be presented to the Executive Committee through him; he shall prepare for the Executive Committee its Annual Report of its operations and condition, and, under its direction, lay before the public such information as may be required in the prosecution of the work of the Commission.[144]

As part of his public information function he also edited the commission's monthly journal—the *American Freedman*.

Although abolitionists were well represented in the organizational leadership, this was not simply a reincarnation of the pre-war antislavery society. Names as prominent as Garrison and Coffin appeared on the commission's roll of officers, but, as Secretary McKim suggested early in the freedmen's aid movement, the end of slavery necessitated a shift in strategy. This organizer of the Port Royal Relief Committee had vividly described the difference in 1862 when resigning as corresponding secretary of the Pennsylvania Anti-Slavery Society. "Iconoclasm has had its day," he wrote at the time. "Scarp and counter-scarp, big guns, and *'Delenda est Carthago'* do very well when the citadel stands defiant and apparently impregnable; but when the enemy hoists the flag of truce, it is time to change our tactics," time to substitute the "hod and trowel" for the "battering ram."[145]

Lyman Abbott, who never laid claim to being an abolitionist, was openly critical of the antislavery crusade's supposed "impracticable methods" and "uncharitable spirit." He would later characterize his views as "progressive" rather than radical. "My sympathies," he generalized in a volume of reminiscences published in 1915, "have been for the most part neither with the radicals nor with the reactionaries, but with the progressives in every reform. I have been an evolutionist, but not a Darwinian, a Liberal, but not an Agnostic; an antislavery man, but not an Abolitionist; a temperance man, but not a Prohibitionist; an Industrial Democrat, but not a Socialist."[146] For this Congregational minister "progressivism" in the early Civil War years had meant opposing slavery and the aristocratic Southern society that institution helped to create. But it also meant believing the federal government had no right to interfere with slavery in the South and that blacks were not prepared for the responsibilities of citizenship. Thus, Abbott reasoned, they should not be granted immediate political equality. "I would confine the administration of Government always," he told his Terre Haute, Indiana congregation in 1863, "to the moral and intelligent." Finally, Abbott's nineteenth-century progressivism did not envision severe punishment for the Confederate states after the war. The main object of the conflict was simply to replace a system of servitude and enforced ignorance with a "pure and genuine democracy."[147]

During Reconstruction Abbott's dual role as American Freedmen's Union Commission secretary and editor gave him ample opportunity to put his ideas into practice. Making full use of the *American Freedman,* he not only advised teachers on matters of racial etiquette but personally influenced the commission's ultimate decision to abandon its stated commitment to integrated education. Aside from McKim and Levi Coffin, few, if any, abolitionist officials had as much impact on the administration of commission schools in the South.[148]

Many antislavery leaders were most active at the local or regional level. Coffin, the famous "president" of the underground railroad, was an organizer and agent of the Western Freedmen's Aid Commission.[149] Baptist abolitionist Joseph W. Parker served as corresponding secretary of his denomination's New England Educational Commission for the Freedmen, visiting the Southern states on several occasions and actually organizing a number of freedmen's schools.[150] Samuel J. May was a mainstay of the Syracuse Freedmen's Aid Society, and his cousin, Samuel May, Jr., established an auxiliary of the New England Freedmen's Aid Society in Leicester, Massachusetts. All were involved to some extent in making educational policy.[151]

Wendell Phillips, Frederick Douglass, and other like-minded abolitionists on the other hand questioned the whole freedmen's aid concept. Douglass contended blacks needed justice more than pity, liberty more than old clothes, rights more than training to enjoy them. Once give the Negro equality before the law, Douglass wrote to McKim in May 1865, "and special associations for his benefit may cease."

> He will then be comprehended as he ought to be in all those schemes of benevolence, education and progress which apply to the masses of our countrymen everywhere. In so far as these special efforts shall furnish an apology for excluding us from the general schemes of civilization so multitudinous in our country, they will be an injury to the colored race. They will serve to keep up the very prejudices which it is so desirable to banish from the country.

Douglass's mission at the time was to work for equal rights. While cooperating in efforts to establish schools for freedmen, he did so under protest, explaining in his letter: "Our home mission societies and others of like character ought to take this class in common with all other ignorant and destitute people (white as well as colored) at the South in hand."[152] The noted black abolitionist later may have been encouraged by the American Freedmen's Union Commission policy on biracial educational opportunities, but neither he nor Phillips ever became AFUC officers.

The emergence of the American Freedmen's Union Commission coincided closely with an important administrative reorganization of the American Missionary Association. Occasioned by a need to improve fund-raising procedures and to fill the gap created by Lewis Tappan's retirement as treasurer, this new plan expanded the organizational structure by setting up three regional offices outside of New York City. District secretaries were stationed at Boston, Cincinnati, and Chicago, each responsible for raising money in his region and all but the Boston officer supervising association activities in assigned areas of the South. The central office in New York staked out the southeastern region for itself, assigning the Chicago secretary the lower Mississippi Valley and Texas while placing Kentucky, Tennessee, northern Georgia, and most of Alabama under the control of the secretary in Cincinnati. Allowing for some changes in boundaries, this would be the basic jurisdictional pattern for the next few years.[153]

As with the AFUC, the American Missionary Association's presidency and vice-presidencies were largely honorary. Titles notwithstanding, the most influential association official between 1846 and 1866 was Lewis Tappan, one of the pillars of evangelical abolitionism and a dominant force on the AMA executive committee. During his twenty years as treasurer, the retired businessman tended to overshadow the two corresponding secretaries—George Whipple and Simeon S. Jocelyn. Only after Tappan stepped down on 1 January 1866 did Whipple begin to take on the leadership role he was to exercise for the next ten years.

Whipple, like his friend John W. Alvord, was a Lane Rebel who entered the abolitionist ranks as an American Anti-Slavery agent in western New York and Ohio. Pursuing his education at Oneida Institute, Lane Seminary, and Oberlin College, this protégé of Theodore Dwight Weld was professor of mathematics at Oberlin before becoming corresponding secretary of the AMA in 1846. Because of his close relationship with Alvord and Commissioner Howard he served as the chief link between the association and the Freedmen's Bureau during the latter half of the 1860s.[154]

Whipple and his principal associates were deeply involved in educational policy matters at every level. Samuel Hunt, a Congregational minister from Massachusetts with some teaching experience, held the difficult office of superintendent of education from 1864 until his resignation on 1 January 1867.[155] Former United States Christian Commission agent Edward P. Smith began as the district secretary at Cincinnati in February 1866 and within a matter of months was elevated to the powerful position of field secretary. Moving to the New York office, his specific function was the direction of work among the freedmen.[156] Smith's successor in the Midwest Department, Erastus M. Cravath, was instrumental in establishing and supervising schools throughout his area of the South. Most notably, the Oberlin graduate and Civil War chaplain helped found the institutions out of which grew Atlanta University; LeMoyne College and Fisk University in Tennessee; and Alabama's Talladega College. In 1875 he would be elected president of Fisk.[157] Western Secretary Jacob R. Shipherd, who was continually at odds with association and bureau personnel, had first gained familiarity with Southern Negro education as a secretary of the American Freedmen's Aid Commission and of the Chicago branch of the American Freedmen's Union Commission. Between February and the middle of June 1866 he represented the AFUC in the nation's capital. After shifting to the AMA he devoted considerable attention to Straight College in New Orleans and the struggling Emerson Institute at Mobile in the two years before his forced resignation in October 1868.[158] Dr. Michael E. Strieby, a minister at Mt. Vernon, Ohio and Syracuse, New York before becoming a corresponding secretary in 1864, spent much of his time handling complaints from missionaries and teachers.[159]

In both the AMA and the AFUC a relatively small group of officials concerned themselves with the day-to-day administration of freedmen's education—selecting and assigning school personnel, defining organizational policy, settling disputes among educators, arranging for transportation and supplies, advising teachers, and terminating their employment when necessary. Voluminous executive correspondence files attest to the activity and influence of these pivotal administrators.

Aid societies staffed and managed the schools, while the Freedmen's Bureau assumed responsibility for coordinating the overall educational effort. Congress's failure to appropriate funds circumscribed the bureau's activities in the first year, but two pieces of legislation enacted in 1866 vastly improved its position. The Army Appropriations Act allocated $21,000 to pay superintendents' salaries and $500,000 for "repairs and rent of schoolhouses and asylums." As interpreted by assistant commissioners in most states, the rent and repair provision also permitted assistance in the construction of new facilities.[160] The Freedmen's

Bureau bill passed over President Johnson's veto in July further empowered the agency "to seize, hold, use, lease, or sell" Confederate property for educational purposes, and instructed Commissioner Howard to furnish the protection necessary for the "safe conduct" of schools.[161] Upon passage of these acts, the program "assumed in all respects a more enlarged and permanent character." The education division instituted a detailed reporting system involving standardized forms to be completed by teachers, district and state superintendents and other bureau officers. Cooperating associations were requested to report their work on these blanks directly to the bureau. In a circular dated 20 February 1867, Howard ordered:

> that the sub-assistant commissioners and agents of this bureau, in each sub-district, will, in connection with their other duties, visit the schools now in operation in their several fields, inducing teachers to report promptly on the blanks furnished by the general superintendent of schools for this bureau.
>
> They will also observe the various plans on which these schools are conducted, suggesting improvements, or noting defects.
>
> They will gather information as to places now destitute of schools, the number of youth and children therein between the ages of six and twenty-one years, the encouragements and the obstacles existing to new schools being opened, if means are furnished.
>
> They will also ascertain what more can be done for the improvement in knowledge of the adult freedmen, all of which will be reported to the assistant commissioner for the State superintendent of schools.
>
> Care should be taken by the officers and agents of the bureau, in the performance of the above duties, not to interfere with the province of the local superintendents or teachers of the several educational associations. But it is essential that both work together in mutual consultation and sympathy.
>
> Great care will be taken to forward to this office all information gained by this circular.

State superintendents were to summarize the data in formal accounts submitted to the education division every month. General Superintendent Alvord then used this information in preparing his semiannual reports to the commissioner.[162]

Upon completion of the school year ending 30 June 1867, Alvord looked back "with astonishment at the amount accomplished." In the cities and larger towns administrators had developed graded systems extending from the elementary level to high school, and the question as to whether black children could advance into the "higher branches" was being answered. There "is increasing evidence that 'God hath made of one blood all the nations of men,' " Alvord generalized, adding that "*equal* endowments substantially, with *equal* culture, will produce that *equality* common to all mankind." In his public statements the general superintendent claimed all doubts about "the ability of colored children to learn, with capacity for higher attainment, were . . . rapidly passing away."[163] Nor were refugees and poor whites overlooked, the reports for the first six months of 1867 recording 1,348 such pupils attending segregated schools maintained especially for them or predominantly Negro schools open to both races. Hovering around 1 percent throughout the remainder of the 1860s, the small proportion of whites on the rolls documents the bureau's sincere but unsuccessful attempt at biracial education on a large scale.[164]

In the year and a half after receiving its first appropriation, the bureau encouraged industrial education and distributed financial aid to high schools, normal schools, and such institutions of higher learning as Fisk; Berea; Atlanta; Howard; Storer College at Harper's Ferry; Wesleyan and Maryville colleges in eastern Tennessee; and Lookout Mountain Educational Institute for "poor whites."[165] Alvord's office paid particular attention to improving teacher-training facilities and weeding out freedmen and native whites who were "wholly unfit" to conduct the most elementary classes. The department previously had regarded these "pay school" instructors as better than nothing, but Alvord thought the time had come when all patrons, and especially the bureau officers, should, if possible, permit no teacher to enter a schoolhouse who had not passed "some form of thorough and appropriate examination."

The superintendent also asked supporting organizations to be more selective in commissioning instructors from the North, white as well as black; for, despite existing criteria applied by the larger associations, some of their teachers were lacking in adaptability, "love for the work, or the desired moral qualities."

Figure 1   Ed.Form, No. 1.

[Ed. Form, No. 1.]

State Superintendent's Monthly School Report to Bureau Refugees, Freedmen and Abandoned Lands for the month of ——, 186 , —— District, State of ——.

A school under the distinct control of one teacher, or a teacher with one assistant, is to be reported as one school.   To be forwarded as soon as possible after the 1st of each month.

*This has reference to the present season.	Number of day schools.	Number of night schools.	Location and name of school.	When opened.*	Societies, &c., patrons.	No. schools sustained by freedmen.	No. schools sustained in part by freedmen.	No. teachers transported by bureau.	No. school buildings owned by freedmen.	No. school buildings furnished by Bureau.	Teachers. Whole number.	Teachers. White.	Teachers. Colored.	Number pupils enrolled. [Both day and night schools.] Male.	Number pupils enrolled. [Both day and night schools.] Female.	No. pupils enrolled last report.	No. left school this month.	No. new scholars this month.	Average attendance.	No. of pupils paying tuition.	No. of white pupils.	No. always present.	No. always punctual.	No. over 16 years of age.	No. in alphabet.	No. spell and read easy lessons.	No. advanced readers.	No. geography.	No. arithmetic.	No. higher branches.	No. writing.	No. needle-work.	No. free before the war.	No. Sabbath schools.	No. pupils in Sabbath schools.
This report is incomplete unless each blank is filled by a number or cipher.																																			
Totals																																			

*This has reference to the present season.

To these questions give exact or approximate answers:

1. How many of the above schools are graded? ——. How many grades? ——.
2. How many day or night schools, within your knowledge, not reported above? White, ——; colored, ——. Whole number of pupils (estimated) in all such schools? ——. Number teachers in all, ——.
3. How many Sabbath schools, within your knowledge, not reported above? White, ——; colored, ——. Whole number of pupils (estimated) in all such schools? ——. Number teachers in all, ——.
4. How many industrial schools? ——. Whole number pupils in all? ——. State the kind of work done, ——.
5. Whole amount of tuition paid by freedmen during the month, ——.
6. Whole amount of expenses for the above schools by the Bureau for the month, ——.
7. Grand total of expenses per month for support of above schools by all parties, ——.
8. Whole number of high or normal schools, ——. How many pupils in all? ——.
9. Remarks: ——.

A. B., *State Superintendent Education.*

Smaller societies and individual churches drew similar criticism for sending volunteers who knew "little of the profession and art of teaching." Alvord reminded these groups that freedmen needed educators "of a high order, with culture sufficient to reduce knowledge to its simplest forms." They must be equipped for a vocation which would "carry them among a peculiar people, of strange habits, with vices germane to a degrading, cruel system, and surrounded by circumstances in public and private wholly anomalous." In such a work every qualification was required, "physical, moral, and intellectual, but especially professional tact and taste acquired by experience, or else possessed by natural endowment."[166]

Alvord was careful to state that most educators sent by the major societies met all of these standards. While seeing room for improvement, he and his staff found ample opportunity to praise the Northern teacher in the South. John Mercer Langston summed up a common feeling in his report on several inspection tours in 1867 and 1868. Langston discovered no "appreciable diminution of zeal on the part of the Christian people of this country to educate and civilize the freed people."

> Sons and daughters, earnest, laborious Christians, educated, refined children of the tenderest culture, accustomed at home to none other than the kindest treatment and most agreeable surroundings, are found ... in goodly numbers in all parts of the south, laboring assiduously as teachers and missionaries among the freed people. Without anything like just remuneration these teachers endure with wondrous resignation the taunts and jeers, the inconveniences and the hardships, which they are so unjustly and cruelly made to suffer.[167]

Jacob R. Shipherd lauded them as the noblest "Army of Civilization" ever sustained by American benevolence.[168] Hostile Southerners considered them meddling "nigger teachers." To many observers they were simply "Yankee schoolmarms." However described, they formed the backbone of black education in the South throughout the critical decade following the Confederate attack on Fort Sumter.

2　Yankee Schoolmarm

　　　　If the cast of characters for D. W. Griffith's *The Birth of a Nation* had included a freedmen's teacher, there is little doubt she would have resembled the Yankee schoolmarm described by Wilbur Cash in his influential study of the Southern "mind":

> Generally horsefaced, bespectacled, and spare of frame, she was, of course, no proper intellectual, but at best a comic character, at worst a dangerous fool, playing with explosive forces which she did not understand.[1]

Blurring the thin line between caricature and historical analysis, Cash completed his satirical portrait by excoriating these educational carpetbaggers for their "meddlesome stupidity." Their interference in Southern affairs, he explained, had no little part in native resistance to Yankee thought.[2]

Although Cash used no footnotes, he easily could have documented this acerbic analysis not only with primary and secondary sources, but with works of fiction such as Constance Fenimore Woolson's *Rodman the Keeper*. Published in 1880, this series of "southern sketches" contains a perceptive short story detailing the Reconstruction experience of David King, a delicate, near-sighted young abolitionist-turned-freedmen's teacher.[3] Like Cash's schoolmarm, King represents a dangerous blend of naïveté and fanaticism. Failing to understand Southern white society, he is equally oblivious to the implicit desires of his black students. Dismayed by the community's approval of his grudging decision to resign in favor of a Negro instructor, he finally admits defeat when told by an old freedman "you hab nebber *quite* unnerstan us, sah, nebber quite; an' you can nebber do much fo' us, sah, on' count ob dat fack."[4]

Had they been aware of their schoolmaster's secret prejudices, blacks at Jubilee Town would have been still more critical. For

King was no practitioner of social equality. He "shrank from personal contact with the other race." Indeed, after dining with any of his students he always "threw away every atom of the food, washed his dishes, made up the fire, . . . and cooked a second supper." It took a great deal of fortitude even for him to go through his daily rounds among them. "He did his best; but it was duty, not liking."[5]

As for political equality, the New England abolitionist "would have given years of his life for the power to restrict the suffrage." Not having this power, he attacked the "emancipation problem" with the only weapon at his disposal—basic academic and moral education. Confronting the question of what to do about "tens of thousands of ignorant, childish, irresponsible souls . . . , he began at 'a, b, and c'; 'You must not steal'; 'You must not fight'; 'You must wash your faces'."[6] King acknowledged Southern claims that freedmen were idle and shiftless but emphasized these traits were "the natural result of generations of servitude and ignorance."[7]

Ultimately, however, this "thin, somewhat narrow-chested" Yankee appears as a thoroughly futile character. Failing successively in his attempts to maintain a school, to organize a free-labor cotton plantation, and to counteract the immoral influence of a grasping carpetbagger, David King dejectedly returns to his district school in New Hampshire.[8]

The Northern teacher portrayed by Cash or Woolson exemplifies but one of the two contrasting kinds of stereotype commonly associated with each of the major groups involved in Reconstruction. The heroine of Charles W. Chesnutt's short story "The March of Progress" illustrates the opposing interpretation. Henrietta Noble approximates the teachers delineated in *The Mind of the South* only in appearance and training; she is "thin, homely, and short sighted" with a "fair education." Otherwise, the similarities are negligible. Clearly not a comic figure, Miss Noble is an angelic reformer who devotes the last fifteen years of her life to educational and missionary work among blacks in Patesville, North Carolina. The "very fair progress" of Patesville's freedmen was, in Chesnutt's estimation, due chiefly to the unselfish labors of Henrietta Noble. In the off chance that readers might miss his allegorical intent, the author interjected that the nature of this latter-day Pilgrim "did not belie her name."[9]

His romantic style notwithstanding, Chesnutt made Miss Noble a believable protagonist, her fictional background corresponding closely to that of many of her real-life counterparts. Raised in a New England household by parents who taught her to fear God and love her fellow man, "she had seen her father's body brought home from a Southern battle-field and laid to rest in the village cemetery."[10] This, in combination with a missionary spirit, a sense of adventure, and a desire to be self-sufficient motivated her participation in freedmen's affairs.[11]

The contrast with Cash is more striking in the case of Mollie Ainslie, the idealized Yankee schoolmarm in Albion Tourgée's *Bricks without Straw*. An attractive, experienced teacher from Massachusetts, Miss Ainslie is a personification of sectional reconciliation after the war. Her marriage to the aristocratic Confederate veteran Hesden LeMoyne symbolizes national reunification based on cooperation between the best classes of both sections. She and freedmen's teachers in general are described as the "cream" of Northern life, one man in the novel saying he has never known "a more accomplished, devoted, or thoroughly worthy" class of women.[12]

Tourgée did not link his teachers with the abolitionist cause. Having remained aloof from radical reform throughout his younger years, the Ohio "carpetbagger" was ambivalent toward the abolitionists in his novels.[13] It thus comes as no surprise that he depicted Mollie Ainslie as a resolutely moderate woman, whose postwar philosophy was epitomized in the statement "I don't think that anything should be done to excite unnecessary antipathy which might interfere with . . . the most important element of the colored man's development, the opportunity for education."[14] In seeking to dissuade the freedmen of Red Wing from staging a parade to the polls on election day, Miss Ainslie reminded them that such a display would naturally prove exasperating to local whites. She "counselled moderation and quietness of demeanor, and told them to re-form their ranks and go forward, quietly vote and return."[15]

Mollie knew the educational process would take time. Reflecting on the abilities of black student-teacher Eliab Hill, she "realized how great is the momentum which centuries of intelligence and freedom give to the mind of the learned—how unconscious is the acquisition of the great bulk of that knowledge which goes to make up the Caucasian manhood of the nineteenth century."

While Hill's desire to acquire knowledge was insatiable and his application tireless, he lacked "that substratum of general intelligence which the free white student has partly inherited and partly acquired by observation and experience, without the labor or the consciousness of study." On one side he seemed a full-grown man of grand proportions, on the other a "pigmy-child."[16]

Compared to the two-dimensional characters portrayed by Woolson and Cash, Mollie Ainslie is a complex individual. Too complex, in fact, to have been a totally fictional creation. As might be expected from a writer whose reputation centered on his ability to dramatize real situations, Tourgée in *Bricks without Straw* was drawing on his own experience. From October 1865 until June 1867 he, along with his wife and in-laws, had operated a freedmen's school just outside of Greensboro, North Carolina.[17]

Still, a stereotype almost by definition involves some degree of oversimplification. The totality of the freedmen's educational experience takes in several thousand Miss Ainslie's, each with a different background and temperament. It is the task of the historian to synthesize these elements without obscuring the inherent diversity.

The incompleteness of existing educational records rules out the possibilty of estimating precisely the number of instructors teaching during Reconstruction. Those employing teachers were asked, but not required, to complete Alvord's standardized reporting forms, and between 20 and 30 percent of the schools known to bureau superintendents failed to do so. Self-supporting instructors and schools sustained by freedmen were especially apt to neglect this paperwork, forcing Alvord to depend on approximate figures supplied by his state and local agents.

Alvord's first semiannual report recorded 1,314 teachers as of 1 January 1866. Over the next five years the total for day and night schools alone increased to 3,300 (see table 3). By the end of the 1870 academic year, incomplete statistics for high schools, and colleges added another 261, and an unspecified number of instructors in 61 industrial schools would bring the final total of teachers in all but sabbath schools to approximately 3,600.[18]

Northern whites constituted the predominant element of the teaching force, both in numbers and influence, for seven of the nine years between the beginning of freedmen's education and the termination of involvement by the bureau. Within this group, the

Table 3   Freedmen's Teachers in Day and Night Schools

	Jan. 1867	July 1867	July 1868	July 1869	July 1870
Teachers in schools regularly reported					
White	972	1,388	1,305	1,279	1,251
Negro	458	699	990	1,176	1,312
Total	1,430	2,087	2,295	2,455	2,563
Teachers in schools not regularly reported					
White	120	109	190	272	285
Negro	91	211	306	566	452
Total	211	320	496	838	737
Total white teachers	1,092	1,497	1,495	1,551	1,536
Total Negro teachers	549	910	1,296	1,742	1,764
Total teachers	1,641	2,407	2,791	3,293	3,300

"average" Yankee teacher was a white, unmarried woman under forty years of age, quite likely living in Massachusetts, New York, or Ohio at the time of her appointment.

A survey of existing records indicates the proportion of female instructors fluctuated in the range of 65 to 85 percent during the first half-decade of Reconstruction. The American Freedmen's Union Commission placed the figure at 69 percent in 1867.[19] While trying to attract more male volunteers, aid societies soon accepted the seemingly inevitable feminization of freedmen's teaching. As early as 1865 an article on teacher qualifications in the New England Freedmen's Aid Society magazine used feminine pronouns in referring to potential applicants, and generally the Yankee schoolmarm became a virtual cliché.[20] When women sought wider employment opportunities after the war, the AMA urged them to consider the domestic mission field as an alternative to such supposedly masculine vocations as business, industry, law, medicine, theology, and politics. Flying in the face of an emerging trend toward women's rights, the AMA argued in a short pamphlet published in 1873 that freedmen's work was appropriate to woman's "special faculty and adaptations." "Here is a demand for her sweetest sympathies and her boundless charity," the pamphlet lectured paternalistically. "How much better this than to be groping about in the dark, as so many of them are, seeking to answer the craving for work in callings that belong more properly to men."[21]

The various committees charged with teacher selection essentially agreed on a few basic qualifications for employment in their schools—health, energy, religious purpose, morality, commitment, and educational experience heading most lists. Each organization had its own variations on these standard requirements. The New England Freedmen's Aid Society insisted their employees "must have earnestness of purpose."

> No mere youthful enthusiasm, love of adventure, or desire of change, will sustain a teacher through the labors and hardships of her work. She must see in the freedmen the representatives of humanity, "the little ones" whom Jesus has told us we serve him in serving. She should feel also the importance of the work in relation to our country: that she is forming the people who are to influence very largely its future, for good or evil. She will need all these motives of religion and patriotism to sustain her in her duties.[22]

Aiming for the best possible combination of energy and maturity, the society's committee on teachers discouraged elderly applicants as well as those under the age of twenty-five. The committee refused even to consider applications from anyone under twenty-two. As for personality traits, they specified "high moral character, purity of heart and mind, self-control, firmness, command of temper, the soldier's spirit of obedience, without its uncomprehending slavishness, frank and honest deportment, self-respect, and dignified propriety of manner."[23]

While the New England society expected its teachers "to be religious in character and influence," it imposed no sectarian tests. Its teachers, like its officers, represented "almost every shade of religious opinion." So far as the editors of the *Freedmen's Record* knew, seven or eight of the society's fifty-four instructors in 1865 were Unitarians, three were Quakers, and the remainder was about equally divided among the Baptist, Methodist, and Congregational communions.[24]

A special committee on education and religion later formulated comparable guidelines for the American Freedmen's Union Commission. Made up of General Secretary Abbott, Rev. E. H.

Canfield, Rev. Octavius B. Frothingham, Francis R. Cope, and Dr. Nathan Bishop, the committee prepared a formal statement defending their organization's nonsectarian policies. ''The education of the South . . . is a truly religious work,'' committee members insisted, ''none the less so because it is undenominational.''

> We desire the more that our schools may be truly Christian because they are unecclesiastical. For this purpose we aim to commission only teachers possessing the spirit of true religion, by which we do not mean persons of any particular doctrinal views, but such as are attracted to the work, not by curiosity, or love of adventure, or its compensation, but by a genuine spirit of love for God and man.

Not allowing ''the peculiar tenets of any particular denomination'' to be taught in its schools, the commission sought educators willing to confine themselves to ''those precepts of morality and teachings of the Christian religion in which all agree.'' Men and women employed by the AFUC would be expected to offer instruction in ''secular knowledge'' and in ''the fundamental duties of the Christian religion as inculcated in the command, 'Thou shalt love the Lord thy God with all thy heart and soul and strength, and thy neighbor as thyself'.'' This secular society was content to leave the inculcation of ''more specific religious truth'' to the churches.[25]

O. B. Frothingham, the distinguished Unitarian member of the special committee on education and religion, presented his own interpretation of the emerging AFUC policy in a letter to the *Independent* published on 12 July 1866, two months before the appearance of the committee's official statement. Less subtle in its condemnation of what Frothingham termed ''parochial education,'' the essay declared unequivocally: ''Practical religion is common ground for both teacher and missionary. Speculative and ceremonial religion belong to the missionary alone, and may be, should be, kept wholly distinct from mental instruction.'' Educational work could be done by ''any intelligent, capable, right-minded, whole-souled, wise and earnest man or woman, whether Calvinist or Universalist, Evangelical or Unitarian, Churchman or Comeouter, advocate of the scheme of salvation or not.'' The work demanded personal virtue, social enlightenment, a deep respect for man as a rational being, and a profound sense of allegiance to recognized moral law, but it did not require "a familiarity with the Bible, a zeal for the sacraments, or a particular belief in regard to the conditions of the future life, or the terms of acceptance with God." Adopting a tone more strident than the committee's statement, Frothingham explained why educators grounded in liberal religion were preferable to evangelical missionary-teachers:

> Rationalists and Unitarians—who reject the scheme of salvation, whose religion is chiefly ethical, who preach up the interests of this life, intellectual culture, domestic virtue, social kindness, the priceless worth of the simply human relations —may mingle such religion as they have with education, because education is their religion. But evangelical men, who are supremely interested in a salvation of souls cannot confound them with secular interests without encountering the dangers of compromising both.

Presumably, this was the kind of language Abbott had in mind when he wrote to Secretary McKim, "I like the general spirit of Mr. Frothingham's article very much, tho' I fear some expressions in the letter may lead to a rejoinder."[26]

Abbott's fears of a destructive newspaper controversy were well-founded. In August the *Boston Recorder* responded with an article asking "Who Shall Educate the Freedmen?" Treating Frothingham's statement as an accurate representation of the AFUC position, this religious newspaper accused the commission of inconsistency in professing a desire to send out "none but Christian men and women" at the same time one of its "leading managers" was questioning the suitability of religious instruction in freedmen's schools. The *Recorder* considered it inevitable that religion would color the teaching of Christian educators. Yet a key member of the AFUC executive committee seemed to be saying this rendered evangelical teachers less prepared to instruct black students in standard academic subjects. In opposition to the views of Frothingham and his sympathizers, the Boston paper argued that "the highest state of civilization is attained where the people are most thoroughly imbued with the principles of evangelical religion." With reference to Southern Negroes, the author of the *Recorder* article lectured: "Their religion is the basis of their domestic and mental improvement."

When this is ignored, or set at naught, the most effective in-
strumentality for their civilization is set aside. How utterly in-
appropriate—to use no harsher term—it is to send these poor
people, whose religion is dearer to them than life itself,
teachers who must be silent on that subject; or who, if they
speak their honest sentiments, must tell them that their
"blessed Saviour" is a mere creature; that there is no hell or
personal devil; that the Book which they are so anxious to be
able to read, has no claim to be regarded as the Word of God;
or that to abandon their church relations is to "come out of
Babylon."[27]

The AMA's decision to reprint the *Recorder* piece in the September *American Missionary* along with an editorial of its own
put AFUC leaders on the defensive. Soon after the release of his
committee's address on religion and education, Abbott requested
that the AMA magazine publish a part of it as proof that the
Recorder had misconceived and misstated commission policies.
The editors honored the request but felt constrained to express
their conviction that the Boston newspaper had fairly stated
Frothingham's position. They perceived little real difference between his article in the *Independent* and the statement prepared
by Abbott's committee. Both allegedly manifested a desire on the
part of the AFUC to take education out of the hands of so-called
"ecclesiastical organizations" and to monopolize in one nonsectarian society "all the means, and all the opportunities for
educating the Freedmen in common or day schools." Emphasizing the AMA's policy of employing Christians from every *evangelical* denomination, association spokesmen dismissed claims
that the American Freedmen's Union Commission was better
fitted for the work simply because it embraced Universalists,
Rationalists, and Unitarians.[28]

Commission officials did their best to play down these differences over liberal religion. They insisted that most AFUC
teachers were orthodox Christians, a contention corroborated
by the organization's manuscript records and publications. In a
sample of sixty-three white teachers who indicated their religious
affiliation, only three were Unitarians, and one of these was listed
as "Unitarian or Congregational." Aside from the one instructor
who espoused Swedenborgianism, this was the extent of religious

liberalism in the group. The more orthodox element included: nineteen Baptists, sixteen Methodists, eleven Congregationalists, eight Presbyterians, and five Episcopalians.[29]

The AFUC was still a secular society, however, and its separation of religion and education obviated any real chance for accommodation with the American Missionary Association. When challenged on its school policies, the AMA answered:

> The school teacher has very peculiar facilities for reaching the Freedmen with sound religious instruction, that must not be lost. None others can so readily win and retain their confidence. This is pre-eminently true of those who, while they instruct them in letters, and in the domestic arts . . . and all that pertains to this life, seek to win them to Christ, and lead them in the way of life eternal. God has thus by His providence indicated the combined work of intellectual and religious instruction, and the most effective instrumentality for its accomplishment, and we can hardly regard as true to Christ and His requirements, the effort to dissever what He has thus joined together, and to take from the Missionary teachers the power, the vantage ground which, by their schools, they have gained, to speak a word for Christ and eternity.[30]

In keeping with this philosophy, the AMA placed "missionary spirit" at the top of its list of teacher qualifications. No one need apply who was not "prepared to endure hardness as a good soldier of Jesus Christ." None should go who were influenced by romantic or mercenary motives, none who sought "the poetry or the pay," none who wished to go South because they had failed in the North. As published in the *American Missionary* of July 1866, the other prerequisites were health, energy, culture and common sense, teaching experience, and suitable personal habits. Marked "singularities" and "idiosyncracies" had no place in the AMA scheme of things:

> Moroseness or petulance, frivolity or undue fondness for society, are too incompatible with the benevolence, gravity, and earnestness of our work, to justify the appointment, or recommendation, of any exhibiting such traits. Neither should any be commissioned who are addicted to the use of tobacco or opium, or are not pledged to total abstinence from intoxicating drinks.[31]

The AMA was nonsectarian, at least with respect to Protestant denominations, and in this limited sense stood apart from bodies like the Freedmen's Aid Society of the Methodist Episcopal Church, the American Baptist Home Missionary Association, the Protestant Episcopal Freedmen's Commission, and the Presbyterian Church's Committee on Freedmen. As distinguished from their AMA counterparts, teachers commissioned by these societies were representatives of a particular denomination. If not ministers themselves, they usually worked closely with denominational missionaries "in elevating and saving the people," and in adding black communicants to the church rolls.[32] That sectarian societies would favor their own denomination was expected and in the case of the Presbyterians was incorporated in official policy. Retaining guidelines developed earlier by the church's General Assembly, the Committee on Freedmen accepted only Presbyterian candidates who had been endorsed by their respective Sessions.[33]

Quaker societies were not sectarian to this extent, but they too favored instructors of their own persuasion. Indicative of this priority were letters written by the secretary of the Instruction Committee of the Friends Freedmen's Association when seeking principals for two or three large schools in North Carolina. Following a familiar pattern, Joseph Potts asked for recommendations, specifying "we would *prefer* Friends or those educated as such, if it be possible, and desire 1st class teachers."[34] On the broader topic of religious lessons for freedmen, the instruction committee advised superintendents and teachers that all of their schools were to be opened with the reading of a "judicious selection" from the Bible, "followed by a silence meet for prayer."[35]

A number of AMA teachers were products of foreign missionary backgrounds, having served in association missions in such locations as Africa, India, and Jamaica. West Africa had been the AMA's primary mission field from its founding in 1846. Indeed, the American Missionary Association was a direct outgrowth of the Amistad Committee, a body constituted in 1839 to provide legal and educational assistance to a group of Mendian slaves accused of piracy and murder. After securing the release of the Amistad captives, the committee had arranged to return the former slaves to their homeland and had set up a mission station among the Mendi people in Liberia. It was at this station that several AMA teachers obtained their missionary experience.[36]

The Jamaican mission was the creation of another AMA predecessor—the Committee for West Indian Missions. This committee had been established in 1844 to support five existing stations on the island maintained by a group of former Oberlin students. Dominated by abolitionists, its members were greatly interested in the success of the West Indian experiment in emancipation as an example to their own countrymen. Jamaica was thus an ideal training ground for many who eventually became involved in freedmen's education. Such was the case, for example, with Jacob Weston, an instructor in a bureau school at Saint Charles, Missouri. Educated in Cincinnati as a physician, Weston before the War had spent several years as a minister in Jamaica and had taught high school in New England. He and his wife had come west to Missouri in 1865.[37]

The home mission field was equally important as a source of talent for the bureau school program. Here again the AMA and Oberlin College led the way. In 1842, Frederick Ayer, a missionary among the Ojibway Indians in Minnesota, visited Oberlin to obtain recruits from among the ranks of the graduating class. Ayer's appeal was successful, and more than twenty students offered their services to the American Board of Commissioners for Foreign Missions. All were refused commissions, however, chiefly because of objections by board members to Finney perfectionism, the theology taught at Oberlin. Still determined to work among the Ojibway, several of the students persuaded the Western Reserve Congregational Association to create a society which would "prosecute missionary operations among the western Indians, and in other parts of the world." The resultant organization—the Western Reserve Evangelical Missionary Society—resolved not to "solicit or knowingly receive the wages of oppression, especially the price of the bodies and souls of men, for prosecution of the work of the Lord." In 1846 the society became part of the AMA.[38]

Ayer himself was a personification of the transition from home missionary to Freedmen's Bureau teacher. Born in Stockbridge, Massachusetts in 1803, he spent most of his early life in New York State, where his father was a missionary. Prevented from going to college by ill health, he left New York in 1829 to become a missionary to the Indians of the Northwest. There he spent the next twenty years organizing schools and churches. Again hampered by illness, Ayer settled in Fort Ripley, Minnesota, where he maintained a school for Ojibway children until the Indian raids of 1863.[39] After a short stint as a farmer, the aging minister and his wife went to Atlanta under the auspices of the AMA. Upon their arrival in the capital city, they took over a small Negro school that had been started by two ex-slaves, James Tate and Grandison B. Daniels. They subsequently established a second school in an obsolescent railroad car, which the association had purchased for $310. Together these two institutions constituted the basis for what later became Atlanta University.[40]

Although Ayer's home mission experience was restricted to the East and Midwest, there were freedmen's teachers who had served in the Far West. Richard Sloan was one such teacher. In the ante-bellum period, he taught among the Comanche Indians at the Witchataw Agency in Kansas. During the Civil War he worked with the Chickasaws and then went to Mexico, where he maintained a school for "the African people." With the onset of Reconstruction, Sloan moved back across the border and established a Negro school at Brownsville, Texas.[41]

Several bureau instructors had done their missionary work among the racial and ethnic minorities of urban centers like New York and Chicago. Charleston teacher Martha Kellogg, for example, had been principal of a Children's Aid Society industrial school for German-American girls in New York City.[42]

The career of a second urban missionary—E. R. Pierce—provides ample proof that not all freedmen's teachers were moral and pious. A merchant and businessman for nine years prior to his becoming a minister in the United Brethren Church, Pierce taught for several years in Negro sabbath and night schools in Chicago. During the Civil War, he served as a missionary, chaplain of the First Alabama Colored Infantry, and bureau superintendent of schools for Memphis, Tennessee. In January 1865, he asked the AMA to send him and his wife as missionaries to Africa. His application was rejected, however, for reasons that are spelled out in a series of letters written by Pierce's coworkers. According to several accounts, Pierce was having sexual relations with a married Quaker woman and was not fit to go as a missionary into Africa or anywhere except "into a *Bar room.*" In addition to philandering, the Memphis educator was accused of drunkenness, smoking cigars, defrauding the army and the American Freedmen's Union Commission, neglecting his educational duties in favor of cotton planting, and taking chloroform as laughing gas. Faced with overwhelming evidence against him, Pierce admitted that he was guilty of some of these indiscretions.[43]

Relatively few Northern white Freedmen's Bureau instructors had had any prior teaching experience among blacks in the South. This was due in large part to ante-bellum Southern resistance to outside educational influences. By the mid-1850s this resistance had risen to the point where citizens' groups throughout the South passed resolutions suggesting that "no teacher should be employed who was not born South, or was not a Northern man with Southern principles."[44] In 1854 a Charleston convention urged the employment of local instructors, explaining that the importation of a "troop of Northern teachers" to organize the city's free schools was an insult since there were "sons of the South sufficient for the Work."[45] Similarly, in 1856 the *Richmond Examiner* complained that the Southern states were being overrun by hordes of illiterate, unprincipled graduates of Yankee public schools who did not deserve the protection of the law.[46]

Despite local opposition, a number of Yankee educators continued teaching below the Mason-Dixon Line. One such teacher was Mrs. H. A. Hart, daughter of Rev. Samuel Newell, the first United States missionary to India. Born in India, Mrs. Hart was raised and educated in Geneva, New York. After graduating from college, she accepted a position as teacher and governess in Liberty County, Georgia. In 1855 she married a widowed planter and immediately established a clandestine school for slaves on his property. Because of their Unionist sympathies, the Harts were ostracized by both neighbors and family. According to a later account, Mrs. Hart was "put down with the dogs and was compelled to beg bread from the Col[d] people." Sherman's march through Georgia and the death of her husband in 1866 made the situation still worse. For several years after the war, she barely existed on a diet of stale bread and dry hominy. It was thus a combination of humanitarianism and financial need which prompted Mrs. Hart to open a freedmen's school on her plantation in the summer of 1869.[47]

Yankee educators encountered severe opposition even in such cities as New Orleans and Washington, D.C. When in 1858 Mrs. Mary Price, a native of Ohio, opened a school for blacks in the Louisiana metropolis, she was constantly threatened by signs placed before her door reading "death to nigger teachers." Despite such threats, Mrs. Price continued her school long enough for it to become a base from which the freedmen's educational movement could be launched in the Department of the Gulf.[48] In Washington, opposition was almost as intense when Myrtilla Miner, a young white woman from New York, established an academy for Negro girls. Still, Miss Miner's school flourished and produced at least one recruit for the Freedmen's Bureau educational program—Emily Howland. Miss Howland was born into a Quaker family in Sherwood, New York. Her parents were abolitionists and her principal reading as a child was that of anti-slavery books and papers. She studied at private schools around Sherwood and, for a short time, in Philadelphia. According to her own account, in 1857 "much against the wishes of the most of my relatives I went to Washington and taught a school for free col-oured girls which had been started some years before by Miss Myrtilla Miner."[49]

A number of freedmen's educators had received their teaching experience in the Negro schools of the North. Mrs. L. W. Stebbins, a bureau instructor in the District of Columbia, had earlier been associated with a sabbath school for free blacks and run-away slaves in Wilbraham, Massachusetts.[50] Similarly, Joseph S. Evans, an AMA employee in Virginia, had been principal of the "Colored Department" of the West Chester, Pennsylvania public schools between 1859 and 1865.[51]

Quaker abolitionist Laura Haviland had devoted the greater part of her adult life to black education. A native of Ontario, Canada, Mrs. Haviland had begun her teaching career in a manual labor school for indigent white children in Michigan Territory. There she instructed the girls in housework, sewing, and knitting, while her husband and brother taught farming to the boys. Soon, however, financial difficulties forced the family to reconstitute the school on "the Oberlin plan" of admitting anyone "of good moral character, regardless of sex or color." As part of the reorganization, several Oberlin students were added to the instructional staff. Together these changes helped to make the school both a financial and a social success. As Mrs. Haviland later explained in her autobiography: "Hundreds of young people who enjoyed the privileges our school afforded came to us with their prejudices against the colored people and our position in regard to them; but they soon melted away, and went they knew not where."[52]

After more than a decade of association with Raisin Institute, Laura Haviland moved to Toledo, Ohio, where she and her daughter Anna established a public school for blacks. Taking advantage of a state law which allocated funds to support a "colored school" in any town where there were fifteen or more regular scholars, the Havilands stayed just long enough to pressure the local school board into continuing support beyond the first term. This accomplished, Mrs. Haviland resigned her post, recommending as her replacement John Mitchell, a black student from Oberlin who later became a freedmen's teacher in Columbus, Georgia.[53] She then returned to Windsor, Ontario, where she opened a school for fugitive slaves.[54] Thus, by the time Laura Haviland began teaching freedmen, she had already devoted over thirty years to Negro education.

The most common form of prior educational experience was that obtained in the predominantly white public and private schools of the North. The institutions represented ranged from the Yates City, Illinois public schools to Yale College.[55] Midway between these extremes were men like Ira Pettibone, a minister who had been principal of a boarding school in Litchfield County, Connecticut for fifteen years prior to accepting an AMA position at Savannah, Georgia.[56] Somewhat atypical was Fisk P. Brewer, a science instructor at Yale who came to Raleigh, North Carolina under the auspices of the American Freedmen's Union Commission.[57] In the post-Reconstruction era, Brewer was elected professor of Greek at the University of North Carolina.[58]

Like many of his fellow freedmen's teachers, Fisk Brewer had grown up in a favorable academic environment. Similarly, William F. Mitchell, a Philadelphia Quaker who served as superintendent of freedmen's schools in Nashville, was born into a family which had produced two nationally known astronomers.[59]

Continuing the tradition begun at Port Royal, a significant proportion of the bureau's teacher corps was recruited from such prestigious institutions as Harvard, Yale, Brown, Amherst, Williams, and Mount Holyoke. An even larger percentage came from relatively obscure colleges like Connecticut Normal School, Oakland Female Institute, and Michigan Central College.[60] A typical representative of the latter group was Mortimer A. Warren, a graduate of Connecticut Normal School's class of 1856. Indeed, Warren seemed to be almost the archetype of the professional educator of the mid-nineteenth century. He was thoroughly conversant with "improved methods of teaching, after some ten years of study and experience as a teacher."[61] He did not hesitate to apply these modern methods to freedmen's education. As he explained when seeking an appointment as principal of a proposed teacher's college in New Orleans:

> Our first move would not be to teach the science of Pedagogy, but to carry on the studies already commenced in the grammar schools. Latin is a favorite study but I am wise enough to see that it would be out of place here. The natural sciences, mathematics, history[,] composition[,] and all the English branches would be all that we should attempt. After a time . . . we might extend this circle[,] but we would not dig up Greek and Latin roots. The Freedmen need to be fitted for a present civilization[,] not for a past and musty one.[62]

Not unexpectedly, Oberlin College contributed more than its share of freedmen's teachers. In most cases these Oberlin graduates were motivated by antislavery ideals. This was certainly true of Sallie Holley and Caroline Putnam, cofounders of the bureau school at Lottsburgh, Virginia. Both were oldline Garrisonian abolitionists, and, in Miss Putnam's estimation, "the only ultra radicals" at Oberlin.[63]

Sallie Holley was a true product of the Age of Reform. Born in the "burned-over district" of New York, her father was active in Anti-Masonry and was an officer of the American Anti-Slavery Society. Myron Holley was the first AASS leader to urge abolitionists to form their own political organization, and in 1840 his persistent efforts in that direction eventuated in the creation of the Liberty Party.[64] With respect to religion, he was a nonconformist. Sallie followed her father's lead in almost every respect. She became an opponent of slavery, a pacifist, a Unitarian, and a temperance advocate. She even considered teaching in a school for young Irish girls in 1847, but decided instead to enroll at Oberlin—this despite her brother's plea not to expose herself to the insults accorded to anyone affiliated with that "nigger school." At Oberlin, Sallie met Caroline Putnam and Josephine S. Griffing, an antislavery lecturer who later became a bureau teacher in Washington, D.C. It was Mrs. Griffing who convinced Sallie Holley to become an active abolitionist. Once converted to the cause, Miss Holley was tenacious in her defense of Negro rights. On one occasion, she went so far as to nominate a black student for president of Oberlin's Ladies' Literary Society. There was an adverse reaction at first, but her candidate was elected. On another occasion, she incurred the wrath of the college president's wife by ignoring her admonition against staying overnight in a Negro household.[65]

During the Civil War, Sallie Holley abandoned most of her Garrisonian principles in favor of those espoused by the Wendell Phillips faction. Rejecting Garrison's antipolitical philosophy, she became an active Republican.[66]

In 1868 Emily Howland convinced Misses Holley and Putnam to establish a school for freedmen at Lottsburgh, Virginia. Sallie Holley remained there until her death in 1893, and Miss Putnam was still instructing the Negroes of Lottsburgh in 1907.[67]

Educators with antislavery backgrounds often had risked heavy fines and even imprisonment by purposefully violating laws designed to protect the rights of slaveholders. Laura Haviland, Clinton Fisk, and John Blevens were representative of hundreds of underground railroad participants who had helped runaway slaves in the ante-bellum years. Blevens had paid the legal price for his covert activities, receiving a sentence of forty years in the Virginia Penitentiary for "the virtuous act alleged, but not proven of assisting a slave to obtain his freedom." The prisoner had completed sixteen years of his sentence when Union forces liberated him (and Richmond) in 1865. He was sixty years old when he left prison and entered the classroom.[68]

Rev. Horace Hovey, one of Blevens's fellow teachers in Richmond, had incurred a different form of punishment by injecting equal rights doctrines into his sermons at the Congregational church in Florence, Massachusetts. In 1863 approximately twenty of his parishioners walked out of the church in protest when the abolitionist pastor preached that "the negro has the same right that we have . . . to obtain a first-rate education and to rise in social position according as he rises in worth; the same right to vote and to sit in legislative and congressional halls.''[69]

As with so many instructors, Emily Bliss and Mary Ames encountered opposition even from their own families. Both were residents of Springfield, Massachusetts, and Mary Ames was the product of a Unitarian household. Yet the two women's families ridiculed their going to Hilton Head, South Carolina and tried to stop them, prophesying that they would return in less than a month.[70]

In contrast to Hovey and Miss Ames were those teachers who had spent most of their lives in an environment conducive to liberal political and racial ideas. One such teacher was Cornelia Hancock, a Quaker abolitionist from Hancock's Bridge, New Jersey. In a town noted for its social and political moderation, Cornelia's family stood apart as a bastion of antislavery partisanship. Indeed, her father was known throughout the township as the one man ''who was foolish enough to vote for Frémont in the election of 1856.'' He was, in Cornelia's words, ''a nonconformist by nature,'' an idealist who ''believed that every man should be a law unto himself.'' He also believed that ''he should carefully avoid interference with the rights of others and take as little interest as possible in other people's affairs.'' Cornelia never knew her father to have an occupation. Instead, he spent his time fishing, reading newspapers, and generally pursuing a lifestyle similar to that made famous by Henry David Thoreau.[71]

Equally important in fostering Miss Hancock's inclination toward social reform was her brother-in-law, Dr. Henry T. Child. Well-known for his involvement in humanitarian causes, Dr. Child laid the groundwork for Cornelia's career in freedmen's education by employing her as an army medical assistant in Pennsylvania and Virginia. After ten years as a school principal at Pleasantville, South Carolina, Miss Hancock returned to join Dr. Child in establishing a social-work agency in Philadelphia. Four years later, in 1882, she helped found the Children's Aid Society of Pennsylvania.[72]

With so many female abolitionists participating in the bureau educational enterprise, it was to be expected that some freedmen's teachers would be veterans of the women's rights movement. The number involved in this type of reform activity is difficult to estimate, but there is sufficient evidence to document the feminist careers of a few of the most prominent Yankee schoolmarms.

Of all the feminist teachers, Josephine S. Griffing is probably the best known. Born, raised, and educated in Connecticut, Mrs. Griffing in 1842 migrated to Ohio's Western Reserve, where her home soon became a station on the underground railroad. In 1849 she joined the Western Anti-Slavery Society as codirector of the lecture corps. At about the same time, she joined the crusade for women's rights. According to Elizabeth Cady Stanton's *History of Woman Suffrage*, Mrs. Griffing "heartily responded" to "the first demand for the enfranchisement of women, . . . and in this re-form . . . was ever untiring in effort, wise in counsel, and eminent in public speech."[73]

Josephine Griffing remained active in the feminist movement after assuming her dual role as social worker and freedmen's teacher in Washington, D.C. There she helped organize the Universal Franchise Association of the District of Columbia in 1867. She was also corresponding secretary of the National Woman Suffrage Association. Rejecting the common abolitionist conten-tion that Negro suffrage took precedence over feminist goals, Mrs. Griffing joined Elizabeth Cady Stanton and Susan B. An-thony in opposing ratification of the Fifteenth Amendment be-cause it did not extend the franchise to women.[74]

Mrs. Griffing did not consider woman suffrage the sole objec-tive of the movement. In a letter written in 1870 she graphically made this point by comparing feminism to a surging tide:

> How grandly the tide is lashing the shore on both sides of the Atlantic, and its voice is the voice of God, commanding once more that ye "let my people go, that they may serve me." Only the foam and the surge are seen to-day—"Woman and the Ballot." But there is overturning and upheaving below, and the great depths shall ere long become the surface. . . . To my mind the issue of to-day in the woman cause is clearly not what Paul taught and thought, nor what God has settled upon her as her dower, nor what the marriage contract makes her, but it is woman as a beneficent genius, next to the angels, against woman below the beasts, in human society under the heel of the Law, in the arms of brute force, crushed to death with passion and lust.[75]

In addition to Josephine Griffing, Ohio's Western Reserve pro-duced several more feminist teachers, including Sallie Holley, Caroline Putnam, and Emily Howland. All three of these young women had joined the movement while students at Oberlin. Each had attended women's rights conventions in Ohio and New York and had thus been exposed to the ideas of such eminent reformers as Fanny Gage, Sojourner Truth, Caroline Severance, and Thomas Wentworth Higginson.[76] Miss Holley had herself attained a degree of prominence at the time of her graduation by delivering an address entitled "The Ideal of Womanhood." The "heretical" ideas in this oration "put bees in the bonnets of the sages, humming as they did with women's right to vote, to preach, and with the brightest humour, poetry, and satire, ranging for illustration from Hans Andersen's 'Ugly Duck' to Wordsworth's 'perfect woman nobly planned.' "[77]

Sallie Holley remained active in the feminist movement throughout the remainder of her life. Between 1868 and 1871, she and fellow teacher Emily Howland engaged in a successful campaign to open the doors of Cornell University to women. And as late as 1888, Miss Holley was still dedicated enough to make the trip from Lottsburgh, Virginia to New York State in order to attend a woman's suffrage convention.[78]

Not all teachers were sympathetic to the woman's rights movement. J. Milton Hawks, for example, would have preferred that his wife abandon her feminist ways and accept the more conventional role of homemaker. He especially regretted that Esther had decided to pursue her own medical career. A husband, according to Mr. Hawks, needed a loving woman rather than a "business man-like worker."[79] His arguments apparently had little effect, however. Instead of staying in South Carolina with her spouse, Mrs. Hawks accepted a bureau teaching post in Jacksonville, Florida.[80]

Nineteenth-century reformers rarely restricted themselves to one cause. Thus it was inevitable that the bureau's educational staff would include not only abolitionists, feminists, and civil rights workers but also temperance advocates, penal reformers, and proponents of Negro emigration.

The influence of temperance crusaders on the educational program was especially evident. Superintendent Alvord was secretary of the Lincoln National Temperance Association, an organization which encouraged sobriety among freedmen. He was also instrumental in establishing the Vanguard of Freedom, a temperance society for students in bureau schools. The superintendent provided space on monthly reports for teachers to describe their progress in organizing branches of the Vanguard. The results were disappointing, however. As Alvord explained in 1869, teachers, "not being especially instructed to organize societies, and very often overworked in other ways . . . have not felt obliged to act in this direction, though themselves favorable to temperance, and seeing daily great need for temperance efforts."[81]

Although Alvord may have overestimated the extent of temperance zeal among teachers, he could safely count on the support of several highly placed bureau officials, including Clinton B. Fisk, the assistant commissioner for Tennessee and Kentucky. Extremely active in the educational affairs of these two states, Fisk was an unabashed prohibitionist. He was so devoted to the cause, in fact, that he ran for the governorship of New Jersey on the prohibition ticket in 1886 and was the candidate of this party in the presidential campaign of 1888.[82]

Fisk's counterpart in the Negro emigration movement was James Redpath, the chief organizer of a spectacular but short-lived campaign to colonize northern blacks in the Republic of Haiti. In 1859 Haitian President Fabre Geffrard, eager to develop his country's natural and human resources, invited Redpath to Haiti and approached him with a proposition to subsidize the emigration of American blacks to the island. Geffrard finally won Redpath over by convincing him that a strong, prosperous Haiti would demonstrate to skeptics the capacity and genius of the Negro race.

Upon his return to the United States, Redpath founded the Haytian Emigrant Bureau and immediately began promoting his grandiose project by publishing a guide to the island republic. In it he described Haiti as the only country in the Western Hemisphere

> where the Black and the man of color are undisputed lords
> . . . where neither laws, nor prejudice, nor historical memories press cruelly on persons of African descent; where the people whom America degrades and drives from her are rulers, judges, and generals, . . . authors, artists, and legislators.[83]

With this type of publicity Redpath persuaded approximately 2,000 blacks to emigrate to Haiti.[84]

Although Redpath's colonization scheme attracted numerous supporters (including Dr. J. Milton Hawks), it also encountered passionate opposition from Negroes who rejected "the infamous doctrine . . . that the white and black races cannot live together upon this continent in a state of freedom and equality."[85] Opposition increased as reports began filtering back from Haiti of mismanagement, disease, financial difficulties, and hostility between natives and immigrants. By 1863 most of the original colonists had either died or returned to the United States. Buckling under such pressure, the Haytian Emigrant Bureau disbanded, and Redpath became a war correspondent for the *New York Tribune*.[86]

It would be a mistake to assume that the decision to become a Freedmen's Bureau instructor was in every case motivated by purely altruistic considerations. In many instances applicants for teaching positions were more concerned about employment than reform.

This was certainly true of Charles C. Arms, who came to Alabama to teach after running out of money while studying medicine in Philadelphia.[87] It was also true of Edward Van Ness, a War Democrat who in the latter part of the Rebellion served in the Connecticut legislature. Obviously aware that his party affiliation might work against him, Van Ness specified in his letter of application:

> Since the conclusion of the War I have been and still am a supporter of the liberal policy of the present administration and should I be placed in charge of freedmen I should endeavor to impress upon them the fact that though emancipated, they still owe to their former masters the respect which a son though of age owes a parent.

Van Ness further specified that, although not destitute, he was sixty-one years old and had no family.[88] There is no notation on the letter indicating whether or not Van Ness received the appointment. Considering his endorsement of the "liberal policy" of the Johnson administration, it seems doubtful.

That such applications were not confined to the office of Superintendent Alvord is amply demonstrated by the admonition of the American Missionary Association that no teachers need apply who wished to go South because they had been unsuccessful in business in the North.[89] It should be pointed out, however, that this admonition did little to discourage applicants who could find no other work. Neither did it prevent the AMA and its sister organizations from employing this type of applicant.[90]

There were, of course, thousands of Union veterans searching for new sources of employment in the immediate postwar period. Many were disabled. In the fall of 1867 Alvord's office received at least three applications from soldiers who had been incapacitated while serving on the front lines. Two were hospitalized at the United States Military Asylum at Augusta, Maine. The third— Will J. Deming—was recuperating at his home in New Caseo, Michigan. "Have taught school considerable," Deming wrote in his application. "I have ever been loyal and am a friend of the Colored people. I am 25 years old & a single man."[91]

Some veterans came South to stay, bringing their families with them. Perhaps the most famous of these Northern emigrants was Adm. Charles Wilkes, the naval officer whose seizure of the British merchant ship *Trent* had provoked an international incident. Forced into a premature retirement by this diplomatic controversy, Wilkes bought 15,000 acres in Gaston County, North Carolina. On his property he established an "iron business" and a "school of 150 colored and 50 white pupils." The school was taught by Mrs. Wilkes and her three daughters.[92]

Veterans who had spent considerable time in the Confederate states often felt they were peculiarly qualified for freedmen's work, especially if they had been officers in black regiments. Thus George W. Williams emphasized in his application that he possessed "some knowledge of the South and the Negro character," having served nearly four years in the army, the last sixteen months of which were spent as an officer of the Forty-Third U. S. Colored Troops.[93] Similarly, prospective teacher J. H. Douglass wrote in 1865:

> I see by the papers that the Freedmen's Bureau has been organized and I suppose that its operations in the South will give employment to many persons as Superintendents, Teachers & c.... Having been an officer of colored troops perhaps I may be better fitted for the duties required to be performed by the employees of this Bureau than persons who have had no experience with negroes.[94]

Veterans like John Ogden and O. W. Dimick had become freedmen's teachers out of a sense of obligation. Both men had been assisted by slaves after escaping from the prisoner-of-war camp at Columbia, South Carolina. Ogden described his experience in an *American Missionary* article entitled "A Peculiar Call to Teach." According to this account, he fled through the swamps of the Palmetto State "half naked and starved, in mid-winter, chased and caught by bloodhounds, thrown into prisons, and befriended on all occasions by the poor slave." "These things," Ogden concluded, "lay me under some obligations to the work."[95]

A number of teachers had political ambitions. In South Carolina, State Superintendent Reuben Tomlinson and his assistant B. F. Whittemore played a prominent part in organizing the state's Republicans. Both men served in the state legislature and Whittemore represented South Carolina in Congress from 1868 to 1870, when he was expelled because he allegedly sold appointments to West Point and Annapolis.[96] Justus K. Jillson, a Massachusetts teacher, represented Kershaw at the organization of the state Republican party at Columbia in 1867 and at the constitutional convention of 1868. In 1868 and again in 1872, he was elected state superintendent of public instruction.[97]

Serving with Whittemore in Congress were two other prominent bureau educators—Charles W. Buckley, formerly state superintendent for Alabama, and C. H. Prince, a native of Maine who had taught a freedmen's school in Augusta, Georgia.

In every Southern state, some freedmen's educators used the bureau school system as a stepping stone to political office. This was certainly true of S. S. Ashley in North Carolina, Henry R. Pease in Mississippi, and Joseph W. Clift in Georgia.

Clift's situation was fairly typical. In a *"Strictly Confidential"* letter to the American Missionary Association in 1867, he admitted:

> I am now engaged in Reconstruction up to my eyes. The colored people in this Congressional district will vote for me for almost anything.... I am organizing Union Leagues everywhere among them and teaching them the importance of learning to read immediately; before the election anyhow.

Clift fully intended to take advantage of this situation by accepting the post of chief register in his senatorial district. He assured the AMA that he sought the office in order to exert influence on behalf of freedmen's education, but he obviously was motivated by more partisan considerations as well. [98]

Any analysis of the backgrounds of Northern white educators would be incomplete without a discussion of discriminatory employment practices. For freedmen's aid societies often let ethnic and religious biases influence their selection of school personnel.

A prejudice against Catholic applicants was particularly evident. Neither the American Missionary Association nor the American Freedmen's Union Commission made much of an attempt to conceal their fears that Rome was making a concerted effort to bring Southern blacks into the Church. Indeed, both organizations seemed intent on proving that they were better equipped than the other to thwart this Catholic plot.

The dispute between the AMA and the AFUC can be seen in microcosm in a series of articles from the *American Missionary*. Published in the December 1867 and January 1868 issues, these articles had originally appeared in the *Christian Intelligencer* under the title "Rome in the Field." Their overall thesis was quite simple: the Pope was engaged in a carefully planned campaign to gain control of the government of the United States. This was to be accomplished by creating a Catholic-oriented political coalition of European immigrants and Southern blacks. To prevent this from happening, it would be necessary not only to educate the freedmen but to instruct them "in the faith and doctrines of the evangelical churches."[99]

To support this thesis, the *Christian Intelligencer* offered its own unique interpretation of the events of the Civil War and Reconstruction. Beginning with the unproven assertion that Bishop John Hughes of New York had engineered an alliance between the Vatican and the Confederacy, the editors went on to accuse Irish Catholics of perpetrating such outrages as the New York draft riots and the assassination of President Lincoln. The *Intelligencer* reminded readers that

> only eight per cent of our grand army were of foreign birth, the balance . . . were native Americans, who returned . . . to find their places on the farms, in the factories, and elsewhere, filled by Irish, who had sought safety and profit at home, while our boys were courting danger and death in battle.

Even more alarming was the fact that Catholics in cities like Saint Augustine, Raleigh, Mobile, and New Orleans had instituted educational programs that had drawn Negro students away from the schools of Northern freedmen's aid organizations. The Society for Propagating the Faith reportedly had given $600,000 in gold for the work among the blacks, an act that convinced the editors that Rome intended to ''control the colored man as she does the Irish.''[100] It is obvious why the *American Missionary* chose to reprint ''Rome in the Field.''

The *Intelligencer* article evoked an immediate response from Rev. Crammond Kennedy, secretary of the New York branch of the American Freedmen's Union Commission. The newspaper printed this response along with its own rebuttal:

> Mr. Kennedy's letter seems to claim support for the Commission as best calculated to prevent encroachments of Romanists, and yet we are met by the fact that the Commission for whose schools such paramount superiority is claimed, cannot without a violation of its boasted liberality, . . . refuse appointment to a well-qualified ''Catholic'' teacher; and we learn, on undoubted authority, that it . . . has appointed such. . . . How can a society seek support as a bulwark against Romanism, which boasts of principles that would send Romanists, as well as Unitarians and rejecters of the scheme of salvation, to enlighten and Christianize an ignorant and naturally religious people?

Not unexpectedly, the *American Missionary* also reprinted this article.[101]

There is little basis for the *Intelligencer's* charge that the AFUC, or any other Northern society commissioned a significant number of Roman Catholic teachers. Almost without exception, Catholic instructors had to depend on their own local churches and religious orders for support. Bureau School Superintendent John W. Alvord professed a willingness to aid and encourage parochial schools for freedmen, but only if the teachers limited themselves to secular education. Few were willing to make such a basic sacrifice.[102]

A letter written by Alabama teacher Charles C. Arms makes it clear that aid societies hired Catholic instructors only under exceptional circumstances. In describing a Tuscaloosa woman whom he had engaged to teach at Northport, Arms wrote: ''She is of Roman Catholic persuasion & *very* poor [,] her mother being both a widow & an invalid. While her religious views are to be regretted [,] her poverty appeals to our charity.''[103]

The Catholic teacher's chances of securing a position were further diminished if the applicant was Irish as well. Although this conclusion is based primarily on the fact that Northern educators frequently exhibited anti-Irish biases, the most cursory survey of bureau rosters reveals the relatively small number of Irish-Americans commissioned by freedmen's aid societies.

Judging from a letter penned by prospective teacher Matthew O'Kean in 1867, Irish-Americans were well-aware of these nativist tendencies. Writing from Merton, Wisconsin, O'Kean assured Gen. Oliver O. Howard that he was not tainted by any deceptive motive:

> Tis true I am originally an Irishman but my Countrymen and me differ altogether politically. . . . I am aware they are ignorant which to my shame I acknowledge it. I go by the Principles of the Great Irish Leader . . . D. O'Connell who always advocated the cause of the Colored Man all over the world. And I will always follow the same principle so long as I live and for which I was wounded at the battle of Prairie Grove. . . .[104]

Unfortunately, there is no notation on the letter to indicate the success or failure of O'Kean's appeal.

Whether successful or not, O'Kean had anticipated most of the objections to employing Irish-American instructors. He obviously knew that Northern nativists viewed Irish immigrants as ignorant, depraved, and disloyal. He may not have known, however, that many supposedly liberal freedmen's educators shared these views. Indeed, O'Kean might have been shocked to hear some of the statements made by reformers like William Channing Gannett, who believed the Irish to be at least as "degraded" as the freedmen of the South. In recording his first impressions of blacks on the Sea Islands, Gannett described them as "wretched and stupid" but added that "to those who are accustomed to many Irish faces, these except by their *uniformity* c[ou]ld suggest few new ideas of low humanity."[105]

Even high-ranking bureau officials were guilty of ethnic and religious discrimination. One of the most blatant examples of such discrimination is recorded in a strictly "private" letter written in 1870 by S. N. Clark, an assistant treasurer for the AMA. Writing to Association Secretary George Whipple, Clark warned that Capt. H. A. Kelly was being considered for the post of bureau school superintendent for Mississippi. "I fear," Clark

explained, "that if Kelly is appointed we shall experience difficulty inasmuch as he is an Irishman, not very friendly to the
Association."[106] For whatever reason, Kelly did not receive the
appointment.

The prejudice against Irish Catholics was clearly the most intense form of nativism manifested by bureau educators. The only
comparable ethnic bias was that directed against the nation's
Jewish population. In the case of Jews, the nature of the bias was
entirely predictable, amounting to little more than a post-Civil
War version of the standard antisemitic argument. Shylock in this
revised standard version simply became a Southern Jewish merchant. He was, in the words of an AMA teacher from Massachusetts, one of the

> many adverse influences at work to crush the negro. The
> planter, trader, bad Yankees, Jews and Catholics license
> ... whiskey and tobacco, have each the hundred hands
> of Briareus, and all are stretched out to grasp, pull down and
> tear these poor ebony victims that here abound.

To illustrate his point, the teacher quoted the Negro residents of
Thomasville, Georgia on the subject of economic exploitation:
" 'pears like we never gits any money to do with. The white
people cheats us, and the Jews cheats us, and the niggers steal
from one another, and there seems to be little chance for a
man."[107]

This same theme was developed in an *American Missionary*
article published in June 1870. Entitled "Sharp Practice," this
piece recounts the story of a freedman who avoids being out-
witted by a "shrewd" Jewish merchant. Hoping to capitalize on
the economic naïveté of his Negro customer, the merchant attempts to entice him into spending the entire proceeds of his
cotton crop on luxury items. The black here resists the tempta-
tion. In a triumph of Calvinist restraint, he purchases ten dollars'
worth of homespun and osnaburgs and then enlists the aid of a
friendly lawyer to help him collect the balance.[108]

Although Jews, Catholics, and Irish-Americans bore the brunt
of this nativist attack, they were not the only victims. With the
possible exception of the British, every major ethnic group received its share of criticism. The vices attributed to the individual
"races" were numerous and varied, but most can be subsumed

under one or two general headings—ignorance and immorality.
Both of these sins of commission were subject to a variety of
interpretations. To the editors of the *American Missionary* "immorality" meant intemperance, card-playing, nonobservance of
the sabbath, and a host of other transgressions. The working
definition of "ignorance" was so flexible, in fact, that it was
commonly employed as a political epithet. Ignorance, according
to this interpretation, was the chief reason for the immigrant's
affinity for the Democratic party. It was on this basis that many
freedmen's aid officials defended the idea of Negro suffrage.
"The black men of the South are ignorant, and many degraded,"
these officials conceded, but no more so than the thousands of immigrants who had settled in New York and other urban centers:

> If any great measure of the Republican party were to be set-
> tled today, by the vote of certain wards in New York City,
> and by the ballots of the freedmen of Charleston, the white
> and black men would vote almost to a man, on opposite sides;
> and who doubts that the black vote would be on the right side,
> and the white vote on the wrong one?[109]

In light of such partisan sentiments it should come as no surprise
that freedmen's educational officials made little effort to recruit
their teachers from among the ranks of America's immigrant
population.

When freedmen's aid societies did employ foreign-born instructors they were often displeased with the results. Such was
the case with an AMA teacher of German descent stationed in
Raleigh, North Carolina. The first complaint registered by her
superiors concerned her immaturity and lack of self-discipline.
"She is only nineteen," a local freedmen's educator explained.
"Her mother died when she was a child, and she has always had
her own way, seems to know nothing about governing herself."
More important from the standpoint of ethnic bias within freedmen's education, her superiors complained "she has never been
accustomed to our kind of society, and it does not suit her. *She is
German*. She associates with the colored people just as she would
with white, sleeps with the girls, and the boys are beaus for her,
just as her school mates at home would be."[110] Clearly the
AMA's local officials expected this teacher to revise her European approach to racial etiquette or risk losing her position.

The case of this German-American teacher illustrates the foremost problem facing those responsible for staffing the bureau educational program—that of finding applicants who conformed to the lofty ideals laid down by the various freedmen's aid societies. It was one thing to specify that instructors should be abolitionists "of the 'right stamp' actuated by pure philanthropic motives."[111] It was quite another to find men and women who fit this description. Consequently, the teaching staff was extremely diverse. There were educators who resembled the fictional characters created by Cash, Chesnutt, Woolson, and Tourgée, but there were also educators who conformed to no simple stereotype, literary or historical.

3   The Black
         Teacher

"It is evident that the freedmen are to have teachers of their own color," Superintendent Alvord reported at the beginning of 1867. Already Negroes made up a full third of the teaching force, and the number was rising steadily as rural districts and plantations gave them preference "even when inferior in qualifications." This early in the school program the demand for competent black educators far exceeded the supply.[1]

Especially in the years before the development of an adequate number of normal schools within the Freedmen's Bureau system, aid societies had to depend heavily on Northern Negroes and those of the South who were fortunate enough to have received some education during the ante bellum period. The group as a whole covered the gamut from nearly illiterate former slaves to college graduates, from charlatans to well-trained professionals.

Alvord recommended that benevolent associations take a chance on the growing number of black teachers applying to the bureau for employment. A portion of them seemed well qualified. "They may not be equal to the accomplished school mistresses of the north," he allowed, "but their services might be accepted on trial, and they could be placed in a grade of schools, perhaps in the interior, where they would be very useful." Their enterprise and willingness to help were "quite worthy of notice and encouragement."[2]

The superintendent pointed out there were schools taught by Negroes in some Southern cities that compared favorably with equivalent Northern institutions. One such school at New Orleans served 300 students and was staffed entirely by "educated colored men." On a visit in 1865 Alvord found that the pupils were advancing in their basic studies and that the higher grades could recite as fluently in French as in English. These results were all the more impressive since this was a free school, wholly supported by the Negro residents of the city, and the students were from "the common class of families." The more affluent, better-educated people of color could afford to send their children to private schools.[3]

An article in the 21 December 1865 issue of the *Nation* helped focus attention on a similar school in Charleston superintended by Francis L. Cardozo. A special correspondent for the magazine described what was obviously a successful operation. "The head-master is a colored man," he wrote, "a graduate of the University of Glasgow, and the various classes are taught by about twenty persons, of whom some are Northern women and some Southern, and of the latter, some are white and some are colored." In one room a class of boys whose parents intended them for professional life was transposing, analyzing, and parsing a passage from Milton's "L'Allegro."[4]

Cardozo's impressive credentials made him one of the most respected Negro educators anywhere in the South. The father of this native Charlestonian was Jewish and his mother reputedly was of mixed black and Indian ancestry.[5] Receiving his early education in local schools, Francis served as a carpenter's apprentice between the ages of twelve and seventeen and practiced his trade for four more years prior to pursuing advanced studies abroad. Upon completion of his program at the University of Glasgow, where he won prizes in Latin and Greek, the ambitious free Negro spent a year at the United Presbyterian Church's theological seminary in Edinburgh followed by three years at the London School of Theology. After being ordained he returned to the United States in May 1864 to become pastor of the Temple Street Congregational Church in New Haven, Connecticut.[6]

Francis L. Cardozo occupied the New Haven pulpit a little over a year, resigning in July 1865 to join his younger brother Thomas in working among the freedmen of Charleston. At the time Thomas was superintendent of American Missionary Association schools in the city, but the revelation that he had engaged in sexual relations with a young female student while teaching in Flushing, New York virtually guaranteed that he would be replaced at the earliest opportunity. When the inevitable happened, Francis assumed responsibility for the operation.[7]

Like his predecessor, the new superintendent had to make do with local resources. "It would be better for the scholars to have all, or nearly all the Teachers from the North," Francis told an AMA official. "But the great expense prevents this, and perhaps it is best to encourage the native Teachers." Under these circumstances he selected one Southern white and reappointed four of his brother's best Negro employees—Frances Rollin, Amelia Shrewsbury, Mary F. Weston, and William O. Weston. The black teachers were all scions of leading free families from the Charleston area. Miss Rollin was one of five attractive, cultured daughters of a French father and a Negro mother. She and her sisters were at the center of Negro social life in Charleston and Columbia. Twenty-two years old in 1865, Frances had received her education at the Institute for Colored Youth in Philadelphia. She would later marry black officeholder William J. Whipper.[8] Amelia Shrewsbury was the sister of Henry L. Shrewsbury, the bureau instructor who went on to become Chesterfield County's delegate to the South Carolina Constitutional Convention of 1868 and a representative in the state legislature. Amelia was twenty-four. A member of the Protestant Episcopal Church who possessed what Thomas Cardozo considered "good attainments," she had "no one to look to for support in the world but herself."[9] Also a member of the Episcopal Church, Miss Mary Weston, the daughter of the prosperous mulatto Jacob Weston, was twenty-six and had kept a school for free blacks over the past six or seven years. In her more private moments she wrote poetry.[10] William Weston at thirty-one was a pious, strictly temperate man, a diligent student who aspired to the ministry. Formerly a bookkeeper for S. & P. Weston Tailors on Queen Street, he had been educated in the common branches and in such advanced subjects as logic, rhetoric, algebra, geometry, surveying, astronomy, Greek, and Latin.[11]

These instructors were generally acceptable to Thomas and Francis Cardozo, but the two brothers considered most local people far less qualified than Northern-trained educators. Thomas had advised the AMA that "the southern teachers are very faithful; and are good Christian young ladies of respectable parentage. But they (with two or three exceptions) do not understand our system of teaching." He believed one experienced Northern instructor could accomplish as much as two Southerners.[12] Francis thought it better "that no colored persons should engage in this work at all, than to have such as would only

disgrace the cause, and retard the progress of their own people.''
In enlarging his staff he necessarily had to take on more native
employees but compensated by putting ''the educated and experienced *white* Northern teachers in the highest and most responsible positions, and the colored ones in the lower and less responsible ones.'' Under this arrangement, the principal expected black
teachers to ''improve by the superiority of their *white* fellow-labor-
ers,'' whose positions they would eventually be able to occupy.[13]

Francis Cardozo's stated preference for Northern teachers initially caused some confusion. Cardozo was afraid AMA Superintendent of Education Samuel Hunt had misinterpreted this
preference in discussions with two Negro missionaries bound for
South Carolina. The concerned principal complained to Hunt:
''Mrs. [Amanda] Wall and Miss [Louisa] Alexander informed me
when they came down here that you had told them I wrote you
requesting you not to send me any *colored* teachers. They naturally felt much hurt.'' ''My request was that I should have all
Northern teachers,'' Cardozo clarified. ''It was and still is per-
fectly indifferent to me whether they are *white* or *colored,* all I
ask is that they be competent for their work, and when I made the
request I did so because *Northern* teachers are more competent
than Southern ones.''[14]

Cardozo's standards were high, but he gladly employed black
instructors whom he considered qualified. A month after assuring
Amanda Wall and Louisa Alexander that he had no intention of
denying persons teaching positions because of their color, the
AMA representative hired Mrs. Wall, the wife of Freedmen's
Bureau Sub-Assistant Commissioner Orindatus S. B. Wall.
Amanda and her husband were from Oberlin, Ohio, where Orindatus had prospered as a shoe and boot merchant before entering
the army as a captain under Gen. Rufus Saxton. Captain Wall was
the brother-in-law of bureau school inspector John Mercer
Langston.[15] Cardozo also recruited his own sister and brother-
in-law, Mr. and Mrs. C. C. McKinney. Having lived in the North
for over seven years, the two relatives were teaching in Thomas
Cardozo's old school in Flushing. Previously, Mr. McKinney had
worked in schools both at Charleston and in Cleveland, Ohio.[16]

American Missionary Association officials and Cardozo agreed
on the propriety of selecting suitable black teachers but purportedly had trouble finding enough with the requisite qualifications.

Cardozo felt there were few yet "*intellectually* fitted"[17] for the work. Those who did measure up were almost always educated members of leading Charleston families such as the Westons, Holloways, and the Shrewsburys.[18]

Charleston and New Orleans had greater numbers of qualified native black educators than most other areas of the South. Rev. Ira Pettibone, the American Missionary Association's school super-intendent in Savannah complained he could scarcely find a black person in that city competent to teach. He claimed nearly all who had an adequate educational background were "still wanting in knowledge of the methods of successful teaching."[19] Bureau school inspector O. H. Howard reached a similar conclusion after completing an official tour through Georgia in 1869. Referring to schools conducted by blacks, Howard asserted that "the present teachers copy the late white teachers literally, and *play* school very successfully without imparting any instruction whatever."[20]

Florida Superintendent C. Thurston Chase claimed there were no more than twenty good Negro teachers in his state. Chase went on to say that "of the others some are ranked as 'unknown vixens & wizards' & teaching in 'unknown alleys & lanes.' They belong to that class of persons known as 'medicine men' who are said to hold mighty incantations for the benefit of their patients over the 'hind leg of a frog.' "[21] Chase's successor, Charles H. Foster, shared this negative view. "The white people of the South will not engage in teaching the colored people," he informed Superintendent Alvord, "and there are very few here of their own class who are competent to instruct."[22]

In assessing the qualifications of potential freedmen's teachers, white educational officials emphasized morality as well as aca-demic ability. G. L. Eberhart, the bureau's first superintendent for Georgia, wrote late in 1866 that "although there is much to commend in the Negroes, under the difficulties which they labor, I am becoming daily more impressed with their total unfitness to assist in the moral and mental elevation of their own race." It appeared to Eberhart "as if Slavery had completely divested them of every moral attribute —every idea that leads to true moral rectitude."[23]

Such negative assessments of the qualifications of black teachers had a definite effect on employment practices. When attempting to staff a freedmen's school in Greenville, Tennessee, for example, Joel Terrell asked AMA Field Secretary Erastus M. Cravath to send two "first rate white teachers." Terrell later explained "I think that white teachers will do better in any school than colored, the *influence* will be better for the cause." Significantly, Cravath was happy to comply with Terrell's request, since the secretary admitted to having little confidence in the "managing ability of colored teachers."[24]

As late as 1869 New England Freedmen's Aid Society officials were also hesitant about placing blacks in positions where "first-class" teachers were required. A member of the society's committee on teachers made this abundantly clear when answering a request for an instructor to be employed in a North Carolina school. "The place now to be filled does not seem to us just the one for a Colored teacher," Miss L. Crocker wrote to Freedmen's Bureau State Superintendent H. C. Vogell. None of them "have had the chances for the best experience in teaching—surely not at the North, as yet—and you need a good grammar school, with the best methods organized and conducted successfully."[25]

Most educators, however, felt they had no choice but to commission some Negroes even when those available were not strictly qualified. As a spokesman for the American Freedmen's Union Commission indicated in 1867:

There are many localities where a negro teacher can carry on a school successfully, to which it is impracticable to send a white teacher from the North; many, where the prejudice against negro teaching would be less than against instruction offered by a Northern teacher.[26]

In certain areas Yankee schoolmarms simply could not find suitable places to live. White residents would neither sell nor rent to them, and rooming with a black family was often out of the question.[27] Negroes themselves sometimes preferred educators of their own race, as in Marlin, Texas, where the former slaves were "disposed to distrust" any white man who would teach a freedmen's school.[28] From Kentucky, Bureau Superintendent T. K. Noble reported in the summer of 1867 that blacks "will accept white teachers in virtue of their superior qualifications, but whenever they can get black ones really competent they receive them with great satisfaction." Noble turned to Oberlin College for qualified Negro recruits, but the supply was still by no means equal to the demand.[29]

The shortage was nationwide. When AFUC Secretary McKim wrote for help from associates in the East, he received little encouragement. His counterpart in the freedmen's aid society at Hartford, Connecticut responded: "I have been beating the bush here for Colored Teachers for you, . . . but I fail to find one who is both qualified and willing to go. The truth is, ver[y] few indeed of the Colored people are qualified for such a work."[30] Closer to home, inquiries at Philadelphia's Institute for Colored Youth failed to turn up any available candidates. While the school's principal and Marmaduke Cope of the Friends Freedmen's Association were gratified to find their graduates in demand, Cope advised McKim "the prospect is that our utmost efforts will fail to meet the demand for colored teachers."[31]

School officials in the South could not always afford to wait until aid societies or emerging teacher training institutions supplied their needs. The majority of native black instructors were inexperienced and defective in their mode of teaching, admitted Alabama Superintendent Charles Buckley, but he used them because they were of service to the cause. "It is our policy," Buckley declared in 1866, "to convert colored pupils into teachers as fast as possible. It is cheaper if not so beneficial, and it has good effects in many ways."[32] At the very least the use of black teachers increased the freedmen's sense of involvement in the educational process. Georgia's bureau superintendent continued to support the school of George Maddox even after a white instructor complained that Maddox knew only the alphabet. In answering this complaint, Col. John R. Lewis assured Miss T. C. Roberts that he agreed with her contention that "ignorant" black teachers generally did more harm than good. But, he defended, "some have been aided because we could do no better & because we wished to get them to do *something* and arouse an interest in the school work."[33]

Beginning in 1867 the Freedmen's Bureau stepped up its efforts to provide educational opportunities for blacks who wished to become teachers. In May of that year Commissioner Howard urged benevolent societies to develop plans for establishing teacher-training facilities throughout the South. He wanted the societies to take the lead in this work but was willing to assist them financially. During the next three years he allotted $407,752 to twenty institutions of higher learning for Negroes. By 1871 there were eleven colleges and universities and sixty-one normal schools that were intended especially for blacks.[34]

Increased emphasis on the employment of blacks is revealed in bureau statistics showing a rise of twenty percentage points over a period of two and a half years, from 33 percent in January 1867 to 53 percent in July 1869. The underlying figures included many student assistants and some who were teachers in name only, but the trend was unmistakable.[35] Between 1867 and 1870 the American Missionary Association's proportion of Negro teachers and missionaries jumped from 6 percent to 20 percent.[36] During these same years, the Presbyterian Committee on Freedmen was making good on its intention "to raise up Ministers and Teachers of their own race for this people." Blacks represented an impressive 53 percent of the committee's teaching staff in 1867 and 55 percent by the middle of 1868.[37]

Proportions varied from state to state. Over the last three years of bureau operations North Carolina and Louisiana consistently reported figures in the area of 50 to 75 percent, whereas South Carolina, Alabama, and Georgia rarely rose above the 35 percent mark. Other states fluctuated somewhere in between.[38] The majority of black teachers during this period were Southerners. The American Missionary Association employed sixteen such educators and missionaries out of a total of twenty-eight in 1867, and seventy-one of one hundred five in 1870.[39] Similarly, a study of Negro political leadership in South Carolina indicates that three out of every four Afro-American teachers who sat in the state constitutional convention or the legislature between 1868 and 1876 were Southern born. Not all of these had stayed in their native region, but the majority were living in South Carolina at the beginning of the war and had been educated locally. A few had been slaves throughout the ante-bellum period.[40]

When representing an Afro-American teacher in *Bricks without Straw*, Albion Tourgée introduced a character who was both a native Southerner and a free black. Based on an instructor from York County, South Carolina, Tourgée's partly fictional creation was born a slave but had been manumitted after his master's neighbors complained that a literate bondsman was a threat to the white community. Far from being dangerous, however, Eliab Hill proved to be a calming influence. During the Civil War this crippled shoemaker and preacher "always counselled the colored people to be civil and patient, but not [to] try to run away or go to cutting up." After Appomattox, Hill enrolled in Mollie Ainslie's school, eventually achieving the status of student-teacher. As Tourgée said of the light-skinned former slave:

> Eliab Hill had from the first greatly interested the teachers at Red Wing. The necessities of the school and the desire of the charitable Board having it in charge, to accustom the colored people to see those of their own race trusted and advanced, had induced them to employ him as an assistant teacher, even before he was really competent for such service.[41]

While a student-teacher Eliab Hill underwent a marked transformation. At first convinced of the need for political action, he soon concluded his race could be made free only through education. "I begin to see that the law can only give us an opportunity to make ourselves freemen," he said. "Liberty must be earned; it cannot be given."[42] Apparently Hill had internalized the reform philosophy espoused by Mollie Ainslie and other Northern white teachers in the town of Red Wing.

Outside the classroom, Eliab Hill was a leader in his community. After the war, he and his friend Nimbus Ware had bought land in Red Wing and had converted it into one of the most productive tobacco farms in the county. By selling plots to other freedmen in the area, Hill and Ware eventually succeeded in establishing a settlement of fifty to sixty families.[43]

As a civic leader Hill revealed the depth of his devotion to moderate reform principles. Convinced of the necessity of attracting Southern white support for equal rights, he helped persuade the freedmen of Red Wing to forego political activism and retaliatory violence. Practicing what he preached, Hill submitted to being beaten by the Ku Klux Klan rather than use his pistol for self-defense.[44]

Mollie Ainslie's future husband was so impressed with Hill's "noble soul" and "rare mind" that he arranged for the Negro student-teacher to attend college in the North. After completing his course of study, Hill rejected an offer of a position in a Northern school, choosing instead to resume teaching at Red Wing.

Upon his return in 1873, he found the situation in his home town greatly changed. Students no longer looked forward to the future with confident expectations. They were no longer subject to the terrible cruelties of slavery, but they saw no hope of regaining the rights which they had achieved during Reconstruction and lost during "Redemption." Still, Eliab Hill retained his faith in the ameliorative power of education. As he said in a letter to Mollie Ainslie:

> I used to think that the law could give us our rights and make us free. I now see, more clearly than ever before, that we must not only make *ourselves* free, but must overcome all that prejudice which slavery created against our race in the hearts of the white people. . . . I know it can only be done through the attainment of knowledge and the power which that gives.[45]

Tourgée made little effort to disguise the identity of his character's real-life equivalent—Elias Hill, a South Carolina freedmen's teacher who had testified before the Ku Klux Investigating Committee. Crippled at age seven and bought into freedom by his father, Elias had learned to read and write from white students in the South. During Reconstruction he served as a Baptist minister, a schoolmaster, and president of a local branch of the Union League.

Hill's published testimony pertained to an incident that occurred in 1870. Shortly after midnight on May 5 of that year, six Ku Klux Klan raiders dragged the Negro teacher from his house and beat him with their fists and with a horse whip. They accused him of setting fire to white dwellings, barns, and gin-houses. He responded by pointing out that he was physically incapable of such acts. They asked if he "didn't . . . tell the black men to ravish all the white women." He answered "no." "When did you hold a night-meeting of the Union League, and who were the officers?" they asked. He admitted he had been the president but added that the league had not met at his house since the fall of 1869. They warned that if he did not publicly renounce the Republican party and promise not to vote, the Klan would return the next week and kill him.[46]

The main difference between Tourgée's fictional black teacher and the real-life Elias Hill was evident in their respective reactions to this violent episode. Whereas the incident had little effect on Tourgée's character, it embittered Elias Hill to the point where he began making plans to emigrate to Liberia. According to the *Yorkville Inquirer,* Hill and his friend June Moore were leaders in a movement to relocate sixty to eighty families in that part of Liberia known as the North Carolina Colony. In his testimony before the Ku Klux Investigating Committee, Hill explained why so many Negroes in York County were willing to leave their native country:

> we all ascribe the same cause for this movement; we do not believe it possible . . . for our people to live in this country peaceably, and educate and elevate their children to that degree which they desire.[47]

Obviously, Elias Hill did not share his fictional equivalent's faith in the healing powers of time, patience, and American education.

Their differences notwithstanding, Elias and Eliab Hill exemplified the type of native freedmen's teacher who had gained a degree of literacy in the prewar era. Northerners were frequently amazed at the number fitting this description in a region known for its laws forbidding or restricting the education of blacks. Certain localities produced an unexpectedly large number of qualified candidates. In eastern South Carolina most of the Negro teachers sponsored by the New England Freedmen's Aid Society were educated at Charleston before the war.[48] From Virginia a school principal informed the *Freedmen's Record* that "in spite of the rigid laws against teaching the negroes, nearly every colored family in Richmond has one or more members who can read." The principal went on to say she had employed Peter H. Woolfolk, whom she described as "one of those brave colored men who had acquired some education in spite of all obstacles, and who had been a teacher in a Sunday School of his own people."[49] In Georgia, AMA representative W. T. Richardson was "surprised to find so much intelligence . . . among the Freedmen of Savannah." On 10 January 1865 he could report that several evinced a competence for teaching and were in the employ of the association.[50]

The experience of Susie King Taylor illustrates a number of options open to blacks in the ante-bellum years. Born a slave on one of the Georgia Sea Islands, this future teacher grew up in Savannah and learned to read and write at a secret school maintained by a free Negro woman who lived about one-half mile from her home. Mrs. Woodhouse and her daughter had twenty-five to thirty students. Neighbors would sometimes see pupils entering the school one by one but assumed the children were learning a trade. "I remained at her school for two years or more," Taylor reminisced in 1902, "when I was sent to a Mrs. Mary Beasley, where I continued until May 1860, when she told my grandmother she had taught me all she knew, and grandmother had better get some one else who could teach me more, so I stopped my studies for a while."[51]

Susie King Taylor's next teacher was Katie O'Connor, a white playmate who attended a convent. Keeping her activities secret from all but her mother, Katie gave evening lessons to Susie for the next four months. When Katie went into the convent permanently, Susie's grandmother persuaded a white high school student to take over. James Blois continued the lessons until the middle of 1861, when his volunteer regiment was called into active service in Virginia. One year later the beneficiary of this makeshift educational process was herself a teacher among the black soldiers of the First South Carolina Volunteers. After the war she returned to Savannah and opened a freedmen's school at her home on South Broad Street. With a few brief interruptions she taught for the next three years.[52]

Milla Granson, a freedmen's teacher at Vidalia, Louisiana, had received tutoring from the children of her indulgent master in Kentucky. This in turn allowed her to teach other slaves in a clandestine school, which generally met between midnight and 2:00 AM. According to one description, "every window and door was carefully closed to prevent discovery. In that little school hundreds of slaves learned to read and write a legible hand. After toiling all day for their masters they crept stealthily into this back alley, each with a bundle of pitch-pine splinters for lights." When, after her master's death, Granson was taken to Mississippi, she established a second school for slaves.[53]

Some freedmen's schools were direct continuations of antebellum efforts. One Negro woman in Savannah, a Miss Deveaux, had been teaching in the same building since 1835.[54] Likewise, Mary Peake was already an experienced instructor when she opened her school for contrabands at Fortress Monroe. Forced to abandon her own schooling after Congress ruled that Virginia's antiliteracy laws applied to the District of Columbia, Peake moved back to her home town of Norfolk and sometime in the 1850s began teaching her husband and "scores of negroes" who came to their cabin by night. This clandestine school was still in operation at the time Union troops captured Hampton in the summer of 1861.[55]

Secret tutoring could be dangerous for teacher and pupil alike. In a typical action Mississippi authorities forced Milla Granson to close her night school when it was discovered, and masters frequently punished slaves who inadvertently revealed their literacy. Mary Chadwick, an American Missionary Association instructor at Beaufort, North Carolina, remembered:

> My master once sent me for a book of Hanna[h] More's. Instead of bringing the whole pile like the rest did, I fetched the one massa wanted. He said why didn't you bring all the books. I said I seed it on the back, massa. He said "who learnt you to read? Bring me the cowhide["] & gave me three or four licks on the head.

Chadwick freely admitted early in 1866 that she had a great deal more to learn before she would be an effective teacher. The ex-slave therefore continued her studies under white instructors at Beaufort while conducting her own school for freedmen.[56]

With so many freedmen seeking an education, Northern school officials in many cases were willing to assign native blacks to teach in beginning classes even though these men and women might not measure up to the usual standards set by the associations. Anna Gardner and the New England Freedmen's Aid Society, for example, "watched with considerable anxiety and interest the primary class taught by Isabella Gibbons, her recent appointment as a teacher of her race being an experiment as to how a colored woman, who had been a slave up to the time of the surrender would succeed in a vocation to her so novel." Gardner, a white educator at Charlottesville, Virginia, was glad to be able to say that the subject of this experiment "has quite equalled my sanguine expectations, especially in the matter of organizing her school, and of governing it without resorting in any instance to severity of discipline."[57]

Less optimistic educators, on the other hand, complained that black instructors deficient in proper pronunciation, spelling, grammar, punctuation, and school discipline passed their own bad habits on to the students.[58] Alvord's assistant superintendent in Mississippi, Henry R. Pease, blamed inefficient bureau agents who had recognized such teachers "without ever taking the pains to ascertain whether they were morally or otherwise qualified to teach." Pease and other officials reacted by cutting off funds from those they deemed incompetent, although in doing so they often encountered charges of racial discrimination. A group of blacks in Natchez reported to Commissioner Howard that Pease as a rule refused to recognize Negro instructors.[59] And when Georgia Superintendent John R. Lewis denied financial assistance to Joseph Morris, the Wilkinson County teacher protested:

> I will Say to you now Mr. Lewis We Callor people are very badly Defrauded out Wright [rights] which was garnantee to ous from the foundasion of the Constistiution and sir Will say to you with good faith that you are the first man Every condentradict my Educasion before since the new mancipasion and will further more say to you Again that it ant anything Supriseing to see white man Defeat a Callor man out his wright.

This letter, followed by Morris's clumsily forged petition attesting to his effectiveness, failed to secure the necessary aid.[60]

Solomon Derry of Union Springs, Alabama showed a slightly greater facility in spelling and written expression but he too was judged unqualified, and bureau authorities attempted to replace him with a white teacher. Derry saw a contradiction between this effort and earlier statements by Superintendent R. D. Harper. "Mr. Harper... you Said we must have Teachers of our own color," Derry reminded. "As you Said the Educational Salvation of my people depend on us & ask us to go in the work." In his own defense, the black minister declared: "So far as my competency are concern, I feel competent of teaching the branches I told you I could."[61]

Harper's office denied any inconsistency. Writing for the superintendent, H. M. Bush answered:

> When Dr Harper told you that the Colored people must depend upon those of their own color for teachers he meant those who had attended school and become competent to teach. We want the best teachers that can be had either white

or black. The ignorant man cannot teach what he does not know himself and I would advise you to turn over your school to the 1st competent teacher that offers. . . .

Bush criticized blacks at Union Springs for refusing to accept Derry's intended replacement. The bureau spokesman alleged they preferred their old instructor not because he was "good and educated" but because he was "black and a minister." In any event, Harper's office balked at paying the rent on a school managed by someone who appeared "totally unfit" for his duties.[62]

Aid societies, especially those in the evangelical camp, often turned down literate applicants primarily on moral grounds. In Norfolk, black political leader J. W. D. Bland found it difficult to obtain a commission from the American Missionary Association even though the principal in the school where he acted as an assistant thought "he would succeed very well in teaching reading and the rudiments of Geography and Arithmetic."[63] This native of Prince Edward County was self-educated until November 1864, when, at age twenty, he began receiving instruction from Mary M. Reed of Falls Village. Both Miss Reed and H. C. Percy, one of the AMA's principal teachers in Norfolk, were impressed with Bland's progress. Percy described him as "very intelligent" and allowed that he was advanced enough to teach elementary reading. Even so, Percy advised the association not to grant Bland's request for a commission to open a school in the small town of Farmville. "He *knows* enough," Percy explained, "but is too careless and dissolute in his habits. He both *smokes* and *swears:* —therefore would never do to represent a *'Missionary Society.'* " Unwilling to give Miss Reed's assistant a school of his own, Percy hired him to do general housework, run errands, and substitute for teachers when they were absent.[64]

Shortly after blocking Bland's application for a commission, Percy gave a strong indication of the type of black teacher he preferred when he asked the association's secretary to send Robert Harris or some other "very intelligent col'd man to take charge of the school at Providence." Percy singled out Harris because he had taught at Providence the previous winter but also because he measured up to the AMA's exacting moral standards. The Ohio Negro's personal code of behavior can be inferred from his temperance activities and from his revealing exclamation following the elections of 1868: "Thank God! The future is brightening before us, and setting ourselves to work, we will make great strides in Education [,] Morality, Temperance, Religion [,] Industry and general progress and improvement." Over the course of the 1860s Harris taught at Providence, Virginia and in Fayetteville, North Carolina.[65]

The black teachers most acceptable to the aid societies were usually Northerners or Southern free Negroes educated in the North. Although some in this preferred group had lived in slavery, relatively few were freedmen in the sense that they had been emancipated during the war. John Wesley Cromwell, one of the best-known instructors endorsed by H. C. Percy, for instance, was born a slave in Portsmouth, Virginia but spent the greater part of his early life in Philadelphia, where he attended the Institute for Colored Youth. In a letter of recommendation, Percy said of Cromwell, who after graduating from the institute in 1864 had taught in Pennsylvania, Virginia, and Maryland:

> He is of dark complexion, of ordinary intelligence, a graduate of a Philadelphia High School, and a teacher of some experience. . . . He identifies himself with the people here,—has their confidence, and is very well-liked by all who know him. I *think* he will prove a better teacher than most col'd persons yet offered to our Association. . . . I have known him but one year, but my acquaintance gives me considerable confidence in his abilities.[66]

Only Cromwell's admission that he had "never embraced Christianity" stood in the way of an AMA commission. He apparently overcame this obstacle, however, by explaining that he fervently desired salvation and that it had been his rule to open classes "by the reading of the Scriptures and the Lord's Prayer; to lead to the distinction between right and wrong; to teach moral principles, thus preparing the mind for religious impressions."[67]

An examination of Cromwell's subsequent career shows that Percy underestimated this former slave's mental capacity. Cromwell certainly was not a man of "ordinary intelligence." In 1874 he obtained a law degree from Howard University and was admitted to the bar in the District of Columbia. At various points in his professional career he was a Treasury Department employee, editor of a Negro newspaper, and an elementary school principal.

Cromwell devoted much of his spare time to intellectual pursuits, serving as president of the Bethel Literary and Historical Association and as secretary of the American Negro Academy. In the 1880s he gained a reputation as one of Booker T. Washington's most influential supporters. Reversing his position at the beginning of the twentieth century, he became a leader among the anti-Bookerites. But racial politics did not divert Cromwell's attention from black education. In 1914 he published *The Negro in American History,* a text designed to make black children aware of the fact that members of their race had gained eminence "as educators, statesmen, artists and men of affairs."[68]

Florida and South Carolina represented two extremes with regard to qualified black instructors. The difference is well illustrated in the contrast between Francis Cardozo's Negro teachers at Charleston and the ill-prepared freedmen described by Florida Bureau Superintendent C. Thurston Chase in 1867. When Chase assumed his post, he found two classes of schools in Florida: (1) those sustained under the auspices of Northern benevolent associations, and (2) those established by individuals with the hope of receiving aid from the state. Most of the black teachers fell into the second category. According to Chase's report for the school year ending 30 June 1867:

> In the latter class are a number of persons of color, who, having been educated in the north, have come to the State and started schools for their own race. Their schools have been highly creditable to them, and deserve a cordial support. Beyond these, and comprising nearly or quite half the entire number engaged in teaching, is a class of freed persons who had acquired a little learning in their bondage. Without questioning their zeal or desire to elevate their race, it must be manifest that their qualifications only enable them to impart the rudiments of learning, and these in many cases but very imperfectly. They can read, spell, and write a little. Their pupils can do as much, and need teachers of higher qualifications.[69]

Chase's successors were faced with the same situation. In 1868 Charles H. Foster called for at least thirty to forty teachers from the North since he considered most of Florida's black instructors "poorly fitted for their work" and many of them "utterly incompetent.''[70] Months later Foster and Assistant Commissioner John T. Sprague were still waiting. "Teachers from the north are daily expected," Colonel Sprague reported, "but school operations can not fairly commence without their assistance. The colored teachers in the interior are sadly in need of education themselves."[71]

At the other extreme, South Carolina had an ample supply of competent native teachers, many of whom were raised and educated in their home state. A predictably large number emanated from Charleston's ante-bellum free-Negro population and had benefited from the educational opportunities open to that segment of society. Through the efforts of self-help organizations and individuals like Thomas S. Bonneau and Daniel Alexander Payne free persons of color had maintained schools of their own at Charleston since early in the nineteenth century.[72] The city's educational and cultural opportunities gave a distinct advantage to those Negroes in the area who had always been free. "One fourth of my school is composed of such," Francis Cardozo informed the AMA in 1866, "and they are advancing towards the higher branches, and anxious to be prepared for Teachers." Cardozo would help perpetuate Charleston's role in training future teachers during the three years he was principal of the school that became Avery Normal Institute.[73]

Free-Negro instructors in the northeastern part of the state made a favorable impression on Superintendent Reuben Tomlinson. The superintendent reserved his greatest praise for Henry L. Shrewsbury at Cheraw, saying this mulatto from Charleston was modest, firm, and conscientious and that his school under all circumstances reflected "the very highest credit upon him." Of Henry E. Hayne and John A. Barre in Marion County, Superintendent Tomlinson wrote: "they belong to the same class of society with Mr. Shrewsbury, and have done with their schools much better than we had any reason to expect."[74] Hayne's background was as an artisan and soldier. He had been a tailor in ante-bellum Charleston before joining Thomas Wentworth Higginson's famous black regiment—the First South Carolina Volunteers. One of the few free Negroes in a unit composed primarily of ex-slaves, Hayne rose to the rank of sergeant by the end of the war.[75] John Barre was born in Charleston, the son of a French father and a West Indian mother, but when John was six years old, his father sent him to Philadelphia to receive a common-school education. After ten years of schooling and four years at sea, Barre worked in Philadelphia until 1865, when he finally returned to South Carolina. In the year before Tomlinson engaged him to teach at Marion, the Northern-trained mulatto earned his living as a shipping and receiving clerk for F. W. Daggett and Company, commission merchants in Georgetown.[76]

The Timmonsville school was in the capable hands of James H. Holloway, a well-to-do mulatto described by Tomlinson as belonging to "one of the best and most intelligent colored families" in Charleston. Although James had just taken charge of the school at the beginning of 1867, he had "already given evidence of capacity and fitness."[77] His forebears' wealth derived from the Holloways' Harness Shop and Carpenter's Establishment, founded in the late eighteenth century, and male members of the family were prominent in the Brown Fellowship Society, an exclusive benevolent and educational association limited to "free brown men." A postmaster and town councilman at Marion in the period after Reconstruction, James himself was to become a vice-president of this bastion of social superiority for Charleston's light-skinned elite.[78]

The importance of Charleston is shown by the fact that seven of the thirteen Negro teachers who sat in the South Carolina Constitutional Convention of 1868 were products of the port city's free population. In addition to Henry E. Hayne, Francis Cardozo, and Henry Shrewsbury, they were: Thaddeus K. Sasportas, William J. McKinlay, Charles D. Hayne, and his brother James N. Hayne. Thaddeus Sasportas came from a family headed by a mulatto butcher who in 1860 owned $6,700 in real estate and five slaves. Joseph A. Sasportas was wealthy enough to have Thaddeus educated in Philadelphia, where he attended private schools and a teacher-training institution before returning home with a unit of Colored Troops.[79] McKinlay's father was a successful tailor and property owner active in the Brown Fellowship Society. Like Joseph Sasportas, the elder McKinlay had acted as a trustee for an ante-bellum Negro school, which incidentally was taught by a white instructor. Between them the two McKinlays amassed a family fortune of about $40,000.[80] The remaining Charlestonians, Charles and James Hayne, were well-educated mulattoes who came to the Barnwell district as bureau employees. Charles was a tailor who belonged to another of Charleston's exclusive societies for "brown" men—the Friendly Moralist Association.[81]

Calvin Stubbs apparently was the only freedmen's instructor at the convention who had been a slave into the war years.[82] W. Nelson Joiner, the delegate from Abbeville County, had gained his freedom during the ante-bellum period, and the other four educator-politicians were free-born natives of Pennsylvania, Vermont, or Kentucky.[83]

The four from outside the Confederacy all had ties with the Union Army, the American Missionary Association, or both. The most prominent of the four, Jonathan Jasper Wright, was a native of Lancaster, Pennsylvania. Born in 1840, Wright had attended Lancasterian University at Ithaca, New York and had read law in the office of Bently, Fith, and Bently at Montrose, Pennsylvania. In the meantime he had obtained a first-class certificate and supported himself by teaching school. Taking advantage of Wright's educational experience, the AMA in 1865 sent him to South Carolina as a teacher and school organizer. After one year in the association's employ, he returned north and became the first Negro admitted to the bar in Pennsylvania. Within a few months of passing the bar examination, Wright was back in Beaufort, spending the next two years as a legal adviser for the bureau, a post which would help prepare him for his election to the state supreme court in 1870.[84]

A second AMA agent, Benjamin Franklin Randolph, represented Orangeburg in the constitutional convention. A native of Kentucky, Randolph had moved to Ohio as a child, received a common-school education, and graduated from Oberlin College. During the war this Methodist minister served as chaplain of a black regiment in South Carolina. Afterwards he edited a newspaper in Charleston and served in the educational division of the bureau, first as a teacher and then as an assistant superintendent of schools. A front-rank leader in South Carolina politics, Randolph was active in Orangeburg and was that county's first Republican state senator. Using his religious position for partisan purposes, he helped establish Republican organizations throughout the state right up to the time of his assassination in October 1868.[85]

Stephen A. Swails and L. S. Langley followed the familiar path leading from the military to bureau service and eventually to political life. Originally from a town near Lancaster, Pennsylvania, Swails moved to Elmira, New York and worked as a boatman until April 1863, when he enlisted in the Fifty-Fourth Massachusetts Volunteers. Rising to the rank of second lieutenant, he remained in South Carolina during Reconstruction to become a bureau agent, a free-school teacher, a political boss in Williamsburg County, a member of the constitutional convention, and a state senator.[86] Langley joined the Fifty-Fourth Massachusetts seven months after Swails and transferred to the Thirty-Third U.S. Colored Troops at the end of April 1864. A mulatto farm owner from Vermont, he taught in military schools near Beaufort prior to the convention.[87]

When the convention delegates set up their organization in January 1868, nearly half of the committee on education consisted of Negro teachers. Francis Cardozo chaired a group which included Langley, Shrewsbury, and Henry Hayne along with white bureau instructor Justus K. Jillson of Massachusetts and four other members.[88] The nine-man committee developed and pushed through an educational plan stipulating that:

1. It would be the duty of the legislature, once public schools had been "thoroughly" organized, to provide for the compulsory attendance in public or private schools of children between six and sixteen for at least twenty-four months.
2. All public schools, colleges, and universities supported wholly or in part by public funds "shall be free and open to all children of this state, without regard to race or color."

Delegates differed on the question of whether or not these provisions mandated compulsory integration of public schools, but, whatever the intent, there was virtually no movement toward racially mixed institutions even though Jillson served as state superintendent of education for the next nine years. During his second term in this elective post, Jillson told a Northern reporter that "should the question arise, he would feel it his duty to decide that negro children were entitled to the benefit of every free school in the State." Yet the constitution of 1868 and subsequent legislation gave him only limited authority in this sensitive area.[89]

Although most of the black educators at the convention continued their political participation beyond 1868, this does not mean that teaching was for them merely a stepping stone to public office. No one illustrates this point better than Francis Cardozo, who served as South Carolina's secretary of state from 1868 to 1872 and as state treasurer between 1872 and 1877. Cardozo stayed active in education even during these years of government service. He was a member of the Board of Trustees of the University of South Carolina in 1869 and two years later accepted a Latin professorship at Howard University. Gov. Robert Scott appointed a deputy secretary of state to take over Cardozo's duties for the last fourteen months of his term. While state treasurer the accomplished Negro educator earned a bachelor of laws degree from South Carolina College. Moving to Washington, D.C. once Conservatives regained control of his native state, Cardozo was appointed principal of a black high school after working as a clerk in the Treasury Department for six years. He remained in public education until 1903.[90]

Fellow delegates Stephen A. Swails, Henry Shrewsbury, and J. J. Wright combined politics and education to a lesser degree. Like Cardozo, Swails served on the University of South Carolina's board of trustees, accepting that position in the midst of his nine-year tenure as a state senator.[91] Shrewsbury, while a representative in the Forty-eighth General Assembly, devoted the time between sessions to teaching, as did Henry J. Maxwell, the Negro senator from Marlboro County.[92] Wright, a colleague of Maxwell's in the senate before being elected to the state supreme court, was forced off the bench in 1877. Four years later he received an appointment as professor of law at Claflin College in Orangeburg, South Carolina. Holding the professorship in 1881, he subsequently moved to Charleston and conducted law classes at his home on Queen Street until his death in February 1885.[93]

The pattern in South Carolina was also evident elsewhere. In most, if not all, former Confederate states the leading black educators were usually either free native Southerners or transplanted residents of Northern and border states. If from the South they often had spent some time outside the region during the antebellum years and in many cases had attended Northern schools. Thomas Cardozo, who was Mississippi's superintendent of education from 1874 to 1876, had left Charleston for New York state in the late 1850s when he was twenty years old. He completed his academic training in the North and spent four years teaching in

New York before returning to Charleston near the end of the war.[94] Georgia school organizer Henry McNeal Turner had been an African Methodist Episcopal minister in the District of Columbia as well as chaplain of the First Regiment, United States Colored Troops.[95] The controversial Aaron Alpeoria Bradley had gone from slavery in South Carolina to a law career in Massachusetts. Along the way he created considerable trouble for himself both personally and professionally. Convicted of seduction in New York at the beginning of the Civil War, Bradley spent two years in Sing Sing Prison. Later he was disbarred in Massachusetts for contempt of court and malpractice. Revelation of these offenses in 1868 led to his expulsion from the Georgia Constitutional Convention as well as his forced resignation from the state senate.[96] James H. Harris, "the black war-horse of Raleigh," grew up as an upholsterer in Warren County, North Carolina but soon moved to Oberlin, Ohio, where he received most of his formal schooling. Living in Indiana during the war, he came back to his native state afterward to take an active part in politics and freedmen's education. An officer of the state council of the Union League, he was appointed to the Raleigh Board of Commissioners in 1868 and represented Wake County in the constitutional convention and the legislature. While pursuing a political career, Harris promoted freedmen's education, operating as a bureau school agent and helping to establish the Colored Educational Association of North Carolina.[97]

As shown in table 4, among those educators prominent in Southern party politics outside of South Carolina there were men from both sides of the Mason-Dixon Line, who had previously worked as artisans, professionals, and especially ministers.[98]

Distinctive as they were, politically prominent instructors had much in common with the larger black teaching force. Among Negro educators in general, free persons of color constituted a majority, and a substantial number were ministers affiliated with the Baptist, Methodist, Presbyterian, AME, or AME Zion churches. In the secular sphere a wide variety of trades and professions was represented. As might be expected, many instructors had previous teaching experience. Pelleman M. Williams, the highly regarded Louisiana educator, had taught both black and white students in the North for twenty-six years.[99] John G. Mitchell, an Oberlin graduate, had been an instructor in Cin-

Table 4   Backgrounds of Negro Educator-Politicians in the
           Reconstruction South

Name and State	Place of Birth	Occupational Background
James Walker Hood (N.C.)	Pa.	Minister (AME Zion)
James E. O'Hara (N.C.)	N.Y.	Lawyer
James H. Harris (N.C.)	N.C.	Upholsterer
James D. Porter (Ga.)	S.C.	Tailor, teacher, church musical director and lay reader
A. A. Bradley (Ga.)	S.C.	Lawyer
Henry M. Turner (Ga.)	S.C.	Minister (AME)
Jonathan C. Gibbs (Fla.)	Pa.	Minister (Presbyterian)
Charles H. Pearce (Fla.)	Md.	Minister (AME)
James D. Lynch (S.C., Ga., Miss.)	Md.	Minister
Thomas W. Cardozo (S.C., Miss.)	S.C.	Teacher

cinnati and at Wilberforce University before coming to Georgia.[100] Florida educators Mary Still and Susan L. Waterman had taught in New Jersey in the ante-bellum period.[101] Mary J. R. Richards, an instructor at Saint Marys, Georgia, had taught in Liberia for four years. Miss Richards's mother was white and her father was part Cuban and part Negro. She was educated at Princeton, New Jersey and during the war was a spy in Richmond for the United States Secret Service.[102]

Also included in the ranks of freedmen's teachers were farmers, blacksmiths, mechanics, businessmen, lawyers, and even editors. William Steward, for example, had been a mechanic for an iron works located near his home in Bridgeton, New Jersey. He had also been a farmer. In the late 1860s, when he obtained a school in Americus, Georgia, Steward had a wife and three children and owned a comfortable farm home in Bridgewater. Extremely "fair skinned," the young New Jerseyan was often treated almost as a white in the South. As Steward explained in 1869: "the whites use me very kindly and in no case among them have I been treated as a colored man—always with the utmost equality among ladies and gentlemen." This situation convinced one black teacher that Steward was a " 'low down' Yankee passing off for a negro."[103] Another middle-class black teacher, J. P. Sampson, had been editor of the antislavery *Colored Citizen* in Cincinnati. A native of Wilmington, North Carolina, Sampson was described in a Southern newspaper as "a young man of ability, liberal education in Northern schools, and somewhat wordy radicalism."[104] A second editor, William Jefferson White, was one of the founders of Augusta Baptist Institute (now Morehouse College). The son of a planter, White distinguished himself during Reconstruction as an educator, minister, journalist, and politician. In the post-Reconstruction era, he joined Judson Lyons and other members of Augusta's light-skinned elite in leading the opposition to Booker T. Washington and his accommodationist policies.[105]

Men like Steward and J. P. Sampson helped to reinforce the middle-class tendencies of the Freedmen's Bureau educational program. Like their white counterparts, they tended to emphasize strict morality, refinement, "responsibility," religion, and economic advancement. Most would have agreed with James Harris when he suggested in 1868 that the Negro race must "make great strides in Education [,] Industry and general progress and improvement."[106]

The extensive papers of Robert Fitzgerald provide a glimpse into the life of a representative middle-class black teacher. Although not wealthy, Fitzgerald was financially comfortable. During his tenure as a freedmen's instructor in North Carolina, he operated a farm, a tannery, and a brick yard. The hard-working educator's financial success in these endeavors obviously affected both his life-style and his social attitudes. In his home he emphasized ambition, self-reliance, culture, and strict morality, and in his community he aided local blacks in establishing lyceums, churches, and schools. The result, according to Fitzgerald, was a marked improvement in the freedmen's "general deportment, industry [,] frugality, &c &c."[107] In school and out, Fitzgerald was a preacher of self-help. "I have bright prospects of a pleasant future," he wrote in his diary on 11 December 1868, "for I find that it lies [in] a man's own energies whether he is successful in life or not."[108]

Considerations of class and status among Negro teachers created significant division within the bureau educational program. In Virginia, State School Superintendent R. M. Manly reported in 1870 that communities made up primarily of free-born Negroes were often "unwilling to accept a teacher born in bondage, unless of a very light complexion." To illustrate his point,

Manly explained that "a community of this sort treated very coldly a black teacher that was sent to them, and withheld their children from school." The boycott lasted one month and ended only after the superintendent made it clear he would not provide funds to maintain a school as long as the town refused to accept a black instructor.[109] Such situations were even more prevalent in Louisiana, where an elite group of mulattoes had flourished since the ante-bellum period. There were about two thousand such elite Negroes in 1866. Many had received a foreign education, and their number included planters, merchants, bankers, and doctors. Although members of this class occasionally allowed a few children of freedmen to attend their schools, their usual policy was to exclude the dependents of former slaves.[110]

Individual free black teachers frequently evinced a sense of superiority over the former slaves. The attitude voiced by Mary J. R. Richards was typical. "I felt that I had the advantage over the most of my Race both in Blood and Intelligence," she wrote in 1867, "and that it was my duty if possible to work where I was most needed."[111] A similar sense of superiority prompted Thomas W. Cardozo to refuse to worship in Negro churches while teaching in Charleston. "I cannot worship intelligently with the colored people," he complained to the American Missionary Association in 1865. Cardozo qualified this statement by saying that Negro Episcopalians worshipped "intelligently." But, he added, "they have . . . a known rebel for their Pastor." Cardozo even considered attending an integrated church. This congregation, however, insisted that all Negroes "sit in the *North Gallery*—the hottest in summer and coldest in winter."[112]

Prejudice based on class and status did not prevent former slaves from playing a major part in freedmen's education. Indeed, the roll of bureau teachers included a number of nationally famous Negro men and women who had been slaves for at least part of their lives—William and Ellen Craft, Sojourner Truth, Harriet Tubman, and Harriet Jacobs. The Crafts served as managers of the Southern Industrial School and Labor Enterprise, a vocational agricultural institution begun in Georgia by a group of Boston abolitionists and philanthropists.[113] Under a *"quasi* commission" from the teachers' committee of the American Freedmen's Union Commission, Sojourner Truth instructed black women in "domestic duties."[114] Harriet Tubman, who could neither read nor write, performed a comparable function for the New England Freedmen's Aid Society.[115]

Harriet Jacobs had come to public attention in 1861 when white abolitionist Lydia Maria Child published Jacobs's slave narrative under the title *Incidents in the Life of a Slave Girl*. Although extremely critical of the "peculiar institution," Jacobs informed readers that her first mistress treated her kindly and taught her to read and spell. I "had always been . . . tenderly cared for, until I came into the hands of Dr. Flint," she wrote. "I had never wished for freedom until then."[116] After thirty years in bondage, Harriet Jacobs escaped to New York and obtained employment as a nursemaid. In the North she constantly encountered discrimination and Jim Crowism. Whenever possible she resisted such prejudicial treatment. In a typical incident in New York, Miss Jacobs was told that she and her employer's child must eat in the kitchen of the hotel where she was staying rather than dining with the white guests. Instead of complying with this demand, she insisted that her meals be sent to her room. Despite objections from white waiters and Negro servants, the determined young woman continued her protest until she began receiving courteous treatment.[117] It was this type of situation that motivated Miss Jacobs to become an active participant in the antislavery movement.

Soon after the end of the war, Miss Jacobs and her daughter established a school in Alexandria, Virginia under the auspices of the New York Society of Friends. The New England Freedmen's Aid Society sent a teacher for the school—Miss Virginia Lawton, "a young colored woman of good education and great worth of character (the grand-daughter of one well known to the fashionable circles in Boston, as the administrator of good things at weddings, christenings, parties, and other merry-makings)."[118]

A number of the most respected black educators had studied at Northern institutions of higher learning. Jonathan Gibbs, who taught freedmen in North Carolina before entering Florida politics, was a Pennsylvanian educated at Dartmouth College and Princeton Theological Seminary. A Presbyterian minister while in the North, Gibbs was Florida's secretary of state from 1868 to 1872 and as superintendent of public instruction from 1872 to 1874 became the chief architect of the state school system.[119] New Orleans teacher Pelleman M. Williams had spent only one year at

Dartmouth in the 1840s, but his advanced education and teaching experience were sufficient to earn him a position as principal of the normal department of the American Missionary Association's Straight University.[120] Port Royalist Charlotte Forten had been first a student and then an instructor at the state normal school in Salem, Massachusetts.[121]

Many had been educated at black colleges or at institutions associated with the antislavery cause. Oberlin, Wilberforce, Lincoln, Oneida, Fisk, Howard, Hampton—all contributed more than their share of teachers. Oberlin and Lincoln were especially prolific. From Oberlin came such notable figures as John Mercer Langston, B. F. Randolph, Arkansas State Superintendent of Education J. C. Corbin, and Mary Jane Patterson, reportedly the nation's first Negro woman college graduate.[122] Lincoln University derived from Ashmun Institute, a Presbyterian school incorporated in 1854 to train black men for religious work in the United States and Liberia. Numbered among its early students were at least three future freedmen's educators—William H. Hunter, a Virginia free Negro preparing for the ministry, Peter Plato Hedges, a New Jerseyan who during Reconstruction would serve as a teacher and state representative in South Carolina, and Robert Fitzgerald, a native of New Castle County, Delaware.[123]

Fitzgerald's diaries and letters give a fairly complete picture of his educational career. Born in 1840, he was the product of an interracial marriage. His mother was a white farm girl from a Delaware family that frequently intermarried with Indians and Negroes. His father was a black farm owner who had been employed as a servant and coachman by his wife's family prior to their marriage in 1834. Robert obtained his elementary education at a Quaker school for Negro boys in Wilmington and his secondary training in Philadelphia's Institute for Colored Youth. He was a student at Ashmun between 1859 and 1861.[124]

Fitzgerald never received his college certificate. In 1861 he left school to join the war effort, serving as an army teamster, a sailor, and a private in the Fifth Regiment, Massachusetts Cavalry. He returned to Lincoln University in 1866 but spent only one year at the institution before becoming a full-time teacher at Amelia Court House, Virginia under the auspices of the Presbyterian Committee on Freedmen. The devoutly religious schoolmaster resumed his studies in the fall of 1867, planning to finish the English course, then to "go forth as a laborer" in his "master's vinyard." Assigned to the freshman class, he pursued a program that included, among other subjects, history, bookkeeping, arithmetic, algebra, chemistry, and anatomy. After a year's absence, however, Fitzgerald found it difficult to keep up with his classmates and decided to seek another teaching position. In January 1868 he took charge of a school at Hillsboro, North Carolina. Although Fitzgerald left this school later in the year, he continued in freedmen's education until 1870, when he became a teacher in the Orange County public schools.[125]

The Presbyterian General Assembly's Committee on Freedmen encouraged Lincoln students to spend their summer vacations as missionaries and teachers among Southern blacks, and many answered the call. Catalogs of the university reported nine volunteer teachers in 1867, eight in 1868, and twenty-eight in 1869.[126] Some of Lincoln's most promising students participated, students of the caliber of Francis J. Grimké, Archibald H. Grimké, and William F. Brooks. When recommending this trio for summer teaching positions in 1868, the president of the university, I. N. Rendall, informed Virginia Bureau Superintendent R. M. Manly: "Three of our young men fully competent to conduct and govern schools have made up their minds to go South. . . . They are the best students in our sophomore class, and are worthy of confidence in all respects."[127] The Grimké brothers were slave-born nephews of the famous white abolitionists Sarah Grimké and Angelina Grimké Weld, a fact which Angelina discovered and openly acknowledged in 1868. After learning of the relationship, Angelina and her husband, Theodore Dwight Weld, accepted the two mulatto students as members of the family and assisted them in financing their collegiate and professional education. When they graduated from Lincoln in 1870, Francis was valedictorian in a class of twelve while Archibald placed third.[128] Both went on to distinguished careers in their respective fields. Francis studied law at Lincoln and at Howard University, earned a bachelor of divinity degree from Princeton Theological Seminary, and served over fifty years as pastor of the prestigious Fifteenth Street Presbyterian Church in Washington, D.C.[129] Archibald developed a successful legal practice in Boston after graduating from Harvard Law School in 1874. Combining public service with scholarly and civil rights pursuits, he acted as United States consul to Santo

Domingo (1894–1898), organized the Boston Literary and Historical Association (1901), and was president of the American
Negro Academy early in the twentieth century. Both he and
Francis were prominent in the struggle for racial equality, initially
supporting the program of Booker T. Washington but later becoming leaders in the N.A.A.C.P. Meanwhile, Lincoln University classmate William Brooks was pursuing his career as a
Presbyterian minister and a professor at Biddle University in
Charlotte, North Carolina.[130]

Many Negro teachers who were not college graduates had
studied at secondary schools in cities like Philadelphia, New
York, New Haven, Cleveland, Boston, and Springfield, Massachusetts.[131] Undoubtedly the most important in this respect
was Philadelphia's Institute for Colored Youth, a Quaker school,
which traced its origins back to the 1830s. Incorporated in 1842,
the institute over the next three decades built a solid reputation as
a training ground for black teachers and ministers and during
Reconstruction maintained close ties with the Friends Freedmen's Association.[132] This and other private or public secondary
schools in the North produced a number of well-qualified bureau
instructors. When describing two "very *light*" Negro teachers
who had attended high school in Massachusetts, for instance,
H. C. Percy noted: "They are thoroughly educated and certainly
very prepossessing. . . . Miss [Fannie A.] Rowland in our family
was their classmate in the Springfield High School, and vouches
for their high standing in society and church, at home."[133] Similarly positive recommendations could be cited for teachers educated at such institutions as the Negro high schools in Cleveland
and New York City's "Colored Grammar Schools."[134]

The trend toward greater reliance on native black teachers accelerated rapidly during the last three years of bureau operations
as Negro colleges and normal schools proliferated in those areas
coming under the federal government's postwar educational program. Toward the end of his last semiannual report, Superintendent Alvord listed over thirty such normal schools along with a
smaller number of predominantly black colleges, universities, and
institutes that devoted some attention to teacher training.

The amount of attention was often considerable. In 1869 Howard University closed its first academic year with 139 students in
the normal and preparatory department, compared to 4 in the
classical course, 8 in medicine, and 21 in law. The university also

maintained a model school in connection with the normal department, "affording opportunities for professional instruction, and for testing the capabilities of students in the art of teaching." The same year Fisk had an enrollment of 41 in its normal department, 68 pursuing the academic course, and 248 in the model school. Atlanta University, according to Alvord, was "designed to accomplish a much-needed work—the preparation of teachers for this region." The student body numbered 37 in the spring of 1869 and 140 in the fall term. Beginning its teacher-training program in November of that year, Straight University attracted 50 students within a couple of months. By this time Howard University had 4 regularly appointed instructors and 12 teachers selected from the higher academic and professional students, with an enrollment of 225. Of the pupils, Alvord reported, "one-half are in the model school pursuing common English branches, and the other half are fitting for college or for school-teaching." The bureau superintendent added enthusiastically: "Seven students have already successfully engaged in teaching, and at the close of the present year some thirty will be ready for that most important work."

Alvord in 1870 deemed secondary and collegiate institutions the most promising feature of freedmen's education. He noted in his final report: "Many hundreds of teachers and leading minds have already been sent forth from them to commence a life work, and make their mark upon the coming generation. These hundreds will be followed by thousands."[135]

Competition between white and Negro religious denominations contributed to the steady increase in the number of black teachers during Reconstruction. From all parts of the South came complaints that representatives of "colored churches" were attempting to draw students away from schools maintained by the freedmen's aid societies. As early as January 1865, Josiah Beardsley reported that an AME minister had made a concerted effort to convince the black Methodist Episcopal congregation at Baton Rouge, Louisiana to join the African conference and "to separate from the white preachers and white teachers."[136] Although this particular minister failed in his mission, black churches became increasingly involved in establishing their own schools, a development that profoundly disturbed many white educators.[137]

It would be easy, however, to overestimate the extent of educational rivalry between black and white churches. Certainly religious leaders in the African Civilization Society, the nation's most important all-black freedmen's aid organization, were anxious to cooperate with their Northern white counterparts. Dominated by Negro ministers from the African Methodist Episcopal, Congregational, Presbyterian, Baptist, and Methodist churches, the society was closely allied with the evangelical wing of the school effort. Indeed, two of the society's most active trustees, Amos G. Beman and Charles B. Ray, had helped found the American Missionary Association. Ray, John Sella Martin, and Society President Amos N. Freeman were all former AMA officers, and both Ray and Beman served as home agents for the association.[138]

By relying exclusively on black instructors the society was seeking "to prove the complete fitness of the educated negro . . . to teach and lead his own race. . . ." The trustees sent two teachers from New York City to Washington, D.C. about the middle of January 1864 and by the end of 1868 employed 129 teachers and assistants, instructing 8,000 students at an expense of $53,700.[139]

To a large extent the African Civilization Society's philosophy of racial self-help was an outgrowth of the National Negro Convention movement, which began in 1830 and continued to function until the end of the nineteenth century. National conventions had been held annually from 1830 to 1835; subsequently, they were held irregularly as the occasion seemed to warrant. After the emergence of the American Anti-Slavery Society in 1833, the movement almost died out completely. Black abolitionist leaders, especially in Philadelphia, argued that the AASS obviated the need for separate conventions. Moreover, these leaders contended there was a serious contradiction involved in promoting integration and legal equality through meetings that were attended only by Negroes. In 1835 the Philadelphia faction gained control of the movement and prevented the calling of another convention for the next eight years.[140]

The campaign to revive the dormant movement began soon after the schism in the American Anti-Slavery Society in 1839 and 1840. Convinced that black abolitionists could not afford to remain inactive while their white colleagues fought among themselves, a group of Connecticut Negroes recommended that a national convention be held in New Haven in September 1840.[141]

Their recommendation gained immediate support from a number of influential New York abolitionists, including Theodore S. Wright, Charles L. Reason, and Rev. Charles B. Ray. Those who favored the proposed convention saw in it a means of self-expression. As Ray, a future African Civilization Society trustee, explained: "If we act with our white friends, the words we utter will be considered theirs, or their echo."[142]

Ray and his supporters eventually achieved their objective. On 15 August 1843, the seventh National Negro Convention assembled at Buffalo, New York. Significantly, two future trustees of the African Civilization Society were elected as officers of the Buffalo meeting. Amos G. Beman served as president and Charles B. Ray as secretary. In addition, two future African Civilization Society executive officers—Rev. Amos N. Freeman and Junius C. Morel—were appointed to the committee responsible for organizing the next National Negro Convention. More than twenty years later Freeman became president of the society, and Morel treasurer.[143]

The rolls of subsequent conventions, held in 1847, 1848, 1853, 1855, and 1864, list the names of still more men who would later become leaders in the African Civilization Society. Richard Harvey Cain, Martin R. Delany, Jabez P. Campbell, Singleton T. Jones, J. Sella Martin, Henry M. Wilson—all participated in one or more national meetings.[144] Of the thirty-two officers and trustees in 1866 at least nine had participated in the National Negro Convention movement.[145]

The published minutes of the conventions of the 1850s make it clear just how important the movement was in shaping the basic philosophy of the African Civilization Society. This is especially evident in the case of the Rochester Convention of 1853. At Rochester the delegates took a more nationalistic position than any of the earlier conventions. The conclave created a national council to promote Negro self-help in the areas of employment, business, publishing, and education. The delegates even made provision for the establishment of a national Negro museum and library. More important with respect to the future development of the African Civilization Society, the convention's committee on social relations issued a report suggesting that Northern blacks develop their own educational policy. Committee members William J. Wilson, William Whipper, and Charles B. Ray argued that schools "constituted, especially for, and wholly directed by the whites" were inadequate to meet the needs of black children. With specific reference to the Negro student, the committee contended that

> the training . . . necessary to propel him, so that he can gain up
> with the whites . . . is to be obtained only in schools adapted to
> his wants; that neither schools nor educators for the whites, at
> present, are in full sympathy with him; and that he must either
> abandon his own state of things which he finds around him,
> and which he is pledged to change and better, or cease to re-
> ceive culture from such sources, since their whole tendency is
> to change him, not his condition—to educate him out of his
> sympathies, not to quicken and warm his sympathies.

While denying that they were advocating separate schools, the three-man committee concluded its discussion of formal education by asserting:

> We are more than persuaded . . . that the force of circum-
> stances compels the regulation of schools by us to supply a
> deficiency produced by our condition; that it should be our
> special aim, to so direct instructors, regulate books and li-
> braries; in fine, the whole process to meet entirely our par-
> ticular exigencies.[146]

This was the kind of thinking that led to the establishment of the African Civilization Society. Making its headquarters in Brooklyn, New York, the society was rooted in evangelical abolitionism. The vast majority of its officers and trustees were clergymen, and many were antislavery activists. Among the trustees were two bishops of the African Methodist Episcopal Church (Daniel A. Payne and Jabez P. Campbell) and two future bishops (Henry M. Turner and Richard Harvey Cain). The society's president, A. N. Freeman, was pastor of Brooklyn's Siloam Presbyterian Church, and General Superintendent of Schools Rufus L. Perry was one of the nation's most distinguished Baptist ministers. Before moving to Brooklyn, Perry had been pastor of churches in Ann Arbor, Michigan, in Ontario, Canada, and in Buffalo, New York.[147]

Two African Civilization Society trustees—Amos Gerry Beman and Charles B. Ray—had been important anti-Garrisonian abolitionists. Beman was one of eight Negroes who had helped found the American and Foreign Anti-Slavery Society in 1840, and both he and Ray had served on that organization's first executive committee.[148] Later Ray and Beman also became deeply involved in the antislavery politics of the Liberty party.[149]

Ray and Daniel A. Payne had been active in the underground railroad. Ray's home was a haven for runaway slaves (fourteen of them walked up the front steps one summer morning).[150] Payne was a member of the Philadelphia Vigilance Committee until it expired in 1844. After that he had continued to assist fugitives on his own.[151]

In setting up the African Civilization Society school program, men like Freeman, Perry, Ray, and Payne hoped to consolidate the gains of the antislavery crusade by preparing blacks for full legal equality. As a consequence, education in ACS schools combined the academic and the utilitarian. Pupils "are pursuing such studies as are generally pursued in common schools," Perry generalized, "with such variations in particular cases as seem best to accelerate the scholar's fitness for practical life." Specifically, students were taught "to have a very clear idea of the personal responsibilities attending their new relation to society, and fully to understand that the state of FREEDOM is the state of SELF-RELIANCE."[152]

Hampered from the beginning by financial constraints, the society in 1866 issued a special appeal for donations from whites, saying: "If our white friends will help us to help ourselves, we will comparatively soon reach the status of self-reliant people, successfully engaged in all the pursuits of civilized life, and constituting an essential element of strength to the Government." Appended to the appeal was a list of past contributions, including one of $150 from Henry Ward Beecher. Most were $25 or less, however, and, despite a continuing series of solicitations, the society was forced to suspend its school activities early in 1869.[153]

Black educational organizations appeared in almost every Southern state. In 1865 Negroes at Little Rock, Arkansas withdrew from the pay schools they had been attending, formed themselves into an educational association, paid by subscription the salaries of teachers, and made the schools free.[154] Two years later James Harris and nine other Negroes from Wake County, North Carolina incorporated an association for the purpose of "establishing schools and encouraging and promoting general education among the colored children of the state.''[155]

Superintendent Alvord himself had a hand in organizing the Savannah Educational Association while he was still secretary for the Boston wing of the American Tract Society. Founded by local black church leaders almost immediately after Gen. William T. Sherman captured Savannah in late December 1864, the SEA opened its first schools at the beginning of January 1865 with teachers selected by Alvord, Rev. Mansfield French, and Methodist Episcopal missionary James D. Lynch. The association initially consisted of the pastors and governing boards of black churches in the Savannah area and was administered by a nine-man executive committee. It soon established ten classes of fifty students each in schools located at the old Bryan Slave Mart and at Oglethorpe Medical College. By summer the total attendance increased to 700, and schools had been started on plantations as far up river as Augusta. "These self-made efforts may not be perfect," Alvord said of the all-Negro SEA system, "these schools are not, perhaps, as good as those taught by men and women from the North, . . . but we want this colored population to become self-reliant at once, though it be in an imperfect way."[156]

According to William Gannett, the SEA's leadership included "men of real ability and intelligence," men who had "a natural and praiseworthy pride in keeping their educational institutions in their own hands." Unlike S. W. Magill, the American Missionary Association agent in Savannah, Gannett respected the desire of SEA members for "assistance without control." Thus, the former Port Royalist and his employer, the New England Freedmen's Aid Society, were willing to help a Negro educational organization without "interfering with the management of a work so well begun." Gannett admittedly felt local freedmen "would make a better beginning if under a more experienced supervision than that which any board of colored men, wholly unversed as they are in such experience, can at present furnish." Still, he believed "it would be much better for them to come to this conclusion, if true, of themselves, and it would be almost cruel to check their ambition."[157]

The American Missionary Association's S. W. Magill, on the other hand, never seriously considered supporting the SEA as originally constituted, since its leaders "started on the principle of managing things themselves & admitting their white friends only to inferior places & as assistants in carrying out their ideas & wishes."[158] The Savannah enterprise would prove a failure, Magill predicted, "unless persons of more head than these Col.ᵈ people yet have, can be in the ascendant."[159] Since the American Missionary Association could not afford to become involved in "such failure and reproach," it must refuse to cooperate with the SEA as long as the black organization maintained a posture of racial "exclusiveness."[160]

Magill's first inclination was to ignore the Savannah association until its inexperienced members realized their inability to administer the schools "on the plan proposed, excluding white control." But when Gen. Rufus Saxton proposed making him director of education for Savannah, the Georgia-born AMA agent began to develop plans for integrating institutions controlled by Negroes into the overall city system. Ideally he hoped to put at least four whites on the SEA executive board and to replace black principals with American Missionary Association teachers.[161]

The extent of resistance to these plans apparently surprised the new director of education. Although he was prepared for the inevitable charges that the AMA discriminated against blacks with respect to hiring them as teachers, Magill underestimated Bureau Superintendent John W. Alvord's commitment to maintaining the SEA as an all-Negro society. Soon after the American Missionary Association representative assumed the directorship, Alvord visited Savannah and encouraged the "Col'd Board to *hold on*" until the bureau could advance them enough money to prevent bankruptcy. Cognizant of widespead fears that the emancipated slave would become a perpetual burden on the nation, Superintendent Alvord was anxious for this experiment in self-help to produce positive results.[162]

Predictably, both Magill and Edwin Cooley, the AMA agent who replaced him as educational director, questioned whether the bureau superintendent's plans for sustaining the Negro organization were advisable or even feasible. If "Alvord had not paid up the expenses of the Association and determined they should be sustained in their present shape," Cooley complained, "I could have brought everything under our control and made what is now working badly more efficient." Cooley insisted that he wanted the SEA to succeed and be self-sustaining if possible, but he doubted

this would happen unless Alvord came to Savannah and personally carried "the thing completely through." As it was, however,
the superintendent intended to begin financing SEA operations
through a voluntary tax among the freedmen. If Alvord followed
this procedure, Cooley advised AMA officials, the Negro board
of education might as well "be called a government institution as
to try to credit the Colored People with doing what they seem to
take but little interest in." Under such circumstances, the American Missionary Association agent had concluded that it was "best
to leave them to navigate alone, and simply manage our own
schools."[163]

Less than two weeks after submitting his report, Cooley had
reason to revise this conclusion. The occasion for such a quick
change of heart was an order from State Superintendent Eberhart
authorizing a reorganization of the freedmen's school system in
Savannah. For Cooley the crucial aspect of Eberhart's new plan
was a provision that the "Colored Educational Board, if it continue, will be recognized as auxiliary only: and all their official
acts must be subject to your approval" and in accordance with
orders issued from the state office.[164] Finally in a position to
influence the administration of SEA programs, Cooley tried to get
Negro board members to see the necessity of Eberhart's proposed changes. He soon discovered, however, that it was virtually impossible to implement the plan without antagonizing the
local black population. Faced with the prospect of intensified
racial conflict in Savannah, both Cooley and Eberhart decided to
revert to the original laissez-faire policy, confident the SEA
would "die a natural death, unless Mr. Alvord once more puts his
Herculean shoulders beneath the load of debt they are ac-
cumulating and lifts it from off them once more."[165]

The confidence of the two Georgia educational officials proved
to be well-founded. By March 1866 all Savannah Educational
Association teachers had withdrawn from the organization and
were seeking employment elsewhere. Acting for the AMA,
Cooley agreed to hire five or six SEA instructors who were willing to come fully under his "control." None of these Negro
schoolmasters, Cooley was careful to point out, would have
charge of their own classes. Rather they would serve as assistants
to the American Missionary Association's Northern white
teachers. Indications are that the director of education would

have balked even at this concession had he not feared that other Northern societies would take on former SEA school principals and in the process gain more pupils than were presently attending AMA institutions. Certainly his decision did not reflect a high regard for the educational qualifications of black instructors like James D. Porter and Louis Toomer. In Cooley's estimation Porter was well educated but "somewhat opinionated" and not a very good disciplinarian. Toomer was not as well prepared academically, although he had considerable executive ability.[166] Generalizing beyond these two examples, Cooley in a letter to State Superintendent Eberhart expressed his belief that a "Yankee girl" could manage one hundred students better than three black teachers could do.[167] Such statements only served to confirm Eberhart's conclusion that slavery's lingering effects rendered Southern blacks totally unfit "to assist in the moral and mental elevation of their own race."[168]

Cooley's actions prompted James Lynch, an SEA official and future secretary of state in Mississippi, to accuse the American Missionary Association of discriminating against Negroes with respect to employing them as teachers. Although Cooley dismissed the accusation as utterly false, available records of the period indicate that some white participants in the bureau's school program for Georgia treated freedmen prejudicially. Since this type of historical evidence is rarely unambiguous, any judgment concerning the *extent* of this prejudicial treatment must be based on inference, but the fact of its existence is beyond reasonable doubt. A study of Cooley's own correspondence reveals that the AMA representative constantly prejudged black educators and invariably assumed they were less competent than white teachers or assistants. Occasionally he did praise certain black teachers, but always these grudging commendations were couched in relative terms. James Porter, he observed in a typically condescending evaluation, was "well-educated for a colored person here."[169]

Considering Porter's accomplishments academically and politically, it seems doubtful that Cooley was unbiased in deciding that this former SEA principal was qualified only for the position of assistant to a white teacher. Certainly the director of schools was more reluctant to recognize the abilities of Negroes like James Porter than were many of the educators not affiliated with the

American Missionary Association. Compare, for example,
Cooley's evaluation of Porter with the newspaper account written
by a Quaker abolitionist instructor just after her arrival in Savannah late in 1865:

> The principal teacher is admirably qualified; for ten years he
> had given lessons on the piano and organ, to black and white.
> All the while he has had a secret school [for local Negroes], . . .
> as well as many private pupils, who have kept their secret
> with their studies; at home.[170]

The biographical information not included in this brief contemporary sketch is equally impressive. Born of free parents in
Charleston, South Carolina, Porter before the war established the
first of his secret schools for blacks denied education by state or
city ordinances. In 1856 he accepted an appointment as musical
director and lay reader in Savannah's African Methodist Episcopal Church. Remaining in Savannah after Lee's surrender, he
opened an eight-grade private school, and later was called to be
principal of the city's first black public school. He left this post to
take charge of a similar institution at Thomasville, a small town
approximately twenty miles from the Florida border. While there,
he published a textbook entitled *English Grammar for Beginners*.
Shifting his emphasis from education to politics, Porter took an
active part in the post-war Negro convention movement and in
1870 won a seat in the Georgia legislature.[171]

The Savannah situation was unusual in the sense that the SEA
need not have been a threat to American Missionary Association
educational interests. Certainly Alvord and others had no trouble
accepting the idea of an autonomous black organization working
alongside integrated societies. More understandable was the
AMA leadership's reaction to supposed attempts by local blacks
to take control of two of its fledgling colleges at Tougaloo and
Atlanta. On 2 April 1870 Mississippi Governor James Alcorn informed AMA Field Secretary Edward P. Smith "that the colored
people in the Legislature are going to insist on an entree to the
State University at Oxford or a University of *their own*, that there
is very little probability that they will at all consent to have
A.M.A., or anybody but themselves run their machine." Governor Alcorn suspected it would be *"necessary* in order to satisfy
them, to put the management [of Tougaloo] into their hands and

appoint colored teachers and managers throughout." If this were the case, Smith knew association leaders would want to sever their ties with the Mississippi institution since Negro control purportedly would bring about its destruction. With black trustees in charge, Secretary Smith predicted, school appropriations would "go principally for the aggrandizement of some Dinah and Sambo until they have floundered through two or three years—perhaps five—experience of incompetency." Much to Smith's relief, the AMA maintained its hold on Tougaloo, and his pessimistic and sarcastic prediction was never put to the test. The state legislature established Alcorn College near Lorman the next year.[172]

In the fall of 1870 Edmund Asa Ware, AMA officer and president of Atlanta University, began to develop a strategy that he hoped would prevent a recurrence of the kind of latent crisis that had threatened the association's position at Tougaloo. As in the Mississippi incident, several Negro members of the legislature had been, according to Ware's account, "rather opposed to aiding us: because they wanted a *'Black College'* managed by black &c &c. . . . I want to kill this feeling as much as possible." He thus advised Field Secretary Erastus M. Cravath that it would be well for the association "to elect several more teachers & mostly colored ones." Specifically, Ware proposed appointing John Mercer Langston "or some good colored man to some Professorship." For whatever reason, Langston did not join the Atlanta faculty, but President Ware nevertheless succeeded in thwarting the plans of those legislators who hoped to convert the AMA institution into a *"Black College."*[173]

A different type of opposition confronted the Georgia Educational Association, an organization with the avowed purpose of encouraging freedmen throughout the state to establish and support schools for themselves. Although ostensibly a Negro self-help organization, the association was largely dominated by J. E. Bryant, a former Freedmen's Bureau agent with definite political aspirations. Indeed, there was reason to believe that Bryant intended to use his position as association president to increase his influence among black voters. Certainly he made no attempt to conceal his partisan activities as editor of the *Loyal Georgian*, president of the Georgia Equal Rights Association, and member of the Republican party's state central committee. Furthermore, he freely admitted that the educational body was at the time of its founding in January 1866, ''a political as well as educational association.''[174]

Whether or not he was motivated primarily by political ambition, Bryant was remarkably successful in his efforts to induce freedmen to establish and manage their own schools. As one bureau educational official reported in 1867:

> This organization ... has ... in not a few communities, developed and stimulated the self-reliant spirit of the freed people. As showing this, we now find that in each of the ten sub-districts of Georgia there is at least one school, and in one or two of them there are not less than twenty.[175]

Bryant claimed even more progress would have been made if State Superintendent G. L. Eberhart had cooperated with the association. With substantial justification, Bryant charged that Eberhart had ''but little confidence in the ability of the colored people to organize associations and support teachers.''[176]

Despite the efforts of the association, white teachers in Georgia continued to outnumber black instructors by a large margin. The gap narrowed in the last two years of the Freedmen's Bureau program, but in July 1870, the ratio of whites to Negroes was still approximately two to one.[177]

Employing black instructors in freedmen's schools was one thing. Treating them as social equals was quite another. Indeed, many white educators discriminated against their black coworkers, either out of prejudice or because of conscious policy decisions to conform to Southern mores in the potentially explosive area of racial intermingling. Soon after the end of the war John G. Fee, the Southern abolitionist and cofounder of Berea College, encountered strong opposition from white teachers at Camp Nelson, Kentucky when he assigned a new Negro instructor to the dormitory and gave her a place at his table. Fee later revealed in his autobiography that ''all the lady teachers (white) sent there by the American Missionary Association and the Freedmen's Aid Society, refused, with two exceptions, to come to the first tables whilst the young woman was eating.''[178]

Although Fee was confident association officials would disapprove of the teachers' actions, segregation was not uncommon in AMA educational facilities. In Virginia, Samuel Chapman Armstrong and H. C. Percy agreed it would be inadvisable to bring Norfolk's "white and colored teachers together in the same household." The two men told Secretary Smith that if the teachers' home were integrated "family relations would be delicate—probably disagreeable, and there would be much bad feeling and talk among the people of Norfolk."[179] This was in 1865. Three years later the issue surfaced again when the AMA, on Percy's recommendation, made plans to commission a black woman then living in New Bedford, Massachusetts. Percy wrote to Smith: "The colored people are taking more than usual interest, just now, in their schools, and as many think you never send out colored teachers, it might make a difference in your receipts here, if this lady could come to Norfolk." The woman in question—Phebe Henson—was the daughter of a Norfolk minister and had attended high school. Percy recommended hiring Miss Henson if her testimonials were satisfactory.[180]

Anticipating such a move, however, the matron in charge of the teachers' home suggested the association send a white schoolmistress instead. Fannie Gleason explained:

> I do not quiet [quite] like the idea of having colored teachers in our family [;] we tried the experiment here in 63 & 64 and it was not a success. . . . I do not like to mix up the two Races [.] Perhaps you will say Im predjuiced [*sic*] to color [.] I will take them seperate [*sic*] without mixing [.]

The matron from Glens Falls, New York apparently had her way. Phebe Henson received a commission from the AMA but was not assigned to Norfolk.[181]

In North Carolina, AMA educator S. S. Ashley contended boarding blacks and whites together would create an intolerable situation for the white teachers:

> We are charged with endeavoring to bring about a condition of social equality between the blacks and the whites. We are charged with teaching the blacks that they have a right to demand from the whites social equality. Now, if they can point to mission families or teachers homes where there is complete social equality between colored and white, they have proved, to their own satisfaction at least, their assertion.[182]

Connecticut teacher Martha Kellogg, who did not wish to be identified with any policy that ignored or repudiated social equality, asked the association to transfer her out of Ashley's bailiwick. In explaining the reason for her request, Miss Kellogg advised George Whipple that the Wilmington school official's policy "has been non-association with the colored people on the same social terms . . . [as] our white friends (such as receiving them to the parlor, at our table and walking them)."[183]

As shown in the case of Rev. Sela G. Wright, the postwar South affected even antislavery veterans. While living in Ohio's Western Reserve, this Oberlin-affiliated missionary was quite egalitarian in his relations with Negroes. Once in the South, however, Wright readily conformed to the region's code of racial etiquette, even when this involved discrimination against black teachers under his supervision. His accommodation was so complete, in fact, that he succeeded in alienating the majority of his staff. John P. Bardwell, one of Wright's colleagues in the bureau school system at Natchez, Mississippi, summarized the situation in a letter to the American Missionary Association:

> Bro[ther] W[right] hates slavery, but is very much influenced by the popular sentiment of those around him, & this has led him into some errors here. His anxiety to propitiate the favor of military officers has led him to do some things that he would not have done in Oberlin. Some things occur[r]ed on the way down, last fall which prejudiced the Col^{d} teachers against him.[184]

The incidents alluded to by Bardwell took place during Wright's initial journey from Oberlin to Natchez. Informed that he was to be accompanied by three black teachers from the college, Wright advised them that "public sentiment" in Mississippi would not allow him to treat them as he would in Ohio. Upon their arrival in Natchez, he arranged to board the women with black families rather than allowing them to room with the white teachers at the mission house. According to Bardwell, the teachers justifiably "felt that they were proscribed on account of their colour, and this naturally awakened in them a spirit of resentment."[185]

In the first three months of 1866, the situation deteriorated still further. When one of the black teachers became ill, Wright allegedly told her that her board was more than the American Missionary Association was willing to pay and that arrangements were being made for her to come to the mission house, where she "would be obliged to room with two of the domestics." According to the young woman's account, he specified that at the house she must not expect to eat at the "first table" with her white coworkers.[186] Such discrimination added further evidence to support her contention that the "distinction between the two classes of teachers (white and colored) is so marked that it is the topic of conversation among the better class of colored people."[187]

Wright answered these allegations by pointing out that local whites had threatened to mob the mission house if the Northern educators practiced "social equality." In light of his overall approach to Reconstruction issues, however, this defense seems more a rationalization than a justification. Not only did he advocate immediate readmission of the Southern states to the Union, but he strongly criticized those educators who encouraged freedmen in the belief that they would soon gain full political equality.[188] Southern blacks, according to Wright, were "not . . . yet qualified for such privileges." "The time may come," he explained, "when they should be entitled to all the privileges of white citizens—but that time is *not yet.* . . . Privileges guaranteed to citizens will be *theirs when* they are qualified to *use them wisely.*"[189] Little wonder that a black resident of Natchez referred to Wright as a "Copperhead Preacher."[190]

In analyzing the backgrounds of black bureau teachers it is extremely difficult to generalize. The one safe generalization is that they were a diverse group. Their ranks included former slaves and free blacks. They varied widely with respect to academic competence. They came from all social classes. Some had extensive teaching experience; some had none at all. There were radicals among them, but there were also teachers closely allied with conservative Southern whites.[191] After Reconstruction, some black freedmen's teachers sided with Booker T. Washington, while others, like Francis and Archibald Grimké, John Wesley Cromwell, and William Jefferson White, became leaders in the anti-Bookerite camp.

Despite the diversity, however, free blacks from both the North and the South were a dominant force. Largely middle class and literate, they tended to share the values of their white counterparts. Like most Northern white teachers, they sought gradual, orderly change in the post-Civil War South.

Many of the black teachers, especially those from the North, were well prepared for the task of educating the former slaves.

Even if few possessed the academic credentials of a Francis L. Cardozo or a Pelleman M. Williams, a substantial number were well educated, and as a whole they constituted an important leadership group not only in education but in religion and politics as well. Many of the race leaders of the post-Reconstruction period first came to prominence as teachers or principals in Freedmen's Bureau schools. On the national, state, and local level the impact of the black teacher would be felt for many years to come.

4   The Southern
White Teacher

"We attribute a great deal of importance to the work of training Southern teachers, for obvious reasons," former Port Royalist William F. Allen wrote from Charleston in May 1865. "By employing them," he elucidated, "we are saved the cost of transportation; we place, in some degree, the work of reconstruction in the hands of native Southerners; and we adopt the very best means to foster the spirit of harmony in this people, which is so essential to our future progress."

When Allen provided his description of Charleston's educational system, there were one hundred teachers under the supervision of city Superintendent of Public Instruction James Redpath—thirty from the North, twenty-five Southern Negroes, and forty-five Southern whites. They taught at schools that accommodated both races together in the same building but in separate classrooms. Allen was pleased to see evidence of closer racial relations among the city's educators and students. He predicted: "The successful working of the schools, and the harmony with which white and colored teachers work together in the same schools, will be a powerful aid in bringing about a feeling of social harmony in this community, and a disposition to acknowledge the great principle of political equality."[1]

Over the South as a whole Freedmen's Bureau General Superintendent John W. Alvord was confident that as prejudice wore away, more and more native whites would be willing to engage in what he termed the "well-paid and useful service" of teaching freedmen. Like Allen, Superintendent Alvord looked forward to the beneficial effects of "mingling in one common and honorable employment persons from opposite sections of the country, and also of different colors."[2]

Alvord and many of his subordinates were remarkably tolerant of the shortcomings of those local citizens who did apply for

teaching positions. Assistant Superintendent R. M. Manly recommended the use of white Virginians even though they were
"generally women in reduced circumstances, or broken-down
schoolmasters—persons sufficiently humbled to be willing to earn
their necessary bread by teaching colored children." "While such
teachers are not the best," wrote Manly, "they are better than
none."[3] State Superintendents R. D. Harper, Charles W.
Buckley, E. B. Duncan, and Davis Tillson concurred in this
opinion.[4]

In contrast, other leading educators strongly opposed the policy of hiring large numbers of native whites. Georgia's Bureau
School Superintendent Edmund A. Ware declared in 1868:

> My experience during the last year shows me that there are
> *very few* Southern teachers, who offer to teach in our schools,
> who are in any way fit to do so. The only qualification most of
> them have is poverty and they seem to think that sufficient. I
> do not know of more than twelve or fifteen in the whole state
> whom I would employ.[5]

Laura Towne, school superintendent for the Pennsylvania branch
of the American Freedmen's Union Commission, claimed that
native white teachers were not only incompetent but dangerous.
Between 1866 and 1869, Miss Towne repeatedly warned AFUC
officials that if Negro schools were placed in the hands of Southerners "it would be a matter of little doubt what kind of political
instruction the rising generation would receive." She thus
suggested that no Southern teachers be employed except as subordinates to Northern principals. According to Miss Towne, it
was the object of the commission "to teach loyalty to government," and such teaching could come only from the North.[6]

Educational officials also expressed doubts about the morality
as well as the racial attitudes of Southern instructors. Typical
were the remarks of W. L. Clark, an assistant superintendent of
bureau schools in Georgia. According to Clark:

> The "good moral character" of average Georgian school-
> masters does not prevent their lounging example of idleness,
> tobacco chewing and occasional bad language. And that ten-
> derness and patience exercised by Missionary teachers in
> themselves so instructive and refining is all wanting. For a
> long time the black people will be called "niggers" and "nig-
> gers" only by one born south of Mason and Dixon's line.[7]

Not unexpectedly, accusations of sexual immorality were especially common. In North Carolina a bureau educational agent charged that a native teacher in Gaston County had been "imprudent" in her relations with black men. According to this agent's report, it was common knowledge that Margaret S. Clark had borne a "Colored child" in 1866 and that she "had been entirely too free with the Colored people."[8] Similar charges were leveled against a number of male teachers in Texas. James Burke, a native white school organizer and agent for the American Tract Society, claimed that a large percentage of the bureau teachers in the Lone Star State were having intercourse with their female students.[9] Although grossly exaggerated, Burke's accusations were not without some foundation in fact.[10]

Texas seems to have had more than its share of "immoral" native white instructors. In a representative case, a resident of Columbus complained that the bureau teacher in that town took all-night buggy rides with an army officer. When State Superintendent Joseph Welch received this complaint, he immediately relieved Josce Stell of her teaching duties.[11]

Many Northerners also suspected that Southern whites who wished to become involved in freedmen's education were motivated more by considerations of self-interest than by a genuine concern for the welfare of blacks. In Alabama, School Superintendent Charles W. Buckley noted that local churchmen often supported the establishment of freedmen's sabbath and day schools, but not always "from the best of motives or any real desire to see the negro educated." To illustrate his point, Buckley quoted a prominent Alabama minister who in 1866 advised his fellow church leaders that they could not prevent Negroes from being taught. If they did not educate the freedmen, Northern teachers would. What class of people would these Yankee instructors be? the clergyman asked. Answering his own question, he asserted:

> They will be men and women of the North whose moral and intellectual culture and whose social position, offers them no higher reward than the compensation received for teaching the negroes of the South. Coming from the lowest class of Northern society, educated to believe that you "Slave Drivers" are the embodiment of the "sum of all villanies" with their ideas of negro suffrage, of social equality, of miscegenation, of agrarianism, and ... they will infuse these things into the minds

of the negroes, and who can . . . foretell the result? If we do
not mean to suffer the distinction of races to be destroyed,
and permit equality in every respect, we must keep these men
from among us. We can keep them out only by ourselves giving these people the instruction they need.[12]

This fear of outside influences, coupled with a sincere desire to
spread religion among blacks, stimulated a great number of the
locally supported educational efforts that surfaced during Reconstruction in the form of Sunday schools and Protestant parochial schools for freedmen.[13]

There were other indications that Southern teachers wished to
control the tone and content of freedmen's education. In
Covington, Kentucky a bureau instructor reported that local
white women taught their black students "*nothing* unless it be the
injunction of the Apostle, 'Servants obey your masters.' "[14] In
Arkansas a planter who had established a freedmen's school on
his place asked Superintendent William Colby not to send him
textbooks "tinctured in the least with Radicalism or
Abolishionism [*sic*]." M. W. McGill closed his letter to the
superintendent with a touch of unconscious irony. "Dont it look
strange," he asked, "that a fireater and secessionist of 1861
should . . . do all he can to advance the interest and prosperity of
our former slaves [?]" Presumably Colby's reaction to McGill's
altruism was somewhat less than enthusiastic.[15]

Leaders of the major freedmen's aid organizations were divided on the issue of employing Southern whites. E. M. Cravath,
the secretary of the Middle West Department of the American
Missionary Association, contended that there were few Southerners who could meet the three minimum requirements for employment by the AMA—"1. Good Christian Character. 2. Good
Qualifications as Teacher. 3. A True *Missionary* Spirit."[16] By
contrast, the chairman of the New England Freedmen's Aid Society's committee on teachers endorsed the use of local instructors
"as an economical measure and as tending to promote a better
feeling towards the schools on the part of the whites."[17] The
American Freedmen's Union Commission followed the lead of
the New England society. As Lyman Abbott explained in a letter
to an AFUC principal who had refused to employ a native white
instructor in her school: "The whole object of the Commission is
to stimulate the Southern people to take up and carry on this work

of educating themselves. . . . The more Southerners we can take into our schools with us, the better."[18]

Despite opposition from some Northern educators, a significant number of Southern whites secured employment in freedmen's schools. In Louisiana, where the Department of the Gulf's board of education had depended heavily on the local population, such instructors constituted over half of the bureau teaching force at the end of the 1867–68 academic year.[19] From Alabama, State Superintendent Charles Buckley wrote in his school report for 1 January 1867: "No difficulty is now experienced in getting competent southern persons who are willing to teach colored schools. Among those already employed are graduates of the State University, and men who have been county superintendents of education."[20] South Carolina began with 12 native whites out of a teaching force of 148 in the 1865–66 school year and expanded from there.[21] By 1869 R. M. Manly could tell General Superintendent Alvord that the number of white Virginians opening black schools or seeking employment through the bureau was "considerable."[22] And a study of freedmen's education in Georgia concludes that at least 200 Southern whites taught in regularly reported schools in that state between 1866 and 1870.[23]

In Florida and Arkansas recruitment presented more of a problem. Florida Superintendent E. B. Duncan was unable to attract many native white teachers even though he took "a decided position" that the educational work should be done by Southerners.[24] Arkansas Superintendent William Colby, who was not nearly so committed to using indigenous resources, advised Alvord as late as 1869:

> In my jurisdiction it has been, and still is, impossible to secure a sufficient number of competent instructors for the children in our schools from either the white or colored residents of the State. Indeed, I have not met with half a dozen thoroughly qualified teachers of both these classes in the State during the past three and a half years.[25]

Existing evidence suggests a major portion of the Southern teachers considered themselves Unionists or at least denied having supported the Confederacy. In Louisiana the dependence on loyalists had been a matter of policy since 1863. Continuing this wartime approach, Freedmen's Bureau State Superintendent

Frank R. Chase told the American Missionary Association: "I employ very few southern teachers who have not been truly loyal during the war, for I do not believe in the constancy of reconstruction."[26] The dismissal of nearly 200 Northern and loyalist instructors by the New Orleans public school system in 1866 strengthened Chase's resolve. There was little doubt these educators were removed because of their Unionist sympathies, and Chase felt it his duty as the bureau's chief school officer in Louisiana "to give them employment in preference to others of doubtful loyalty."[27]

Many agreed with the Louisiana superintendent's emphasis on Unionism, and some were even more explicit in their stated preferences. Georgia bureau agent J. H. Caldwell, who, like Chase, was a Southerner, assured his superiors he would engage "none but those truly loyal and such as heartily accept the situation as it is." Caldwell went further: "All the teachers I employ are not only qualified for the work, but thoroughly loyal [,] in fact staunch Republicans, . . . who will sustain the government against all its enemies."[28]

There are numerous examples of instructors who conformed to the specifications spelled out by Chase and Caldwell. David Mahoney, an experienced teacher from Watkinsville, Georgia, defied local sentiment in his hometown by voting the Radical ticket in state elections.[29] P. L. Walker, a teacher at Belton, South Carolina, adhered to the principles of the South Carolina *Republican*.[30] William B. Thompson of Rome, Georgia had served in the Union army.[31] Mary E. Carr was the daughter of a loyalist state senator representing Dinwiddie, Virginia.[32] A school official at Pocahontas, Tennessee hired William S. Holley "because of his experience in teaching, and also for his undoubted Loyalty to the Government & sympathy with the Col^d Race."[33]

Many of the professed Unionists saw in teaching a means of alleviating the serious financial reverses that they had suffered during or immediately after the Civil War. This was true, for example, of an unnamed Baptist clergyman mentioned by Frederick Ayer in the summer of 1866. In a letter to the American Missionary Association, Ayer described "a school of 25 taught by an aged Baptist clergyman—a Southern Union man, who lost all his property by the war, a part of which was 15 slaves." "He is penniless." Ayer added, "and teaches (much to the disgust of some) ex-slaves for a livelihood."³⁴ A similar situation faced John J. Judge, a teacher from Enfield, North Carolina. According to Judge's own account, he had lost his fortune in the Rebellion, and owing to bad crops and many other disadvantages was in "grate need [*sic*]." Moreover, he had been denied employment around Enfield because of his active support for the Republican party. He had thus "concented to teach a collord scholl [*sic*]."³⁵

For some of these Republicans there was virtually no other means of support available. This was true in the case of Thomas P. Henley, an instructor employed by the New England Freedmen's Aid Society. At the outbreak of the war Henley had left his home in Richmond to join the Union Army, eventually becoming a guide and spy for Gen. George B. McClellan. Thus, when he returned to Virginia after Appomattox, Henley was regarded as a "carpetbagger," making it impossible for him to obtain work. This lack of employment opportunity, coupled with a desire to repay Southern blacks for their assistance during his service as a spy, led Henley to seek out a position as assistant teacher in a freedmen's school at Culpepper.³⁶

Bureau educational officials often had difficulty determining whether destitute Southern teachers were sincere in their pretensions of loyalty to the Union. In Virginia, Gen. Orlando Brown initially denied a Richmond teacher's request for school aid because he believed her "plea of union sentiment was grounded upon *present* necessities." The teacher, Mrs. H. G. Cadwallader, responded by assuring Brown that she had always been loyal to the United States. She further stated that she had been "a firm friend, and, as far as the law of Virginia would allow, a teacher of the colored people." She concluded her reply to Brown's charges by informing him that as a freedmen's teacher she had received "every insult that malice, envy, revenge, ignorance, and disappointed ambition could tempt women, children, officers of justice and the editors of the Richmond press to heap upon a woman whose only sin . . . [was] the loyalty they now profess[ed] to feel." Whether or not General Brown was convinced by Mrs. Cadwallader's defense of her loyalism, he reversed his initial decision and instructed School Superintendent Manly to do all he could for her.³⁷

Not all Northern educational officials shared Brown's concern about past affiliations, however, and in a surprising number of instances they were even willing to hire former Confederates and Confederate sympathizers. Several representative biographical sketches show what types of people gained positions in Negro schools.

Fred J. Collier, who taught on the Boykin plantation in Kershaw County, South Carolina, was born in nearby Cheraw and had received his education in Camden. Before the war, Collier had been a clerk in a Camden drug store; during the war he had been a corporal in a South Carolina regiment.[38]

A Professor Morton, who maintained a school just outside Millidgeville, Georgia, was a Virginian by birth who had served as a chaplain in the Confederate army. He owned a large number of slaves before the war but lost his fortune during the Union invasion of Georgia. After Appomattox he became a professor at the university in Millidgeville and a correspondent for the *New York News*. Although at first Morton was skeptical about the prospects for the bureau's educational enterprise and considered Northerners too ignorant of the Negro character to work successfully for their improvement, he changed his mind after visiting some of the more successful freedmen's schools at Macon.[39]

Samuel J. Danforth had served in the Confederate army before taking a teaching position on a Georgia plantation. The bureau assistant superintendent for Augusta described Danforth as "a sensible sort of man but not very thoroughly educated." He also had "been known to go on a 'spree'."[40] James McMaster, an instructor at Wharton, Texas, had served as a justice of the peace from 1863 until he was removed in April 1869 because he could not take the iron-clad oath. He regained his position in the next election after his political rights were restored.[41] The teacher at Van Buren, Arkansas had been a Confederate officer. Yet, in the words of a Northern instructor, "he seems thoroughly interested in the education and elevation of the colored race, and appears to be doing much good."[42] Another Northern instructor reported that most of the women employed in a school supported by the Presbyterian church at Tuscaloosa, Alabama "are now or have been teachers, and some of them originally from the North, but they are ardent supporters of the 'lost cause' nevertheless." The Yankee instructor doubted that Northerners "could out-do them in their active zeal for this school."[43]

One of the most prominent Confederates involved in freedmen's education was Rev. Anthony Toomer Porter, a native South Carolinian who had been chaplain of the Washington Light Infantry and the Twenty-Fifth South Carolina Regiment. Born in 1828, Porter was the son of a state legislator. His mother originally was from Elizabeth, New Jersey. When the elder Porter died in 1829, Elizabeth Porter and her two sons inherited a plantation with a complement of eighty slaves. It was on this plantation that Anthony spent his early years. In 1844 the young aristocrat enrolled in Mount Zion College at Winnsborough and began his preparation for the ministry. When his education was completed, Anthony Toomer Porter served as an Episcopal minister among both blacks and whites.[44]

At age twenty-one Porter took possession of five of the slaves that his father had willed him. In 1895 the distinguished Episcopal clergyman recalled his initial reaction to his new status:

> I believe I realized the solemn responsibility of holding my fellow creatures as slaves. I did all I could to house my people well, to feed them plentifully, to clothe them warmly, and to provide for their religious instruction, while their daily tasks of labor were such as they could easily fulfill. I worked harder in the countinghouse . . . than any slave I ever owned.[45]

Like many Southern ministers, Porter regarded the importation of African slaves as "the greatest missionary work ever done by man." In characteristically frank language, he argued that if Negroes had remained in Africa, "their descendants would be naked . . . savages still."[46] His views on the beneficial effects of the peculiar institution notwithstanding, Porter claimed that he "was born opposed to slavery." He added, however, that he was not such a "philanthropist" as to be willing to make himself a "pauper" by emancipating his own slaves.[47]

Porter was a firm believer in Negro inferiority. "I love the African race," he declared in 1865, "and think they are the most wonderful people (taking all their history) of the present day, and yet, I believe they are an inferior type of men, and the mass of them will be hewers of wood and drawers of water till the end of time—at the least, to the end of many generations. Do for them as we will, a black man will never be a white one."[48]

Although Porter was opposed to secession, he voluntarily enlisted as a chaplain in the Confederate army. Immediately after the war, however, he declared himself a true friend of the Union and advised planters to accept as a fact the freedom of their slaves. He called on Southerners to support freedmen's education and even advocated that the franchise be granted to blacks who "could read, write, and cipher, and owned five hundred dollars of freehold property."[49]

Porter's motives were not completely altruistic. He hoped that these concessions would help Southern whites keep the freedmen as friends, "and not drive them over to the Northerners, whom they would look upon as their deliverers." With regard to black education, Porter believed native white teachers could impress upon the ex-slaves the fact that "liberty was not licentiousness."[50] Moreover, the decision to become personally involved in freedmen's education was stimulated by Porter's knowledge that officials of the reunified Protestant Episcopal Church intended to support Southern clergymen and teachers rather than sending missionaries from the North. Less than six months after the church's General Convention endorsed this policy of non-interference in local affairs, he accepted a position on a committee appointed by the Episcopal Convention of South Carolina to establish Negro schools throughout the state.

Early in 1866 Porter travelled north to raise funds for a proposed freedmen's school in Charleston. Wherever he went on his fund-raising mission he encountered reactions that ranged from cordiality to skepticism to outright hostility. In New York the South Carolina clergyman angered many members of his audience when he characterized the Freedmen's Bureau as an unwelcome intruder in the South. By contrast, A. A. Low, a wealthy New York businessman and officer of the American Union Commission, was so impressed with Porter that he offered to endow his school if he would consent to become pastor of an Episcopal church in Brooklyn. On the whole the trip was a success. Porter raised a total of $66,000 to be divided between the black school and a white theological seminary that he proposed to establish in Charleston.[51]

The South Carolina minister's success at fund raising was attributable in large part to his moderate approach to sectional issues. Indeed, when he later described one of the addresses that he delivered in New York, Porter asked Southerners to remember "that this was in April 1866, and that the sermon preached had been submitted to Mr. George A. Trenholm, late secretary of the Confederate Treasury, and had received his commendation and approval." In 1898, when Porter offered this explanation, such a disclaimer was necessary since he by that time had established a reputation as a bitter critic of "carpet-bag rule" and "negro supremacy" in the South.[52]

Porter used a part of the money that he raised in the North to employ Southern Episcopalians to teach Negroes in his Franklin Street School. Subsequently, he visited O. O. Howard in Washington, and together they obtained the use of the United States Marine Hospital in Charleston to house another school, which was to be supported by the Freedmen's Commission of the Protestant Episcopal Church. For Porter this was the beginning of an involvement in Negro education that would continue for two more decades.[53]

In almost every Southern state there were outspoken Confederate sympathizers who had no trouble gaining employment in the bureau educational system. This was true of James R. Smith, a minister and physician from Sandersville, Georgia who claimed that he was no secessionist but that he believed his state "had the *Right* to secede." Early in 1866 Smith began serving both as a bureau educational agent and as a freedmen's teacher. Maintaining a combination sabbath and day school in Sandersville, Smith quickly won the respect of Bureau State Superintendent G. L. Eberhart. This despite the fact that Eberhart was fully aware of Smith's strong anti-Northern feelings.

The interaction between Eberhart and Smith is well illustrated in an exchange of letters in the spring of 1866. In early April Smith wrote a letter accusing Northern leaders of persecuting the South and its people. On April 24 Eberhart replied with a firm defense of the North. And on June 4 Smith wrote to clarify his position. He advised the superintendent:

> You certainly misunderstood my letter—or I wrote what I did not intend—if I accused the whole north of malevolence toward the south. I have never believed, not even during the fury of our struggle for National Independence, but that there were and are thousands at the north... as pure minded and noble as can be found on earth.... And when I spoke of malevolence I had only reference to those whose every act

shows a determination to degrade and destroy us. To those who having sworn to support the Constitution have violated every provision that interfered with or would have restrained them in their designs to ruin us. Tell me not of the sympathy of the "Radical" majority in Congress. I would as soon believe in the sympathy of the Devil for the damned spirit that he has lured to its destruction and then plunged into Hell.

Smith reminded Eberhart that the defeat of the Confederacy was "no proof that the north was right." Southerners "have not yet learned to kiss the foot that spurns us. . . . Nor can we exactly regard as friends of Civil Liberty, or as particularly entitled to our love those who deny us the Right of Representation." The Georgia physician warned that unless Congress ceased in its determination to "oppress" the Southern states "there never can be unanimity of feeling between the two sections." Smith ended his letter, however, on a positive note. "The education and moral elevation of the African race on this continent is a great and glorious work," he asserted. "In this I can and will co-operate with you."[54]

Although the bureau state superintendent may have objected to some of Smith's more extreme statements, he made no attempt to dismiss the Sandersville resident from his dual position as bureau agent and part-time freedmen's teacher. On the contrary, Eberhart tried to convince the pious Southerner to become a full-time bureau instructor at a respectable salary of $50 per month.[55] Smith refused this initial offer, saying he could not afford to abandon his medical practice since a teacher's salary would not support his family.[56] In 1867, however, serious financial reverses prompted him to reconsider Eberhart's offer. "I believe that God has called me to this work . . . of educating the African," Smith proclaimed. It "is my intention to devote my life to it so long as I can live by it." He informed the superintendent that he favored granting the vote to literate freedmen and promised to do all he could to qualify his students for that privilege.[57]

Compared to some other native white teachers, James R. Smith and Anthony Toomer Porter were quite restrained in their sectional attitudes. In fact, several Southern freedmen's instructors were known to be "bitter Rebels." Laura Towne described two such employees in a diary entry dated 3 March 1867. "They were tawdrily dressed," wrote Miss Towne, "and were in the war undoubted rebels. Indeed, we hear that they whip the children in their school and make them call them 'Massa' and 'Missus,' as in the old time." But they are " 'nigger teachers,' so I did my duty by them as agreeably as I could."[58]

Few bureau educational officials regarded pro-Southern feelings as automatic grounds for dismissal. Thus, when Texas State Superintendent Joseph Welch received a letter from a Northern teacher complaining about the employment of "a bitter rebel" woman at Victoria, he filed it away with the notation: *"No action to be taken. This matter will regulate itself."*[59]

School officials were equally tolerant of educators who had been slaveholders. In Tennessee, Bureau School Superintendent Burt gave substantial financial assistance to Lorinzo Lea, a resident of Jackson who had owned more than 100 slaves. The state superintendent may have been influenced by Lea's assertion that he had always "felt a deep interest in the fortunes of the colored race, & would have at any time voted for their gradual emancipation." Burt may also have been influenced by the fact that Lea was organizing freedmen's schools for a religious denomination, namely, the Methodist Church South.[60] In Texas black teacher and politician George I. Ruby praised the educational efforts of a Rev. Mr. Myers. Ruby described Myers as "a Texan gentleman of middle age, who from his own account has 'seen better days, having at one time held slaves; but who conscious of wrong doing in the past has latterly felt the necessity and importance of personally assisting in the elevation of a class so long down trodden and oppressed.' "[61]

In Virginia a Mrs. Dr. Brown, the daughter of a slaveowner, had begun her involvement in black education *before* the war. Accepting her parents' contention that it was a "Christian duty" to provide Negroes with instruction in religion and reading, she had devoted a good deal of her time to the mental and spiritual training of slaves on her family's plantation. After emancipation, she continued her involvement in Negro education, explaining:

Since the Negroes were made free, I have regarded their being educated as more important than ever both as fitting them for thier [sic] new duties and responsibilities, and also as being highly obligatory on us at the South, among whom God has placed and left so many of them in my opinion in order that we may thus try to discharge this our Christian duty towards them.[62]

When Mrs. Brown opened her school at Charlotte, Bureau Commissioner O. O. Howard and General Superintendent John W. Alvord offered encouragement, and State Superintendent R. M. Manly offered financial assistance. "It is so rare to find such Christian feeling and devotion to this unfortunate race among those who formerly owned them as slaves," wrote Alvord, "that we would gladly encourage it in every way we can."[63]

Some bureau school officials were even willing to overlook evidence of blatant racial prejudice on the part of Southern teachers. Nowhere is this better illustrated than in the correspondence between Georgia State Superintendent Edmund A. Ware and two freedmen's teachers in the town of Eatonton. The exchange began on 9 June 1868 when one of the teachers, Miss Vallie Meriwether, informed Ware that she had refused to allow a black bureau agent to examine her school. Although she based her refusal on the fact that her school was no longer directly subsidized by the bureau, Miss Meriwether's real reasons were racial in nature. Anxious to avoid antagonizing Superintendent Ware, she assured him that she would continue to submit school reports to the bureau and that she would receive and treat respectfully "any *white* gentleman" who wished to inspect the classes that she and her mother held in their home. At the same time she defended her action with regard to the Negro agent. "I have always moved in the best of society," she explained, "but if I had allowed this man who has no interest in my affairs to examine them, as I would a white gentleman[,] I should soon fall from that station."[64]

Four months later Miss Meriwether and her mother decided to ask Ware for financial aid for their school. The superintendent agreed but stipulated that if the aid were accepted "I shall expect that anyone whom I may send to visit your school will be allowed to do so."[65] Mrs. R. C. Meriwether replied immediately. "I am willing to recieve [*sic*] this aid," she wrote, "but object to having a colored man to visit my school."

Now hear my reason [:] it is because I have no male person in my family. Myself and daughter are alone, and it would not be in accordance with the rules of propriety. Think Mr. Ware if you have mother or sister, and act accordingly. I will receive any white gentleman you may send.[66]

The final disposition of the matter is uncertain, but it is significant that Superintendent Ware was willing to support teachers who had openly demonstrated their racial bias (few Southern white teachers, however, were so blatant in their expressions of prejudice).

Many of those involved in freedmen's education were actuated by motives more pragmatic than idealistic. Such was the case with the large number of planters throughout the South who maintained schools to prevent their laborers from leaving the plantation in search of greater educational opportunities.[67] This was certainly true of Matthew W. Jackson of Charlotte Court House, Virginia. On 26 October 1867 the veteran teacher and Presbyterian minister asserted that his decision to open a freedmen's school was based on a desire to further the interests of *both* races. Alluding to Southern blacks in a letter to Assistant Commissioner Orlando Brown, Jackson wrote: "I feel very much for them in their ignorant & destitute condition, & also we have cause to feel concerned for our own safety if they are not properly taught. . . . Indeed I always thought that Southern slavery was a greater curse to the whites than to the blacks."[68]

Similar sentiments motivated J. H. Caldwell, a resident of La Grange, Georgia, who served as the bureau's district superintendent of schools for the western part of the state. Caldwell entered the work of freedmen's education for a variety of reasons. Foremost among these was the belief that "a common school system is indispensable to the welfare of all inhabitants of the State." The importance of this consideration is revealed in a letter that Caldwell wrote to bureau official J. R. Lewis in 1867. Assessing the effects of the bureau educational program in western Georgia, he explained:

It is one of the most hopeful signs of the times . . . that throughout my entire district when the benign influences of education and religion have prevailed, the Colored population have been marked for their morality and industry. No crime of any magnitude has been committed and they are everywhere rising above the dominion of those vices which were nurtured in the slavery. They are cultivating a desire . . . to prove themselves worthy [of] the exalted privileges bestowed upon them by a wise and beneficent government, and I sincerely hope that they may show in the great experiment about to be made at the ballot box that they are worthy to be trusted with the . . . right of franchise.[69]

Clearly, Caldwell regarded freedmen's education as a deterrent to social disorder in the postemancipation South.

Although most of the Southern white teachers seem to have come from the middle class, the entire social spectrum was represented. A "poor white" woman with seven fatherless children taught in Polk County, Texas.[70] At the opposite extreme were instructors like R. P. Taylor and Miss H. C. Shield. Taylor was a wealthy landowner who taught in a school that he had built at his own expense a few miles from Oxford, North Carolina.[71] Miss Shield was a scion of one of the first families of Virginia, a family that, it should be noted, was strongly opposed to her decision to teach in a Negro school at Yorktown.[72]

A number of occupations and professions were represented. Clergymen and educators predominated, but there were also local government officials and skilled tradesmen. A. P. Abell, the chairman of the board of trustees of a school at Charlottesville, Virginia, was a justice of the peace before the war.[73] A. J. Talmadge, a New Yorker who had lived in Georgia for more than ten years, was a carriage maker.[74]

Many of the native educators had previous teaching experience or were otherwise qualified for the task of managing a freedmen's school. Baptist leader Rev. Robert Ryland had served as president of Richmond College more than a quarter century before teaching briefly in the institution for Negroes that later became Virginia Union University.[75] J. N. Murdock of Wellville, Virginia had taught in white schools for almost ten years. When applying for a bureau post, Murdock informed Superintendent R. M. Manly that he did not use the "whip stick" or strap and explained his reason for wanting to educate blacks:

My reasoning is: that as they are citizens they cannot be expected to be good ones without education. I think that putting books into their hands, will force upon them habits of thought & compel them to industriously use their leisure moments, will make them generally industrious.[76]

Murdock regarded education as an experiment that "must prove" whether Negroes "are people or entirely of animal creation, as they have always been considered & treated." The bureau gave the Wellville resident money to establish a freedmen's school even though he refused to operate the institution on an integrated basis.[77]

In Georgia, Julia A. Shearman praised the teaching ability of "a poor little broken hearted southern widow, whose husband was conscripted by the rebels, captured before doing service, & carried to Camp Chase to die of small pox." "Mrs. Setzer is doing quite finely in a primary school at Atlanta," Miss Shearman reported in 1867.

> The condition of her scholars[,] their discipline & improvement[,] were in advance of some of our Northern teachers[,] & I was glad to be able to encourage the poor toiling creature[,] whose bread depends both for self & three children in this effort, & who throws heart and soul into her labor.[78]

In 1870 the bureau's state superintendent for Texas endorsed J. T. Zealy of Brenham despite rumors that his school "was organized just before the last election by political enemies of the Republican party and for ... political purposes."[79] Welch explained in his July 1869 report to General Superintendent Alvord that prejudice against teaching freedmen was so strong in Texas that Zealy was the only "Southern man of standing" with enough "moral courage to adopt teaching a colored school as a profession." According to the state superintendent, Zealy was "a man of culture and good capacity."[80]

At the opposite pole were a large number of Southern teachers who failed to measure up to the standards set by their Northern counterparts. A bureau assistant superintendent at Bainbridge, Georgia claimed the native teachers in that town were "quite incompetent." Some "good men" had applied for positions, but the "kind of work and the moderate returns" persuaded them "to turn their hands to something else."[81] An instructor at Eufala, Alabama advised the American Missionary Association in August 1869 that 99 percent of the local white males who were willing to teach in order to make money were incompetent. "There are," the instructor conceded in a second letter to the AMA, "a few white teachers here capable of conducting a school, but they are all intensely Southern in their feelings & prejudices and so wouldn't lift a finger to help us.''[82]

Intense local opposition to freedmen's schools made it difficult to secure and retain qualified native teachers. The extent of this opposition is indicated by an encounter between Alfred J. Rose of Madisonville, Louisiana and a former friend. Rose described the incident in a letter to the bureau state superintendent dated 25 October 1865. According to Rose's account, the friend advised him to have nothing to do with teaching blacks. Rose quoted the friend as saying:

> I do not blame you for making money out of it if you can, but you know that the people will soon have the State in their hands, and that the Negroes will have nothing to say.... You know that the people do not want to pay taxes for educating the Negroes. *Look out or some of these wild fellows will shoot you full of holes.*[83]

Rose defiantly refused to be intimidated, but other Southern teachers took such threats more seriously. An instructor in Henry County, Georgia obtained protection from the bureau agent in the area after his house was stoned.[84] Similarly, a Unionist minister teaching in the Roefish Island Creek district of North Carolina informed bureau officials that his school was "sternly opposed by Hot Headed Secessionists" to the point where the work would have to stop unless the military could guarantee his safety.[85]

Such vehement opposition was the most important factor preventing the Freedmen's Bureau and the aid societies from achieving one of their major objectives—a rapid and smooth transition from Northern to Southern control of black education in the former Confederacy. Unfortunately for those who sought to achieve this goal, native opposition outlasted the bureau school program.

5   Educational Objectives and Philosophy

District Superintendent of Schools S. S. Ashley was anxious to gain local support for the freedmen's school that he proposed to establish at Lumberton, North Carolina. Early in February 1866 he made contact with some of the town's most influential residents in an attempt to determine the feasibility of such a project. Thus it was that on February 7 he wrote to Col. N. A. McLean explaining the bureau's plan of operations and soliciting McLean's opinion concerning Negro education in the South.

In his letter Ashley informed McLean that the business of Northern educators was not only to teach freedmen a knowledge of the three *R*'s

> but to instruct them in the duties which now devolved upon them in their new relations—to make clear to their under- standing the principles by which they must be guided in all their intercourse with their fellowmen—to inculcate obedience to law and respect for the rights and property of others, and reverence for those in authority; enforcing honesty, industry and economy, guarding them against fostering animosities and prejudices, and against all unjust and indecorous assumptions, above all, indoctrinating them in the Gospel of our Lord and Saviour Jesus Christ.

Ashley concluded by assuring McLean that he and his colaborers had "no other desire or purpose than to promote the peace and prosperity of the South" by removing the "causes of dissentions & strife."[1]

Two weeks after mailing this letter Ashley received the type of reply he wanted. Colonel McLean admitted he did not believe "any demonstrations of *delight* would be manifested" but he ex- pected no opposition if bureau teachers acted "*discreetly*" and evinced a "harmonizing spirit." McLean explained further that "a due observance of law and order, an improvement in morals, a *decent* respect for the rights and opinions of others—properly inculcated & impressed on the minds of the Freedmen . . . [would] be the surest passport to the attainment of the objects aimed to be accomplished.''[2]

Ashley and McLean were in basic agreement. The district superintendent of schools had already expressed a desire to promote "law and order" in the southern part of North Carolina. As he specified in his initial letter to the colonel: "We start with the principle that to rescue the Freedmen from vice and crime, they must be intelligent and virtuous[,] they must be taught.''[3]

This correspondence between Ashley and McLean neatly summarizes the major nonacademic goals of the educational program of the Bureau of Refugees, Freedmen and Abandoned Lands. Obedience to law, respect for personal and property rights, honesty, industry, economy, sectional and racial harmony—all are mentioned as desirable objectives. Taken together they constitute the bureau school system's formula for a peaceful and orderly transition from slavery to freedom.

Although this conservative educational philosophy clearly represented an attempt to gain the support of Southern whites, it also reflected a genuine apprehension on the part of bureau educators that emancipation might result in social chaos. As General Superintendent Alvord explained in a discussion of the purposes of freedmen's education: "a nation, especially like ours, will be short lived unless it has a *virtuous educated people.*"

> Wealth will be solid [only] when ignorant masses are not beneath and around it. Capital . . . must employ *intelligent* labor, and so also it is that political power when permanent emanates only from the masses *who think;* men not to be controlled by demagogues; who have *character* and *interests* at stake.[4]

Alvord left little doubt as to the consequences of denying education to the ex-slaves. "This great multitude will rise up simultaneously, and ask for an education," he asserted in 1866. "With it they will at once start upward in all character. Without it they will as quickly sink into the depravities of ignorance and vice; free to be what they please, and, in the presence only of bad example, they will be carried away with every species of evil.''[5]

Spokesmen for both the American Missionary Association and

the American Freedmen's Union Commission echoed Alvord's sentiments. In August 1865 the *American Missionary* printed an editorial stressing the need for a national system of education. With obvious reference to both freedmen and Northern immigrant groups, the editor asserted that "it is the duty of every government to provide against crime, pauperism, and wretchedness, by providing against ignorance."[6] Five months later, James Miller McKim, corresponding secretary for the AFUC, made a similar point in a letter to William Lloyd Garrison. According to McKim, the nation was just beginning to realize the importance of the work "of lifting up its ignorant & degraded masses, of relieving its perishing classes, & saving *itself* from its dangerous classes."[7]

Southern whites connected with the bureau educational program were more explicit in discussing the consequences of allowing freedmen to remain uneducated. Typical were the observations of Dr. William Hauser, a physician who maintained a Negro school near his home in Barton, Georgia. Describing the situation around Barton in 1867, the Southern doctor noted: "There are hundreds of bright eyed, smart little darkies hereabouts . . . who must become educated and useful citizens of the country, or they will relapse into barbarism, and become a curse to themselves and the country."[8]

It is obvious then that bureau educators from both sides of the Mason-Dixon line believed that the proper type of freedmen's education would promote social stability and order in the post-Civil War South. Less apparent but inescapable is the conclusion that most school officials hoped to achieve this goal by convincing blacks of the need for moderation and patience in their pursuit of equal rights.

Nowhere is this purpose more evident than in Gen. O. O. Howard's widely publicized address to the freedmen of Lynchburg, Virginia. Delivered in the latter part of 1865, Howard's speech constituted an appeal for *gradual* change. In it he advised freedmen to make contracts with their former masters or with others and to observe these agreements to the letter. The bureau commissioner further advised freedmen to "be faithful, industrious, obedient, and thus to live down the predictions of many that they were unfit for freedom." He took special care to dispel the illusion that the federal government planned to parcel out confiscated Confederate lands to Southern Negroes. According to one eyewitness account, Howard emphasized that

> the government had no lands to give: it had no right to take them from their owners, and it would not be best if it had the right; and that if lands were given them now, with their want of experience in managing for themselves, and lack of means, they would not find it to their advantage, and would, most probably be cheated out of them by sharpers.

The commissioner concluded by telling his black audience that it would be best for them "to work for others faithfully, learn experience, be industrious and economical, and try to save enough from their wages to buy themselves homes after a while."[9] Howard later pinpointed the role of education in this gradualist approach, saying it underlay every hope of success for the freedmen. He reasoned that through education, embracing moral and religious training, prejudice against blacks could be overcome. They themselves would thus be in a position to demand and receive the rights that others found it difficult to guarantee them.[10]

The race's contribution to its own elevation was a common theme, aptly expressed by Rev. Ira Pettibone soon after the end of the war. An AMA educator from Connecticut, Pettibone advised students how to act in their "new condition" by telling them: (1) that they should cherish no unkind feelings toward their former masters, (2) that they should realize that freedom did not mean liberty to be idle, wild, or lawless, but that it was the privilege of working for themselves and their families, and (3) that now the eyes of the entire nation were upon them to see whether they were capable of working out their own prosperity and happiness, so as to convince even their enemies that emancipation was "a great blessing."[11]

To these admonitions other freedmen's aid participants added suggestions that blacks should soften their demands for immediate legal equality. In their July 1865 issue, the editors of the *Freedmen's Record*, commenting on an address just given at Charleston by Salmon P. Chase, frankly admitted they liked the Chief Justice's advice to freedmen to be patient if they did not get their rights immediately.[12] Months earlier the magazine had printed a selection applauding the self-restraint of Afro-Americans who were in attendance when Henry Highland Garnet became the first Negro minister to preach in the United States Senate. The writer proudly reported that although it was thought by some that blacks in the audience would exercise their "admitted right to occupy any seats they please," they "modestly" took possession of one side of the gallery.[13]

Passage of the Civil Rights Act of 1866 and the adoption of the Fourteenth Amendment did little to dilute the old idea that members of the race would have to raise themselves by their own bootstraps. The premise that prejudice was largely based on the *"condition"* of Negro Americans suggested to many the means of eliminating racial bias and discrimination. "It cannot be done by expostulation or complaint," spokesmen for the New England Freedmen's Aid Society argued characteristically, "still less by self assertion and pushing on the part of those who feel agrieved; but mainly, if not solely by their persevering effort to elevate themselves morally and intellectually, and in all the fields of exertion opened to them ... to compete for the rewards of talent and industry."[14]

Bureau educators were quite specific about the ways in which freedmen's schools might help to reduce racial prejudice in the South. They were also quite pragmatic. Realizing the depth of Southern fears concerning the economic and social effects of emancipation, school officials sought to convince white leaders that education would transform the recently freed slaves into efficient, dependable, and contented laborers. Even Superintendent Alvord advanced this argument. In his first semiannual school report he warned Southerners that it would be difficult to retain Negro laborers in the rural districts if they were denied educational advantages available in the larger towns and cities. Combining his most salient points into one sentence, Alvord informed readers that:

Liberal minded and northern men, who are preparing for
crops, are earnestly asking that schools be established,
knowing that they concentrate and keep the people contented,
greatly stimulating industry, and especially that labor is valuable just as it becomes intelligent.

More specifically, Alvord concluded that "popular education cannot well be opposed; free labor is found to be more contented with its privileges."[15]

Imbued with a strong Puritan work ethic applicable to both races but especially relevant to freedmen in a period of extreme economic uncertainty, most Northern school officials felt a pressing obligation to discourage idleness and vagrancy among the former slaves. Many feared that protracted financial assistance would destroy incentive. Bureau State Superintendent Manly in Virginia asserted idealistically "there is but one kind of 'Freedman's Aid' that is entirely free from doubtful results and evil influences—*that is aid in educating them*. This aid tends to make all aid unnecessary." In support of his statement Manly quoted fellow educator Samuel Chapman Armstrong to the effect that "it is far better to build up character, self-respect and intelligence, which are the conditions of all right living, than to fill this people with meal, meat and herring, which teach the degrading lesson of dependence."[16]

In South Carolina, Superintendent B. F. Whittemore impressed upon freedmen the necessity of doing all they could for themselves, "assuring them of the motto of the North—'we will help those who help themselves.' "[17] Putting this philosophy into practice, the bureau school official, a minister in Massachusetts before the war, helped establish a Young Men's Enterprising Society, an extracurricular organization undertaking "to inspire *goaheaditiveness* & self reliance among a people impelled in the past alone by whip & paddle."[18]

The most prominent advocate of the Negro self-help approach was Booker T. Washington's strong-willed mentor, Samuel Chapman Armstrong. Even before becoming principal of Hampton Institute, General Armstrong showed that he was willing to use extraordinary means to combat idleness, vagrancy, and poverty. While still serving as a bureau agent and school superintendent in eastern Virginia, he developed an "exhaustive and vigorous scheme" for getting the large number of impoverished freedmen in his district back to work. His plan envisioned having the bureau offer freedmen a chance to settle in Florida or some other suitable location. If they "stupidly" refused, Armstrong suggested that bureau officials *"let them suffer."* Anticipating charges that such a solution was callous or inhumane, the general justified his scheme by saying, "they have got to learn something through the school of hard experience—they have no philosophy or forecast."[19]

At Hampton Institute, General Armstrong persisted in his determination to implement a policy of Negro self-help. Consequently, he began his tenure as principal by attempting to get freedmen in the area to pay a pro-rata educational tax. This initial attempt was unsuccessful, but Armstrong was not easily discouraged. He was convinced he knew the reasons why the former slaves had failed to contribute their share of school costs. The difficulty in obtaining financial support from freedmen was, according to Armstrong, "a complex one, resulting from the absolute poverty of some; the bad faith of others; . . . their inability to put forth organized effort; want of mutual confidence, and of a true perception either of the importance of education or their obligation to do their share in providing it for their children. . . . All is summed up in the word *ignorance*," Armstong concluded, "and for *that* they are not responsible."[20]

Quite naturally, the principal of Hampton expected freedmen's teachers to deal with ignorance and other adverse effects of slavery. As he explained in his discussion of the school tax failure: "It is only the educators . . . who begin to comprehend the curse of slavery. The Freedman is expected to work harder to get the means of schooling his children; but he don't know what it is to work harder; only patient pleading, earnest appeal and holding absolute necessity before him will rouse him. The best treatment, I might almost say, is tender violence." Armstrong ended the discussion by urging educators to continue their efforts to promote self-help among the freedmen even "at the expense of some apparent suffering."[21]

In the spring of 1869, Armstrong carried his campaign one step further by requiring AMA teachers in his district to turn away students who did not pay a mandatory tuition fee of ten cents a week. In justifying this policy, the general argued that free education would help some freedmen but would make paupers of others. "No class of people is so easily pauperized as Anglo-Africans," he asserted. "It is almost impossible to give to them largely without doing as much harm as good."

The reaction was immediate. Approximately one-third of the students in the district had to leave school. And despite

Armstrong's assurances that most of these pupils were "disorderly and indifferent," several teachers decided to defy the directive and allow the evicted students to return to classes. Still, the future mentor of Booker T. Washington defended his policy and expanded it to include the idea that students should work their way through school.[22]

This bootstraps philosophy became the basis for Hampton Institute's venture into agricultural and industrial education for blacks. "From the first it has been true to the idea of education by self-help," Armstrong said of the school twenty-two years after its founding, "and I hope it will remain so."[23] Like many of his fellow educators, Hampton's founder believed in an evolutionary ladder of "civilization" on which the Negro race occupied a lower rung. Thought to be backward if not inferior, blacks, according to this common line of reasoning, needed practical education to overcome hereditary limitations and the retarding effects of centuries of servitude. The chief difficulty with Negroes was supposedly a deficiency in "character," which manifested itself in such destructive traits as ignorance, laziness, dependence, and immorality. The function of education then was to build character by teaching industrious habits. Armstrong and his school preached the gospel of hard work, insisting that moral strength was more important than "polished scholarship." Through its periodical the *Southern Workman,* Hampton said to freedmen all during Reconstruction:

> Be thrifty and industrious. Command the respect of your
> neighbors by a good record and a good character. Own your
> own houses. Educate your children. Make the best of your
> difficulties. Live down prejudice. Cultivate peaceful relations
> with all. As a voter act as you think and not as you are told.
> Remember that you have seen marvellous changes. . . . In
> view of that be patient—thank God and take courage.

Armstrong considered this conservative approach essential since he subscribed to the prevalent theory that racial advancement was a slow, almost imperceptible, process of human evolution. In the short run only a foundation could be laid "for a bright future for the negro race."[24]

Assistant Commissioner Orlando Brown and School Superintendent R. M. Manly both agreed with Armstrong's sense of priorities. "It should be borne in mind," said Brown, "that the pupils are from the hovels of slavery and need civilizing quite as much as they do educating in letters. In fact if their personal habits, social morality, superstitious prejudices and modes of living and of labor are not brought under an enlightened and thorough discipline it is doubtful whether the value of mere book learning, as a means of their elevation, has not been overestimated."[25] Manly concurred. He believed the Hampton system provided just what the freedmen needed—teachers of their own race, who while they were "missionaries of the spelling book," could also be "teachers of a better civilization as symbolized in the broom."[26]

The Hampton plan obviously did not spring full-grown from the head of Samuel Chapman Armstrong. First coming to prominence in the Jacksonian era as an economic and educational program for working-class whites, industrial education was soon expanded to include Northern blacks. In 1831 antislavery leaders Simeon S. Jocelyn, Arthur Tappan, and William Lloyd Garrison proposed to the first national Negro convention the establishment of a self-supporting manual-labor college "for the education of Young Men of Colour, on such basis, as cannot but elevate the general character of the coloured population—" Under this plan, students might "cultivate habits of industry and obtain a useful mechanical or agricultural profession, while pursuing classical studies." Opposition from residents of New Haven, Connecticut, the site selected for the proposed school, forced abolitionists to abandon the idea. But subsequent exertions by ante-bellum reformers resulted in the founding of such vocational institutions as Peterboro Manual Labor School in New York; Emlen Institute in Mercer County, Ohio; Union Literary Institute of Spartanburg, Indiana; and the predecessors of Philadelphia's esteemed Institute for Colored Youth.[27]

Industrial schools proliferated during the Reconstruction years. As early as 1864 and 1865 various societies established institutions where trades such as sewing and shoemaking were taught in order "to develop ideas of self-dependence and self-support," which had been "crushed out by slavery."[28] By the end of June 1867 Superintendent Alvord could report a total of 35 industrial schools with an overall enrollment of 2,125 pupils, most of whom were working at "sewing, knitting, straw-braiding, repairing, cutting, and making garments.[29] By this time Alvord had also set in motion a number of school-related organizations designed to promote temperance and financial responsibility. Moreover, in his capacity as corresponding secretary of the Freedmen's Bank he had directed the cashiers of all local branches to encourage teachers to set up savings programs for their students.[30] A pioneer in the postwar version of industrial education for blacks, the bureau's school division promoted practical training for adults as well as for children. The government-supported effort included among its objectives: "the instruction of freedmen in civil affairs; the improvement of home life and the family condition; the encouragement of intelligent industry, thrift, and the accumulation of property; the establishment of families, as soon as possible, in homesteads, where the duties of the citizen will be realized, and where the school, the church, and town affairs will be interests of their own."[31]

School-related reform societies anticipated the moral emphasis of Armstrong's Hampton Plan. Closely connected with the conventional curriculum, these organizations aimed at suppressing vice and immorality by encouraging such virtues as temperance, clean language, chastity, and marital fidelity. The most important of these societies, the Vanguard of Freedom, was established in Washington, D.C. on 11 June 1867. Members were required:

1. To abstain from all intoxicating drinks.
2. To abstain from the use of tobacco in any form.
3. To abstain from all profane and vulgar language (including objectionable terms like "fool," "liar," "thief," and "nigger").[32]

The purpose of these reforms was both moral and financial. As one teacher explained at the end of the 1867 school term: "Many reasons of a social, moral, and religious character could be urged for immediate action, but I propose to call attention to a consideration of mere finance—the waste; the enormous expense to which the freedmen are subjecting themselves, even in their poverty and dependence." The teacher estimated that freedmen spent at least $20,000,000 per annum on tobacco alone. This sum, he emphasized, "would equal the whole amount expended by the North for their educational and physical wants."[33]

Local school officials established their own organizations. In

Vicksburg, Mississippi J. P. Bardwell, a school superintendent for the American Missionary Association founded the "New Reform Society," an organization dedicated to reversing the effects of slavery with regard to smoking, drinking, profanity, and sexual promiscuity. Students joining the society pledged themselves:

> to hold sacred and inviolable the marriage relation, and to discountenance any separation of husband and wife, save for the cause of fornication or adultery, and to use our influence in every proper way to prevent any violation of the seventh commandment: "Thou shalt not commit adultery"; to promote chastity and moral purity among all classes, and especially, to guard the young of both sexes against the vice of lewdness, and to the utmost of our abilities to reform those who have already fallen under the influence of this vice.[34]

Superintendent Alvord applauded the efforts of men like Bardwell, but he also felt more drastic measures were necessary. He was especially concerned about the plight of black women in the South. "The effect of slavery on female character has been fearful," he asserted. "There was no binding matrimony, no family sacredness, nothing which could be called a *home* in slavery." It was amazing to Alvord that after 200 years of such influence any trace of feminine delicacy remained.

Alvord was extremely concerned about the effects of female immorality on the education of young Negro women. He was certain that freedmen's schools were constantly "hindered by the counter teaching of a vicious home life." To obviate this situation, the superintendent proposed the creation of "girl's departments" in black high schools and the establishment of female seminaries "to prepare colored lady teachers for the schools, and leading women for their race." In these seminaries students could "receive in connection with intellectual culture, that refinement in virtue, that taste and idea of domestic elegance, which, though in poverty, reveal their charms, and endow their possessor of whatever rank with an undefined power always possessed by the well-bred cultivated woman."[35]

This emphasis on getting black students away from their home environments served a useful purpose at a time when freedmen's aid societies were shifting their focus from elementary education for the masses to high school and college training for future race leaders. Spokesmen for the societies constantly reminded potential college applicants that institutions of higher learning would give them a chance to live in an atmosphere conducive not only to scholarship but to culture and refinement.[36] Apparently this argument had some effect. By 1871 there were eleven colleges and universities in the nation that were especially intended for Negroes, and sixty-one normal schools. Most of these institutions combined what were thought to be the best elements of a secondary school and a home. At Fisk University teachers inspected the rooms of all students daily to make sure that they were "kept with the most scrupulous neatness." A bathroom was provided for each building, and students were required to bathe at least twice a week.[37] The regimen at Hampton was equally stringent and familial, involving an "inspection of men," "family prayers," inspection of quarters, and evening prayers. Little wonder that Samuel Chapman Armstrong was considered a second father by students like Booker T. Washington.[38] At Talladega Normal School a similar system seemed to produce beneficial results. After inspecting the institution in 1869, Edward P. Smith reported to the American Missionary Association:

> The first Normal class and their first schools have helped
> my misgivings and confirmed my hopes for the race. They
> have also confirmed my belief that we make our best and most
> economical expenditures in their behalf when we take *them in
> hand,* not merely in the school, five hours per day, but when
> we put them under Christian family influence, and constantly
> inspire them with a proper idea of true living.[39]

When Samuel Chapman Armstrong assumed the leadership of Hampton Institute, the foundations of industrial education had already been laid. It was Armstrong, however, who stood out as the foremost promoter of the concept as a basis for accommodation between racial and sectional factions in the aftermath of the Civil War. Stressing the value of vocational and moral training for supposedly backward, dependent dark-skinned races, the general's Hampton Idea drew support both from conservative Southerners and from Northerners who believed Negroes to be near the bottom of a human evolutionary scale, if not innately inferior. A paternalist in the most literal sense, Hampton's founder regarded freedmen as children who would improve their socio-economic status only if they allowed benevolent whites to assist them in

eliminating the self-defeating vices characteristic of the slave—
"improvidence, low ideas of honor and morality, and a general
lack of directive energy, judgment, and foresight." Convinced
that Negro agitation for immediate legal equality would discourage cooperation from Northern as well as Southern whites, he
advised blacks to abstain from politics and civil rights activity in
order to concentrate on improving their moral and economic condition. The implication was that prejudice and discrimination
were understandable responses to Negro shortcomings and that
full citizenship rights would be granted when the race made
significant progress in education, labor, financial management,
and family life. Believing the time required for these changes
might be measured in centuries rather than years, the general
apparently expected blacks to accept their inferior status in-
definitely.[40]

All through Reconstruction and the remainder of the nineteenth
century Hampton concentrated on turning out "an army of black
educators" who would exemplify the values taught at the Institute and pass them on to others. Owing to financial considerations as well as to underlying philosophy, technical training at
the Institute and such other schools as Atlanta and Tougaloo was
restricted to agricultural, domestic, and trade skills.

Not everyone approved of the post-Civil War version of industrial education for blacks embodied in the Hampton Plan. Henry
M. Turner, the outspoken AME bishop and former African
Civilization Society officer, accused Hampton Institute of perpetuating the idea of Negro inferiority. After a visit in 1878 Turner
wrote of Hampton's instructors: "The graduates they send out
cannot be called educated by any means, for they have not near
the learning given by a respectable grammar school. . . . Besides, I
think colored children are taught to remember 'You are Negroes,'
and as such, 'your place is behind.' " When Turner inquired
about the "higher branches"—mathematics, science, and classical languages—a white faculty member replied: "Oh, the colored
people are not prepared for those studies yet. They are too ignorant. It will be time enough to talk about that, years from this
time."[41]

Additional criticism of industrial education came from Dr. William A. Sinclair, a Negro physician who attended the freedmen's
school at Georgetown, South Carolina before going on to Claflin,
the University of South Carolina, Howard, and Meharry Medical

College. In his book *The Aftermath of Slavery,* published in 1905, Sinclair praised freedmen's educators for refusing "to regard the colored race as a special race, and therefore needing a special kind of education." It was his contention that

> If they had yielded to a "craze" for industrial education, . . . the colored race could not have gained in a hundred years the great advance in civilization and the splendid achievements which now . . . [stood] to its credit after only a single genera-tion of endeavor. For emphasis on industrial education would have circumscribed the mental vision, limited the aspiration, narrowed the ambitions, stunted all higher and broader growth, and held the race close down to the lines of hewers of wood and drawers of water.[42]

Such criticism was more than counterbalanced by enthusiastic praise from high-ranking bureau officials like Oliver O. Howard and E. W. Mason. As early as December 1865, Commissioner Howard declared, "there is no institution that seems to be more useful in aiding the colored people in the transition state, than the industrial school."[43] Four years later, Mason, who was superin-tendent of schools for Louisiana, made a strong case for con-tinuing vocational education beyond the life of the bureau. He asserted that the founding of more industrial schools "would tend to the elevation of the colored race more than any plan yet de-vised." He observed that the streets of Louisiana's cities and large towns were crowded with idle boys between the ages of ten and sixteen. If industrial schools were established in these loca-tions, "many such boys would form habits of industry, and be better fitted to take part in the great drama of life."[44]

Teachers and officers of the American Missionary Association saw in industrial education an opportunity to offer vocational alternatives to blacks who normally would seek to enter the over-crowded fields of education, the ministry, or domestic service. It was this rationale that motivated Edward P. Smith in 1866 to propose the establishment of a manual labor school near Atlanta. And it was this rationale that prompted Mrs. A. L. Tade to rec-ommend increased instruction for women in trades such as tailoring, dressmaking, and millinery. Negro women cannot all be teachers or servants, argued Mrs. Tade, "and it is quite evident that culture and self-respect cannot make her the indolent con-tented Dinah of the slave kitchen, much less, the rude unthinking field hand of former times." The freedwoman would, according to Mrs. Tade, either have to seek new occupations or yield to "degrading and ruinous temptations."[45]

It is clear then that most major arguments for and against vocational schooling were well developed by the time bureau operations ended in 1870. It is also apparent that by this date the American Missionary Association was on its way to becoming the principal practitioner of industrial education for blacks, although liberal arts remained predominant in the AMA program and would continue to do so.

If freedmen's educators feared the effects of an ignorant black labor force, they were equally concerned about the need to fit Negroes for their future role as voters. Most school officials believed, along with J. Miller McKim, that "democracy without the schoolmaster is an impossibility" and that "universal suffrage without universal education would be universal anarchy."[46]

Prior to passage of the Fourteenth Amendment, those concerned with freedmen's affairs warned that if Southern Negroes were "left to the power of intemperance, to the intimidations of their former masters, or to the wiles and control of demagogues," the suffrage would be a curse to themselves and to the nation.[47] Some advocated a literacy test that would be applied impartially to blacks and whites alike. Others suggested that the government append qualifications of "intelligence and morality" to any suffrage amendment to the Constitution.[48]

Still, most advocates of "impartial" suffrage considered it unlikely that Congress would disfranchise illiterate whites. They therefore placed great emphasis on convincing skeptics that freedmen were as qualified for citizenship as Northern immigrants or lower class Southerners. In some cases, officials of freedmen's aid organizations frankly admitted their desire to use the votes of educated Negroes as a "counterpoise" to the ballots of European immigrants, poor whites, secessionists, and other stalwarts of the Democratic party. Without this "counterpoise," they argued, freedmen and Southern loyalists would be at the mercy of those who had supported the Confederate rebellion against the United States.[49]

For public consumption at least Northern educators repeatedly emphasized they were interested in politics only as it related to the social and civil welfare of freedmen and other loyal elements in the South. Downplaying or rationalizing the involvement of some American Missionary Association employees in partisan affairs, AMA spokesmen claimed the organization deemed "ephemeral and inconsequential" any party questions that did not touch such vital issues as civil rights, education, and religion. Leading association officials sincerely believed the work of "deepest significance" was not political but educational and moral. Freedmen must be elevated both in intelligence and character "to guide them in the right use of the ballot, and to save them from becoming the dupes of demagogues."[50]

The stated goals of this idealized approach to politics were simple and direct: (1) to aid freedmen in gaining an intelligent understanding of their rights and duties, (2) to make black citizens aware of unscrupulous campaign practices, which might be used to control their votes, and (3) to instill in Southern Negroes the type of morality that would help them resist the blandishments of corrupt and immoral politicians.[51]

These avowed goals were linked to more concrete political objectives, including educational and civil rights legislation, campaign reform, and even legal restraints on the sale of liquor. It was intended that educators would help convince black voters to support these types of measures.[52] For the vast majority of freedmen's teachers more direct participation in partisan politics was discouraged. Convinced that party rivalry intensified opposition to Negro education, bureau and aid society officials frequently advised instructors to avoid open involvement in politics. Some forbade employees to hold local or state office and dismissed those who concentrated too heavily on political instruction.[53]

In contrast were the better-known teachers and school officials who used their power and influence to further the interests of the Republican party. Although not officially endorsed by the bureau, political involvement was often tolerated and sometimes encouraged by Commissioner Howard, Superintendent Alvord, and their subordinates.

In the academic sphere, freedmen's educators generally regarded the bureau school system as an ideal laboratory for testing and refuting popular theories of racial inferiority. Teachers and school officials fervently hoped that Negro educational achievements would be sufficiently impressive to dispel doubts about the race's mental capacity and its ability to survive in a highly competitive society.

Yankee reformers were well acquainted with the arguments used to support the idea of Negro inferiority. Since early in the nineteenth century, liberals in both the North and the South had been confronted by assertions that Negroes belonged to a separate and inferior species of mankind; that they were deficient in reasoning power; that they were incapable of taking care of themselves in freedom and might easily revert to barbarism; that they would always be hewers of wood and drawers of water; and that, "in competition with superior races, they must inevitably succumb and perish."[54]

Those who argued the case for Negro inferiority could cite such respected scholars as Thomas Carlyle, Josiah Nott, and Louis Agassiz to support their conclusions. As early as 1849, Carlyle had advanced the proposition that the Negro race would "retrogress" when released from bondage. In his influential "Occasional Discourse on the Negro Question," written soon after emancipation was completed in the West Indies, he had predicted that freed blacks would gradually revert to the level of civilization of their African ancestors and ultimately would become extinct.[55] The credibility of such speculation was enhanced by the ethnological findings of Nott, Agassiz, and others associated with the "American School" of anthropology. These scientists purported to have proved that the various races of mankind constituted separate species and that Negroes were at the bottom of the scale.[56]

During Reconstruction Southern conservatives adapted the conclusions of men like Carlyle, Nott, and Agassiz to suit their own purposes. Writers used Carlyle's theory of "retrogression," for example, to show that freedmen still needed the supervision of their former masters. In a typical article, published in September 1866, Bishop T. V. Dudley of Kentucky asserted that: "Separated from . . . their neighbors and their friends the Negroes must retrograde toward the barbarism whence they are sprung."[57] Later the same year, Rev. J. Stuart Hanckel of South Carolina cited evidence purportedly showing that the race was already on its way to becoming extinct. He claimed the mortality rate for blacks was rising sharply, although the percentage of increase was lower among those who were under the "supervision and care" of white Southerners.[58]

It is clear from J. W. Alvord's official reports that the superintendent placed a great deal of emphasis on refuting this type of argument. Indeed, Alvord in these reports addressed himself to almost every major theory of racial inferiority then current. He began by challenging "the assumption that some races are naturally so inferior that, in competition with superior races, they must inevitably succumb and perish." The superintendent admitted that this neo-Darwinian assumption would be plausible "if mankind had remained barbarians, subject only to brute forces." "But," he countered, "we have a better theory. The human race, though diverse in characteristics, is progressive. Culture, with opportunities and right conditions of improvement, overcomes every deficiency." Addressing himself to Nott and other anthropologists who claimed Negroes were a separate species of mankind, Alvord cited the book of Revelation as proof that God had "made of one blood all nations of men." Thus the superintendent saw no convincing evidence, either scientific or Scriptural, to support the hypothesis that the "colored race" was destined for "gradual extermination."[59]

Alvord was confident education would obviate the possibility that blacks would retrogress. He made this abundantly clear in his 1867 school report when he asked rhetorically: "If brought into conditions of comfort, with the home life of a frugal, industrious class; if recovered from vices...and advanced generously by education, shall we not have the guarantee that this race will not deteriorate?" Immediately answering his own query, the superintendent asserted: "Civilization does not tend to extinction; knowledge and virtue in a people do not cause their falling into decay."[60]

Alvord was equally emphatic in denying claims that Negroes were deficient in reasoning power and thus were incapable of advancing into the "higher branches" of education. Less than one year after becoming superintendent of schools, he felt able to answer this argument practically as well as theoretically. To this end he published statistics showing that 1,573 of the 53,092 pupils enrolled in bureau schools were studying such advanced subjects as mathematics, science, literature, and foreign languages.[61] In 1870 Alvord reported 9,690 advanced students out of a total enrollment of 114,516, figures which did not even include those attending college.[62]

In addition to statistics, Alvord could cite the testimony of hundreds of teachers and bureau officials who agreed that freedmen were capable of succeeding in the "higher branches." This testimony appeared frequently in the superintendent's printed reports and in the publications of the various freedmen's aid societies. In the *Fifth Semi-Annual Report on Schools for Freedmen* Assistant Commissioner Orlando Brown challenged predictions that black pupils would "decline in good scholarship in proportion as they advanced in studies requiring more particularly the exercise of the reflective and reasoning faculties." "No such indications appear in the highest classes of our advanced schools," Brown observed. On the contrary, these classes were said to be "the most promising and encouraging of all."[63] Similarly, H. E. Simmons informed the New York wing of the American Tract Society in 1865:

> I can only confirm my opinion expressed a year ago, that this people exhibit a surprising aptness in acquiring knowledge. Those who have attended school during the year have made as good progress as any children could do, and as yet have shown no signs of reaching that point, which some predict may come, where they will not go any further.[64]

Some freedmen's teachers believed the educational experiment had demonstrated that black students learned fully as quickly as white children. One instructor concluded that if there were any difference in intelligence between the two races in Virginia, "the advantage is on the side of the colored people."[65]

Most educators and bureau officers were more restrained in assessing the intellectual and educational potential of Southern blacks. Superintendent Alvord freely admitted that he considered it unrealistic to expect a race so long enslaved could at once compete with white children, who from the beginning had had "high advantages."[66] Spokesmen for the New England Freedmen's Aid Society were even more cautious. According to the April 1865 issue of the *Freedmen's Record*, the society did not "enunciate any mooted theory of the equality of races."[67] The editors of the *Record* elaborated on this statement in August of the same year:

> While we do not admit the absolute inferiority of any race . . . there can yet be no question that races, like nations and individuals, have their peculiarities. All elements are present, but they are blended in various proportions. In the negro race we believe the poetic and emotional qualities predominate, rather than the prosaic, mechanical, and merely intellectual powers.[68]

Like many other abolitionists and freedmen's aid advocates, these editors spoke of racial "peculiarities" and "differences" rather than inferiority. At times, however, the distinction between the terms was almost meaningless. Semantic niceties aside, the editors of the *Freedmen's Record* were simply saying that the Negro was innately inferior to the Caucasian in some ways and superior in others. They admitted as much when they stated in the April 1865 article that blacks "have as yet shown themselves inferior as respects many of the traits which characterize some of the white races."[69]

The editors did suggest that Negroes might eventually overcome their inferiority and rise on the scale of civilization. In an article entitled "Superiority of Race," published in the November 1865 issue of the *Record,* they wrote:

> History shows that races and people, like individuals, have their ups and downs; and that those who at one period are paramount, are at another among those lowest in rank. . . . Races, it would . . . seem, change . . . not only under the influence of time and under different political institutions, but mere change of residence has a great influence. . . . What bearing these general laws may have upon the future of the Negro race in America; whether change of place, circumstances, institutions, will work as beneficially upon their prospects as their friends hope and prophesy—time only can show.[70]

This tentative faith in the future prospects of the Negro race helps explain why the editors argued so vehemently against those who contended blacks were "incapable of civilization and destined to extinction." Writers for the *Record* repeatedly asserted that Northerners who were discouraged about the progress of the race did not make due allowance for the Negro's previous condition. They cautioned readers not to declare the freedman "hopelessly incapable and inferior" just because he did not, "at once and with a bound, attain to the civilization" that it had taken other races many generations to reach.[71]

In an article appearing in the November 1868 issue of the *Record,* the editors emphasized that Negroes might well progress upward on the scale of civilization if they were properly educated. This article was published in response to a selection from the *Atlantic Monthly* entitled "The Man and Brother." Written

by bureau agent J. W. DeForest, "The Man and Brother" provided a rather gloomy picture of freedmen's affairs in South
Carolina. DeForest admitted that his experience among Southern
blacks had raised doubts in his mind about the freedman's capacity for holding his ground "against the vigorous and terrible
Caucasian race." With specific reference to freedmen's education, he had written:

> It is a mooted point whether colored children are as quick at
> learning as white children. I should say not; certainly those
> whom I saw could not compare with the Caucasian youngster
> of ten or twelve, who is "tackling" French, German, and
> Latin; they are inferior to him, not only in knowledge, but in
> the facility of acquisition. . . . I am convinced that the negro,
> as he is, no matter how educated, is not the mental equal of
> the European. Whether he is not a man, but merely, as
> "Ariel" and Dr. [Samuel] Cartwright would have us believe,
> "a living creature," is quite another question. . . . Human or
> not, there he is in our midst, four millions strong; and if he is
> not educated, mentally and morally, he will make us trouble.[72]

Such pessimism from a bureau official who had himself organized
freedmen's schools around Greenville, South Carolina was
shocking indeed. The editors of the *Record* responded by charging that DeForest was unduly influenced by the present degrada-
tion of the race and reminding him that most freedmen's teachers
considered the Negro "equal, as respects ability to acquire
knowledge, to white children."[73]

The gist of the New England Freedmen's Aid Society position
as expressed in the *Record* was that educated blacks, even if
inferior in some respects, could become successful workers and
citizens. In an article entitled "The Prospects of the Negro in
America," published in 1868, the editors conceded it was probable "that in the hardier qualities,—perhaps in those which constitute greatness, pre-eminent distinction,—the African is inferior
to the Anglo-Saxon race." But, they asked, "does it follow that
therefore the colored people are doomed henceforth to be only
the barbers and waiters and stevedores and porters and servants
that they are for the most part [?]" The answer was a qualified
"no." In the words of the article, "there are a good many people
in America who somehow succeed in being something more than
these even though they cannot proudly boast of Anglo-Saxon

1   The Hooper School on the South Carolina Sea Islands, 1866.
From the Rufus and S. Willard Saxton Papers, Yale University Library.

2   Freedmen's teacher Lizzie Langford with two of
     her students from the Hooper School in June 1866.
     From the Rufus and S. Willard Saxton Papers, Yale Uni-
     versity Library.

3 A class in the primary school for freedmen at Vicksburg, Miss. The artist who drew this picture observed in 1866: "These scholars, embracing all ages from the grandam down to the infant are attentive, and master their tasks without any appearance indicating that the labor is irksome." From *Harper's Weekly,* 23 June 1866.

4   Noon recess at the Vicksburg school.
From *Harper's Weekly*, 23 June 1866.

5   The Abraham Lincoln freedmen's school in
New Orleans. Opened on 3 October 1865 in a
building belonging to the University of Louisiana,
this institution employed fourteen teachers for over
eight-hundred students. At the end of April 1866 it
was said to be the largest freedmen's school in the
United States.

From *Harper's Weekly*, 21 April 1866.

6   John W. Alvord, Freedmen's Bureau general
superintendent of education, in a story from *The
Freedman's Third Reader,* published by the Boston wing of the American Tract Society.

LESSON CXXXVIII.

church	as-sign	com-mun-ion	ar-range-ment
stretch	oys-ter	pro-ces-sion	op-por-tu-ni-ty
through	shoul-der	ex-am-ine	or-gan-i-za-tion

SCHOOLS IN SAVANNAH.

Rev. Mr. Alvord, whose picture is on this page, was in Savannah when the first colored schools were formed, and assisted in organizing the "Educational Association." We
give his description of the scene when the members were admitted to the Association.
The admission-fee was three dollars.

THE large church was full; and, as soon as opportunity was offered, the crowd came forward.
About the communion-table they pressed, stretching

7   A lesson from *The Freedman's Third Reader* on
Negro poet Phillis Wheatley. The piece concluded:
"The life of Phillis Wheatley gives most interesting
proof of the power of talents and virtues, crowned
with 'the pearl of great price,'—the love of
Christ,—to raise one from the lowest position to
the notice and the esteem of the wise and good."

LESSON XXXIX.

bought	pleas-ant	daugh-ter	ap-pear-ance
chalk	char-coal	learn-ing	ea-ger-ness
health	six-teen	al-though	in-ter-est-ing

PHILLIS WHEATLEY.

PHILLIS WHEATLEY, whose likeness is on
this page, was brought to this country from Africa in the year 1761. She was then between seven
and eight years old. She was bought by Mrs. John
Wheatley, a Boston lady, who chose her from a crowd
of robust negroes, although she looked feeble and
slender, because of her modest appearance and pleasant face.

8   Title page from *The Freedman's Spelling-Book,*
published in 1866.

THE FREEDMAN'S

SPELLING-BOOK.

PUBLISHED BY THE

AMERICAN TRACT SOCIETY,

NO. 28 CORNHILL, BOSTON.

9   A practical lesson from *The Freedman's Second Reader*, published by the Boston wing of the American Tract Society, 1865.

LESSON XV.

cock	wash	pig	too
crows	dawn	dig	two
food	bound	hoe	scrub
wake	clean	plow	bake
home	know	noise	eyes
cheer	knives	kneel	school

What letter is silent in hoe? in clean?   Say just, not *jist*; catch, not *cotch*; sit, not *set*; father, not *fuder*.

THE FREEDMAN'S HOME.

SEE this home! How neat, how warm, how full of cheer, it looks! It seems as if the sun shone in there all the day long. But it takes more than the light of the sun to make a home bright all the time. Do you know what it is? It is love.

lineage. People sometimes emerge from very humble callings who are not of Anglo-Saxon blood, and who further are by no means exceptional persons intellectually."[74] In short, there was hope for the Negro race.

Although few freedmen's aid officials were this explicit, many accepted the idea that blacks were inferior or "different." The head of the Freedmen's Aid Society of the Methodist Episcopal Church spoke openly of "Caucasian superiority," "negro inferiority," and the need to "Americanize" the African race.[75] Similarly, Lyman Abbott of the American Freedmen's Union Commission challenged the literal interpretation of Thomas Jefferson's assertion that all men are created equal:

> No sane man supposes that all men are created equal in character or capacity. They are not equal in . . . nerve or brain development. . . . By the doctrine of human equality is simply meant that all men have a right to an equal opportunity. . . . The wisest and best friends of the freedmen do not aver that the African race is equal to the Anglo-Saxon. Neither do they admit any race inferiority. They simply assert that the negro must be accorded an opportunity for development before his capacity for development can be known.[76]

Like most other freedmen's aid leaders, Abbott believed that Negroes, even if inferior, should be given the same educational opportunities as whites. In practical terms this meant Abbott and his colleagues rejected the notion that industrial training for blacks was more important than academic instruction:

> Any scheme of education which proposes to furnish the negro race only with manual and industrial education is a covert contrivance for putting him in serfdom; it tacitly says that the negro is the inferior of the white race, and therefore we will educate him to serve us. The race must have an education which in its final outcome shall be complete for the *race as a race*, which shall open opportunities for the highest culture of which any individual of that race is capable.[77]

Lyman Abbott and many bureau educators believed Negroes must be allowed to study advanced subjects in order to demonstrate their intellectual capabilities. This was certainly in the mind of Negro teacher Francis L. Cardozo when he established college-preparatory classes in his school at Charleston, South

Carolina. Cardozo was confident students who successfully completed these courses would be important in "providing the capacity of colored young men to the *Southerners.*"[78]

Similar considerations prompted a native white teacher in Atlanta to introduce Latin, Greek, Geometry, and Algebra into her curriculum. In January 1870 she reported the results of this experiment in the *American Missionary:*

> There is about as much white blood as black in our school,
> variously distributed. Several have the usual African
> physique, while it would puzzle even Nasby to decide whether
> others were "darkies," or specimens of the superior race. Our
> blackest are just as good scholars as the whitest. It's all stuff
> about their being an inferior race.[79]

At the time this report was published the teaching of Latin, Greek, and mathematics was no longer a novelty; for by 1870 a number of prominent aid societies were committed to building a permanent system of black education that would extend from elementary school through college. The goal of this proposed system was to prepare freedmen to enter such fields as teaching, the ministry, government service, and the professions. The emphasis was on establishing a new and enlightened leadership class, which would guide and inspire the entire Negro race.

Officials of evangelical freedmen's aid organizations placed particular emphasis on training black ministers, a group which had exerted an enormous influence over Southern Negro society since the eighteenth century. This was especially true of the American Missionary Association, whose officers and employees considered the "ignorant" black preacher one of the foremost obstacles to reforming Negro religion in the former Confederacy. AMA leader C. L. Woodworth explained in June 1870:

> The old heathen churches still bear sway, and hinder the
> moral progress of the race. Their preachers, ignorant, and
> many of them vicious, still have a mighty hold upon the race.
> The more rational, quiet, and orderly worship, which the Association has introduced, advances slowly, and only attracts
> the few who have cultivation enough to appreciate its simplicity and beauty.[80]

Two years later, Howard University Professor John Mercer Langston made the same point in a published report on the condition of freedmen in the South. The former bureau school inspector warned the AMA that ignorant and immoral ministers were setting a bad example for their congregations. At one religious meeting Langston "counted no less than twelve colored ministers very drunk," an occurrence which helped confirm his conviction that "an earnest, intelligent and pious clergy is greatly needed among these people." In order to provide for this need, the Negro educator strongly advised the American Missionary Association to continue its support for theological schools such as those recently established at Howard, Lincoln, Atlanta, and Straight universities.[81]

The importance of these religious objectives is obvious when it is realized that most private black colleges founded in the latter half of the nineteenth century were connected, at least informally, with a church involved in proselytizing among the freedmen. The Methodist Episcopal Church North developed a sizable black membership and established such important institutions as New Orleans University (later merged with Straight to form Dillard University), Clark College, and Claflin University. The Baptists founded Shaw University, Morehouse College, and Virginia Union University. The predominantly Congregational American Missionary Association between 1865 and 1871 established Atlanta University in Georgia, Fisk University in Tennessee, Talladega College in Alabama, and Tougaloo College in Mississippi.[82]

None of these institutions advanced far beyond the high school stage in the Reconstruction era. Even the best Negro colleges maintained elementary and secondary school programs well into the twentieth century. In 1878 the Freedmen's Aid Society of the Methodist Episcopal Church supported five so-called colleges, but the total number of genuine college students in all five institutions was only seventy-five. Talladega did not have even the barest beginnings of a college department until 1879 and did not grant a single degree until 1895. Tougaloo was originally a normal and industrial school and did not develop a liberal arts program until around 1900.[83]

The development of a system of bona fide black colleges was never a primary goal of the freedmen's aid societies during Reconstruction. Indeed, it is doubtful Negro higher education in the South would have made the limited progress that it did if the leaders of these organizations had not been committed to training

Southern black teachers and ministers to continue the work that Northerners had begun.

Throughout Reconstruction freedmen's educators were chiefly concerned with reversing the effects of slavery and with fitting the ex-slaves for useful and productive citizenship. Advanced academic training took a back seat as school officials concentrated on raising the level of "civilization" of the masses through instruction in the three *R*'s and "practical" or industrial education.

6 Reading, 'Riting, and Reconstruction: The Content of Instruction in Freedmen's Schools

The school is located in an abandoned Baptist church, shaded by lofty live-oak trees, with long, pendulous moss everywhere hanging from their wide-spreading branches, and surrounded by the gravestones of several generations of white communicants. The walls of the makeshift classrooms are adorned with pictures of Lincoln, Garrison, Phillips, and Whittier. On the only blackboard in the school is written: "Try, try again" and "Knowledge is power."[1]

By 10:00 A.M. all of the 145 pupils are in their seats and busily engaged in reading, spelling, or arithmetic. One class of 12 students reads an exercise from Clark's *First Lessons in English Grammar:*

Columbus discovered America.
Fulton invented steamboats.
Howard alleviated suffering.[2]

The teacher interrupts briefly to explain that General Howard is commissioner of the Freedmen's Bureau.

Meanwhile, another class in the same room has just completed a selection from Willson's Reader entitled "Going Away." They had not read the passage before but went through it with little spelling or hesitation. They then recited the first five pages of Towle's Speller and the multiplication table as high as fives.[3]

The teacher of an advanced class is leading her pupils in a prepared oral exercise on the subject of government and citizenship:

What was the wisest country of old times?
Egypt in Africa.
What are the people of the United States called?
American citizens.
What are the rights of an American citizen?

Life, liberty, and the pursuit of happiness.
What are his duties?
To obey the laws, defend the country, and vote for good
men.[4]

Pointing to a picture on the wall, the instructor continues:

Who is that?
President Lincoln.
Was he a good man?
Yes, yes!
What good thing did he do?
He set the colored people free.[5]

The class for older children and adults is reading from *The
Freedman's Third Reader,* published by the American Tract Society. The story for today is about Toussaint L'Ouverture, the
slave who led the successful Haitian revolt against French rule. A
student begins reading on page 81:

Toussaint L'Ouverture has been very justly called "one of
the most extraordinary men of an age when extraordinary men
were numerous." Born a slave in St. Domingo, his first employment was tending cattle on the plantation of his master.
As a child he was gentle, thoughtful and of strong religious
tendencies. He early learned to read and write, had some
knowledge of arithmetic, geometry, and Latin, and was diligent in gathering stores of information which fitted him for a
higher sphere.
2. Toussaint's good conduct and ability gained the love and
esteem of his master, and he was soon promoted to offices of
trust and honor. . . .
War having broken out in St. Domingo between the French
and Spaniards, involving both the free people of color and the
slaves, Toussaint joined his brethren in arms, and stepped in a
moment from slavery to freedom. Yet, while struggling for the
rights of his race, he had no feelings of revenge to gratify, but
was the same amiable and charitable person as ever.
3. When his late master and family were in danger he risked
his own life for their escape, sent them to a safe retreat in
America, with provision for their support, and afterwards re-
mitted to them not only all he could save from the wreck of
their fortune, but also valuable additions from his own
property.[6]

As the hour approaches 2:30 P.M., teachers conclude the day's lessons and instruct their students to assemble in the main hall for closing exercises. As always, these exercises begin with a song. Led by a pleasant-toned melodeon, the entire school joins in a chorus of "Howard at Atlanta":

> We are rising as a people, with the changes of our land,
> In the cause of right and justice let us all united stand.
> As we rose amid the conflict, when the battle storm was high,
> With returning peace we're rising, like the eagles to the sky.[7]

This was followed by renditions of Whittier's "Song of the Negro Boatmen" and "John Brown's Body."[8]

With the completion of "John Brown's Body" a white teacher from Massachusetts reads a geography lesson on Africa from *The Freedman's Third Reader:*

Africa is less known than any other portion of the globe. Many parts of the interior have never been visited by Europeans. The greater part of the inhabitants are either in a savage or a barbarous state.

The climate being warm, they need little shelter or clothing. Their houses are therefore poor mud huts, or slight tenements made of leaves or branches of trees. Their dress is often but a single piece of cloth tied around the waist. They are, however, a cheerful race, and spend much of their time in various amusements.[9]

The school day ends with the singing of the traditional closing song:

1

> Silently ! silently
> Ope and close the school-room door;
> Carefully ! carefully
> Walk upon the floor.
> Let us, let us strive to be
> From disorder ever free;
> Happily ! happily
> Passing time away

2

Cheerfully ! cheerfully
Let us in our work engage,
With a zeal, with a zeal
Far beyond our age;
And if we shall chance to find
Lessons that perplex the mind,
Persevere ! persevere !
Never borrow fear.

3

Now we sing ! now we sing,
Gayly as the birds of spring,
As they hop, as they hop
on the high tree-top.
Let us be as prompt as they
In our work and in our play;
Happily ! happily
Passing time away.[10]

Promptly at 3:00 P.M. classes are dismissed, and the children are admonished to return to their jobs in the cotton fields as soon as possible. Classes will resume at 10:00 A.M. on Monday morning.

In the absence of detailed information on any one freedmen's school, this composite picture gives some idea as to the type of educational exercises used by bureau instructors throughout the South. While subject to many of the limitations involved in reconstructing past events, it is by no means fictional. Rather, it is based directly on contemporaneous accounts written by teachers, missionaries, soldiers, agents of the federal government, and other interested observers from both sides of the Mason-Dixon Line.

By modern standards these exercises seem quite tame. During the passionate post-Civil War period, however, they were the subject of heated and often violent controversy. Southern whites continually complained that freedmen's teachers used their classrooms to belittle the South, to stir racial hatred, and to propagandize on behalf of the Republican party. As one Virginia editor explained to an instructor from Nantucket, Rhode Island, "The idea prevails that you come among us not merely as an ordinary school teacher, but as a political missionary; that you communicate to the colored people ideas of social equality with the whites." The editor claimed that he approved of education for freedmen, but regarded such teaching of "politics and sociology" as "mischivous" and likely to "disturb the good feeling between the two races."[11]

The Sumter, South Carolina *Watchman* in 1866 printed a vivid example of the type of lesson that most alienated the former Confederates. The subject was the hated antislavery militant John Brown:

> Who talks of deeds of high renown?
> I sing the valiant martyr Brown.
> I love the Doctor of the West,
>   May his pure soul in quiet rest.
> Let Nations weep the martyr's death.
>   Let children lisp with early breath,
> The name of Brown, above all men,
>   Who e'er have lived in mortal ken.[12]

A more common form of tribute to "Old Ossawatomie" was manifested in the widespread use of the song "John Brown's Body" (also known as "John Brown's Soul"). Indeed, it appears to have been an indispensable part of the school curriculum. Much to the disgust of Southern whites, Negro students especially enjoyed the version that referred to hanging Jefferson Davis "on a sour apple tree." In Norfolk, Virginia this line prompted one student to ask her teacher if the recently captured president of the Confederacy had been hanged yet. On being told "no," the student was extremely disappointed.[13]

Many educators continued to use "John Brown's Body" even after it became readily apparent how deeply Southern whites resented its lyrics. Francis Cardozo seemed almost proud to report that residents of Charleston could scarcely control their rage when they heard his students singing "Rally 'round the Flag," "John Brown's Soul," and "other patriotic songs." The black principal's defiant attitude intensified resentment. One woman, "very finely dressed, and apparently quite lady like," stopped at the door of Cardozo's school while the children were singing and said "Oh, I wish I could put a torch to that building! *the niggers.*"[14]

In North Carolina the John Brown song became the symbol for all such invidious attacks on the Confederacy and its leaders.

Thus it was that a Jackson County delegate to the state's constitutional convention offered an amendment that would forbid
the teaching of certain sentiments, such as those contained in
"John Brown's Soul," especially with the added parts ridiculing
"Old Jeff Davis."[15]

Such allusions to Jefferson Davis were especially evident in the
period immediately after the assassination of President Lincoln.
In May 1865 Miss L. D. Burnett asked her students in a Norfolk
school where Davis was captured. An eight-year-old student answered: "Running away in the woods, with his wife's dress &
petticoat on." On another occasion, Miss Burnett asked who was
happier—Lincoln, "who was murdered," or Jeff Davis. The answer: "Mr. Lincoln 'cas' he's in Heaven." Finally, the bureau
instructor asked if Davis wouldn't be just as happy "if we would
let him go to some country & live there unmolested." The answer: "No he'd think of the folks he's killed."[16]

After his vetoes of the civil rights bill and the Freedmen's
Bureau bill, President Andrew Johnson replaced Jefferson Davis
as the chief villain of these politically oriented school lessons.
Perhaps the best illustration of this trend is an undated poem
found among the papers of Lucy and Sarah Chase, two Quaker
teachers from Worcester, Massachusetts:

> Then came Buchanan to execute the law
> Who plunged the country into civil war
> Then Abraham Lincoln, the honored & brave
> Who passed through the Red Sea his country to
>   save
> Then Johnson came in martyred Lincoln's place
> The promised Moses of the colored race
> A traitor he, a curse to our free land
> Soon in his place brave Grant shall stand.[17]

The official bureau position on this kind of political instruction
remained conveniently vague and ambiguous. The closest thing to
a definitive policy statement is found in the Education Division's
Fourth Semi-Annual Report, compiled in 1867. Written by Reuben Tomlinson, state superintendent for South Carolina, the
statement declared:

> In the present state of society in the south, any tuition
> which does not include some information upon the character

and condition of our whole country will fail of producing what is most needed, an intelligent and loyal population. But the statement that politics, in a partisan sense, are taught in the schools is without foundation in fact.[18]

One year later Tomlinson gave some indication as to what these generalizations meant by pointing out that South Carolina's black students were receiving instruction in "the chief points in the Constitution of the country, the duty of its higher officers, and their own duties as citizens and voters."[19]

As was true to a lesser extent in Northern public schools, the distinction between civics instruction and political indoctrination was not always clear. Teachers frequently had their students read from the Emancipation Proclamation, acts of Congress, and speeches by such Radical Republican stalwarts as Owen Lovejoy and Samuel Shellabarger.[20] Some instructors even involved their classes in Union League activities. And in Andersonville, Georgia, the closing exercises of the 1869 term included a debate on the question "Whether the Legislature of Georgia had a right to expel its colored members."[21]

Experience showed partisan lessons were not appreciated by local whites. In the spring of 1867, John Tamblyn, a Canadian teacher in South Carolina, was severely beaten for informing Negroes of their rights under the Reconstruction Acts.[22] Southern white instructor J. N. Murdock encountered a less physical form of resistance while working at Wellville, Virginia. Totally ostracized by his neighbors, Murdock complained:

> Matters might have assumed a different character had not I when questioned by the voters, advised them to vote and adhere to the privilege, as an inheritance with their freedom . . . I explained fully and freely and truthfully their new position, as citizens, not slaves or serfs, but citizens entitled to all the rights claimed by any white person. . . . This doctrine did not suit my neighbors and it seems to me never will be accepted and recognized practically by but very few if any of the whites in my extensive acquaintance.[23]

In retrospect it appears these extreme Southern reactions were often based on widespread misconceptions about the nature of political instruction in freedmen's schools. Southerners had no way of knowing, for example, that many of the political speeches included in bureau school lessons were essentially moderate and conciliatory. As demonstrated in Lydia Maria Child's pioneering textbook for freedmen, this was true even of speeches by such bona fide radicals as Henry Wilson and William D. Kelley. Instead of publishing one of Wilson's acid indictments of slavery or segregation, Mrs. Child extracted a homiletic lecture to the freedmen of Charleston, South Carolina delivered in April 1865. While this speech dwelt briefly on slavery and the slave power, its main emphasis was on the "duties" of a free people. "Remember," Wilson had told his audience, "that you are to be obedient, faithful, true, and loyal to the country forevermore."

> Remember that you are to be industrious. Freedom does not mean that you are not to work. It means that when you do work you shall have pay for it, to carry home to your wives and the children of your love. . . . I want every man and woman to understand that every neglect of duty, every failure to be industrious, to be economical, to support yourselves, to take care of your families, to secure the education of your children, will be put in the faces of your friends as a reproach. . . . For more than thirty years we have said that you were fit for liberty. . . . The great lesson for you in the future is to prove that we were right. . . . We simply ask you . . . to show by your good conduct, and by efforts to improve your condition, that you were worthy of freedom; to prove to all the world, even to your old masters and mistresses, that it was a sin against God to hold you in Slavery, and that you are worthy to have your names enrolled among the freemen of the United States of America.[24]

Mrs. Child's extract from a speech by Congressman Kelley reiterated exactly the same theme. Kelley merely added a brief discussion of the economics of prejudice, Northern as well as Southern:

> Your friends in the North appeal to you to help them in the great work they undertook to do for you. We want you to work *with* us. We want you to do it by working here in South Carolina, earning wages, taking care of your money, and making profit out of that money. Work on the plantation, if that is all you can do. If you can work in the workshop, do it, and work well. . . . If you respect yourselves, others will respect you. There are Northerners who are prejudiced against you; but you can find the way to their hearts and consciences through their pockets. When they find that there are colored

tradesmen who have money to spend, and colored farmers
who want to buy goods of them, they will no longer call you
Jack or Joe; they will begin to think that you are Mr. John
Black and Mr. Joseph Brown.[25]

Although Mrs. Child's textbook was published in 1865, it is representative of the type of teaching materials used throughout the
Reconstruction era. A detailed analysis of "political" exercises in
The Freedmen's Book and similar works published by the American Tract Society suggests that Southern whites tended to overestimate the extent of "radical" or "partisan" instruction in
bureau schools.

Other evidence suggests that some Southerners purposely
exaggerated the degree of radicalism. This was almost certainly
true of Gen. James H. Clanton, the powerful Ku Klux Klan leader
from Alabama. During his appearance before the congressional
committee investigating the Klan in 1871, Clanton claimed that
Yankee teachers themselves were to blame for Southern prejudice against the bureau educational system. To support this contention he cited the example of one school program at which a
"radical" delivered an address reciting the "wrongs" Negroes
had suffered at the hands of whites. "The school was under radical regime," said the general, "white teachers were strangers to
us, and it was a political nursery to prejudice the race against us.
As the negroes number three to one white person among us it is a
very serious question." Implicit in Clanton's testimony was the
notion that such a palpable danger largely justified Klan violence
against bureau teachers and their schools.[26]

Most Southern whites were unaware of persistent bureau efforts to discourage manifestations of excessive partisanship and
sectional bias by freedmen's teachers. Perhaps the best evidence
of the sincerity of these efforts is found in a short note from
Mississippi School Superintendent Joseph Warren to Rev.
George Kitchen. Dated 22 March 1866, this note informed
Kitchen that he was being sent as a teacher to the plantation of
William Pugh in Chicot County, Arkansas. According to Warren's explanation, Pugh, a bachelor, wanted to provide schooling
for some mulatto children "of his own begetting." "Let me advise that you go there," Warren directed, "as a devoted Christian
Minister, teaching faithfully, letting politics alone, and avoiding
all participation in the quarrels that blacks may have with whites.

Let all see that your influence with the blacks is in favor of honesty, industry, chastity, & c. Say nothing at all to Mr. Pugh about
the children being his own.''[27]

Hoping to build white support for the educational enterprise,
Warren offered to supply bureau instructors to other plantation
owners in his district. Anticipating objections from native Mis-
sissippians, the superintendent assured planters that he did not
believe there was among the Northern teachers ''one fanatical
agitator or one whose work will not be beneficial to the employer's interests as well as the laborer's.'' Warren emphatically
denied allegations that these educators were ''unchaste mis-
cegenationists, promoters of social equality between whites and
blacks, and of discord between employers and laborers.''[28] Becoming more specific, he challenged newspaper reports that certain teachers were having their students sing inflammatory songs.
In a general policy statement addressed to the editor of *The Sunny
South,* Warren declared he would reprimand anyone teaching
songs that were insulting to the South, that exulted over its defeat, or held its people up to contempt. ''None of us approve of
vituperation or unmanly exultation,'' he explained, ''even though
we may be called trash, stinking Yankees, and the like.''[29]

S. G. Wright, the controversial American Missionary Association official from Oberlin, carried this policy of accommodation
one step further. He strongly criticized two Baptist Home Missionary Society instructors for encouraging black students in
Natchez to hope they would soon become citizens ''with all the
rights & privileges of the same.'' In reporting this incident to the
association, Wright made it clear that he discouraged this type of
instruction in AMA schools:

> I often say to our teachers & others that the great results of
> emancipation are not by any means yet developed. What these
> results shall be will depend *greatly* upon the character of the
> instructions given by the teachers and missionaries *now* on the
> ground laboring among them. I cannot think it right to refer
> very often to the *past* and I think it is *exceedingly* unwise &
> *dangerous* to inculcate the feeling among these ignorant
> peoples that they are now to be elevated to all the rights of
> citizens.[30]

Bureau officials in Georgia evinced a similar concern for the feelings of native whites. In the spring of 1865 Assistant Superinten-

dent W. H. Robert paid an official visit to Americus after hearing complaints that a teacher there was planning a public celebration in which students were to sing "Down with the Traitors & up with the Stars." Robert advised the teacher that such a celebration "would *embitter the feelings of the community, array the prejudices of each race against the other,* and inculcate hate & venom." He ordered her to delete the song from the program.[31]

Robert's desire to avoid antagonizing local whites was shared by bureau officials throughout the state. The attitude of Charles Raushenberg, a school agent in Albany, was typical. Raushenberg conceded that white Georgians were "prejudiced against . . . northern teachers and look[ed] upon them as radicals and social equality propagandists." But, he added, "no matter how unfounded and unjust this presumption may be in a large majority of instances, it nevertheless exists and without using some influence to counteract and mitigate it and to show the whites that only simple primary school instruction is aimed at, these country schools will be opposed and all possible means to interfer[e] with them and to break them up will be used."[32]

Raushenberg was sincere in his desire to make freedmen's schools as acceptable to whites as possible. In a report to Bureau Superintendent Edmund Asa Ware, he strongly emphasized the necessity of fitting adult freedmen "for the performance of their duties and the exercise of their rights & privileges as men and citizens." To further this goal Raushenberg proposed the creation of a series of freedmen's readers, "gotten up with the particular view of not only teaching them to read; but at the same time to impart to their minds in an easey [*sic*] comprehensible and attractive form that particular information on their duties and rights and their relation to the white race which is of the most practical value for them in everyday life."[33]

Ware undoubtedly was sympathetic to Raushenberg's suggestions. He had himself established a solid reputation for sensitivity to the feelings of Southern whites. The extent of respect for the superintendent among Georgians was graphically illustrated in 1867 when a Macon newspaper charged that the "sole mission" of bureau educators in Atlanta was "to stir up strife and sow the tares of hate and evil in the minds of their pupils." Instead of endorsing this viewpoint, the editors of the *Atlanta Daily Opinion* defended Ware and his teachers. According to the *Daily Opinion:* "No one here, who knows anything about the management of these schools, can be made to believe that Mr. WARE, or any of his co-laborers, seek, to stir up strife between the races. On the contrary, it is a notorious fact that the colored people are more polite and deferential to the whites than are the generality of negroes."[34]

An article in the 9 December 1866 edition of the *Atlanta Daily New Era* suggests the type of instruction that helped make bureau institutions more acceptable to residents of the capital city. The subject of the article was the dedication of Storr's school, a precursor of Atlanta University. Of particular interest to the reporter from the *New Era* was a song with distinct overtones of sectional reconciliation:

> Boys and girls are all for union,
> North and South and East and West,
> All the States in loved communion,
> Heart and Land with freedom blest.[35]

Presumably, E. A. Ware, the first principal of Storr's school, had played some part in selecting this piece. Subsequently, during his years as president of Atlanta University, the New England abolitionist encountered resistance on such matters as antislavery books in the library and the practice of having white faculty members eat with the resident students, but Ware's diplomacy and willingness to compromise staved off threatened punitive action by the Georgia legislature with regard to the school's subsidy from the state.[36]

Generally bureau teachers were more interested in preparing freedmen for responsible citizenship than in converting them to Radical Republicanism, a situation well illustrated by the case of AMA instructor David Todd. To be sure, Todd's lessons in "national affairs" drew upon political speeches by men like Owen Lovejoy, but they also included numerous selections from the Bible relating to the freedmen's "duties to themselves & others." The tone of these selections leaves little doubt as to the main thrust of Todd's civics instruction:

> MATTHEW 7:12—Therefore all things whatsoever ye would that men should do to you, do ye even so to them.
> SECOND THESSALONIANS 3:10—For ever when we were with you, this we commanded you, that if any would not work, neither should he eat.

MATTHEW 25:21—His lord said unto him, Well done, thou good and faithful servant: Thou hast been faithful over a few things, I will make thee ruler over many things.[37]

In every Southern state high-ranking bureau officials frequently used their considerable influence to prevent freedmen's teachers from becoming too political or too vindictive in their approach to sectional issues. Predictably, they were not always successful. Instructors who were truly intent on exploiting the political potential of their schools were not easily deterred.

Southern whites were generally unimpressed by the bureau's efforts to minimize sectional bias in freedmen's instruction. The reaction of the *Norfolk Virginian* was typical. According to the *Virginian,* it was the grossest form of insult

> to have sent among us a lot of ignorant, narrow-minded, bigoted fanatics, ostensibly for the purpose of propagating the gospel among the heathen, and teaching our ... negroes ... to read the Bible and show them the road to salvation, just as if we were Feejee Islanders and worshippers of African Fetish gods, snakes, toads and terrapins, but whose real object was to disorganize and demoralize still more our peasantry and laboring population.

The writer claimed Virginians would have been willing to let these "impudent assumptions pass with the contempt of silence" if bureau educators had "confined themselves merely to teaching the objects of their idolatry the rudiments of our English education—to read, to write, and to cypher." But, the *Virginian* concluded, "they failed to confine themselves to these harmless objects, and at once set to work assiduously to array the colored race against their former masters and natural protectors."[38]

As the *Virginian* article clearly indicates, Southerners deeply resented any implication that their region was "backward" or inferior to the North. Perhaps the most emphatic expression of this sentiment appeared in the *Memphis Avalanche* in 1866. "The South never learnt anything from New England," according to the *Avalanche.* "The Pharisaical religion, the morals, the 'isms' of that land of hickory hams and wooden nutmegs have never obtained foothold among us, and never will. These 'isms' are sprouts to be planted among us by these 'schoolmarms' and the South will rejoice when the last one has left us."[39]

The editor of the *Avalanche* was basically correct in his assertion that freedmen's aid leaders were attempting to "northernize" the former Confederate states. As Lyman Abbott freely admitted in 1864, "we have not only to conquer the South—we have also to convert it. We have not only to occupy it by bayonets and bullets—but also by ideas and institutions." The two great essentials for successful democracy, he believed, were popular intelligence and popular morality, in other words free schools and free churches. "The South now possesses neither of these," he said. The North should supply them.[40]

Rev. Daniel A. Payne of the AME Church was more emphatic. After visiting several of Charleston's Negro schools in 1865, he was convinced that "New England ideas, sentiments, and principles" would "ultimately rule the entire South."[41]

In pursuit of this goal bureau teachers frequently admonished their black pupils to emulate their Northern counterparts and to strive to become "good Yankees." One instructor disciplined her students by reminding anyone who misbehaved that a "Yankee boy would be ashamed to do as they were doing."[42]

Evidence of a strong Northern bias could also be found in the textbooks used in freedmen's schools. Indeed, this was almost inevitable since the bureau and the various aid societies were forced by financial considerations to depend primarily on donations of old second-hand works, many of which reflected the sectional biases of the ante-bellum period. These were some of the same histories, geographies, spellers, and readers that had provoked what has been called a Southern educational revolt in the period between 1830 and 1860.

Southerners generally found texts published after the war more acceptable. During Reconstruction *DeBow's Review* noted approvingly efforts "to furnish the infancy and youth of the South with books and prints more congenial to the true sentiment and traditions of their country."[43] *DeBow's* was no less positive in its review of one of the most important of the works directed specifically at Southern blacks—Clinton B. Fisk's *Plain Counsels for Freedmen*. The magazine's review editor offered an opinion that "Gen. Fisk has given good counsel, and the circulation of the work among Freedmen would effect good, supposing that it were read and acted upon." The only major source of disagreement was General Fisk's assertion that masters would naturally feel "severe" toward their former slaves:

Now, General, we take issue on that point. . . . The old masters
do *not* feel "unkindness." We are one of them. Dinah and
Cudgo begin to understand this very well, too. *Pity* is the sentiment evoked, and this leads to a thousand acts of good-will,
now as when slavery existed. Doubtless the negroes expected
to find enemies in their old masters. They were so instructed
by designing persons. It was not these masters that reduced
them to bondage. . . . The slave-ships and the slave-traders
who fastened the system upon America, as every historian
knows, *were all from . . . New England,* and only ceased the
traffic when the traffic ceased to be profitable. Had Gen. Fisk
mentioned the fact, it would have caused upon the part of the
Freedmen even greater respect towards their old masters!

The Southern periodical was willing to forgive Fisk's misstate-
ment, however, since his little volume was "prepared in good
spirit."[44]

Textbooks written especially for freedmen are excellent
sources of information on exactly what messages authors and
publishers wanted to convey to those making the welcome but
difficult adjustment to a new condition. Detailed examination reveals more about the underlying philosophy of educational Reconstruction than one might at first expect.

The most prolific of the publishers in this specialized area were
the Boston and New York wings of the American Tract Society,
an organization established in 1825 "to diffuse a knowledge of our
Lord Jesus Christ as the Redeemer of sinners, and to promote the
interests of vital godliness and sound morality, by the circulation
of Religious Tracts, calculated to receive the approbation of all
Evangelical Christians." The phrase "all Evangelical Christians"
was significant since the society by 1830 claimed 2,606 local units
in every state and territory of the Union. These three words were
intended to "restrain" the ATS from "political and partisan
alliances. . . , from sectional entanglements, and from all *ists* and
isms involving angry controversy and divisions among evangelical Christians."[45]

Although the ATS in the ante-bellum period did publish books
and tracts indirectly touching upon the subject of slavery, abolitionism was one of the "isms" which the society avoided. As an
officer said in 1855, "not a dollar was ever contributed to the
Society, with a view to 'anti-slavery propagandism'."[46] Occa-

sionally ATS editors even resorted to publishing expurgated versions of works containing antislavery passages that might offend Southern members.[47]

Toward the end of the prewar era the society's publication policies concerning slavery precipitated serious divisions within the organization, and in 1858 the Boston branch declared its independence from the parent body. The Bostonians resolved to publish their own tracts and to purchase others, not only from the society in New York, but also from antislavery publishers. As the schism developed, some New England tract societies shifted their allegiance from New York to Boston, while new groups were established in competition with loyal New York auxiliaries. The New York faction in 1859 responded by setting up a New England Branch Society in Boston.[48]

Not until the 1860s did the American Tract Society in New York begin to issue truly antislavery works. The first tangible evidence of a policy shift came in 1863 when the ATS president proudly cited the recent publication of two books dealing with slavery as proof of "an advance of the Society's testimony on that subject."[49]

This advance came at about the time the New York society entered the field of freedmen's education. Beginning in March 1862, the organization carried on its instruction, first in Duff Green's Row in Washington, D.C.; then at Camp Barker near the junction of Twelfth and R Streets in the city; and finally at Freedmen's Village on the Arlington, Virginia estate formerly owned by Robert E. Lee. During the early days of the society's involvement the schools in effect constituted a testing ground for textbooks and teaching materials. The first product developed by the New Yorkers for use in these institutions was a set of ten cards designed to aid students in learning to read. The cards were three by four feet, "filled with large letters embracing the alphabet and short words and sentences, mostly passages of Scripture," which could be seen and read "at the same time by a whole congregation in a church." Eventually the cards were distributed throughout the South and the material on them adapted for use in a twenty-four page pamphlet entitled *First Lessons.*[50]

The distinction of publishing the first freedmen's textbook, however, belongs to the Boston wing of the society, which brought out *The Picture Lesson Book* around 1862. Consisting of thirty-two pages, the little volume was described soon after publication by a writer for the *Chicago Tribune:*

> On the title page, a neat vignette presents a colored child and
> a white teacher. Turning the leaf, and before an open cabin
> door, we see seated a white teacher and his black pupil. . . .
> This book is the initial volume of a reform that turns a
> new page in history. It is the first book ever printed for the
> elevation and education of the black race,—the American
> slave. It is designed for the use of the contrabands at Fortress
> Monroe and Port Royal and Kansas. In its general aspects, it
> is just such a stepping-stone to knowledge as you would throw
> down before the feet of your pet child,—neat and bold in typog-
> raphy, ornate with wood cuts, elegant in embossed muslin.
> But, in its purpose and intent, it is eloquent with suggestions
> of the era now opened.[51]

During the seven years following the publication of this initial volume, the Boston and New York organizations produced an impressive number of freedmen's texts, including primers, readers, spellers, and an instructional newspaper. New York initiated its United States Series before the end of the war with the printing of an illustrated primer, followed later by a first and a second reader. Boston had its own four-volume Educational Series. In addition, both wings published works containing practical advice to aid the ex-slaves in adjusting to their new condition, namely *John Freeman and His Family* by Mrs. Helen Brown; *Plain Counsels for Freedmen* by Clinton Fisk; Jared Bell Waterbury's *Friendly Counsels for Freedmen;* and two editions of Isaac Brinckerhoff's *Advice to Freedmen.* Donated or sold at a modest price, freedmen's publications saw extensive service in the classroom and in the community at large. A year after introducing its *Picture Lesson Book* the Boston society claimed 21,000 copies were in actual use, and Virginia Bureau Superintendent R. M. Manly in 1867 had no trouble securing New York's contribution of 5,000 copies of the *United States Primer.*[52]

Most textbooks written specifically for Southern blacks bore the imprint of one or the other of the American Tract Society parent bodies. The principal exceptions were Lydia Maria Child's *Freedmen's Book,* published by Ticknor and Fields in 1865, and the *Freedman's Torchlight,* an instructional newspaper put out by the African Civilization Society beginning in December 1866.

Along slightly different lines, Port Royal veteran J. C. Zachos introduced his *Phonic Primer and Reader* "designed chiefly for the use of night-schools where adults are taught, and for the myriads of freed men and women of the South, whose first rush from the prison-house of slavery is to the gates of the temple of knowledge." With Zachos the emphasis was entirely on new phonetic techniques as they applied to "the unlettered classes" rather than on a special content in reading lessons.[53]

Although each of the more conventional freedmen's school-books had a distinctive style and content, a common theme ran through all of them. In Rev. J. B. Waterbury's *Friendly Counsels,* a statement of this theme appeared on pages 3 and 4. Anticipating the immediate dangers of emancipation, Waterbury advised freedmen:

> Your condition is in some respects much better, and in others somewhat worse, than when you were slaves. Your master, if he was kind, took good care of you. Now that you are free, you have got to take care of yourselves. . . . In slavery you had little or no care, except to see that your task was done. Now that you are your own men, you have got to *think* and *work* both. . . . Don't fall into the mistake of some, that freedom means idleness.[54]

Mrs. Helen E. Brown reiterated the same theme on pages 10 and 11 of her *John Freeman and His Family*. In this passage John Freeman, a fictional ex-slave from Hilton Head, South Carolina, explains to his children what it is to be free:

> It is not to be let loose like the wild hogs in the woods, to root along in the bogs and just pick up a living as we can. No; we are to do just what free men do. You look round and you see every free man, black and white, works for a living. . . . He works in some 'spectable profession.[55]

Like most other early freedmen's readers, *John Freeman* made little mention of the evils of slavery. In fact, Mrs. Brown portrayed most of the slaveholding families in her work quite sympathetically. When describing John Freeman's owners, she specified that they "treated their people far more kindly than many slaveholders." Similarly, when introducing the owners of a slave woman named Sally, the author emphasized that "although they were godless people, they were humane towards their servants; so that she had no cause to complain of hunger, cold, nakedness, and stripes, as had many of her brethren in bondage.''[56]

Mrs. Brown left no doubt that her black characters welcomed the chance for freedom when it finally came, but at times she made slave life appear almost idyllic. In describing the experience of John Freeman's daughter and son-in-law she wrote:

> While they were on the plantation she and Prince had lived together in as easy and happy a way as slaves could live. Their work was light, their master and mistress kind, and at dusk they were usually at liberty to lead the dance on the green, or to sit and chat lovingly by the crackling fire. But freedom tried them. Liberty is always a test of character, and their new life tested theirs.[57]

More openly critical of the South's peculiar institution, Gen. Clinton Fisk in *Plain Counsels for Freedmen* reminded black readers:

> You were owned, bought and sold like cattle and horses. You could not defend your own life, could not claim your liberty, nor own any property.... Indeed, your children were not yours, but were the property of your masters, and they had the power to take them from you and to sell them to whomsoever they pleased.[58]

But even this explicit discussion was chiefly a preface to one of the book's main themes—forgiveness. "You must...think kindly of your old master," the author wrote in lecture 2.

> he is your master no longer, and I earnestly advise you to live on good terms with him.... It is natural...that he should feel severe toward you. It is true you did not, in your servitude, agitate the questions of the day; you did not meddle with politics...; you did not begin the war.... Still, whenever he sees you he can not but think of the great change, and can not avoid blaming you for it.... I have noticed he desires to see you do well in life. Be frank, then, with him, and treat him with respect.... Do not think that in order to be free, you must fall out with your old master, gather up your bundles and trudge off to some strange city.[59]

Interpreting the Scriptures literally, Fisk advised black students to turn the other cheek. "White people have old, strong preju-

dices," he asserted, "and you should avoid every thing you can
which will inflame those prejudices. . . . If you are bent on being
good and kind, and return soft answers to hard words and good
for evil, you will have few troubles with white men."[60]

Fisk advised freedmen that moral and economic improvement
were their only weapons against race prejudice. "White men are
very much influenced by a man's success in making a good living," he wrote, "and if you are thrifty and get on well in the world
they can not help respecting you."[61]

The author of *Plain Counsels* was quite specific in his prescrip-
tion for moral and economic success. "Get good steady work as
soon as you can," he recommended:

> Do not attempt to live on the little jobs you may pick up about
> hotels and places of business. Do not be content with cold
> victuals, old clothes, and a blanket on the floor. Be a MAN.
> Earn money and save it. Do not spend it at suppers, parties,
> and dances.
>   You have no time to spend in kicking up your heels. . . . It
> may be dull, hard work, for awhile, to sit down and study
> your book, while Peter Puff is hopping around the ball-room
> like a monkey, with Betty Simple, but it will become easy
> after awhile, and it will pay richly in the end.[62]

Fisk told students not to be ashamed even of menial labor. As
he elaborated in lecture 9:

> The blessed Saviour himself worked . . . at the carpenter's
> trade. . . . And yet, some very silly people are above work,—
> are ashamed to have hard hands,—and do their best to get
> through the world without honest toil.
>   But this was not the case with Abraham Lincoln. . . . He
> used the hoe, the ax, and the maul, cleared ground, and
> fenced it with the rails he had split, and was ready to turn to
> any honest work.

The author admitted it was quite natural that some freedmen
would associate work with slavery and freedom with idleness because they had "seen slaves working all their lives, and free people doing little or nothing." But, explained Fisk, "a slave works
all his life for others. A free man works for himself,—that is, he
gets pay for his labor, and if he saves what he earns and manages
well, he can get on so well that he may spend the afternoon of his
life in his own pleasant home and never want for anything."[63]

Fisk's advice on how to save money reflected his Calvinist up-bringing. Blending simple economics and morality, he warned freedmen that they could not afford to smoke fine cigars, to drink any kind of spirituous liquors, or to be idle. He further reminded students that "every man is, under God, just what he makes himself; it matters not whether he be white or colored." "Now you have yourself in charge," he concluded, "and I want you to make a man of yourself."[64]

These were the kinds of attitudes that motivated President Andrew Johnson to support the general's appointment as bureau assistant commissioner for Kentucky and Tennessee. "Fisk ain't a fool," Johnson reportedly said, "he won't hang everybody."[65]

Rev. Isaac W. Brinckerhoff produced a freedmen's textbook that closely paralleled Fisk's *Plain Counsels*. The missionary author had been associated with the American Tract Society since he was twelve years old. Born at Ithaca, New York in 1821, Brinckerhoff went to work in the society's New York City depository in 1834 and remained there until 1857. Enlisting in the freedmen's aid enterprise early in 1862, Brinckerhoff served as a plantation superintendent, school manager, and teacher on the South Carolina Sea Islands through the end of January 1863, when he went to St. Augustine as a missionary. As a direct outgrowth of these activities in the South, the Baptist minister from New York produced three tracts for Southern blacks—*Advice to Freedmen, A Warning to Freedmen against Intoxicating Drinks,* and *The Freedman's Book of Christian Doctrine.* Two of these were published by the American Tract Society, New York, while the book of Christian doctrine was issued by the American Baptist Publication Society. According to a handwritten note by Brinckerhoff in a copy of his doctrinal tract, he was prompted to prepare the volume when "an intelligent colored woman (a Catholic) inquired for a statement of what Baptists believed."[66]

The impetus for *Advice to Freedmen* came from further north. In the summer of 1863 a New York physician and philanthropist suggested to the secretary of the New York society "the desirability of publishing a tract of 'Advice to Freedmen' in the new condition they were in." The secretary recommended I. W. Brinckerhoff "as a capable person to do it," and Brinckerhoff accepted the assignment. The first edition appeared in 1864. Its tone is evident from the titles of the individual chapters:

How You Became Free.
Be a True Christian.
Be Industrious.
Be Economical.
Be Truthful and Honest.
Be Temperate.
Guard the Family Relation.
Provide for Your Family.
Educate Yourself.
Educate Your Children.
Punctuality.
To Educate Your Children You Must Provide Schools.
Support the Gospel.
Take Care of Your Sick Poor.
Respect One Another.
Be Good Citizens.
Be Soldiers.[67]

Although restrained in his approach to racial issues, the author nevertheless angered some Southern whites by discussing such sensitive topics as slavery and secession and by referring to the war as a "rebellion." He did not hesitate to discuss the adverse effects of the peculiar institution or to condemn the South for starting a "wicked and cruel" armed conflict.

Whether or not Brinckerhoff was aware of Southern objections to his work, he published a revised edition after the war. In this second edition, the author deleted almost everything that could conceivably alienate the former Confederates. In the introduction to the first edition, he described Negroes as "a dependent and enslaved" race.[68] In the revised edition he dropped the words "and enslaved."[69] Changes in the chapter entitled "How You Became Free" were more drastic. In the first edition Brinckerhoff told his black readers that Southern whites had started the war in order to maintain their peculiar institution:

You know we are now engaged in war. One part of our nation is fighting against the other part. . . . The object of those who commenced this wicked and cruel war was to secure you and your people as slaves for ever. God has so ordered events, that instead of their accomplishing their design, you have obtained your freedom.

The President of the United States saw that the rebels were

making use of you and your labor to sustain the rebellion, and he issued his proclamation and declared you free.[70]

The same section in the revised edition treated slavery as a national, rather than sectional, manifestation. Describing the process by which Southern blacks obtained their freedom, the author wrote:

> The blessing came to you unexpectedly. Still the work was not one of an hour, a day, or even of a year. The way for its accomplishment had been preparing for many years.
>
> Slavery was introduced into this country in 1620. . . . A little more than one hundred and fifty years later . . . our forefathers . . . secured freedom and the right of government for themselves. When preparing the Constitution of the United States, the true friends of freedom, among whom were George Washington, Thomas Jefferson, and others, themselves slaveholders, were desirous that *all* classes should enjoy its benefits, and endeavored to extend it to all. Serious difficulties were interposed; still, progress was eventually made. . . . In the course of a few years most of the Northern states gradually emancipated their slaves; but in the South the star of hope seemed to have passed behind an almost impenetrable cloud. It was apparent that deliverance was alone with God; and from him deliverance at last came.
>
> Our country was visited by the scourge of civil war. The glorious result of this war has been, that slavery or involuntary servitude, except as punishment for crime, . . . can no longer exist within the United States, or any place subject to their jurisdiction.[71]

If the response of the *Christian Index and South Western Baptist* is at all indicative of native white sentiment, the Southern reaction to the new edition was favorable. In 1868 the editor of this Atlanta-based newspaper praised the little tract in an article on "Conciliation." Comparing the two editions, he wrote:

> The first edition . . . speaks of the southern people as engaged in "rebellion"—in a war wicked and cruel on their part. This may or may not have been well enough at the time, for the issue then was a *living* one, and the closing pages of the tract were employed in urging the colored men of the nation to engage heartily and earnestly in the work of "crushing the South." But since the cessation of armed hostilities, a revised

edition of the "Advice" has been published, from which the phraseology implying the wrong of secession disappears, and we read instead simply that "our country was visited by the scourge of civil war."

Hoping to shame other Northern writers into following Brinckerhoff's example, the editor concluded by asking "Now was it misbecoming or detrimental action on the part of the [American Tract] Society and the author to make these changes for the sake of harmony? Would it be unwise to copy their example with an eye to that result?"[72]

By 1868 neither wing of the ATS needed prodding to tone down its language with regard to sectional issues. As demonstrated in the Boston society's monthly newspaper-textbook, the *Freedman*, a moderating process had begun soon after the end of the war. Certainly the paper, under the general control of publications editor Israel P. Warren, printed nothing comparable to an article in the August 1864 issue, which asked students to solve subtraction problems involving the capture or killing of "rebels" by freedmen.[73]

In many ways the *Freedman* reflected changing Northern attitudes between 1864 and 1869. During these years its editors took a definite stand in favor of Negro rights and against the policies of President Johnson. Like many Northerners, the editors were optimistic about Johnson in the early months of his presidency but soon became disenchanted by his vetoes of legislation intended to aid the former slaves. In December 1866 the newspaper-textbook even reprinted an article from the *Independent* on Congress's power to impeach the president.[74]

By the time the House actually impeached Andrew Johnson in 1868, however, the *Freedman* was noticeably more objective in its treatment of Reconstruction issues. The passage of the impeachment resolution was reported without editorial comment, and the announcement of the trial's outcome stated simply: "The President has been acquitted by the Senate, the number for conviction lacking one of two-thirds."[75]

The person in charge of the *Freedman*, Israel Perkins Warren, had been editor of publications for the Boston society since 1859. A native of Connecticut, he suffered from a lack of funds in his early years but managed to put himself through Yale College largely by teaching school. Graduating in 1838, he spent the next three years at Yale Divinity School, followed by a decade and a half as pastor of Congregational churches in Granby, Hamden, and Plymouth, Connecticut. Early in his ministry he began writing for religious periodicals and in 1856 became secretary of the American Seamen's Friend Society in New York as well as editor of the *Sailor's Magazine*. When the American Tract Society at Boston declared its independence, John W. Alvord and Warren were chosen as secretaries, Warren assuming responsibility for the New York district.[76]

As editor of publications from 1859 until the reunion of the Boston and New York societies in 1870 Warren supervised the publication of over 300 volumes, approximately 700 smaller works, and four periodicals. Those books prepared for the former slaves were, beginning with the four titles making up the Educational Series: *The Freedman's Spelling-Book, The Freedman's Primer; or, First Reader, The Freedman's Second Reader, The Freedman's Third Reader, John Freeman and His Family* by Helen E. Brown, and *Plain Counsels for Freedmen* by Clinton B. Fisk. The editor himself compiled at least two of the Educational Series volumes—the third reader and the speller.[77]

Boston's tract society summarized the purposes of its texts soon after publication of *The Freedman's Primer:* "This is designed to be the first of a series of books for the use of the Freedmen in their schools, families, & c. While it teaches to read and write, the series will aim to communicate also religious and moral truth, and such instruction in civil and social duties as is needed by them in the new circumstances in which they are placed."[78] Prices were set low enough to encourage widespread use. The primer sold for twenty cents, the speller and second reader for thirty, and the third reader for sixty-five. The *Freedman* was intended for gratuitous distribution among the former slaves or could be purchased at prices ranging from twenty-five cents per year to an annual rate of three dollars for twenty copies of each monthly issue.

The textbooks put together under Warren's direction combined traditional nineteenth-century school lessons with exercises aimed directly at the freedmen. Even the simple *Freedman's Spelling-Book* contained a few references to Abraham Lincoln and freedom, along with such topical passages as "The abolition of slavery has made an alteration in the condition of the freedmen, and laid upon them corresponding duties."[79]

The most advanced of Warren's readers—the third—followed the same pattern, although its format and length allowed for more extended discussions of contemporary issues. Still, the main purpose was religious rather than educational. As the American Tract Society explained in an introductory note:

> If we would adequately supply the Freedmen with religious truth, we must connect it with their early efforts in reading. This is the ground on which we have proceeded in publishing our series of Christian Readers.
>
> This Third Reader is believed to be adapted to the wants of the Freedmen in the following particulars:—
> 1. It contains elementary instruction in respect to the history and government of our country.
> 2. It contains interesting biographies of colored persons.
> 3. It presents to the Freedmen the life and words of ABRAHAM LINCOLN.
> 4. It is thoroughly Christian, containing numerous selections from able and interesting writers on religious subjects, and from the Word of God.[80]

An examination of the Negro biographies in the *Third Reader* sheds further light on the intentions of its author. Without exception the subjects of these biographies were described as pious, industrious, humble, and eager to obtain an education. Paul Cuffe was praised for his Christian approach to business; Toussaint L'Ouverture for his determination "to establish order and discipline" among the liberated blacks of Santo Domingo; Lott Carey for his "devoted piety, rare talents, good judgment, and pure benevolence." The biography of Frederick Douglass concentrated on his conversion experience. "After this I saw the world in a new light," Douglass is quoted as saying. "I loved all mankind, slaveholders not excepted, though I abhorred slavery more than ever." The life of Phillis Wheatley was cited as "proof of the power of talents and virtures, crowned with . . . the love of Christ, . . . to raise one from the lowest position to the notice and esteem of the wise and good." An exhortation to black students to emulate these race heroes was hardly necessary, but just in case they might miss the point the author included full-scale essays on such topics as "Love to Enemies," "Humility," "Pride of Dress," "Labor," and "Temperance."

Although *The Freedman's Third Reader* stressed racial accommodation, it did include selections that were likely to antagonize some Southern whites. Such was the case with a piece entitled "All Mankind of One Blood." According to the short essay: "As God is one, so also the entire race of man, whatever their habits, customs, character, or color, are one. This is a wonderful thing. Some people do not believe it, and many more act as if they did not; but it must be true, for God has told us so."[81] Similarly, a piece entitled "The Marriage Tie" asserted that "one of the worst evils of slavery has been the contempt which its practices threw upon . . . [the] divine law of marriage, and the frequent violations of that law which it encouraged, and often forced upon its victims." The essay concluded with a general indictment of slavery as a "cruel and wicked system of oppression."[82]

A supporter of the Civil Rights Act of 1866, Warren also included selections praising those who had led the fight for racial equality in the United States. In treating the life of Paul Cuffe, he devoted considerable space to the young shipbuilder's successful crusade to secure full citizenship rights for Negroes in Massachusetts. According to Warren, it was an "honorable day" for Cuffe when in 1783 the state legislature passed a law granting free blacks "all the privileges of white citizens." "But," Warren added,

the young man's influence was felt beyond his own State, for other States followed the just and humane example of Massachusetts; so that the exertions of Paul and his brother affected the welfare of the colored people all over the country, and are helping, this day, to solve the question of the rights of man as man.[83]

Even more objectionable to Southern whites was a poem lauding black troops who had fought in the Civil War. Entitled "No Slave Beneath the Flag," the piece eulogized the men who had died in such engagements as Port Hudson and Fort Wagner:

1

No slave beneath that starry flag,
    The emblem of the free!
No fettered hand shall wield the brand
    That smites for Liberty!
No tramp of servile armies
    Shall shame Columbia's shore;

For he who fights for Freedom's rights
Is free for evermore!

2

Go tell the ashes of the brave
Who at Port Hudson fell;
Go tell the dust whose holy trust
Stern Wagner guards so well:
Go breathe it softly—slowly—
Where'er the patriot slave
For right has bled, and tell the dead
He fills *a freeman's grave*!

3

Go tell Kentucky's bondmen true,
That he who fights is free!
And let the tale fill every gale
That floats o'er Tennessee;
Let all our mighty rivers
The story southward pour,
And every wave tell every slave
To be a slave no more.[84]

Such lessons prompted criticism not only from Southerners but from conciliatory Northern educators like R. M. Manly. Although the Virginia superintendent of bureau schools praised American Tract Society textbooks for teaching "correct morals and pure christianity," he objected to those features "which would naturally restrict their use to the Freedmen." In a letter to ATS editor William C. Child dated 25 June 1866 Manly wrote: "To a limited extent white children, and to a great extent free negroes (always free) attend these schools. It is hoped and expected that the number of whites . . . will increase. Now I think your books would be offensive to both these classes—exceedingly so to the whites."[85] The *American Freedman* also objected to the exclusive nature of Tract Society schoolbooks, but for a different reason. Why have a *Freedman's Primer* "any more than a Dutchman's Primer or an Irishman's Primer?" the editors asked.

> We hold that the emancipated are *men*; that they are entitled to the best literature which American authorship can produce, and to nothing inferior or different from that used by the rest of us . . . . What would be said of "The Poor-man's Primer"? The "Freedman's Primer" is in principle no better.[86]

Few Northern educators shared this position. On the contrary, most teachers felt "a great need of more Sabbath school books and tracts published expressly for the Freedmen."[87] Even the *American Freedman* was forced to admit that ATS textbooks were "excellent little volumes, well adapted to their purpose."[88]

Bureau educators were especially pleased with student reaction to these publications. A teacher at Hilton Head noted that pupils "seemed to take in every word" of J. B. Waterbury's *Friendly Counsels for Freedmen.* " 'That is the truth' they would say 'we must do just so, like it says if we want to get the good of our freedom.' "[89] Similar favorable comments led another instructor to write that "the whole Educational Series published by the 'American Tract Society' . . . is admirably adapted to the wants of the colored schools."[90]

American Tract Society texts contained few of the passionate antislavery references found in the *Freedman's Torchlight* or Lydia Maria Child's *Freedmen's Book*, both of which dealt explicitly with the worst aspects of the South's peculiar institution—the slave driver's whip, the middle passage, the sadistic overseer, separated families, "tyranny and hatred, cruelty and despair."[91] The antislavery tenor of these two works is best illustrated in Mrs. Child's chapter on William and Ellen Craft. In describing William's life prior to his escape from bondage, the author explained that "he had not been tortured in his own person, but he had seen other slaves cruelly whipped and branded with hot iron, hunted and torn by bloodhounds, and even burned alive, merely for trying to get their freedom."[92] By comparison, antislavery passages from American Tract Society schoolbooks were extremely mild.

Considering Mrs. Child's abolitionist background, her indictment of slavery in *The Freedmen's Book* is not at all surprising. In fact, this textbook represents a direct outgrowth of some of her earlier polemical writings, including *An Appeal in Favor of That Class of Americans Called Africans, An Anti-Slavery Catechism,* and *The Right Way, the Safe Way.*

The central themes of Mrs. Child's abolitionist works were the injustice of slavery and the advisability of immediate emancipation. To illustrate these themes she meticulously traced the history of involuntary servitude and the condition of Negroes from the ancient world to modern America, especially emphasizing the emancipation experience of the West Indies. In *An Appeal*, for example, she confronted the popular argument that sudden emancipation "occasioned the horrible massacres of St. Domingo." In her opinion this "vilified island" furnished "a strong argument *against* the lamentable necessity of slavery. In the first place, there was a bloody civil war there before the act of emancipation was passed; in the second place enfranchisement produced the most blessed effects; in the third place, no difficulties whatever arose, until Bonaparte made his atrocious attempt *to restore slavery* in the island."[93]

The overall effect of emancipation in the West Indies was, according to Mrs. Child, entirely favorable. Freed slaves continued to work on the plantations and generally conducted themselves with restraint and dignity. There was no real desire for retaliation against the former masters. Mrs. Child discerned a similar pattern in the northern United States. She reminded Southern readers that in the North "slaves were manumitted without bloodshed, and there was no trouble in making free colored laborers obey the laws."

Again addressing herself to Southern whites, Mrs. Child conceded the possibility that free blacks in the slave states were "peculiarly ignorant, idle and vicious." "But," she added, "we trust the civil power to keep in order the great mass of ignorant and vicious foreigners continually pouring into the country; and if the laws are strong enough for this, may they not be trusted to restrain the free blacks."[94]

Mrs. Child cited numerous examples to demonstrate the salutary effects of emancipation. In a chapter entitled "Possibility of Safe Emancipation," she recounted the experience of a group of 774 slaves who escaped from their masters during the War of 1812. At the end of the war these Negroes settled in Trinidad as free laborers, where, according to the author, they were "earning their own livelihood with industry and good conduct." Nearly half of the property of the island was said to be in their hands, and it was generally agreed that they were "rapidly advancing in knowledge and refinement." Later in the same chapter Mrs. Child quoted one observer's impressions of a group of slaves who had escaped from Kentucky to Canada:

Captain Stuart, who lived in Upper Canada from 1817 to 1822, was generally acquainted with them, and employed several of

them in various ways. He found them as good and as trust-
worthy laborers, in every respect, as any emigrants . . . from the
United States, or as the natives of the country. They had purchased a tract of woodland, a few miles from Amherstburgh,
and . . . though poor were living soberly, honestly and industriously, and were peacefully and usefully getting their own
living.[95]

Nearly thirty years after the publication of *An Appeal*, Lydia
Maria Child revived the theme of peaceful emancipation and
made it the central focus of her *Freedmen's Book*. Again she used
the West Indies as her prime example. In a chapter devoted to
"The Beginning and Progress of Emancipation in the British West
Indies," she quoted a Mr. Phillippo as saying:

> The conduct of the newly emancipated peasantry would have
> done credit to Christians of the most civilized country in the
> world. . . . Their behavior was modest, unassuming, and dec-
> orous in a high degree. . . . There was no dancing, gambling,
> or carousing. All seemed to have a sense of the obligations they
> owed to their masters, to each other, and to the civil au-
> thorities.[96]

In a chapter entitled "Advice from an Old Friend," Mrs.
Child drew the obvious parallel between the West Indian experience and the situation in the post–Civil War South. She warned
Negro students that whites would do many things to "vex" and
"discourage" them, just as slaveholders in Jamaica had done
after emancipation there. According to her account, Jamaicans
"seemed to want to drive their emancipated bondmen to in-
surrection, that they might have a pretext for saying: 'You see
what a bad effect freedom has on negroes!' " "But, " she added,
"colored people of Jamaica behaved better than their former
masters wished them to do. They left the plantations where they
were badly treated, or poorly paid, but they worked diligently
elsewhere." The author of *The Freedmen's Book* advised Southern blacks to do the same.[97]

In addition, Mrs. Child called on freedmen to improve themselves to the point where skeptical whites would be forced to
concede the advantages of emancipation. "There are still many
slaves in Brazil and in the Spanish possessions," she explained in
her closing chapter.

If you are vicious, lazy, and careless, their masters will excuse
themselves for continuing to hold them in bondage, by saying:
"Look at the freedmen of the United States! What idle vag-
abonds they are! How dirty their cabins are! How slovenly
their dress! That proves that negroes cannot take care of themselves, that they are not fit to be free." But if your houses look
neat, and your clothes are clean and whole, and your gardens
well weeded, and your work faithfully done, whether for your-
selves or others, then all the world will cry out, "You see that
negroes *can* take care of themselves; and it is a sin and shame
to keep such men in Slavery."

In short, Mrs. Child asked freedmen to prove they were equal to
whites. "Be always respectful and polite toward . . . those who
have been in the habit of considering you an inferior race," she
advised. "It is one of the best ways to prove that you are not
inferior."[98]
A careful study of the Negro biographies in Mrs. Child's
textbook suggests the types of character traits she sought to encourage among Southern blacks. In each case the author emphasized virtually the same values—industry, morality, charity,
humility, and moderation. Thus Ignatius Sancho was described as
"sober and industrious"; Benjamin Banneker as "modest and
unobtrusive in his manners"; William Boen as temperate, truthful, and scrupulously honest; Toussaint L'Ouverture as kind and
forgiving; Frederick Douglass as intelligent and religious; Ellen
Craft as modest and ladylike; William Craft as honest, energetic,
and law-abiding.
The moderate tone of these biographical sketches is clearly
illustrated in the chapter devoted to Phillis Wheatley, a chapter
that stresses the Negro poet's conduct even more than her talent.
According to Mrs. Child, "her character and deportment were
such that she was considered an ornament to the church. Clergymen and other literary persons . . . took a good deal of notice of
her. . . . Most young girls would have had their heads completely
turned by so much flattery and attention; but seriousness and
humility seemed to be natural to Phillis."[99] The author of *The
Freedmen's Book* went so far as to commend Miss Wheatley for
her willingness to tolerate racial prejudice. "Sometimes, when
she went abroad, she was invited to sit at table with other
guests," Mrs. Child explained, "but she always modestly de-

clined, and requested that a plate might be placed for her on a side-table.''

> Being well aware of the common prejudice against her complexion, she feared that some one might be offended by her company at their meals. By pursuing this course she manifested a natural politeness, which proved her to be more truly refined than any person could be who objected to sit beside her on account of her color.[100]

Thus, despite her militant abolitionism, Lydia Maria Child produced a textbook almost as moderate as those published by the American Tract Society. Close analysis of her work fails to support the charge that she taught racial hatred or encouraged blacks to abuse their newly acquired freedom. On the contrary, she advised freedmen to forgive their masters and to return to work on the plantation. And like Clinton Fisk, she advised the ex-slaves to turn the other cheek when abused by Southern whites. As she explained in her final chapter:

> If they use violent language to you, never use impudent language to them. If they cheat you, scorn to cheat them in return . . . . If they propose to women such connections as used to be common under the bad system of Slavery, teach them that freedwomen not only have the legal power to protect themselves from such degradation, but also that they have pride of character. If in fits of passion, they abuse your children as they formerly did, never revenge it by any injury to them or their property. It is an immense advantage to any man always to keep the right on his side. If you pursue this course you will always be superior, however rich or elegant may be the man or woman who wrongs you.[101]

In addition, Mrs. Child strongly emphasized respect for the law. ''Heretofore you had no reason to respect the laws of this country.'' she explained, ''because they punished you for crime, in many cases more severely than white men were punished, while they did nothing to protect your rights.'' But now that emancipation was complete freedmen would be ''restrained from doing wrong'' just like their white counterparts. ''It is,'' she wrote, ''one of the noblest privileges of freemen to be able to respect the law, and to rely upon it always for redress of grievances, instead of revenging one wrong by another wrong.''[102] Clearly, the author of *The Freedmen's Book* was fully committed to orderly emancipation.

This interpretation of the underlying themes of Mrs. Child's textbook is supported by the abolitionist author's own letters written prior to publication of the work. "I am preparing a book for the Freedmen," she wrote to a friend on 19 June 1864. "My object is to encourage them by honorable examples of men of their own color, and to convey moral instruction in a *simple* attractive form." "I also intend," she added in a remarkably unambiguous statement of purpose, "that the general tone shall inspire them with forgiving feelings toward their old masters."[103] Elaborating another familiar educational theme in a letter written soon after the completion of the manuscript, she indicated that "though the book was prepared solely for the freedmen, and carefully adapted to their comprehension, it is well calculated to help the Suffrage Question, because it proves the capabilities of Sambo, beyond all dispute."[104]

Letters written after the appearance of *The Freedmen's Book*, reveal that the author hoped to "stimulate and cheer the poor freedmen" by "showing them what their race is *capable* of becoming," and that she aimed to teach simple morality from a nonsectarian standpoint.[105] According to Mrs. Child's own testimony, the pursuit of these objectives was not always easy. Seeking American Missionary Association assistance in circulating the textbook, she found AMA leaders unwilling to help "unless they could be allowed to cut out several articles, and in lieu thereof insert orthodox tracts about 'redeeming blood,' &c." Despite the fact that Mrs. Child had already paid $600 of her own money to finance publication of *The Freedmen's Book,* she refused to accept the association's terms, arguing that the work "contained not one sectarian word, except here and there an *orthodox* phrase in articles written by colored people." With obvious reference to the AMA and other sectarian aid societies, Mrs. Child emphasized her conviction "that all creeds, which make *faith in doctrines* of more importance than the *practice of morality* have an injurious effect on character."[106]

Mrs. Child's concern for morality and orderly emancipation was shared by the editors of the *Freedman's Torchlight*, a combination newspaper-textbook published by the African Civilization Society. According to their statement of purpose, the *Torchlight*

was "devoted to the temporal and spiritual interests of the
Freedmen: and adapted to their present need of instruction in
regard to simple truths and principles relating to their life, liberty
and pursuit of happiness." Moreover, the *Torchlight* would teach
Southern Negroes "the simplest elementary principles of...
moral science and political ethics; and guide them in their
mental, moral, social and political duties."[107]

The tenor of the *Torchlight* is best illustrated in an editorial
entitled "Address to Our Southern Brethren" appearing in the
first issue. Written by Negro minister Rufus L. Perry, the address
concentrated both on the abuses of slavery and the responsibilities of freedom. "Brethren awake!" the article exhorted.

> The Sun of life is up and the sky is lit up and brilliant with its
> brightness and glory. The crack of the slave driver's whip and
> the sound of the day-break horn are heard no more. But hark,
> the voice of Duty calls you. It says, arise ! to work !
> Not for a master without pay; but for yourselves and your
> families.
> Duty says, get up ! dress, and pray; order your children to
> prepare for school, and proceed to work .... The idle, worth-
> less *freeman* is worse in the sight of God and has less sympathy
> from an enlightened and Christian public, than an industrious
> and well meaning *slave*.[108]

The *Torchlight* elaborated on this theme in a list of "Maxims to
Guide a Young Man." The list included such advice as:

> Keep good company or none.
> Never be idle. If your hands cannot be usefully employed,
> attend to the cultivation of your mind....
> Good character cannot be essentially injured except by your
> own acts.
> If any one speak evil of you, let your life be so virtuous that
> none will believe him.
> Good character is above all things else....
> Drink not intoxicating liquors.
> Ever live, misfortune excepted, within your income....
> Keep yourself innocent if you would be happy....
> Read some portion of the Bible every day.[109]

Always the emphasis was on self-improvement as a means of eliminating racial prejudice.

Evidence concerning the student response to textbooks written for freedmen is sparse but revealing. It seems likely that black pupils tended to reject the Southern white contention that these texts exaggerated the negative aspects of slavery. As one teacher indicated in a discussion of her class's reaction to Lydia Maria Child's *Freedmen's Book*: "Their appreciation of all allusions to slave life and hardships is very marked. Sometimes they say, 'Ah, Miss Alice, we could tell you bigger things than that!'"[110] Mrs. Child herself encountered a student who heartily approved of the antislavery lessons in *The Freedmen's Book* and confessed "If I hadn't been a fool, I should have run away years ago, as Frederick Douglass and William Crafts did."[111]

Blacks also appreciated history lessons that dealt with their recent transition from slavery to freedom. The reaction of a Richmond student upon seeing a picture of slaves celebrating their emancipation was typical. As Lucy Chase explained in 1868:

> I have some classes in the "Lincoln Primer" which has a picture of freedmen dancing in honor of liberty. One day a very black, thick-lipped, broad-nosed, savage looking boy of mine . . . made the discovery of the picture and made merry, from his wooly crown to his shambling shoes, "So glad they're free, dun gone and put it in a book!"[112]

A similar sense of relief was manifested by a South Carolina black woman after listening to a selection from *The Freedmen's Book*. While a young boy was reciting James Madison Bell's poem "Emancipation in the District of Columbia," the old woman "was so affected that she vented her feelings with a *heavy sigh*, from a heart that had ached oft on account of the evils of . . . slavery."[113]

Educators welcomed evidence that students already understood or were learning the ethic being taught in freedmen's schools. Sarah Chase was thus pleased when one of the black soldiers whom she was teaching in 1864 made it clear he recognized the oft-emphasized relationship between freedom and responsibility. When asked whether he was now free to run and do just as he pleased, the soldier-student replied: "Oh no, . . . I'm free to hold myself, to learn, to show my best behavior to everybody, to serve my country, and to be always a gentleman but I'm not free to do anything else. I want to do all I can to show the white people our race is of some account."[114]

The proposition that freedmen would have to convince whites of their fitness for freedom was also illustrated in a poem recited by a black student at Hempstead, Texas:

1

Pray look at me
Why don't you see
How tall and strong I am?
I stamp my foot
And shake my fist
Just like a great big man.

2

I clap and sing
Like any thing,
And when I grow some bigger,
I'll read and spell
So very well
You'll never call *me* nigger.

The recitation occasioned a hearty laugh from an audience that included several leading local merchants and former slaveholders.[115]

Asa B. Whitfield, an adult pupil from Augusta, Georgia, attested to the prominence of the themes of forgiveness and racial harmony in Northern instruction. He wrote to the American Missionary Association: "All men are created equal. And therefore they should be friends. We must learn these things. Let us not look upon ... any set of men as our enemys. ... Now the white people south says that the Yankee are no friend to the Southern people. That's a mistaken idea. The northerners do not advise us to be at enmety [*sic*] against any race. They teach us to be friends."[116]

The Northerners themselves praised, and sometimes exaggerated, the moderating effects of education. In 1867 Port Royal pioneer Edward L. Pierce boasted: "Our schools and teachers have ... had ... a most important influence in restoring social order, in establishing relations of confidence between the planters and the laborers, and in promoting sobriety, cleanliness, industry,

thrift, and fidelity to contracts, on the part of the freedmen.''
Referring specifically to the racial conflict that erupted in the
first two years of the Johnson administration, Pierce concluded
by declaring: ''It is impossible to overestimate the conservative
influence which the teachers have exercised over the freedmen
during the reign of violence and oppression which followed the
accession of the present chief magistrate of the nation.''[117]

American Missionary Association teacher John Scott discerned
a similar trend among the black students of Staunton, Virginia. In
a letter written on 28 February 1866 he asked AMA officials to
imagine ''400 colored persons passing quietly through the
streets,—and all dressed as well as they can dress and with due
attention to cleanliness.'' Scott contrasted this situation with the
state of affairs that existed prior to the establishment of a bureau
school in Staunton. According to Scott, local freedmen previously had been ''idle-ignorant-and vile, often insulting the white
citizens with taunts, feeling that Yankee bayonets would protect
them.'' He boasted that this was no longer true.[118]

Even native Southern bureau educators like J. H. Caldwell
appreciated the social impact of freedmen's education. Caldwell,
who served as Alvord's superintendent for western Georgia, reported in October 1867:

> It is one of the most hopeful signs of the times . . . that
> throughout my entire district, when the benign influences of
> education and religion have prevailed, the Colored population
> have been marked for their morality and industry. No crime of
> any magnitude has been committed and they are everywhere
> rising above the dominion of those vices which were nurtured
> in them in the times of slavery. They are cultivating a desire . . .
> to prove themselves worthy [of] the exalted privileges
> bestowed upon them by a wise and beneficent government.[119]

Teachers and school officials undoubtedly attributed too much
to education. Freedmen were never exceptionally disorderly or
vengeful and many already realized their responsibilities.
Nonetheless the educators' emphasis on order, morality,
middle-class values, and forgiveness obviously played a part in
maintaining social stability in the post-emancipation South. The
basic pattern of freedmen's education followed that of Northern
public schools. Both the curriculum and teaching materials were

adapted from familiar models; the end product, however, was something new. Even more than the education for immigrants in Northern cities, it focused on the concrete goal of preparation for citizenship and a drastically altered place in society. Despite some doubts about the advisability of special instruction for the former slaves, it was a fact of Reconstruction life. As never before, teachers and writers addressed themselves in a major way to the particular needs of blacks. The message was hardly revolutionary, but the freedmen's school experiment itself represented the beginning of an extensive educational effort encompassing both the industrial and liberal arts traditions of the 1860s.

7   Political and
Social Issues

Like some abolitionist leaders, American Missionary Association educator S. W. Magill had mixed feelings about the assassination of President Lincoln. While saddened by this unexpected occurrence, he was at the same time convinced the president's death would prove to be a blessing. As he explained to the AMA secretaries less than a month after the event, "the nation will be key'd up to a sharper & better tone in regard to punishment of traitors, and the carrying out of the great measures for which Lincoln became a martyr."[1]

There was reason to believe Andrew Johnson would prove more severe than his predecessor in dealing with the Confederate states. A steadfast Unionist who blamed the war on the policies of the planter class, Johnson equated secession with treason and had said on more than one occasion that traitors must be punished and "impoverished," their social power broken. They must be made to feel the penalty of their crime.

The belief, or at least the hope, that Lincoln's successor favored what would later be called "radical" reconstruction policies was shared by a number of freedmen's educators in 1865. Two years before his appointment as bureau inspector of schools, John Mercer Langston publicly expressed "the highest confidence" in the new president and, according to one newspaper story, predicted that before Johnson "got through reconstructing the South, all would find that he would exact from the lordly aristocrats complete protection and equal justice before the law for the freedmen." Langston reportedly "had full faith in President Johnson; endorsed his policy, and believed in his honesty."[2] J. Miller McKim was less enthusiastic but confident the chief executive would support equal rights legislation for political if not for humanitarian reasons. "I share your fears in regard to President Johnson," the Pennsylvanian admitted to a fellow abo-

213

litionist, "and yet my hopes exceed my fears."[3] Suspicious as she was of Johnson's intentions, even Lydia Maria Child did not rule out the possibility that he would change his policies in response to the pressure of congressional action and public opinion.[4]

The facility with which the South's old leadership was regaining political power under presidential Reconstruction caused an erosion of this spirit of hope and forbearance. Amnesty, easy pardons, the election of Confederate soldiers and civil officials to positions of authority in Reconstruction governments, and the passage of so-called "black codes" spelled the beginning of the end for the president's grace period. Francis Cardozo, for one, thought whites in his state had been entrusted with power too soon. As he assessed the situation in the fall of 1865:

> They are still disloyal at heart, and are most traiterous; they are trying their best to have civil power fully restored, and are willing to adopt *any means* for that purpose.
> The feeling of hate and revenge toward the colored people seems to me fiendish. They are throwing every obstacle in ... [the] way of their progress, and then pointing to their difficulties as argument for re-enslaving them.[5]

Cardozo, Jonathan Jasper Wright, and Richard Harvey Cain were all present at the Colored People's Convention that met in Charleston's Zion Church in November 1865 to protest the work of the state constitutional convention and legislature. The meeting berated South Carolina authorities for depriving Negroes "of the rights of the meanest profligate in the country," and asked Congress to place "the strong arm of the law over the entire population of the state," to grant "equal suffrage," and to abolish the "black code."[6]

Between May and December 1865 blacks held protest conventions in North Carolina, Virginia, Mississippi, and Tennessee, as well as in South Carolina. At a meeting preliminary to the North Carolina gathering, the resolutions committee, headed by freedmen's instructor John Randolph, detailed the grievances common to Negroes throughout the state—continued enforcement of the slave codes, "which prohibit us from the privilege of schools, that deny us the right to control our families, that reject our testimony in courts of justice"; outrages committed against the freedmen; reneging on wage contracts; and the denial of the franchise.[7] At the convention itself, held from September 29 through October 3, delegates initially were inclined to demand equal political rights, including suffrage, but in the end adopted more restrained resolutions introduced by A. H. Galloway and school organizer James H. Harris. Addressed to the state reconstruction convention, the memorial was couched in the most respectful terms. Omitting all reference to the vote, it asked for protection, education, fair wages and working conditions, and an end to discriminatory legislation.[8]

For many, Johnson's veto of the bureau bill on 19 February 1866 was the last straw. J. Miller McKim interpreted this action as final proof that the president had taken his stand with the "secessionists." "He is a man of coarse nature & strong prejudices," McKim declared, "with antecedents & habits which forbid the hope that he will be the willing instrument of Providence & the people in bringing to a triumphant issue the great work of Enfranchisement."[9]

Even after the veto, however, some freedmen's aid officials continued to hold out hope for the president. Perhaps the most conspicuously optimistic were the editors of the *Freedmen's Record*. In an editorial appearing in the April 1866 issue of the magazine they attempted to show the bright side of the existing social and political situation. They began by admitting that this was a dark period for freedmen. But, they hastened to add, Negroes were better off than they had been in slavery. Blacks had the bureau to give them aid, and Congress was anxious to provide for their welfare. The editors were still optimistic about the intentions of the chief executive. "It now looks," they wrote, "as if the President, not finding support in quarters where he expected it, and, on the other hand, receiving it from persons whose approval is disgrace, will be more inclined than he has hitherto been to meet Congress half way." This plus indications that Johnson endorsed the principle of impartial suffrage convinced the editors "that there is not now so great a difference of opinion between the Executive and Congress as there seemed a few weeks ago."[10]

By the end of 1866 few freedmen's aid officials or educators were defending Andrew Johnson. On the contrary, they complained bitterly that presidential policies cut into educational resources, encouraged Southern defiance, stimulated violence, and generally made life more difficult for teachers and their students. In the opinion of one angry instructor at Raleigh, North Carolina, Reconstruction was "the Johnsonian name for dealing vengeance to the colored race, as under the old regime."[11]

The impact on freedmen's education was immediate. In Louisiana the president's decision to approve the suspension of a school tax effectively crippled the system created by the Board of Education of the Department of the Gulf. Empowered by General Order 38 to tax real and personal property, including crops and plantations, the board during wartime had never succeeded in raising enough money to support its schools. It had operated on borrowed funds and, after the war, passed on a considerable debt to the bureau. In an attempt to save the system, Assistant Commissioner Thomas Conway announced plans for stepping up collection of the tax, threatening to confiscate property when necessary. This, along with Conway's determined advocacy of Negro suffrage drew opposition from Gov. J. Madison Wells, New Orleans Mayor Hugh Kennedy, and most local whites. Complaints reaching the president resulted in Commissioner Howard's sending bureau inspector J. S. Fullerton to investigate. Fullerton concluded Conway was endangering the bureau's future by opposing presidential policies and secured Johnson's authorization to halt collection of the school tax. Louisiana's economically oppressed population, Fullerton argued, could ill afford the added financial burden.

Freedmen's Bureau School Superintendent Henry R. Pease hinted this suspension was motivated by a desire on the part of the president to destroy the bureau's educational system in Louisiana. Whether or not Pease was right, it had the effect of dismantling the old framework everywhere in the state except New Orleans as efforts to make Negro institutions self-supporting fell short of the mark. Conway, after being replaced as assistant commissioner, claimed Johnson's action had made it much more difficult for blacks to gain their rights. Discussing Negro suffrage in a speech at Boston on 12 March 1866, Conway asserted that Louisiana freedmen were as intelligent as the majority of the state's white inhabitants. He claimed: "When President Johnson strangled the school system of the Bureau in that State, one-half the freedmen could read; and, if let alone for two years, ninety per cent of them would have been able to read the Constitution, and sign their names at the bottom."[12]

The process John Hope Franklin has termed "Reconstruction, Confederate style" affected black education in every Southern state. Francis Cardozo complained in 1866 that the president had ordered the Morris Street School in Charleston returned to local authorities. "Thus," he explained in a letter to the American Missionary Association, "the Four Public Schools accommodating 2,500 pupils have all been restored to the Rebels, and the colored people here will be completely destitute of all school accommodations by the end of the term, for mine will be restored then too."[13] As it turned out, Cardozo was only partially correct; when the Charleston school board recovered the use of its buildings, the Morris Street School was set aside for Negro children, and three others were opened for the exclusive use of whites.[14] One year after Cardozo wrote his letter to the AMA, Assistant Commissioner Wager Swayne warned association leaders that Johnson was preparing to remove O. O. Howard as bureau commissioner, a move that would defeat all of Howard's plans for the educational work in Alabama and presumably in other Southern states as well.[15]

Both the AFUC and the AMA demanded an end to discriminatory legislation enacted by Southern governments. An editorial in the July 1865 issue of the *American Missionary* pointed out in reference to the legal status of the region's black residents: "Their voices cannot be heard in courts of justice, they have no part in reconstructing State Governments, and even loyal southern States are framing enactments to bind heavy burdens on them which will make their pretended liberty a solemn hideous farce." The editorial insisted that "no *reconstructed* State government should be suffered to exercise authority over them, or adjudicate concerning their interests, until these rights are secured."[16] Later in the year the magazine printed an article summarizing the views of AMA teachers and missionaries on various subjects, including Negro rights. The article revealed that almost all of these employees said of freedmen:

> that there is nothing in their nature, their disposition or their condition, that should shut them out from the right of suffrage. Their unswerving, and universal loyalty entitles them to the first privilege of this kind in the States lately in rebellion. Give

them the opportunity to purchase the land, equal rights in courts of justice, the jury room, and at the ballot box, and furnish them in their transition state with christian teachers, and schools, and they will speedily give a satisfactory reply to the question, "What shall be done with the Negro?"[17]

In the early postwar period educators were especially concerned about the franchise. Predictably, a large number advocated universal suffrage.[18] More surprising is the fact that a substantial percentage argued for restrictions that would apply to whites as well as to blacks. Although South Carolinian Anthony Toomer Porter favored both property and literacy requirements, most teachers and school officials advocated only an educational qualification.[19] As one teacher wrote in a letter published in the *Freedmen's Record*, "make your educational standard your criterion of intelligence, high or low, as pleases you best; only let the test be applied to all men, irrespective of color."[20]

Several articles in freedmen's aid publications made the point that Negroes were as qualified to vote as many whites. A piece in the *Freedmen's Record* contended that if the experiment of granting the franchise to blacks were tried, "it will show that they will exercise the right of the free citizen quite as well for the good of the country as do thousands of emigrants whose ignorance and inferiority work no disqualification." "It may appear," the article continued, "that the same will hold true when comparison shall be made between them and their white neighbors; multitudes of whom have had as little school-knowledge as they have, and whose very small share of political knowledge has been learned in the school of Calhoun and Jefferson Davis."[21] A similar piece in the *American Missionary* was considerably more harsh. Reprinted from the *Christian Examiner*, the article exclaimed:

> Enough of this misnamed "democracy" which intrusts political power and privilege to aliens, criminals and fools,—to the classes which make the dread and shame of all great cities,— while refusing it where there is no just bar, but only that of blood! The monstrous abuses of universal suffrage in our great cities would be in no way mended by *merely* extending it to the multitudes whom slavery has kept so long in ignorant barbarism. They can be fairly met only by some system of probation, limiting that great trust by some test of competence and worthiness.[22]

In the July 1865 issue, the *American Missionary* also published a portion of James Redpath's school report in which he suggested that the imposition of a literacy requirement was the only way to convince illiterate Southern whites to seek an education.[23]

Several articles printed in the *American Missionary* tend to confirm the natural supposition that freedmen's aid officials and educators viewed Negro suffrage as the most suitable means of counterbalancing the Democratic vote among Northern immigrants and Southern whites. In the summer of 1865 the magazine published a selection recording the political views of a freedmen's aid official who had just returned from a visit to New Orleans. According to the editors, the trip had helped convince this official that it was unnecessary "to make the suffrage of the blacks dependent upon their being able to read and write" and that they should be enfranchised in order to secure loyal representation and legislation and to control the "disunion" whites.[24] A more explicit article quoted resolutions passed at a recent meeting of the Freedmen's Aid Union as saying the "dangers" of universal suffrage could be met "by popular education." The piece continued:

> The black men of the South are ignorant, and many of them degraded; but they are, on the whole, as well qualified to vote as are thousands of emigrants freshly arrived from Europe. If any great measure of the Republican party were to be settled today, by the vote of certain wards in New York City, and by the ballots of the Freedmen of Charleston, the white and black men would vote, almost to a man, on opposite sides, and who doubts that the black vote would be on the right side, and the white on the wrong one. Or who believes that Messrs. Wood would have been sent to Washington to represent New York, if the black voters there had been as numerous as the Irish voters.

The article went on to say that freedmen were equal to the poor whites of the South "on the score of intelligence and political knowledge." "Why not," it concluded, "use their votes as a counterpoise to the ballots of these?"[25]

As the movement for equal political rights accelerated in the latter part of 1865 most of those involved in freedmen's education lent their support to such measures as the Supplementary Freedmen's Bureau bill, the Civil Rights bill, and the Thirteenth, Fourteenth, and Fifteenth Amendments.[26] Aid societies and their employees set about preparing blacks for the day when they would assume the rights and responsibilities of full citizenship. The American Freedmen's Union Commission published a *Handbook for American Citizens* to be used in the schools. The *Handbook* contained printed copies of the Declaration of Independence, the Constitution ("with the latest amendments"), and the Emancipation Proclamation, as well as a code of parliamentary rules, a list of presidents, and a chronology of American history.[27] Late in 1865 an AFUC instructor in South Carolina allegedly was beaten by local whites for explaining to freedmen "their rights under the Reconstruction Bill." And when Negroes in Davis Bend, Mississippi established their own judicial system in 1866, one teacher provided legal instruction for the court officials.[28]

Obviously, not all educators took a radical or liberal stance on every issue. Some teachers of both races were close enough to the conservative position to be labelled "secessionists" by colleagues.[29] And school officials like S. G. Wright tended to favor a prompt readmission of the seceded states. Wright, whose rhetoric occasionally masked his generally conciliatory attitude toward Southern whites, wrote to American Missionary Association Secretary George Whipple in 1866:

> I doubt very much whether there will ever be the least change in the views & feelings of the leading men of the South, that is—they will *never admit* that they were *morally* wrong in seceding. . . . I think no real good will be attained by keeping the Southern members out of Congress any longer except it be on the ground of expediency. *They* will be no *more worthy* while they *live* than they are now.[30]

Whatever his opinions regarding Southern whites, Wright was in essential agreement with the president on the issues of early readmission.

Other officials acquiesced in government policies that they opposed but felt they had to accept, the prime example being President Johnson's decision to return confiscated lands to the previous owners. Regardless of their private views these bureau officers and educators considered it their duty to persuade freedmen to relinquish property they occupied when ordered to do so by the federal government. Commissioner Howard, although personally in favor of making land available to the former slaves, frequently advised freedmen, missionaries, and teachers to abide by the directives of the executive branch. In an address delivered before a convention of Midwestern freedmen's aid representatives in August 1865 he berated Northern "fanatics" and "fools" who came South "to teach . . . [freedmen] wrong things," telling them that confiscated land belongs to the former slaves. The commissioner continued: "We have left, whether it was strictly right or not, the title of [Southerners'] property where it was, and I believe it is better that it should be so. It is better for the freedmen to begin at the bottom and work up, that he may learn how to preserve the property he acquires."[31]

One month later Reuben Tomlinson advised bureau educational officials not to settle Negroes on confiscated estates since a recent order seemed to restore all such property to the original owners. In Tomlinson's opinion, "it is much better that the colored people should not get the impression that the land belongs to them, as it will be that much more difficult to reconcile them to the change when it comes."[32] Local school officials like James W. Hawley took it upon themselves to disabuse freedmen of the prevalent notion "that government would divide up the plantations & distribute them to the negroes."[33]

Willingness to facilitate the execution of established policy, however, did not preclude expressions of dissent. The depth of dissatisfaction is suggested in a letter penned by C. B. Wilder in October 1865. Writing to the American Missionary Association from Fortress Monroe, Wilder declared he had lost faith in his country. "If I am rightfully informed," Wilder raged, "our government has decided to restore rebels to full citizenship with all their former possessions in face of law, justice, & good faith, and if the country sustain the government in such a prostitution of its solemly pledged assurances of protection & care to its loyal defenders & their families I say today of my country I disown thee, I loath[e] and abhor thee as I see thee on thy knees trying to conciliate & purchase the flattery & votes of a class of men . . . more nearly in sympathy with Satan than any other class of men known to history." Wilder emphasized that the government had promised "protection, care & support" to the families of blacks who enlisted in the Union army. "Now," he complained, "those pledges are withdrawn, the . . . lands given back to treason plotters & . . . murderers, and the poor colored man is told that the nation has no land to give as it had promised."[34] The bureau's superintendent of schools for Alabama, C. W. Buckley, went so far as to suggest an "amendment" to President Johnson's Amnesty Proclamation. Buckley thought black farmers at Union Springs had earned the right to their own farms, and he favored confiscation to gain it for them.[35]

Many educators perceived Johnson's restoration policy as a direct threat to the self-help concept inherent in the freedmen's school program. A Virginia instructor proposed, "If Uncle Sam would only divide these large plantations of confiscated land among these people, instead of returning them to their former owners, . . . there would soon be no further need of taxing the Missionary Societies to send out teachers among them, for they would be able to employ their own teachers."[36] Horace James, acting as the American Missionary Association's school superintendent for North Carolina in 1865, strongly believed that "the ownership of real estate is . . . [the freedmen's] strongest incentive to industry."[37] Two years later another North Carolina educator argued "it is useless to send clothes and rations to these people without doing anything that *tends to* lessen their wants or enable them to help themselves."[38]

Educators also advanced more pragmatic arguments for providing land for Southern blacks. Negro instructor Robert Harris suggested in the spring of 1866 that unless freedmen could "get land of their own, they must always remain in a sort of vassalage to the landowners."[39] On a more partisan note, S. S. Ashley, the Massachusetts teacher who was elected as North Carolina's superintendent of public instruction in 1868, warned that Negroes would desert the Republican party if they were not aided in their efforts to obtain property.[40] Ashley also cautioned that "a great landless class will *per force* be lawless and vicious."[41] Emancipation was not enough, argued the *American Missionary*.

> We created a Freedman's Bureau that supplied rations to a limited extent, and fostered education, but no provision was made for homes or lands for the ex-slaves. The result is a partial paralysis of labor, a subserviency of the laborer to the landowner, and the corruption of morals by vagrancy for want of homes, and licentiousness from herding together the sexes in huts with single rooms.[42]

A few educators were in a position to act on these arguments. In the South Carolina Constitutional Convention of 1868 Francis

L. Cardozo made it clear he opposed confiscation of plantations but believed that since slavery had been abolished the plantation system should be destroyed. Considering this system "one of the greatest bulwarks of slavery," he contended that "freedom will be of no effect if we allow it to continue." On March 3 he presented to the convention a petition addressed to Congress, asking it to allot to "citizens of South Carolina who are destitute and deserving" the unsold portion of lands in the state acquired by the United States because of nonpayment of taxes.[43] Another Negro delegate to the convention, Richard Harvey Cain, was in essential agreement. According to this prominent school organizer and African Civilization Society trustee, it was a well-known fact that over 300,000 freedmen were homeless and landless. How were they to live?

> I know the philosopher of the *New York Tribune* says "root hog or die . . ." My proposition is simply to give the hog some place to root. . . . I want these lands purchased by the Government, and the people afforded an opportunity to buy from the Government. . . . I propose to let the poor people buy these lands, the government to be paid back in five years time.[44]

More tangible results were achieved by the American Missionary Association and the American Freedmen's Union Commission. In 1868 the AMA began purchasing property for resale to Southern blacks. On most tracts of land the association established a church and school, and several small villages grew up around these AMA centers. Association officials preferred this plan to any system based on providing lands for freedmen under the Homestead Act. The editors of the *American Missionary* explained that even if these lands could be obtained they usually consisted of "large, isolated tracts." This would mean the freedmen located on these plots would be separated from whites. And, the editors asked,

> is not contact with the industrial and business habits essential to the best development of the activity and thrift of the colored race? . . . In short, should not the purchase of lands for the freedmen by Northern benevolence be confined mainly to aiding the enterprising few who have a little capital and a good deal of energy—such as our teachers, and others, could readily select in the different localities—and should not the main efforts of the North be given to the educational and religious elevation

of the "unfortunate masses," that, mind and heart being developed, they might win their way to lands and houses, as well as to other and better things?[45]

The AFUC also had a small fund for the purchase and resale of farms to the freedmen.[46]

Educators, especially those in government, had to strike a balance between Negro rights and the interests of white Southerners, a balance that necessitated compromise either out of conviction, pragmatism, or a combination of the two. Most who sat in the constitutional conventions and legislatures were disinclined to impose draconian reconstruction measures that might exacerbate native hostility and resistance. It was not unusual to find educator-politicians supporting moderate proposals regarding political disabilities, taxes, confiscation, Negro suffrage, and other equally sensitive issues.

In the educational sphere, attempts to promote such controversial causes as integration met with little success either in Freedmen's Bureau schools or in the developing state systems. Commissioner Howard believed the two races could learn together as well as separately, but he was quite willing to tolerate segregated schools on the pragmatic assumption that Southerners would not accept any other arrangement. Published statistics indicate that the percentage of whites in bureau schools generally fluctuated between 1 and 2 percent, with most states reporting less than one hundred white pupils at any given time. Subtracting those attending all-white schools lowers this small percentage still further.[47]

There were times when it looked as if integration might become more prevalent, particularly after the American Freedmen's Union Commission at its inception adopted a constitution stipulating that no school should be established that recognized any distinction of caste or color. In February 1866 the chairman of the AFUC teachers committee Ednah Cheney elaborated on the application of this policy in a directive to Jane Hosmer, an instructor at Summerville, South Carolina. "This sentence is to be carried out in full force," Cheney emphasized.

White children are to be received on precisely the same footing, and no other, with blacks; that is to say, they are to occupy the same rooms, recite in the same classes, and receive the same

attention as the blacks. You cannot control public opinion outside of the school; but, within its limits, you must secure entire
respect from every pupil to every other. You must not allow
blacks, from their vantage-ground of loyalty, to insult the
whites; nor the whites to insult the blacks from any fancied
superiority.[48]

Similar instructions were later sent to other commission teachers.
"We believe," Lyman Abbott explained in the *American Freedman*, "that even-handed justice to the blacks will conciliate the
whites and bring them to a recognition of their equality sooner
than any deference to Southern prejudice or fear of Southern
violence."[49]

Miss Hosmer, a native of Concord, Massachusetts, welcomed
the opportunity to admit destitute whites to her school.[50] On
March 5 she informed AFUC officials that Negroes and whites
"occupy the same seats, and stand side by side, in their classes,
behaving in all respects as I would have them towards each
other." Citing a specific example of racial harmony in the school,
Hosmer described how William Daniels, a white student, won the
friendship of a Negro girl by turning the other cheek when she
called him "poor white buckra."[51] Two months later AFUC agent
E. B. Adams visited the school and noted that black and white
pupils studied from the same books, recited in the same classes,
and took recess together. The visit relieved Adams's doubts
about the possibility of the commission establishing schools in the
South, "irrespective of caste or color." He was convinced integrated schools were a possibility if educators consulted with
Southern whites and conformed to local customs and habits within
reason.[52]

The *American Freedman* made the most of early successes,
reporting in the August 1866 issue: "The children of the poor
whites have already come into the schools in Virginia and North
Carolina to a small extent. Say in a dozen schools about one white
to fifty colored. These have been admitted at the request of their
mothers, who said they could not give them an education, being
too poor to do so."[53] It was a small beginning that seemed to offer
hope for the future.

Not all educators favored strict adherence to the integration
clause of the AFUC constitution. In the spring of 1866, Fisk
Brewer, the commission's general agent in North Carolina, ad-

vised Lyman Abbott that separate schools seemed desirable in
the cities, where whites would "scarcely appreciate" any reasons
"for not allowing them to attend a school exclusively by
themselves."[54] Abbott replied that there should be no attempt to
prohibit children from attending institutions of their preference;
each might choose to attend school with companions of his own
race, but no pupil could be barred from any commission school if
he chose otherwise. "I at first inclined to think we had better
move gradually in this matter, and come to mixed schools by and
by," Abbott explained, "but further reflection has convinced me,
that if we begin by putting the children in separate schools we
shall find it more difficult afterward to unite them."[55]

Almost as soon as the influential AFUC official formulated this
policy, however, he began to have second thoughts. In the spring
of 1866 he sent out a circular letter to various educational leaders,
asking whether it was possible to establish "mixed schools" in
their respective states. To his surprise, most answered nega-
tively. The reply of Clinton Fisk, then bureau assistant commissioner for Tennessee and Kentucky, was one of the most emphatic. "You cannot gather the whites and blacks into the same
school," Fisk declared. "Both races rebel against it. Separate
schools under the same organization can be successfully conducted. I know of no successful experiment of mixing them in the
same school. I do know of signal failure." From Virginia, R. M.
Manly predicted the commission "would lose rather than gain by
any proposition to mingle whites and blacks in the same school."
G. L. Eberhart, bureau school superintendent for Georgia, held
no hope for integrated schools, saying such an attempt would
engender charges of social equality against freedmen's teachers
and would perhaps destroy their usefulness entirely.[56] Abbott
later wrote in his *Reminiscences* that these letters were among the
first influences to change his opinion "respecting the desirability
of the co-education of the races."[57]

As a result of opposition in both the North and the South, the
organization never really developed a system of integrated
schools. Toward the end of the bureau program, an AFUC official
observed that the schools were essentially the same as before the
merger between the American Freedmen's Aid Commission and
the American Union Commission; a few white children occasionally attended classes with blacks, but prejudice still kept poor
whites away from predominantly Negro institutions.[58]

The American Missionary Association had an added incentive for establishing integrated schools. Association leaders feared Roman Catholics were attracting black members by eliminating segregation in their churches and educational institutions. Expressions of this fear were especially evident in *American Missionary* articles published during the last three years of the bureau program. In a representative piece in the July 1868 issue, the editors cited testimony from a *Chicago Evening Journal* correspondent showing that Catholics in Baltimore were "making great progress in securing to their church the adhesion of the colored people in the South." According to the correspondent, these gains were largely attributable to the fact that Catholics in Baltimore allowed Negroes to sit with whites in church and to attend predominantly white parochial schools. The journalist learned from an interview with a local black man that Baltimore Negroes were free to send their children to a Catholic white school if they wished. "We have separate schools," the source explained, "but it's our own choice."[59] The March 1869 issue of the *American Missionary* cited figures that supposedly showed 170,000 to 200,000 black children were receiving instruction in Catholic schools in the United States. The editors pointed to these figures as proof that the Roman Catholic church was attempting to take over the country. "Only give her votes enough," the editors warned, "and she will take the land, and rule it in Papal interest. She is seeking to do this through the colored people; and we have only to leave the children of that race to be educated in her schools, and she wins the balance of power and rules the country in spite of us."[60]

But regardless of fears about the Catholic "threat," many American Missionary Association schools were segregated, either because whites refused to attend or because AMA leaders were reluctant to force teachers in schools for poor whites to admit Negroes.[61] The same was apparently true of schools supported by the Methodist church. In Tennessee, for example, the Methodists secured federal support for East Tennessee Wesleyan University by agreeing to Commissioner O. O. Howard's stipulation that the school establish "a Normal Department open to pupils, irrespective of color." The trustees of the institution, although "fearful of an uproar among the people," accepted Howard's offer. They received $7,000 from the bureau in 1866 and 1867. In return, the university included in its prospectus a statement specifying "that the Normal Department of the college will open, irrespective to color to all desiring to become teachers." In 1870, however, a bureau investigator informed Superintendent Alvord "that the Normal Department promised for the benefit of . . . the colored people has not been established." When confronted with this charge, Northern Methodists explained that the agreement was made in good faith, but plans for the school were aborted by the failure of blacks to apply for training. Assistant Commissioner William P. Carlin rejected this defense and convinced General Howard to cut off funds to the university. Rather than change its policy, the school stepped up efforts to obtain private donations, reminding potential contributors that East Tennessee Wesleyan was the only Methodist university in the South "for the . . . training . . . of the white race."[62] This was not an isolated incident. By the middle of the 1870s Northern Methodism recognized the principle of "separate but equal" privileges for its members in the South.[63]

Separate institutions were still more prevalent in public education. Despite the efforts of a number of politically powerful educators, only Louisiana actually tried racially mixed public schools to any extent, while seven Southern states followed the opposite course by giving legal sanction to separate facilities—Tennessee and Arkansas in 1867, Alabama in 1868, North Carolina in 1869, Virginia and Georgia in 1870, and Texas in 1876. Florida omitted references to race in its 1869 school law but followed a de facto policy of segregation throughout the remaining Reconstruction years.[64]

Even in those states that left open the possibility of mixed schools, integration was minimal. For one thing policy makers differed in their objectives. At the South Carolina Constitutional Convention both J. J. Wright and the chairman of the education committee Francis Cardozo made it clear they expected separate institutions to predominate under the new system. Unlike educators L. S. Langley, B. F. Randolph, and Justus K. Jillson, they did not interpret provisions regarding integration and compulsory education to mean that most white children outside of private schools would be forced to attend school with blacks. Wright believed prejudice would dissolve eventually, but at the moment he contended neither race wanted integrated facilities. Along the same lines, Cardozo assured his fellow delegates, "I have no doubt, in most localities, colored people would prefer separate schools, particularly until some of the present prejudice against their race is removed." Cardozo and Wright did insist, however, that black children should be given the right to attend white schools in sparsely populated areas where the expense of separate facilities would be prohibitive.[65]

Except at the University of South Carolina, integration in the Palmetto State was more a possibility than an accomplished fact. In 1873 Justus K. Jillson as superintendent of public instruction made a concerted effort to integrate the School for the Deaf and Blind at Cedar Springs but was forced to close the facility when white faculty members resigned in protest. The school reopened in 1876 only after Jillson accepted the necessity of separating the children by race.[66] The situation in Mississippi was no different. Near the beginning of his term in the office of state school superintendent, Thomas Cardozo informed visiting Northern journalist Edward King "that he had in only one case endeavored to insist upon mixed schools, and that was in a county where the white teachers had refused to teach negro scholars." Four years later, in 1878, the legislature specifically prohibited instructing blacks and whites in the same school building.[67]

Louisiana alone achieved more than a nominal level of integration in its public primary and secondary schools, although this success was largely limited to New Orleans during the early 1870s. Statutes passed in 1869 and 1870 left ample room for evading the state constitution's specification that schools be open to all children regardless of race or color. What gains were made owed a great deal to the exertions of Thomas Conway, the Freedmen's Bureau assistant commissioner who held the post of state superintendent of public instruction between 1868 and 1872. Conway himself, however, was ambivalent about compulsory desegregation. While opposed to the idea of exclusion on racial grounds, he doubted "that liberty of choice would be interfered with by a forcible attempt to mix the schools in localities where such action is undesired by any."[68] When tried, intervention yielded meager results at best. One student of Southern education has estimated that approximately one-third of some seventy public institutions in New Orleans were racially mixed during the first half of the 1870s, but in rural parishes integration made very few advances.[69]

In the minds of many Southerners the whole freedmen's educational program smacked of "social equality." No less an authority than Commissioner Howard claimed much of the early opposition to bureau schools stemmed from the belief that teachers were fostering this unpopular concept.[70] Any significant degree of interracial contact was suspect, and the occasional necessity of boarding with a black family could raise the old hue and cry of miscegenation. Those who stepped too far beyond the bounds of local mores ran the risk of personal physical abuse or the destruction of their schools. Educators consequently could not afford to ignore Southern racial etiquette, although reactions varied from school officials who advised teachers against socializing with freedmen to a few instructors who married across racial lines.[71]

The fear of Southern white opposition to social intermingling between teachers and freedmen was entirely justified. As an article in the *Raleigh Biblical Recorder* shows, local citizens preferred teachers who confined their relations with blacks to the classroom. The *Recorder* praised one Northern instructor by saying, "she is quite elderly for a young lady, quiet, gentle, amiable, very pious and charitable, minds her own business, and does not associate *socially* with the freedmen among whom she moves as a teacher and missionary."

The teacher referred to in the article, however, was not anxious to accept this compliment in its entirety. She disclaimed not associating socially with the freedmen, pointing out that she had "constantly attended their church and sat at table with them as occasion required."[72]

Some white teachers were quite giddy about their early social contacts with Negroes. In her diary entry for 8 May 1867, Esther W. Douglass asked, "What do you suppose sister would have said had she seen me last night promenading with *gentlemen* as black as the blackest?"[73] Likewise, in a letter published in the *American Missionary* Julia Shearman, a teacher from Brooklyn, invited AMA officials to come to Georgia to have tea with her and Uncle Abraham, one of the "wittiest" of her Negro friends in Augusta. She promised the officers "a first-rate entertainment, with a man whose face is as black as coal." This was high praise indeed, coming as it did from a teacher who one year earlier had complained that it was impossible that the Negroes at Lexington,

Virginia could "in their present condition" afford white teachers the "mental refreshment" that could be obtained by contact with their "equals."[74]

Instances of teachers marrying across racial lines naturally created more of a sensation. At Enterprise, Mississippi, R. F. Campbell was arrested under a statute that classified as a vagrant any man who lived "with a colored woman as a wife." Campbell allegedly had "boarded with an old negro" for at least eight months.[75] From Columbus, Georgia Miss S. S. Stansbury wrote AMA Field Secretary Edward P. Smith that she had been informed of an engagement between a Northern white schoolmarm and an "intelligent, unassuming and handsome" Negro physician. "The rebs have reported a number of such matches," Miss Stansbury added sarcastically. "Now they can have their sensation and a real cause."[76]

One year after receiving Miss Stansbury's letter, Secretary Smith became more directly concerned with a situation involving interracial marriage. The incident began when Sara G. Stanley, a teacher from Cleveland, Ohio, informed the American Missionary Association's superintendent of Negro schools at Mobile of her decision to marry a black man and requested permission to hold the ceremony at the AMA Teacher's Home. When AMA school official George L. Putnam refused to give his permission, Miss Stanley complained to Association Secretary J. R. Shipherd, declaring she was "surprised, indignant and grieved by this manifestation of a spirit of caste and prejudice." In a followup letter, the disillusioned teacher informed Shipherd that Smith had assured her the association would not support Putnam in this matter. Moreover, she said Smith had offered to solemnize the vows himself if necessary. Shipherd was not convinced. Rather than confront the issue directly, he created a new rule stating that "no teacher can be married until her resignation is first accepted at this office."[77]

The *Charleston Daily Courier* attempted to use humor to ridicule white teachers who married Negroes. According to a joke in the 23 June 1866 issue: "An ex-slave of Beauregard's is said to have married a New England school marm. She must have chosen her Beau-regardless of color."[78] A Texas newspaper was much more serious in its treatment of this emotional subject. In an article entitled "a Carpet-Bagger Hung By His Colored Brethren," the *Denton Monitor* gave its version of a lynching that supposedly took place in 1869:

> We are reliably informed that a white-skin teacher of a Negro school, was hung in Tarrant County last week, by a colored mob, for procuring a license to marry one of the pupils. His license was tacked to the trunk of the tree on which he was hung, as a warning to the rest of the whites. It seems the negroes apprehended that if miscegenation was not checked, the whites would soon get all the best-looking wenches.[79]

A second newspaper scoffed at the *Monitor's* claim that freedmen lynched the teacher, arguing that "the only party interested in preventing white men from marrying colored women are the chivalry; they desire to keep up the old practices and the example of legalizing the intercourse between the colors would be disastrous to their programme." This newspaper confidently asserted that "if the man was hung, it was done by the Ku Klux, and the murder charged upon the colored people, upon the most improbable grounds."[80]

Serious as it was, however, interracial marriage was largely a symbolic issue. It was a manifestation of and the ultimate argument against any form of social equality. As such it commanded a disproportionate amount of attention but did not deter those who fought for Negro rights during the course of the nineteenth century.

Educators like Jonathan Gibbs, J. J. Wright, and James Miller McKim had joined in the civil rights crusade before the end of the Civil War. Gibbs and Wright both were active in the Pennsylvania State Equal Rights League from its beginnings in October 1864, while McKim fought a vigorous but unsuccessful battle to secure for Philadelphia Negroes the right to use that city's horse-drawn streetcars.[81]

In the postwar period the emphasis shifted to the South, where educators witnessed and frequently experienced the direct effects of prejudice and discrimination. Francis Cardozo protested bitterly in 1866 that black instructors travelling on Arthur Leary's steamers between New York and Charleston not only paid more than their white colleagues but were required to ride in steerage. Cardozo's sister, accompanied by another Negro schoolmarm, refused to accept these conditions and booked passage with another company.[82] The same year Harriet Jacobs (the author of *Incidents in the Life of a Slave Girl*) and her daughter Louisa were forcibly removed from a boat bound for New York. The two women had been able to purchase first-class tickets at Savannah only because the ticket agent thought Louisa was white. When passengers discovered she had "colored blood in her veins," Miss Jacobs and her mother were "put off the boat in a very rough manner." Recounting the incident in October 1866, the *Freedmen's Record* commented, "we hope the matter will be followed up, and the right of citizens in public conveyances will be secured."[83] Attacks on discrimination of this sort became a recurrent theme in aid society publications as well as in bureau reports.

For obvious reasons these sources were much less inclined to publicize evidence that some of their own school personnel abused or discriminated against blacks. Complaints about such behavior by teachers were usually handled internally with a minimum of public attention, as, for instance, in the cases of Mrs. E. A. Lane, Mr. B. F. McClelland, a Miss Smith, and Gottfried Schermack. Mrs. Lane and McClelland both referred to their students as "niggers" or "My Nigs," while Miss Smith reportedly "made herself exceedingly hateful to the more influential class of colored people . . . by refusing to treat them in a proper manner." J. C. Haskell, one of Miss Smith's fellow teachers at Norfolk, provided an example. According to Haskell, Smith once asked G. T. Watkins, pastor of the African Methodist Episcopal church on Bute Street, to visit her home in order to discuss a business matter. When he arrived, "she happened to be at dinner, and sent word to him by a servant that *he might go round* and *sit in the kitchen* while she was ready to see him—all of which . . . Mr. W. refused to do, sending back word . . . that if she wished to see him she would do so at his house." Haskell commented that it would not take many repetitions "of such treatment as that to render any person very odious to the colored people."[84]

Gottfried Schermack was accused of inflicting brutal physical abuse upon his students. A teacher at Fayetteville, Texas charged in a letter to the bureau's state school superintendent that Schermack had beaten small children until the blood streamed over their clothes, that he had "laid children across benches & flogged them *until they were senseless*...," and that he had pinched a piece out of a student's ear. Melville Keith told the state superintendent that he could provide more examples of Schermack's cruelty but emphasized the matter should be kept quiet since publicity would reflect discredit on other teachers. Amazingly, Keith recommended only that Schermack be *transferred!*[85]

Another Texas instructor, Hugh Ames, was convicted and fined $38.50 for "whipping a female pupil with over Severity." One year later Ames was tarred and feathered by a group of four whites and three blacks when he and the wife of a Negro man allegedly were discovered making love in his school at Seguin. Bureau Superintendent Joseph Welch dismissed the troublesome teacher on 30 August 1869. On November 4 Ames advised the superintendent that he was starting a new freedmen's school in Caldwell County.[86] The resulting situation was all too familiar; for despite the fact that educational officials frequently took action against unfit teachers, these administrators could not prevent determined former employees from striking out on their own. Under such circumstances guaranteeing Negro rights in the schools was no easy task.

Some of the most prominent black educators concerned themselves with the special problem of segregation in the labor movement. The Colored National Labor Convention, which met in Washington, D.C. in December 1869, was called because the National Labor Union insisted on separate black and white organizations within the parent body. Dominated by politicians, educators, and religious leaders, the convention showed as much concern with politics as with trade unionism as it debated the issues of race and work. Its Cooperative Executive Committee included five men who were, or had been, involved in freedmen's education—John Mercer Langston, James Lynch, Richard Harvey Cain, Jonathan Gibbs, and Rev. B. T. Tanner. An educator-politician, James H. Harris, was elected as the convention's president.[87]

The influence of freedmen's educators on the convention was obvious. The resolutions stressed education as one of the strongest safeguards of the republic. They declared the masses should be encouraged to learn trades and professions and taught (1) that all labor was honorable and (2) that education, industry, economy, and temperance would elevate the Negro race. John Mercer Langston served on the committee of five appointed to draft a plan for the organization of Negro mechanics and artisans, in order to secure recognition for them in the labor market and to convince the trade unions to drop their racial barriers. The committee's recommendations led to the formation of a Colored National Labor Union. Although primarily a Negro organization, it was to make no discrimination as to race or nationality. The convention summed up its viewpoint by asserting: "Our mottoes are liberty and labor, enfranchisement and education! The spelling-book and the hoe, the hammer and the vote, the opportunity to work and rise . . . we ask for ourselves and our children."[88]

Leaders like John Mercer Langston and James Harris helped give the Negro labor movement a strongly political tinge. Both men stressed equal citizenship rights and civil liberties and argued that the Republican party had shown itself to be the best guarantor of these privileges. Langston and Harris were as interested in keeping the Negro loyal to the party as they were in his problems as a workingman or union member. This partisanship led to conflict with the predominantly Democratic white unions and helped to sidetrack efforts to build a strong black labor movement.[89]

Whereas the average freedmen's teacher had relatively little to do with politics, there were educators who used their influence with Southern blacks for partisan purposes; a few succeeded in reaching the upper echelons of state or national government. The careers of the most prominent Negro officeholders have already been covered in some detail.[90] By way of summary, Francis Cardozo, James D. Lynch, and Jonathan Gibbs were secretaries of state respectively in South Carolina, Mississippi, and Florida during congressional Reconstruction, and Cardozo was treasury secretary in his state from 1872 to 1877. In addition, Jonathan Jasper Wright spent seven years on the South Carolina supreme court.

A number of freedmen's educational officials from both races went on to become state superintendents of public instruction—Gibbs in Florida; Justus K. Jillson in South Carolina; Charles H. Prince in Georgia; Mississippi Bureau Superintendent Henry Roberts Pease; and Samuel S. Ashley in North Carolina. Negro religious leader James Walker Hood was assistant superintendent under Ashley, while others associated with the bureau program later acted in various capacities at the state and local levels.[91]

Four served in Congress during Reconstruction. Bureau Superintendent Charles W. Buckley represented Alabama in the House (1868–73), where he was joined by C. H. Prince from Georgia, and Reuben Tomlinson's assistant in South Carolina, B. F. Whittemore. Mississippi's H. R. Pease, subsequent to his term as superintendent of public instruction, won a seat in the United States Senate and served on the education committee.[92]

The political side of freedmen's education, however, can be overemphasized. Publicly Northern educators played down partisanship, but most aid society leaders were sincere when they claimed their interest in politics related primarily to the social and civil welfare of blacks and other loyal elements in the South. Convinced that political disputes intensified opposition to the school program, bureau as well as society officials frequently advised teachers to limit their active involvement in partisan affairs.[93]

Commissioner Howard and General Superintendent Alvord tolerated, and in some cases condoned, political activism on the part of bureau educators, but the two men did little to initiate such participation. This was amply demonstrated during the dispute in Mississippi between State Superintendent Pease and Assistant Commissioner Alvan C. Gillem, whose conservative policies elicited charges that he was one of those generals who needed "reconstructing" themselves. On 19 October 1867 Gillem prohibited all Mississippi bureau employees from running for public office or taking "any active part in political affairs." Three days later, Pease informed Alvord that he intended to defy General Gillem's order. Seeking Alvord's approval for this decision, Pease proudly asserted: "I have taken . . . an active part in reconstructing this state on the Congressional basis. I attended the State Republican party Convention . . . I have organized over a hundred Leagues and Republican Clubs in the state. I have done it 'on the sly[.].' I am President of a Council of the U.L.A. [Union League of America] . . . I am also Grand Dpy for the state am also a member of the state executive committee[.]"[94]

The general superintendent of schools soon replied to his chief lieutenant in Mississippi that he had conferred with Howard about Pease's letter. Alvord wrote: "I am not, of course, at liberty to report to you the remarks of the General thereon as official, but will say on my own responsibility, that if you pursue a wise and steady course, much like that indicated in your letter, there is nothing to fear." Alvord thought that perhaps political offices should not be taken while in the bureau, "but personal action and influence should be strong and constant on the side of *the right*," as Pease conceived of it. "We know the man you have to deal with," Alvord confided. "His plan undoubtedly is to stop the mouths of radicals, and thus give conservatism (falsely so called) a chance."[95]

Most critics of the bureau program, both past and present, have stressed that politically active educators were generally aligned with the Republicans against the Democrats and Conservatives. While essentially correct as far as it goes, this simplistic generalization virtually ignores factionalism within the Republican party. It would be difficult to find a single Southern state in which freedmen's educators were unified politically. Personal ambitions, racial considerations, and ideological conflict all helped create internal dissension.

In the Mississippi case, it is important to note that in 1869 Superintendent Pease was as critical of Assistant Superintendent James Lynch as he had been earlier of the conservative General Gillem. Differences between Pease and his black colleague surfaced during the spring of 1869 when Commissioner Howard made Lynch a bureau educational agent. Pease, who obviously saw in the up-and-coming Republican leader a threat to his own power as school superintendent wrote confidentially to J. W. Alvord:

> I was surprised at his appointment by Gen. Howard in view of the fact that there is not a colored man in the United States who has so little sympathy with the General and so openly and persistently opposed his administration of the Bureau for the past two years. . . . The truth is . . . all his efforts among the people are for James Lynch. . . . There is . . . more solid worth and ability natural and acquired in John [Mercer] Langston in a moment than he can attain in a lifetime.

When the state superintendent learned the full extent of Lynch's powers under the recent appointment, he felt compelled to add a postscript informing Alvord that on 8 June 1869 "the Rev. James Lynch was arrested and confined in the jail of Jackson for drunk-

enness and disorderly conduct.'' Passing on rumors that Lynch
had been seen drunk frequently, Pease suggested Provisional
Governor Adelbert Ames wished to keep the incident of June 8
''quiet'' since ''it would be used by the enemies of reconstruction
against him and his administration.'' Pease closed this fascinating
letter by advising Alvord that he ''felt a delicacy in this matter''
because he expected to be a candidate for superintendent of public instruction and Lynch was powerful enough politically to
thwart this ambition.[96]

Subsequent to writing this letter, Pease took steps to have
Lynch removed as assistant superintendent. Lynch attempted to
save his job by writing to General Howard. ''It must certainly be
apparent,'' he explained, ''that my removal was sought for political purposes. Parties were anxious that it should take place before
our nominating convention met.'' Unable to understand the state
superintendent's opposition to him, Lynch informed Howard,

> I supported Capt Pease as candidate for the office of Sup't
> Education in order to harmonize with him the stupendous
> work of saving this State from the democracy. To resign my
> position now would greatly injure the party here, the dem-
> ocrats would take advantage of it.[97]

To support his defense, the embattled assistant superintendent
included endorsements from R. C. Powers, chairman of the Republican State Committee and a candidate for lieutenant governor, and from Governor Ames. Powers wrote:

> I regard the representations made against the Rev. James
> Lynch as a species of persecution unjust and uncalled for. His
> course has been such as to meet the approval of the Re-
> publican party of Mississippi, and his removal from office
> would work an injury to our cause.[98]

Governor Ames had earlier explained to Howard that Pease was
''running on the extreme republican wing,'' whereas Lynch was
''more moderate.'' In his endorsement to Lynch's letter, he advised: ''I think it would be unwise to force Mr. Lynch's resignation. Capt Pease has I fear forgotten certain Christian virtues in
his hostility to him. I would advise that both be continued as they
now are. 'Twill be best for the cause.''[99] Howard reacted by
asking Pease to place party unity ahead of ''personal con-

tentions.'' Pease did so and won election as superintendent of public instruction, while Lynch became Mississippi's secretary of state. Immediately after the election Howard accepted Lynch's resignation.[100]

In Virginia, Assistant Commissioner Orlando Brown and Superintendent of Schools R. M. Manly used the powers of their bureau offices to marshal support for the faction headed by Henry H. Wells. The Wells group occupied a position in the Republican party midway between the Pierpont moderates on the one hand and James W. Hunnicutt's ''ultraradicals'' on the other. Specifically, this meant that Brown and Manly supported the policies of congressional Reconstruction but resisted what they considered an overemphasis on Negro political rights.[101] As might be expected, this stance brought the assistant commissioner and the school superintendent into conflict with some of their black teachers. During the 1869 state election campaign, they particularly antagonized many black instructors by strongly opposing the Negro convention called by Dr. Daniel Norton and Dr. Thomas Bayne. In this convention, black political leaders questioned whether Northern officials were treating Virginia Negroes fairly. They emphasized that Northerners in the state had done little to increase the number of black candidates or officeholders and had not secured the freedmen's right to sit on juries. Members of the convention were determined to press for these rights and privileges during the campaign, even though this might create dissension within the Republican party and thus contribute to a Democratic victory.[102]

Whatever their views on these issues, however, a majority of freedmen's educators apparently supported Governor Wells against conservative Norfolk resident Gilbert C. Walker in the special gubernatorial election of 1869. Ratification of the Underwood Constitution became one of the main issues of the campaign. Drafted in 1868, the constitution conferred the right to vote and hold office on Negroes and disfranchised those whites who had supported the Confederacy. The Wells faction advocated adoption, whereas Walker called on voters to defeat the disqualifying clause and the test-oath article.

As in the elections of 1868, Brown and Manly used their control over school funds and teacher assignments to political advantage. Working against the Norton-Bayne forces, they sought to unite the party behind Wells—but without success. The incumbent lost the governorship to his conservative Republican challenger by over 18,000 votes.[103]

Ubiquitous internal conflict in Georgia came to a head after March 1869 when Georgia Educational Association leader J. E. Bryant broke with Republican governor Rufus Bullock, resigning his chairmanship of the party's state executive committee and his seat on the state central committee. At a time of tenuous alliances and barely concealed political opportunism in both parties, Bryant was supported by the Democrats in 1870 when he ran unsuccessfully against the nominee of the Bullock Republicans for the speakership of the Georgia House of Representatives.[104] Bureau School Superintendent J. R. Lewis, by contrast, continued his active support of a governor struggling to retain a hold on middle-of-the-road Republicans. "I believe Bullock is a good man and may be trusted," the school official said in a letter to a teacher stationed in Thomasville. "I have been assisting him all in my power during the six weeks I have been in Washington." Lewis asked the instructor to "strengthen Bullock" as much as possible, claiming "he can & will do more for us... than any other man."[105]

When South Carolina Republicans split in the election of 1872, veteran teachers and school officials could be found on both sides. The party convention nominated Franklin J. Moses for governor, and despite widespread charges that the candidate was blatantly corrupt, three freedmen's educators accepted positions on the ticket. Henry E. Hayne ran for secretary of state, Francis Cardozo for treasurer, and Justus K. Jillson for attorney general. The bolting "reform" faction meanwhile nominated former Bureau School Superintendent Reuben Tomlinson to head its ticket. Although Tomlinson was a Republican and scrupulously honest, the Bolters attracted support from conservative whites and from several prominent Northern politicos of dubious integrity. Included in this latter class were B. F. Whittemore, the teacher and Methodist minister who had admitted taking money for a West Point cadetship, and Stephen A. Swails, the dominant Republican leader in South Carolina's Williamsburg County.[106]

Factionalism was less pronounced with regard to the major national issues. As already indicated, Andrew Johnson had almost no support among leading freedmen's educators after the spring of 1866, and when Congress failed to make good on its attempt to remove the president from office, most pinned their hopes on the election of Ulysses S. Grant. "Hold on a little longer," Superintendent Alvord exhorted Mississippi State Superintendent Henry R. Pease in October 1868. "We will give you Grant and Colfax, and then all other things you need will follow."[107] If AMA Secretary Edward P. Smith's answer to a Virginia teacher's political query is any indication, there was little support for alternative candidates like Salmon P. Chase. When R. G. Patten inquired of Smith what to tell Negroes who asked why they could not vote for the chief justice, Smith replied: "Judge C. is not yet before the people for President & is not likely to be unless the Democrats & Copperheads take him up. . . . If he consents to be made pres.' by Copperheads & Negro traitors I sh^d hardly feel like advising my col^d friends to vote for him—would you?"[108]

Two months after Smith penned this reply, S. S. Ashley assured AMA officials that the Chase movement had very few adherents among Republicans in North Carolina.[109] Negro teacher Robert Fitzgerald was so confident about Grant's chances that he composed a song before the election to be sung at a victory parade to be held in Hillsboro, North Carolina after the results were announced:

> Hurrah! Hurrah! From Seymour we are free
> Hurrah! Hurrah! For Grant our man shall be.
>> We'll Forever sing this chorus from Hillsboro to the sea,
>> We'll cherish our country and Freedom!
>
> The Democrats enslaved, but God & Grant hath set us free,
> The Republicans hath saved us and Republicans we'll be.
> And we'll stand by the Union, God, Grant & Liberty.
>> We'll cherish our Country & Freedom!
>> Chorus: "Hurrah" &c
>
> F. P. Blair & Seymour sad and bereft
> Very Rash and importunate have gone to their Death
> And we'll take them up so tenderly yes we'll bury them with care,

> That they may not mar our happines[s] & Freedom!
>   Chorus: "Hurrah," &c
>
> Then Fare thee well poor Seymour but never!
>   never! there
> To Disturb Old Butler's Congress or the Presiden-
>   tial chair,
> Or we'll tow you up Salt River with your Partner
>   F. P. Blair
> And then cherish our country and freedom.
>   Chorus: "Hurrah" &c[110]

Presumably, a large number of teachers shared E. P. Smith's delight when Grant was elected. Commenting on the effect of the election from Talladega, Alabama, the AMA secretary wrote:

> Humanly speaking, the election of General Grant saved the country. Very few white men voted for him in Talladega, but I believe fewer still of men of influence and property in the town are not glad he is President. Every one admits that all business in town and in the country around has revived since the election was announced, and the most ardent democrat, if he has any pecuniary interest at stake, will tell you he is glad we are to have a settled government for the next four years.

Eagerly anticipating improved conditions under the Grant administration, Smith concluded by saying:

> The truth is this Southern people, to be satisfied, must either govern or be governed. Johnson's mistake was in asking them how the North should govern them. The true way is for those who have the power to determine what is right and then do it. If Grant has a "policy" may it be this.[111]

If aid society officers expected the war hero's election to raise the declining fortunes of freedmen's education in the late 1860s, they were soon to be disappointed. The eroding of popular and political support had gone too far. As early as 1867 most societies dependent on private contributions were already feeling the effects of waning interest in Northern-based reform efforts. The April 1867 issue of the *American Freedman* observed that "the enthusiasm which accompanies a new movement, one especially which appealed so strongly to philanthropic and humane considerations as did this during the desolations of war, has somewhat passed away and left as its supporters only those who are attached to it by cardinal and well-considered principles."[112] By October 1867 Philip C. Garrett of the Friends Freedmen's Association was asking its teachers to form fund-raising organizations among Southern blacks since, in his words, "the zeal of the Northern people is beginning to flag perceptibly." Public meetings no longer raised enough money to finance existing educational programs, and the association had no choice but to trim its sails.[113]

The autumn of 1868 found AFUC executives discussing the advisability of dissolving their commission at the end of the school year. The decreased level of activity could be handled more efficiently by the constituent societies, most agreed, and continuing to press the cause of the Negro before an increasingly unreceptive public might well precipitate a reaction against him. The election of Grant on a "let us have peace" platform and the establishment of reconstructed governments in the South were thought to have removed the necessity for Northern involvement in educating freedmen. Disbanding in 1869, the AFUC looked to state officials to fill in the educational structure that freedmen's aid societies had begun.

Under the terms of the Supplementary Freedmen's Bureau Act, the bureau was itself scheduled to expire in the summer of 1868 but had its life extended through a law passed over Johnson's veto on July 25 of that year. The last-minute legislation, which set a termination date of 1 January 1869 for all agency activities other than education and the payment of veterans' claims, effectively prolonged government school operations until the end of 1870.[114]

When dwindling financial resources eventually forced John W. Alvord to resign the superintendency in October 1870, he stressed that the bureau's educational initiatives must be continued and perfected. "The masses of these freedmen are, after all, still ignorant," he cautioned in his last semiannual report. "Nearly a million and a half of their children have never as yet been under any instruction. Educational associations, unaided by Government, will of necessity largely fall off. The states south, as a whole, awake but slowly to the elevation of their lower classes. No one of them is fully prepared with funds, buildings, teachers, and actual organizations to sustain these schools."[115]

Although public school legislation was already on the books in every former Confederate state except Texas, prospects for effective implementation with regard to blacks were uncertain. After completion of the final academic year under bureau auspices, the general superintendent sent out a circular letter soliciting assessments as to how much would be done in the area of freedmen's education "by the several States, or by the freedmen themselves, without aid from the General Government." Among those surveyed were educators, governors, bureau agents, Freedmen's Bank cashiers, and aid society representatives. Most doubted even promising public systems could meet the needs of Negroes if dependent solely on their own resources.

Alvord was skeptical of assertions by Arkansas Governor Powell Clayton and Louisiana Superintendent of Public Instruction Thomas Conway that Northern-supported freedmen's schools were no longer necessary in those two states. Commenting on General Clayton's request for the federal government to turn over all school buildings and property to the state board, the departing bureau official responded: "This may be best, though we regret to receive testimony from reliable sources that in some of the counties there is yet great want of interest in the education of freedmen."[116] Elsewhere in his published report Alvord summarized Conway's reply to the circular with the curt observation: "The State superintendent . . . is full of hope for the future, and believes that the schools will now be placed on a permanent basis." Not included in the document was Conway's argument favoring a decided shift from freedmen's schools to public education in Louisiana. The Irish-born minister who five years earlier had been removed as bureau assistant commissioner gave two reasons for wanting to phase out the educational program developed during the 1860s:

1. Freedmens Schools are no longer necessary in this state. Their continuance aids in perpetuating a spirit of caste and our state system has so far disposed of that spirit as to make our schools absolutely public—as free to the freedmen as to the children of the former masters from whom they were delivered.

2. Freedmen's schools, sustained by the General Government or by charitable Societies do much to keep the freedmen themselves from proper exertion, and the State from using the

means at her control at this time which, in my judgment, are abundantly adequate to meet all educational wants.

According to Conway, people in the North and West had been "taxed long and severely for the support of schools for freedmen." It was his position that Louisiana no longer needed substantial outside assistance. As he had described the situation to Alvord, "there is now in the state an efficient system of education which makes no distinction whatever between blacks and whites, and which within another year, will have extended its benefits all over the State."[117]

Neither Alvord nor E. W. Mason, the bureau superintendent in Louisiana, were so optimistic. Despite provisions supposedly guaranteeing equal access to education in the state constitution and in the 1870 school law, Mason expected little change around New Orleans much less in the rural parishes. His long acquaintance with members of the new city school board convinced him they had no intention of creating a truly integrated system. Moreover, the buildings furnished for black institutions were "far inferior" to those for whites. They were often in poor repair, overcrowded, and generally ill suited for their intended purpose. One was described as "a miserable den of a building" and another as "a disgrace to a civilized community."[118]

If the New Orleans system, one of the best organized in the South, had such deficiencies, the necessity of continued federal involvement seemed obvious to Alvord and many of his subordinates. Bureau inspector John Mercer Langston specifically advocated extending the agency's educational work for two more years, by which time he hoped public schools would be in a better position to provide adequately for Negro education.[119] With the early enthusiasm for Reconstruction social programs rapidly fading, however, Congress was in no mood to vote the requisite funds.

Alvord's final report to General Howard gives a rough idea of the extent and nature of freedmen's education at the close of bureau operations. Table 5 is based on figures from that report. Reflecting increases over the past three years, high and normal schools in the seceded states now numbered sixty, with an attendance of 6,023, while thirty industrial schools served 820 students.[120]

The demise of the bureau further strained the declining re-

Table 5   Freedmen's Bureau Educational Statistics for the Six Months
            Ending 1 July 1870

	Confederate States	Other States and Washington, D.C.	Total
Day and night schools	1,968	709	2,677
Teachers	2,456	844	3,300
Students	114,795	34,786	149,581

sources of the major benevolent organizations still in the field—
the American Missionary Association, the Freedmen's Aid Society of the Methodist Episcopal Church, the Presbyterian General Assembly's Committee on Freedmen, the American Baptist Home Mission Society, the New England Freedmen's Aid Society, and the principal Quaker associations. Over the course of the next eight to ten years these, along with most of the smaller societies, had to retrench or suspend educational activities altogether. By January 1871 the New England organization saw its work as nearing an end. Acting on the premise that the rise of Southern public education and more Negro self-help would soon obviate the need for NEFAS involvement, the society now limited itself to aiding a few teacher training institutions and those schools in which local people took "sufficient interest to pay a large proportion of the expense." Under this policy, the number of NEFAS schools dropped from seventy to seven in a matter of three years. At a final meeting in 1874 the society gave up all educational work except for two normal schools in Georgia and Virginia.[121]

Financial difficulty was accompanied in the 1870s by a heightened sense of disillusionment with the freedmen and with Reconstruction. Beginning early in the decade the American Missionary Association's editors published an increasing number of articles revealing the disappointments of the postwar years. At first the articles were relatively mild. In October 1870 the *American Missionary* printed a letter from a Northern teacher who admitted "we have not accomplished all we anticipated, for we were unreasonable in our expectations. We underestimated the benumbing, degrading effects of centuries of slavery."[122] By the middle of the decade the articles were openly critical of blacks and especially of black legislators. According to a piece appearing in the April 1874 issue:

The Freedmen have not thus far shown themselves to be
successful as legislators and rulers. The results in South
Carolina and Louisiana are by no means encouraging. These
colored people are ignorant and depraved, and are easily made
the tools of worse men than themselves. There is ... little satisfaction in saying that white legislators in the North are also
corrupt. Nor is it any relief to know that we must blame slavery as the remote cause.

The article concluded on a familiar note: "The colored people
must be educated and their moral character formed on the Christian model."[123]

A close examination of *American Missionary* articles reveals
that even ardent abolitionists like James Redpath and James
Freeman Clarke were experiencing a change of heart. After a trip
to Mississippi, Redpath wrote to the *Independent:*

I never experienced so keen a sorrow ... as during my visit
to Mississippi. I never had so profound a contempt for what is
called the conservative Republican policy. We ought never
have given the negro a vote, or we ought to have forced him
to learn to read, and built a school for him in every township.
He has shown that he is not fit to rule in Mississippi. He is the
dupe in peace of black and white demagogues. The negro governments in Mississippi bore the same relation to orderly Republican administrations, that negro minstrelsy burlesques
bear to the divine symphonies of Beethoven.

Redpath asked readers to remember "that ... the negro has
duties; and that ... the rebel has rights too."[124]

Clarke, a former officer of the New England Freedmen's Aid
Society, contended the continued existence of the Ku Klux Klan
was "naturally to be expected after the occurences in Louisiana,
South Carolina, and Alabama...." The Boston minister believed
the Klan was a reaction to "tyrannical ignorance and carpet-
baggery...." He claimed that if the Southern white man ever had
"any exaggerated fears as to a too free assumption of civil rights
by his ex-slave," those fears had been "accented tenfold" since
he had seen the injustice practiced by Negroes where they had
"attained supreme, unrestricted power."[125]

By 1878 freedmen's aid stalwarts like J. P. Thompson and Dr.
William Patton were calling for an end to the emphasis on civil

rights legislation. Thompson publicly advised the federal government to "refrain from all further legislation or interference on behalf of the negro as such." The old abolitionist expected federal authorities to protect freedmen against riots and discrimination in the courts, "but all this without making a point of caring for the negro in distinction from any other man."[126] In his inaugural address as president of Howard University, Dr. Patton stated firmly that

> neither special legislation, nor military protection nor favor extended by those in power, nor the peculiar regard and effort of philanthropists, will, of themselves, avail to procure the abolition of caste-feeling, and the elevation of the colored people to an entire equality with the whites. The effects of ages of slavery are not to be removed in a day, by a mere legislative vote. An amendment to the Constitution alters no fact of ignorance, of poverty, of moral debasement.... [Prejudices] will vanish gradually in the presence of increasing evidence of a noble manhood. Developed intellectual power, the higher education, success in industrial pursuits, and acquirement of wealth and culture and character will cause them to disappear.[127]

While political, economic, and legal reforms fell by the wayside in a headlong retreat from Reconstruction, education retained its appeal as the most appropriate means of improving the Negro's lot in society without posing a serious threat to the position of Southern whites. Architects of the freedmen's school program had from the beginning worked to fashion policies generally acceptable to these local citizens, realizing that public support, or at least acquiescence, was essential both in the short run and in the not-too-distant future, when Southerners would regain control of their own institutions. Tactical considerations and the racial views of the Northern participants themselves combined to moderate the tone of freedmen's education well before the end of Reconstruction. Emphasis on black self-help, practical training, the refutation of prejudice through education, and gradual improvement of racial conditions is most often associated with what some have called the Age of Accommodation or the Age of Booker T. Washington, but this approach had its first large-scale application in the South during the 1860s.

The decade after the end of bureau operations saw a reduction in the number of aid societies supporting black education and in the income of those that survived, a trend caused both by declining Northern enthusiasm and the economic depression following the Panic of 1873. Toward the end of the 1870s, however, financial support for the remaining missionary societies was again on the rise. In succeeding years these societies would help to develop some of the South's most important black secondary schools and colleges, largely leaving elementary education to the emerging public school systems of the region. Industrial and liberal arts traditions were to develop side by side, although not always harmoniously, in a continuation of the Reconstruction experience. The day of the Yankee schoolmarm had passed. The era of Booker T. Washington and W. E. B. DuBois was about to begin.

Notes

Preface

1. [Caroline F. Putnam] to [name omitted], 27 September [1868], Emily Howland Papers, Cornell University Library, Ithaca, N.Y.
2. W. E. Burghardt DuBois, "Freedmen's Bureau," *Atlantic Monthly*, March 1901, p. 358.

Chapter 1

1. This school was not the first started for freedmen but the first such to be supported by a Northern benevolent association. The earliest known school for "contrabands" was that established by a freedwoman named Mary Chase on 1 September 1861. It was located in Alexandria, Virginia, then a part of the District of Columbia. See John Watson Alvord, *Fifth Semi-Annual Report on Schools for Freedmen, January 1, 1868* (Washington, D.C.: Government Printing Office, 1868), pp. 4–5; U.S. Education Office, *Special Report of the Commissioner of Education on the Condition and Improvement of Public Schools in the District of Columbia* (Washington, D.C.: Government Printing Office, 1871), p. 285.
2. Lewis C. Lockwood, *Mary S. Peake: The Colored Teacher at Fortress Monroe* (Boston: American Tract Society, [1863]), pp. 30–33; *American Missionary* 5 (November 1861): 288; ibid. 6 (February 1862): 30, 33.
3. *History of the American Missionary Association: Its Churches and Educational Institutions among the Freedmen, Indians, and Chinese. With Illustrative Facts and Anecdotes* (New York: S. W. Green, printer, 1874), p. 12. See also *American Missionary* 6 (April 1862): 83.
4. Alvord, *Fifth Semi-Annual Report*, p. 4; *American Missionary* 6 (April 1862): 82–83.
5. American Missionary Association, *16th Annual Report . . .* (New York: American Missionary Association, 1862), p. 33; Clara Merritt De Boer, "The Role of Afro-Americans in the Origin and Work of the American Missionary Association, 1839–1877" (Ph.D. diss., Rutgers University, 1973), pp. 224–25. For a useful treatment of the association's ante-bellum activities, see Clifton H. Johnson, "The American Missionary Association, 1846–1861: A Study of Christian Abolitionism" (Ph.D. diss., University of North Carolina, 1959). Before the Civil War, the AMA paid the salaries of two teachers at Berea College.
6. Boston Educational Commission for Freedmen, *First Annual Report . . . , 1863* (Boston: Boston Educational Commission for Freedmen, 1863), pp. 3–4; *Boston Transcript*, 27 January 1862; Julius H. Parmelee, "Freedmen's Aid

251

Societies, 1861–1871," in Thomas Jesse Jones, ed., *Negro Education: A Study of the Private and Higher Schools for Colored People in the United States*, United States Department of the Interior, Office of Education, Bulletin, 1916, no. 38. 2 vols. (Washington, D.C.: Government Printing Office, 1917), 1:272.

7. Boston Educational Commission for Freedmen, *First Annual Report*, pp. 4, 7. See also Willie Lee Rose, *Rehearsal for Reconstruction: The Port Royal Experiment* (New York: Random House, Vintage Books, 1967), pp. 35–38; and James M. McPherson, *The Struggle for Equality: Abolitionists and the Negro in the Civil War and Reconstruction* (Princeton: Princeton University Press, 1964), p. 160.

8. See Harold F. Williamson, *Edward Atkinson: The Biography of an American Liberal, 1827–1905* (Boston: Old Corner Book Store, 1934), pp. 4–8.

9. For more detailed discussions of the two organizations see: Clifton H. Johnson, "The American Missionary Association: A Short History," in *Our American Missionary Association Heritage* (New York: American Missionary Association, 1966); Richard B. Drake, "The American Missionary Association and the Southern Negro, 1861–1888" (Ph.D. diss., Emory University, 1957); Rose, *Rehearsal for Reconstruction*, pp. 35–39; McPherson, *Struggle for Equality*, pp. 156–60.

10. *History of the American Missionary Association*, p. 13; *National Freedmen's Relief Association Organized in the City of New York on 22nd of February 1862* (New York: National Freedmen's Relief Association, 1862); Parmelee, "Freedmen's Aid Societies, 1861–1871," p. 276; Rose, *Rehearsal for Reconstruction*, pp. 40–42.

11. *Circular of the Port Royal Relief Committee, Signed March 17, 1862* (Philadelphia: Port Royal Relief Committee, 1862), pp. 3–4; James Miller McKim, *The Freedmen of South Carolina: An Address Delivered by J. Miller McKim in Sansom Hall, July 9th, 1862* (Philadelphia: Ellis P. Hazard, 1862), pp. 3–4; *Liberator*, 7 March 1862.

12. William Channing Gannett, "Steamer Atlantic" journal, entry for 7 March 1862, William Channing Gannett Papers, University of Rochester, Rochester, N.Y.; Edward L. Pierce, "The Freedmen at Port Royal," *Atlantic Monthly*, September 1863, pp. 298–300; Isaac W. Brinckerhoff, "The Port Royal Gazette," 7 March 1862, Isaac W. Brinckerhoff Papers, Rutgers University Library, New Brunswick, N.J. The "Gazette" was either Brinckerhoff's journal or a handwritten newsletter for friends and relatives in the North.

13. William H. Pease, "Three Years among the Freedmen: William C. Gannett and the Port Royal Experiment," *Journal of Negro History* 42 (April 1957): 98–117.

14. Pierce, "The Freedmen at Port Royal," p. 300; Charlotte L. Forten, *The Journal of Charlotte L. Forten, a Free Negro in the Slave Era*, ed. Ray Allen Billington (New York: Collier Books, 1961), pp. 152–53.

15. *Dictionary of American Biography*, ed. Allen Johnson and Dumas Malone, 22 vols. (New York: Charles Scribner's Sons, 1928–44), s.v. "Zachos, John Celivergos" (hereafter cited as *DAB*).

16. Gannett, "Steamer Atlantic" journal, entry for 2 March 1862; Pierce, "The Freedmen at Port Royal," pp. 305–6.

17. Isaac W. Brinckerhoff, "Autobiographical Links in a Life of Fourscore Years," manuscript written in 1899, revised and enlarged in 1902, pp. 83–140,

Brinckerhoff, "The Port Royal Gazette," 7 March 1862–6 February 1863, both in Isaac W. Brinckerhoff Papers. Brinckerhoff spent over twenty years in various capacities at the American Tract Society depository in New York City, resigning in 1857 on the eve of a schism over the society's reluctance to publish antislavery literature. When he returned to tract work from the spring of 1859 until February 1862, it was as a New York agent for the newly independent American Tract Society, Boston.

18. Pierce, "The Freedmen at Port Royal," p. 303; Laura M. Towne, *Letters and Diary of Laura M. Towne, Written from the Sea Islands of South Carolina, 1862–1884,* ed. Rupert S. Holland (Cambridge, Mass.: Riverside Press, 1912), p. 88.

19. Towne, *Letters and Diary,* p. 55.

20. Boston Educational Commission for Freedmen, *First Annual Report,* p. 11. For a similar statement of priorities see [William Channing Gannett and Edward Everett Hale] "The Education of the Freedmen," *North American Review,* October 1865, p. 529.

21. See Edward Atkinson, "The Reign of King Cotton," *Atlantic Monthly,* April 1861, pp. 451–65; E. S. Philbrick to [?], 19 February 1862, published in Elizabeth Ware Pearson, ed., *Letters from Port Royal* (Boston: W. B. Clarke Co., 1906), p. 1; Rose, *Rehearsal for Reconstruction,* pp. 37–50.

22. Towne, *Letters and Diary,* p. 26.

23. Ibid., p. 87; Pierce, "The Freedmen at Port Royal," pp. 303–4; [Charlotte Forten] "Life on the Sea Islands," *Atlantic Monthly,* May 1864, p. 591.

24. Pierce, "The Freedmen at Port Royal," pp. 305–7.

25. Towne, *Letters and Diary,* p. 97.

26. Pierce, "The Freedmen at Port Royal," p. 303.

27. Ibid. The textbooks mentioned by Pierce were: George S. Hillard, *The Second Primary Reader* (Boston: Brewer & Tileston, 1858); Marcius Willson, *The Second Reader* (New York: Harper & Bros., 1860).

28. Pierce, "The Freedmen at Port Royal," p. 306.

29. Forten, *Journal,* p. 218. Mrs. Hunn was the wife of John Hunn, a Quaker from Delaware who before the war had been convicted of helping runaway slaves and left "utterly destitute" by the heavy penalty. He and his daughter came to the Islands to open a store where blacks could purchase goods at reasonable prices. See William Still, *The Underground Railroad* (Philadelphia: Porter & Coates, 1872), pp. 712–19.

30. Pierce, "The Freedmen at Port Royal," p. 306.

31. Towne, *Letters and Diary,* pp. x, 8.

32. Forten, *Journal,* pp. 149–50.

33. Boston Educational Commission for Freedmen, *First Annual Report,* pp. 13–14.

34. For biographical details see *DAB,* s.v. "Allen, William Francis"; obituary in *Madison* (Wis.) *Democrat,* 10 December 1889; *Dictionary of Wisconsin Biography* (Madison: State Historical Society of Wisconsin, 1960), pp. 8–9.

35. William F. Allen diary, entries for 10 November 1863, 6 December 1863, and 19 June 1864, William F. Allen Papers, State Historical Society of Wisconsin, Madison, Wis. This is a typescript copy of Allen's manuscript diary, the original having been lost.

36. Forten, "Life on the Sea Islands," p. 591.

37. [William Channing Gannett and Edward Everett Hale] "The Freedmen at Port Royal," *North American Review*, July 1865, p. 4.

38. Ibid., pp. 2–4. After having spent less than four months as a freedmen's teacher, Gannett became a plantation superintendent on the Islands, a post he held for nearly three years. See Pease, "Three Years among the Freedmen."

39. Gannett and Hale, "The Freedmen at Port Royal," p. 3.

40. See Parmelee, "Freedmen's Aid Societies, 1861–1871," pp. 268–301; Robert Stanley Bahney, "Generals and Negroes: Education of Negroes by the Union Army, 1861–1865" (Ph.D. diss., University of Michigan, 1965).

41. *Freedmen's Record* 1 (December 1865): 189. See also the "Minute Book" of the American Freedmen's Aid Commission, Cornell University Library, Ithaca, N.Y.; *American Freedman* 1 (June 1866): 37.

42. Parmelee, "Freedmen's Aid Societies, 1861–1871," pp. 270–71.

43. For information on the sectarian societies see: American Baptist Home Mission Society, *Reports*, 1864–70 (New York: published by the society, 1864–70); *Home Evangelist*, 1863–66; Presbyterian Church, *The Report of the Eastern Committee for the Education of the Freedmen* . . . (Philadelphia: published by the committee, 1865); Presbyterian Church, General Assembly's Committee on Freedmen, *Annual Reports*, 1866–70 (Pittsburgh: published by the committee, 1866–70); Freedmen's Aid Society of the Methodist Episcopal Church, *Reports, 1866–1875* (Cincinnati: Western Methodist Book Concern, [1893]); Ralph E. Morrow, *Northern Methodism and Reconstruction* (East Lansing: Michigan State University Press, 1956).

44. Friends Freedmen's Association Records, Friends Historical Library, Swarthmore College, Swarthmore, Pa.; Friends' Association of Philadelphia and its Vicinity for the Relief of Colored Freedmen, *Report of the Executive Board* . . . (Philadelphia: C. Sherman, Son & Co., 1864); Youra Qualls, " 'Successors of Woolman and Benezet': The Beginnings of the Philadelphia Friends Freedmen's Association," *Bulletin of Friends Historical Association* 45 (1956): 82–104; Henrietta Stratton Jaquette, "Friends' Association of Philadelphia for the Aid and Elevation of the Freedmen," ibid. 46 (autumn 1957): 67–83.

45. *Freedman's Torchlight* (Brooklyn, N.Y.), December 1866; H. M. Johnson to John W. Alvord, 15 April 1869, "Bureau of Refugees, Freedmen, and Abandoned Lands Records, Education Division," letters received, September 1866–May 1869, Navy and Old Army Records Division, Record Group 105, National Archives, Washington, D.C. (hereafter cited as "Bureau Records, Education Division"); Carter G. Woodson, *The History of the Negro Church* (Washington, D.C.: Associated Publishers, 1921), pp. 211–12; Lillian G. Dabney, *The History of Schools for Negroes in the District of Columbia, 1807–1947* (Washington, D.C.: Catholic University of America Press, 1949), pp. 58–59; *Christian Recorder*, 20 February 1864 and 2 April 1864; *National Freedman* 2 (15 January 1866): 25; ibid. 2 (15 February 1866): 49.

46. John Eaton, *Report of the General Superintendent of Freedmen Department of the Tennessee and the State of Arkansas* (Memphis: published by permission of the U.S. Army, 1865), pp. 3–6; idem, *Grant, Lincoln and the Freedmen: Reminiscences of the Civil War with Special Reference to the Work for the Contrabands and Freedmen of the Mississippi Valley* (New York: Longmans, Green, & Co., 1907), pp. 5, 26–27; U.S., War Department, *War of the Rebellion: A*

Compilation of the Official Records of the Union and Confederate Armies, 130 vols. (Washington, D.C.: Government Printing Office, 1880–1901), ser. 1, vol. 52. pt. i, p. 301 (hereafter cited as *OR*).

47. In a letter to Elihu Washburne dated 30 August 1863, Grant had written: "I never was an abolitionist, not even what could be called anti-slavery; but I try to judge fairly and honestly, and it became patent to my mind early in the rebellion that the North and South could never live at peace with each other except as one nation, and that without slavery." The letter is published in Edward McPherson, *The Political History of the United States of America during the Period of Reconstruction...* (Washington, D.C.: Philip & Solomons, 1871), pp. 294–95. For Grant's recollections of the establishment of the program see Ulysses S. Grant, *Personal Memoirs of U. S. Grant,* 2 vols. (New York: C. L. Webster & Co., 1885), 1:424–26.

48. Information on Eaton is taken from the biographical sketch by Ethel Osgood Mason in Eaton, *Grant, Lincoln and the Freedmen,* pp. ix–xxxiv. The quotation is from pp. xv–xvi. See also Philip Wade Alexander, "John Eaton, Jr., Preacher, Soldier, and Educator" (Ph.D. diss., George Peabody College for Teachers, 1940); *DAB,* s.v. "Eaton, John."

49. Eaton, *Report of the General Superintendent of Freedmen,* pp. 5–87; idem, *Grant, Lincoln and the Freedmen,* p. 194; Mark Mayo Boatner III, *The Civil War Dictionary* (New York: David McKay Co., [1959]), p. 259; Warren B. Armstrong, "Union Chaplains and the Education of the Freedmen," *Journal of Negro History* 52 (April 1967): 108–15; John Blassingame, "The Union Army as an Educational Institution for Negroes, 1862–1865," *Journal of Negro Education* 34 (1965): 153.

50. Order No. 26 quoted in Eaton, *Report of the General Superintendent of Freedmen,* pp. 85–86. On pp. 82–83 of the report, Eaton noted: "It was intended that schools and teachers should be maintained on the leased plantations; but experience has proved that men who entered upon cotton cultivation, with the intention of making a great fortune in a single year, were not to be expected voluntarily to meet our intentions in this respect." See also John Eaton, *Extracts from Documents, Office of the General Superintendent of Refugees and Freedmen* (Memphis: Freedmen's Press, 1865), pp. 1–20.

51. Eaton, *Report of the General Superintendent of Freedmen,* pp. 7–8, 75, 86; idem, *Grant, Lincoln and the Freedmen,* p. 196; Allen diary, entry for 12 November 1864. For biographical information on Charles Waldron Buckley, see Thomas McAdory Owen, *History of Alabama and Dictionary of Alabama Biography,* 4 vols. (Chicago: S. J. Clarke Publishing Co., 1921), 3:248; U.S., Congress, *Biographical Directory of the American Congress, 1774–1971* (Washington, D.C.: Government Printing Office, 1971), p. 662.

52. Eaton, *Report of the General Superintendent of Freedmen,* pp. 68–87; idem, *Grant, Lincoln and the Freedmen,* pp. 198–201; Allen diary, entry for 17 December 1864.

53. James E. Yeatman, *A Report on the Condition of the Freedmen of the Mississippi...* (St. Louis: Western Sanitary Commission, 1864), pp. 11, 13; Eaton, *Report of the General Superintendent of Freedmen,* pp. 52, 69; Allen diary, entries for 30 November 1864, 25 December 1864.

54. Eaton, *Report of the General Superintendent of Freedmen,* p. 83.

55. Allen diary, entry for 26 September 1864.

56. Eaton, *Report of the General Superintendent of Freedmen*, p. 75.

57. Eaton, *Grant, Lincoln and the Freedmen*, p. 204; See also Blassingame, "The Union Army," p. 153.

58. J. G. de Roulhac Hamilton, *Reconstruction in North Carolina*, Columbia University Studies in History, Economics and Public Law (New York: Columbia University, 1914), pp. 87–89; *DAB*, s.v. "Stanly, Edward."

59. *Appleton's Cyclopaedia of American Biography*, ed. James Grant Wilson and John Fiske, 6 vols. (New York: D. Appleton & Co., 1894), 1:700; *OR*, ser. 1, vol. 9, pp. 399–402; Edward Stanly, *A Military Governor among Abolitionists: A Letter from Edward Stanly to Charles Sumner* (New York: n.p., 1865), pp. 19, 30–32.

60. Vincent Colyer, *Brief Report of the Services Rendered by the Freed People to the United States Army in North Carolina in the Spring of 1862 after the Battle of Newbern* (New York: by the author, 1864), pp. 44–52; Charles Sumner, *The Works of Charles Sumner*, 15 vols. (Boston: Lee and Shepard, 1870–83), 7:112.

61. U.S., Congress, Senate, *Congressional Globe*, 37th Cong., 2d sess., 2 June 1862, pp. 2477–78; U.S., Congress, House, ibid., p. 2495.

62. *OR*, ser. 1, vol. 9, pp. 401, 403; ibid., vol. 11, pt. 3, p. 221; Abraham Lincoln, *The Collected Works of Abraham Lincoln*, ed. Roy P. Basler, 9 vols. (New Brunswick, N.J.: Rutgers University, 1953–55), 5:259–60, 445, 7:158; Colyer, *Brief Report*, pp. 51–52.

63. Horace James, *Annual Report of the Superintendent of Negro Affairs in North Carolina, 1864* (Boston: W. F. Brown & Co., [1865]), pp. 38–39.

64. *OR*, ser. 3, vol. 3, pp. 1139–44; New England Freedmen's Aid Society, *Second Annual Report . . .* (Boston: by the society, 1864), pp. 22–34. One year prior to their appointments, Wilder and Brown responded to a questionnaire from the Emancipation League of Boston that included questions on educational progress and the freedmen's "capacity and desire to learn." Wilder perceived no particular difference between blacks and whites in capacity. Brown asserted that the freedmen's ability to learn to read was fully equal to that of whites but thought black students might be "slow mathematicians" since memory seemed "better developed than any other of their mental faculties." See The Emancipation League, *Facts Concerning the Freedmen. Their Capacity and Destiny* (Boston: by the league, 1863), pp. 5–7.

65. The table is made up of statistics reported by General Superintendent Kinsman and District Superintendent James. These figures were published in New England Freedmen's Aid Society, *Second Annual Report*, pp. 32–33, 71–72. The difficulty in getting accurate figures is suggested by the fact that Captain Wilder estimated there were at least 1,300 students in his First District, whereas the official returns showed only 794.

66. See New England Freedmen's Aid Society, *Second Annual Report*, pp. 31–32.

67. James, *Annual Report*, p. 39; [William Channing Gannett and Edward Everett Hale] "The Education of the Freedmen," *North American Review*, October 1865, p. 531. All but a few of the Northern teachers in James's district were commissioned by the New England Freedmen's Aid Society, the American Missionary Association, or the National Freedmen's Relief Association.

68. U.S., Army, Department of the Gulf, Board of Education for Freedmen,

Report . . . for the Year 1864 (New Orleans: U.S. Army, 1865), p. 12.

69. Thomas Conway to Nathaniel Banks, 1 June 1863, George Hepworth to Banks, 15 June, 2 July 1863, all in Nathaniel P. Banks Papers, Library of Congress, Washington, D.C.; Lincoln to Banks, 5 August 1863 in Lincoln, *Collected Works*, 6:364–66; *OR*, ser. 1, vol. 26, pt. i, p. 704; Charles Kassel, "Educating the Slave—A Forgotten Chapter of Civil War History," *Open Court*, April 1927, pp. 241–42.

70. New England Freedmen's Aid Society, *Second Annual Report*, p. 48; William F. Messner, "Black Education in Louisiana, 1863–1865," *Civil War History* 22 (March 1976): 45–46; C. Peter Ripley, *Slaves and Freedmen in Civil War Louisiana* (Baton Rouge: Louisiana State University Press, [1976]), p. 128; Howard A. White, *The Freedmen's Bureau in Louisiana* (Baton Rouge: Louisiana State University Press, [1970]), p. 167. The New England Freedmen's Aid Society report stated that "anti-slavery sentiments" were made one of the qualifications for teachers.

71. *OR*, ser. 1, vol. 34, pt. ii, p. 228.

72. General Orders No. 38, 22 March 1864, *OR*, ser. 3, vol. 4, pp. 193–94; U.S., Army, Department of the Gulf, Board of Education for Freedmen, *Report . . . for the Year 1864*, pp. 22–23; Charles Kassel, "Edwin Miller Wheelock," *Open Court*, September 1920, pp. 564–69; Kassel, "The Herald of Emancipation: A Memory of Edwin Miller Wheelock," ibid., April 1925, pp. 232–33; Edwin Miller Wheelock, *Harper's Ferry and Its Lesson: A Sermon for the Times* (Boston: by the fraternity, 1859).

73. *OR*, ser. 3, vol. 4, pp. 193–94; U.S., Army, Department of the Gulf, Board of Education for Freedmen, *Report . . . for the Year 1864*, pp. 12, 22; G. Darling to George Hanks, 18 July 1864, Banks Papers.

74. Circular issued 27 June 1864, published in U.S., Army, Department of the Gulf, Board of Education for Freedmen, *Report . . . for the Year 1864*, p. [26].

75. Ibid., p. 7.

76. Ibid., pp. 8–9.

77. Ibid., p. 7.

78. Ibid., p. 13; Messner, "Black Education," pp. 48–49.

79. Charles Strong to George Whipple, 7 May, 23 June, 5 August 1864, Edwin M. Wheelock to Whipple, 1 July, 12 September 1864; Isaac Hubbs to Whipple, 17 June 1864, all in American Missionary Association Archives, Amistad Research Center, New Orleans, La.; Ripley, *Slaves and Freedmen*, pp. 131–35; Messner, "Black Education," pp. 47–48.

80. Isaac Hubbs to S. S. Jocelyn and George Whipple, 23, 24 September 1864, Hubbs to Whipple, 16 September, 13, 15 October 1864, Thomas Conway to Whipple, 4 October 1864, all in AMA Archives; E. M. Wheelock to Messrs. Barnes and Burr, 21 October 1864, "Bureau Records, Education Division," Louisiana, Board of Education and General Superintendent of Schools, letters sent, 15 April 1864–18 December 1865; Ripley, *Slaves and Freedmen*, pp. 133–34; Messner, "Black Education," p. 48.

81. Frank H. Greene to George Whipple, 16 February 1865, John C. Tucker to M. E. Strieby, 7 August 1865, Myra B. Buxton to Whipple, 30 June 1865, all in AMA Archives.

82. Wheelock to William Lloyd Garrison, 8 February 1865, in *Liberator*, 3

March 1865. The letter appeared under the heading "Gen. Banks Vindicated by a 'John Brown' Abolitionist."

. 83. *OR*, ser. 1, vol. 15, pp. 666–67, and vol. 34, pt. ii, pp. 227–31. See also Fred H. Harrington, *Fighting Politician: Major General N. P. Banks* (Philadelphia: University of Pennsylvania Press, 1948), pp. 104–10.

84. See, for example, the *Liberator*, 11 March 1864; *National Anti-Slavery Standard*, 23 April 1864; *New York Tribune*, 16 July 1864; *Independent*, 5 May 1864 and 7 April 1864; McPherson, *Struggle for Equality*, pp. 289–90; Harrington, *Fighting Politician*, pp. 105–10.

85. *New York Herald*, 28 December 1864.

86. George S. Denison to Salmon P. Chase, 29 March 1863, in "Diary and Correspondence of Salmon P. Chase," American Historical Association, *Annual Report for the Year 1902*, 2 vols. (Washington, D.C.: Government Printing Office, 1903), 2:373. Denison graduated from the University of Vermont in 1854 and went to Texas in 1854. He taught in San Antonio for nearly three years and remained in the state until 1860. See Denison to Chase, 15 May 1862, ibid., pp. 298–99. For more on the Treasury Department's relationship to the Banks program see Bahney, "Generals and Negroes," pp. 211–17.

87. *New Orleans Tribune*, 8 December 1864; Ripley, *Slaves and Freedmen*, pp. 73–75.

88. B. Rush Plumly to William Lloyd Garrison, 6 September 1864, in *Liberator*, 23 September 1864. See also Plumly to Garrison, 20 October 1864, ibid., 11 November 1864.

89. E. M. Wheelock to Garrison, 8 February 1865, *Liberator*, 3 March 1865. See also ibid., 30 September 1864 for an educational report originally published in the *New Orleans Times* on September 2.

90. "The Freedmen of Louisiana. Gen. Banks Defends and Explains His Labor System," *Liberator*, 19 November 1864; Elizabeth Cady Stanton to Susan B. Anthony, 29 December 1864, published in Elizabeth Cady Stanton, *Elizabeth Cady Stanton as Revealed in Her Letters, Diary and Reminiscences*, ed. Theodore Stanton and Harriot Stanton Blatch, 2 vols. (New York: Harper & Bros. [1922]), 2:103–4.

91. U.S., Army, Department of the Gulf, Board of Education for Freedmen, *Report . . . for the Year 1864*, pp. 5–6, 14, 17–21; *Liberator*, 30 September 1864.

92. U.S., Army, Department of the Gulf, Board of Education for Freedmen, *Report . . . for the Year 1864*, pp. 14–15.

93. Louisiana, Constitutional Convention, 1864, *Official Journal of the Convention for the Revision and Amendment of the Constitution of the State of Louisiana* (New Orleans: W. R. Fish, printer to the convention, 1864), p. 175. E. M. Wheelock to William Lloyd Garrison, 8 February 1865, printed in *Liberator*, 3 March 1865.

94. R. B. Fulks to E. M. Wheelock, 4 January 1865, "Bureau Records, Education Division," Louisiana, letters received, 1864–66; Isaac G. Hubbs to S. S. Jocelyn and George Whipple, 8 January 1864, AMA Archives; Kassel, "Educating the Slave," pp. 239–56; Gannett and Hale, "The Education of the Freedmen," p. 531; John Watson Alvord, *First Semi-Annual Report on Schools and Finances of Freedmen, January 1, 1866* (Washington, D.C.: Government Printing Office, 1868), p. 6.

95. Extract of a discourse delivered in the Unitarian church at New Bedford, Mass. on 14 July 1863, published in *National Anti-Slavery Standard*, 27 July 1861.

96. *Liberator*, 6 February 1863. For a New York Anti-Slavery Society resolution advocating a bureau of emancipation see *National Anti-Slavery Standard*, 7 March 1863.

97. *OR*, ser. 3, vol. 3, pp. 73–74.

98. Ibid., pp. 447–48.

99. U.S., Congress, Senate, *Message of the President of the United States Communicating a Letter Addressed to Him from a Committee of Gentlemen Representing the Freedman's Aid Societies of Boston, New York, Philadelphia, and Cincinnati . . .*, 38th Cong., 1st sess., 1863, S. Exec. Doc. 1, pp. 2–3. The memorial was signed by Stephen Colwell, Edward Atkinson, George Cabot Ward, J. M. Walden, Francis George Shaw, Henry Ward Beecher, Henry W. Bellows, C. R. Robert, J. Wheaton Smith, Ellis Yarnell, Francis R. Cope, Adam Poe, Edward Harwood, Levi Coffin, and J. M. Forbes.

100. *Congressional Globe*, 37th Cong., 3d sess., 19 January 1863, p. 381; ibid., 38th Cong., 1st sess., 10 February 1864, pp. 566–70; ibid., 38th Cong., 2d sess., 2 February 1865, pp. 563–66; ibid., 13 February 1865, pp. 766–68; ibid., 22 February 1865, pp. 983–90; ibid., 3 March 1865, pp. 1348, 1402.

101. *Act To Establish a Bureau for the Relief of Freedmen and Refugees*, U.S., *Statutes at Large*, 13 (1865): 507–9.

102. Oliver O. Howard to his mother, 4 January 1857, Oliver Otis Howard Papers, Bowdoin College Library, Brunswick, Maine.

103. Howard, *Autobiography*, 2:98–99.

104. U.S., Congress, House, *Report of the Committee on Freedmen's Affairs*, 40th Cong., 2d sess., 1867–68, H. Rept. 30, p. 2; Howard, *Autobiography*, 2:207; *National Freedman* 1 (1 June 1865): 164; *Freedmen's Record* 1 (July 1865): 107; John A. Carpenter, *Sword and Olive Branch: Oliver Otis Howard* (Pittsburgh: University of Pittsburgh Press, 1964); Robert C. Morris, "Reading, 'Riting and Reconstruction: Freedmen's Education in the South, 1865–1870" (Ph.D. diss., University of Chicago, 1976), pp. 24–32; George R. Bentley, *A History of the Freedmen's Bureau* (Philadelphia: University of Pennsylvania Press, 1955), pp. 52–56.

105. Howard, *Autobiography*, 2:208; U.S., Congress, House, *Message from the President of the United States Transmitting Report of the Commissioner of the Bureau of Refugees, Freedmen, and Abandoned Lands*, 39th Cong., 1st sess., 1865–66, H. Exec. Doc. 11, pp. 2, 43.

106. U.S., Congress, House, *Report of the Committee on Freedmen's Affairs*, 40th Cong., 2d sess., 1867–68, H. Rept. 30, p. 22; U.S., Congress, *Message of the President*, S. Exec. Doc. 11, pp. 2–3, 49; Howard, *Autobiography*, 2:216, 271; Paul S. Peirce, *The Freedmen's Bureau, A Chapter in the History of Reconstruction*, State University of Iowa Studies in Sociology, Economics, Politics, and History, vol. 3, no. 1 (Iowa City: University of Iowa, 1904), pp. 47–49; Alvord, *Fifth Semi-Annual Report*, p. 6.

107. U.S., Congress, *Message of the President*, S. Exec. Doc. 11, pp. 44–49; U.S., Congress, *Report of the Committee on Freedmen's Affairs*, H. Rept. 30, p. 22; U.S., Congress, House, *Letter from the Superintendent of Freedmen's Bureau . . .*, 41st Cong., 2d sess., 1869–70, H. Exec. Doc. 142, p. 11.

108. For biographical information on Alvord (1807–80) see Asa A. Stone to Theodore Dwight Weld, 1 November 1832, published in Gilbert H. Barnes and Dwight L. Dumond, eds., *Letters of Theodore Dwight Weld, Angelina Grimké Weld, and Sarah Grimké, 1822–1844*, 2 vols. (New York: D. Appleton-Century Co., 1934), 1:88. See also ibid., 1:218, 227, 248, 259–61, 301, 317, 326–27, and 2:697.

109. Charles Grandison Finney, *Memoirs of Charles G. Finney Written by Himself* (New York: A. S. Barnes & Co., 1876), p. 324.

110. Finney to Theodore Dwight Weld, 21 July 1836, in Barnes and Dumond, *Letters*, 1:318–19.

111. Alvord to Theodore Dwight Weld, 9 August 1836, ibid., 1:326–27. See also Alvord to Weld, 9 February 1836, ibid., 1:260; and Sereno W. Streeter to Weld, 20 July 1836, ibid., 1:317.

112. Alvord to Weld, 29 August 1838, ibid., 2:696; American Tract Society, Boston, *Forty-Fifth Annual Report . . . , 1859* (Boston: American Tract Society, 1859), pp. 3–11; American Tract Society, New York, *Thirty-Fifth Annual Report . . . , 1860* (New York: American Tract Society, 1860), pp. 37, 64–69, 351–55; American Tract Society, Boston, *Forty-Ninth Annual Report . . . , 1863* (Boston: American Tract Society, 1863), pp. 32–33, 97–98; Alvord, *Fifth Semi-Annual Report*, p. 5; *American Missionary* 9 (November 1865): 256.

113. Eaton, *Grant, Lincoln and the Freedmen*, p. 196; Owen, *History of Alabama*, 3:248; U.S., Congress, *Biographical Directory*, p. 662.

114. Kassel, "Edwin Miller Wheelock," pp. 568–69.

115. See Morrow, *Northern Methodism*, pp. 154, 177 n. 5; *American Freedman* 1 (January 1867): 154; William T. Alderson, "The Freedmen's Bureau and Negro Education in Virginia," *North Carolina Historical Review* 29 (January 1952): 67; Frank W. Nicolson, ed., *Alumni Record of Wesleyan University, Middletown, Conn.*, 4th ed. (New Haven: Tuttle, Morehouse & Taylor Co., 1911), p. 92.

116. Nicolson, *Alumni Record*, p. 92.

117. *The National Cyclopaedia of American Biography*, 13 vols. (New York: James T. White & Co., 1892–1906), 12:389; U.S., Congress, *Biographical Directory*, pp. 1522–23.

118. *DAB*, s.v. "Ware, Edmund Asa"; Howard, *Autobiography*, 2:403.

119. John Mercer Langston Papers, Fisk University Library, Nashville, Tennessee; John Mercer Langston, *From a Virginia Plantation to the National Capital* (Hartford, Conn.: American Publishing Co., 1894); idem, *Freedom and Citizenship* (Washington, D.C.: Rufus H. Darby, 1883); William F. Cheek, "John Mercer Langston: Black Protest Leader and Abolitionist," *Civil War History* 16 (June 1970): 101–20; Benjamin Quarles, *Black Abolitionists* (London: Oxford University Press, 1969), pp. 69, 96, 175–76, 189; William J. Simmons, *Men of Mark: Eminent, Progressive and Rising* (Cleveland: Geo. M. Rewell & Co., 1887), pp. 510–23.

120. Howard to Thomas L. Tullock, 6 June 1867, "Bureau Records, Office of the Assistant Adjutant General," letters sent, 3:261; Samuel Willard Saxton to Edmund A. Ware, 7 April 1868, Rufus and S. Willard Saxton Papers, Yale University Library, New Haven, Conn.; Bentley, *Freedmen's Bureau*, pp. 188–89.

121. *New York Times*, 16 April 1865; *Nation*, 21 December 1865, p. 799; Ben-

jamin Quarles, *The Negro in the Civil War* (Boston: Little, Brown & Co., 1953), p. 328; James Redpath to Oliver O. Howard, 5 September 1865, and Howard to Rufus Saxton, 15 September 1865, both in the Howard Papers; Reuben Tomlinson to J. Miller McKim, 20 September 1862, 17 October 1862, and 16 January 1863, James Miller McKim Papers, Cornell University Library, Ithaca, N.Y.

122. Colby wrote in 1868 that he had been an abolitionist since early manhood. See Colby to Mary B. Hitchcock, 27 March 1868, "Bureau Records, Education Division," Arkansas, letters sent, 1868–69.

123. Wheelock, *Harper's Ferry*, pp. 3–4; Charles Kassel, "A Knight-Errant in the Department of the Gulf: Episode in the Life of Edwin Miller Wheelock," *Open Court*, September 1925, pp. 563–76; Kassel, "Edwin Miller Wheelock," pp. 564–69; Kassel, "Edwin Miller Wheelock and the Abolition Movement," *Open Court*, March 1923, pp. 171–72.

124. *National Freedman* 1 (15 August 1865):233–34.

125. John Watson Alvord, *Third Semi-Annual Report on Schools for Freedmen, January 1, 1867* (Washington, D.C.: Government Printing Office, 1868), p. 15; H. H. Moore to George F. Shaw, 18 April 1866 and 22 April 1866, McKim Papers. Duncan succeeded Moore as bureau superintendent.

126. G. L. Eberhart to Oliver O. Howard, 5 December 1866, "Bureau Records, Education Division," letters received, September 1866–May 1869.

127. Report of E. B. Duncan, Tallahassee, Florida, 8 November 1866, ibid., letters received, September 1866–May 1869.

128. *Floridian*, 21 June 1867; Bentley, *Freedmen's Bureau*, pp. 191–92.

129. G. L. Eberhart to Samuel Hunt, 23 May 1866, AMA Archives.

130. Eberhart to Hunt, 4 June 1866, AMA Archives.

131. See Howard's report to the secretary of war, December 1865, in U.S., Congress, *Message of the President*, S. Exec. Doc. 11, p. 13.

132. Alvord to O. O. Howard, 1 July 1866, "Bureau Records, Education Division," letters sent, 1 January 1866–10 October 1867; John Watson Alvord, *Second Semi-Annual Report on Schools and Finances of Freedmen, July 1, 1866* (Washington, D.C.: Government Printing Office, 1868), p. 7.

133. *DAB*, s.v. "Redpath, James."

134. *Freedmen's Record* 1 (April 1865): 61–64.

135. Alvord, *First Semi-Annual Report*, pp. 2–3; American Union Commission, *The American Union Commission: Its Origin, Operations and Purposes* (New York: Sanford Harroun & Co., 1865), pp. 3–4.

136. Alvord, *First Semi-Annual Report*, pp. 2–8. At the time of Alvord's first report, the northern part of Alabama was within the Department of the Tennessee and administered by the bureau commissioner for Tennessee and Kentucky. By the end of 1865 there were eleven schools in this section, located at Huntsville, Athens, and Stevenson. See ibid., p. 5.

137. Parmelee, "Freedmen's Aid Societies, 1861–1871," pp. 269–71; Richard Paul Fuke, "The Baltimore Association for the Moral and Educational Improvement of the Colored People 1864–1870," *Maryland Historical Magazine* 66 (winter 1971): 369–404.

138. *American Freedman* 1 (June 1866): 37.

139. Hannah E. Stevenson to Sarah and Lucy Chase, 18 February 1866, published in Lucy Chase and Sarah Chase, *Dear Ones at Home: Letters from Con-*

traband Camps, ed. Henry L. Swint (Nashville, Tenn.: Vanderbilt University Press, 1966), pp. 198–99. Among those listed by Stevenson as opponents of the merger were: Edward L. Pierce, Ednah D. Cheney, Jacob M. Manning, Charles Lowe, Mr. and Mrs. William B. Rogers, Mrs. Samuel Cabot, and William Endicott, Jr. Three of these —Pierce, Endicott, and Cheney—later served as AFUC officers.

140. J. Miller McKim to "My dear Friends," 30 March 1866, McKim Papers. See also Laura Towne to McKim, 26 March 1866, and Francis J. Child to McKim, both in the McKim Papers. Towne doubted that the union of the two societies would conciliate Southern whites in favor of freedmen's aid, she being of the opinion that "the South will never be conciliated till it is whipped into it."

141. McKim to Dr. C. G. Hussey, 3 April 1866, McKim Papers. For letters supporting the McKim position see Samuel May, Jr. to McKim, 21 April 1866 and Oliver Johnson to McKim, 26 April 1866, both in the McKim Papers. May at first had doubts about the merger but believed "that to insist on separate schools for the freed people would be a disservice to them in the long run."

142. American Freedmen's Union Commission, "Executive Committee Minute Book," 31 January 1866–29 March 1869, p. 1, Cornell University Library, Ithaca, N.Y.; *American Freedman* 1 (May 1866): 19–20, 1 (June 1866): 37–40; *National Freedman* 2 (15 March 1866): 74–75; Parmelee, "Freedmen's Aid Societies, 1861–1871," pp. 271, 276.

143. American Freedmen's Aid Commission, "Minute Book," Cornell University Library, Ithaca, N.Y.; American Freedmen's Union Commission, "Executive Committee Minute Book," pp. 6, 11–12, 36, 54; "The American Freedmen's and Union Commission," an undated circular printed around February 1866 and enclosed in Lyman Abbott to Samuel May, Jr., 23 February 1866, McKim Papers. This circular lists twelve officers and executive committee members based in New York, three each from Philadelphia and Chicago, two from Boston, and one apiece from Baltimore and Cincinnati. As shown in the AFUC's "Executive Committee Minute Book," there would be some changes in the composition of the committee between 1866 and 1869.

144. American Freedmen's Union Commission, "Executive Committee Minute Book," pp. 11–12, 54.

145. McKim to Oliver Johnson, 22 January 1862, *National Anti-Slavery Standard*, 3 May 1862. See also *Liberator*, 9 May 1862 and William Cohen, "James Miller McKim, Pennsylvania Abolitionist" (Ph.D. diss., New York University, 1968).

146. Lyman Abbott, *Reminiscences* (Boston: Houghton Mifflin Co., 1915), p. ix.

147. For representative quotations from Abbott's sermons during the Civil War era see Ira V. Brown, *Lyman Abbott, Christian Evolutionist: A Study in Religious Liberalism* (Cambridge: Harvard University Press, 1953), pp. 27–32. See also Abbott, *Reminiscences*, pp. 98–107; *American Freedman* 1 (July 1866): 51.

148. Evidence of Abbott's role in the formulation of AFUC policy is found throughout the McKim Papers, the American Freedmen's Union Commission's "Executive Committee Minute Book," and the *American Freedman*. More specifically, see Abbott, *Reminiscences*, pp. 265–70; Brown, *Lyman Abbott*, p. 48; *Freedmen's Record* 1 (April 1865): 55; *American Freedman* 1 (April 1866): 5–6; ibid. 1 (June 1866): 43; ibid. 1 (July 1866): 51; ibid. 1 (August 1866): 71–74; ibid. 1 (November 1866): 114–16.

149. Levi Coffin, *Reminiscences of Levi Coffin, the Reputed President of the Underground Railroad* . . . (Cincinnati: Western Tract Society, 1876). Numerous letters from Coffin to freedmen's aid officials are located in the McKim Papers.

150. McPherson, *Struggle for Equality*, pp. 170, 388.

151. Samuel J. May to J. Miller McKim, 28, 31 January, 1, 16 February, 13 May, 9, 20, 26 July, 15 August 1866, 18 July, 21 October 1867, McKim Papers; George B. Emerson and Thomas J. Mumford, eds. *Memoir of Samuel Joseph May* (Boston: Roberts Bros., 1873).

152. Douglass to J. Miller McKim, 2 May 1865, McKim Papers; *National Anti-Slavery Standard*, 6 May 1865; *Liberator*, 13 January, 6 May 1865.

153. The chief sources for this study's discussion of AMA officials were: the AMA Archives; Johnson, "The American Missionary Association, 1846–1861"; Drake, "The American Missionary Association"; Augustus Field Beard, *A Crusade of Brotherhood: A History of the American Missionary Association* (Boston: Pilgrim Press, 1909).

154. Barnes and Dumond, eds., *Letters*, 1:51n, 57–58; Gilbert H. Barnes, *The Antislavery Impulse, 1830–1844* (New York: American Historical Association, 1933; reprint ed., Gloucester, Mass.: Peter Smith, 1957), p. 233n. Whipple taught at a school in Kentucky (1831–33) and at Lane Seminary (1833–44). He became principal of Oberlin's preparatory department in the fall of 1836 and from 1838 to 1847 was professor of mathematics.

155. Hunt to Whipple, 2 July 1866, and Hunt to M. E. Strieby, 7 December 1866, both in AMA Archives; *National Cyclopaedia of American Biography*, 13:41–42. Hunt was born at Attleboro, Mass., 18 March 1810. He graduated from Amherst College in 1832, tutored in Massachusetts, and taught in Rhode Island. Hunt studied theology in West Medway, Mass. and at Andover and Princeton theological seminaries. Subsequent to being ordained, he acted as pastor of congregational churches in Natick and Franklin, Mass. From 1867 to 1872 he was clerk of the United States Senate Committee on Military Affairs.

156. *American Missionary* 10 (February 1866): 34; Drake, "The American Missionary Association," pp. 47, 85, 90.

157. *National Cyclopaedia of American Biography*, 1:309–10; *DAB*, s.v. "Cravath, Erastus Milo." Born in Homer, N.Y., Cravath attended New York Central College, an integrated institution founded by abolitionists. His family moved to Oberlin, Ohio in 1851. He graduated from Oberlin College in 1857 and completed his training at the theological seminary three years later. After serving as pastor of the Congregational church at Berlin Heights, Ohio, Cravath enlisted as chaplain of the 101st Regiment of Ohio Volunteers in December 1863.

158. Jacob R. Shipherd Letterbook, 13 February 1866–14 June 1866, Cornell University Library, Ithaca, N.Y.; Drake, "The American Missionary Association," pp. 89–92.

159. Beard, *Crusade of Brotherhood*, pp. 267–69. Strieby graduated from Oberlin College and Seminary. He was a pastor in Ohio for eleven years and organized a church at Syracuse, N.Y. Forty-nine years old in 1864, he held the corresponding secretary post for thirty-five years.

160. *Act Making Appropriations for the Support of the Army for the Year Ending Thirtieth of June, Eighteen Hundred and Sixty-Seven*, U.S., *Statutes at Large*, vol. 14, sec. 3, p. 92; Alvord, *Fifth Semi-Annual Report*, pp. 8–9.

161. *Act To Continue in Force "An Act To Establish a Bureau for the Relief of*

Freedmen and Refugees," U.S., *Statutes at Large,* vol. 14, secs. 12–13, p. 176.
   162. Alvord, *Fifth Semi-Annual Report,* p. 8 and *Third Semi-Annual Report,* pp. 36–37. Monthly reports of assistant superintendents may be found in the bureau educational records at the National Archives. For further information on the operation of the education division's Washington office see the Saxton Papers. A printer by trade, Willard Saxton was associated with George Ripley's Brook Farm from 1845 until its dissolution in 1846. During the Civil War he served on his brother Rufus's staff and then on that of General Howard. In 1866 he left the army to join the education division, soon becoming chief clerk.
   163. John Watson Alvord, *Fourth Semi-Annual Report on Schools for Freedmen, July 1, 1867* (Washington, D.C.: Government Printing Office, 1868), p. 2; Alvord, *Fifth Semi-Annual Report,* pp. 8–9.
   164. Alvord, *Fourth Semi-Annual Report,* p. 2 and *Fifth Semi-Annual Report,* p. 9. A large percentage of the white pupils recorded in these reports attended all-white "refugee" schools. The American Missionary Association supported two such institutions in Richmond—a day school for 375 students and an evening school for 50 adults. The AMA also maintained a refugee school at Athens, Tenn. and contributed to a large collegiate institute established at Lookout Mountain by Christopher R. Robert, a former American Union Commission officer from New York City. See Howard, *Autobiography,* 2:272.
   165. Alvord, *Fifth Semi-Annual Report,* p. 10; idem, *Eighth Semi-Annual Report on Schools for Freedmen, July 1, 1869* (Washington, D.C.: Government Printing Office, 1869), pp. 77–79; idem, *Ninth Semi-Annual Report on Schools for Freedmen, January 1, 1870* (Washington, D.C.: Government Printing Office, 1870), p. 63.
   166. Alvord, *Fourth Semi-Annual Report,* p. 61.
   167. John Watson Alvord, *Seventh Semi-Annual Report on Schools for Freedmen, January 1, 1869* (Washington, D.C.: Government Printing Office, 1869), pp. 52–53.
   168. Shipherd to Lyman Abbott, 24 February 1866, Shipherd Letterbook.

Chapter 2

   1. Wilbur J. Cash, *The Mind of the South* (New York: Random House, Vintage Books, 1960), p. 140.
   2. Ibid., p. 141.
   3. Constance Fenimore Woolson, *Rodman the Keeper: Southern Sketches* (New York: D. Appleton & Co., 1880), pp. 254–75. The chapter is entitled "King David."
   4. Ibid., pp. 266, 274.
   5. Ibid., p. 259.
   6. Ibid., p. 256.
   7. Ibid., p. 262.
   8. Ibid., pp. 255, 261, 275.
   9. Charles W. Chesnutt, "The March of Progress," *Century Magazine,* January 1901, p. 423. Chesnutt's fictional "Patesville" was actually Fayetteville, N.C.
   10. Ibid., p. 422.

11. Ibid., pp. 422–23.

12. Albion W. Tourgée, *Bricks without Straw* (New York: Fords, Howard, & Hulbert, 1880), p. 70.

13. See Otto H. Olsen, *Carpetbagger's Crusade: The Life of Albion Winegar Tourgée* (Baltimore: Johns Hopkins Press, 1965).

14. Tourgée, *Bricks without Straw*, p. 145.

15. Ibid., p. 160.

16. Ibid., pp. 166–67.

17. Albion Tourgée to F. A. Fiske, 2 December 1867, "Bureau Records, Education Division," North Carolina, letters received, 1867; Report dated 1 December 1865 in the "Minutes of the Instruction Committee of the Friends Freedmen's Association, 1864–1867," Friends Freedmen's Association Records, Friends Historical Library, Swarthmore College, Swarthmore, Pa. Tourgée's school was located on his West Green Nursery property. He and the members of his family alternated teaching duties.

18. These figures and those in table 3 are taken from John Watson Alvord, *Third Semi-Annual Report on Schools for Freedmen, January 1, 1867* (Washington, D.C.: Government Printing Office, 1868), p. 2; idem, *Fourth Semi-Annual Report on Schools for Freedmen, July 1, 1867* (Washington, D.C.: Government Printing Office, 1868), pp. 2–3; idem, *Sixth Semi-Annual Report on Schools for Freedmen, July 1, 1868* (Washington, D.C.: Government Printing Office, 1868), pp. 4–7; idem, *Eighth Semi-Annual Report on Schools for Freedmen, July 1, 1869* (Washington, D.C.: Government Printing Office, 1869), pp. 4–10, 64; idem, *Tenth Semi-Annual Report on Schools for Freedmen, July 1, 1870* (Washington, D.C.: Government Printing Office, 1870), pp. 4–7, 52–54. Figures for high schools, normal schools, and colleges are taken from both the ninth and tenth reports.

19. These statistics and the generalizations about the "average" Northern teacher are based on lists and tables found in: *American Missionary* 11 (April 1867): 73–78; ibid. 14 (June 1870): 121–28; *National Freedman* 1 (15 August 1865): 219; ibid. 1 (15 November 1865): 341–43; ibid. 1 (15 December 1865): 380–83; ibid. 2 (15 January 1866): 36–38; ibid. 2 (15 February 1866): 55, 68–70; ibid. 2 (15 May 1866): 156–57; *American Freedman* 1 (December 1866): 139–42; Horace James, *Annual Report of the Superintendent of Negro Affairs in North Carolina, 1864* (Boston: W. F. Brown & Co., [1865]), pp. 41–42; Presbyterian Church, General Assembly's Committee on Freedmen, *Annual Reports, 1867–70* (Pittsburgh: published by the committee, 1866–1870); "Minutes of the Instruction Committee," Friends Freedmen's Association Records. See also Ronald Eugene Butchart, "Educating for Freedom: Northern Whites and the Origins of Black Education in the South, 1862–1875" (Ph.D. diss., State University of New York at Binghamton, 1976), pp. 273–76; Jacqueline Jones, "The 'Great Opportunity': Northern Teachers and the Georgia Freedmen, 1865–73" (Ph.D. diss., University of Wisconsin, 1976), pp. 15–27; Henry L. Swint, *The Northern Teacher in the South, 1862–1870* (Nashville: Vanderbilt University Press, 1941), pp. 175–200.

20. "Our Teachers," *Freedmen's Record* 1 (May 1865): 70–71. See also: "Men Wanted," *American Missionary* 8 (January 1864): 11; ibid. 9 (February 1865): 35–36; Presbyterian Church, General Assembly's Eastern Committee for the Education of the Freedmen, *Report . . . Presented . . . May, 1865* (Philadelphia: published by the committee, 1865), pp. 9–10.

21. *Woman's Work for the Lowly, As Illustrated in the Work of the American Missionary Association among the Freedmen* (Boston: South Boston Inquirer Press, 1873), pp. 3–4.

22. "Our Teachers," pp. 70–71.

23. Ibid.; "The Situation," *Freedmen's Record* 2 (July 1866): 125–26.

24. *Freedmen's Record* 1 (April 1865): 49–50. Because a large number of Negroes served by the New England society were Methodists, the committee on teachers noted in July 1866 that it might favor applicants of that denomination in the selection process for the coming school year. See ibid. 2 (July 1866): 126.

25. "Education and Religion," *American Freedman* 1 (September 1866): 94–96; *American Missionary* 10 (October 1866): 225. Cope and Abbott played leading roles in the formulation of this statement. Abbott wrote the initial draft. See minutes of AFUC executive committee meetings for 25 April, 9 May, and 12 September 1866 in American Freedmen's Union Commission, "Executive Committee Minute Book," Cornell University Library, Ithaca, N.Y., pp. 44, 47–48, 64. The views of Unitarian leader O. B. Frothingham may be found in *American Missionary* 10 (September 1866): 193–95, 202–4.

26. O. B. Frothingham, "Education and Religion," *Independent* (New York), 12 July 1866; Lyman Abbott to J. Miller McKim, 18 July 1866, James Miller McKim Papers, Cornell University Library, Ithaca, N.Y.

27. "Who Shall Educate the Freedmen?" *Boston Recorder*, 10 August 1866.

28. *American Missionary* 10 (September 1866): 193–95; "Education and Religion," ibid., pp. 202–4; "Am. F.U. Commission," ibid. 10 (October 1866): 225; "Education and Religion," ibid., pp. 226–28; "The Union Commission," ibid. 10 (November 1866): 247–49.

29. These figures are based on detailed teacher listings in the McKim Papers and in the *American Freedman*, April 1866–July 1869. In a letter to Miss M. A. Estlin, McKim wrote that the AFUC did not inquire into a person's theology as a requirement for appointment as a teacher and that most of the commission's teachers were "orthodox" in religion. McKim to Estlin, 8 April 1867, McKim Papers.

30. "Education and Religion," *American Missionary* 10 (October 1866): 227.

31. "Teachers: Their Qualifications and Support," ibid. 10 (July 1866): 152–53. See also "The Home Missionary," ibid. 8 (January 1864): 12.

32. The quotation is from Freedmen's Aid Society of the Methodist Episcopal Church, *Fourth Annual Report* (Cincinnati: Western Methodist Book Concern, 1871), p. 5.

33. Presbyterian Church, General Assembly's Committee on Freedmen, *First Annual Report* (Pittsburgh: published by the committee, 1866), p. 7.

34. Joseph Potts to A. Smiley, 3 August 1866 and Potts to Augustine Jones, 3 August 1866, Friends Freedmen's Association, letters sent, 1866–1867, Friends Freedmen's Association Records. The more formal name for the Association was the Friends' Association of Philadelphia and its Vicinity for the Relief of Colored Freedmen.

35. "To our Superintendents and Teachers in Freedmen's Schools," Friends Freedmen's Association, "Minutes of the Instruction Committee, 1864–1867," Friends Freedmen's Association Records.

36. See Henrietta Matson to George Whipple, 17 June 1870, S. J. Whiton to

Whipple, 9 December 1865, AMA Archives, Amistad Research Center, New Orleans, La.

37. Jacob Weston to [Oliver O.] Howard, 18 November 1867, "Bureau Records," letters received, September 1866–May 1869.

38. For a concise summary of this intricate subject see Clifton H. Johnson, "The American Missionary Association: A Short History," in *Our American Missionary Association Heritage* (New York: American Missionary Association, 1966), pp. 5–40.

39. Biographical information on Ayer is taken from an unsigned letter in the AMA Archives for Georgia in a file dated 24–31 December 1867. See also *American Missionary* 11 (November 1867): 257.

40. *Atlanta Daily New Era*, 9 December 1866; Myron W. Adams, *A History of Atlanta University, 1865–1929* (Atlanta: Atlanta University Press, 1930), pp. 1–12; Clarence A. Bacote, *The Story of Atlanta University* (Atlanta: Atlanta University Press, 1969).

41. Richard Sloan to General [Edgar M.] Gregory, 10 February 1866, "Bureau Records, Education Division," Texas, letters received, 1866–1867.

42. Martha Kellogg was the daughter of the Reverend Bela Kellogg, the first pastor of the Congregational church at Avon, Conn. She taught in Connecticut and Ohio before moving to New York. *American Missionary* 13 (May 1869): 114–15.

43. E. R. Pierce to [George] Whipple, 17 January 1865, J. P. Bardwell to [M. E.] Strieby, 24 January 1865, L. H. Cobb to Whipple, 13 February 1865, Rose M. Kinney to Whipple, 18 February 1865, T. E. Bliss to Whipple, 21 February 1865, E. R. Pierce to Whipple, 5 March 1865, all in AMA Archives.

44. Joseph H. Ingraham, *The Sunny South* (Philadelphia: G. G. Evans, 1860), pp. 271–72.

45. *DeBow's Review*, o.s., 16 (June 1854): 638; ibid. 18 (May 1855): 655; ibid. 22 (May 1857): 555.

46. *Richmond Examiner* quoted in "Reply to Abolition Objections to Slavery," ibid. 20 (June 1856): 646.

47. William A. Golding to J. R. Lewis, n.d., Mrs. H. A. Hart to Lewis, June 1869, Hart to Lewis, 23 July 1869, "Bureau Records, Education Division," Georgia, letters received, 1869–1870.

48. U.S. Army, Department of the Gulf, Board of Education for Freedmen, *Report . . . for the Year 1864* (New Orleans: Office of the True Delta, 1865), p. 45.

49. Caroline F. Putnam to Ralza Morse Manly, 9 August 1869, "Bureau Records, Education Division," Virginia, letters received, 1868–1869; Sallie Holley, *A Life for Liberty: Anti-Slavery and Other Letters of Sallie Holley*, ed. John White Chadwick (New York: G. P. Putnam's Sons, 1899), pp. 203–4.

50. James L. Smith, *Autobiography of James L. Smith* (Norwich, Conn.: Press of the Bulletin Co., 1882), pp. 58–59, 144.

51. Joseph S. Evans to M. E. Strieby, 17 July 1865, AMA Archives.

52. Laura S. Haviland, *A Woman's Life Work: Labors and Experiences of Laura S. Haviland* (Cincinnati: Walden & Stowe, 1881), pp. 34–35.

53. Ibid., pp. 178, 183; John G. Mitchell to John W. Alvord, 12 October 1869, "Bureau Records, Education Division," letters received, 1869–1870; J. R. Lewis to John G. Mitchell, 13 November 1868, ibid., Georgia, letters sent, 27 July

1869–1 February 1870; Mitchell to Lewis, 9 November 1869, ibid., Georgia, letters received, 1869–1870.

54. Haviland, *A Woman's Life Work*, p. 192.

55. A. C. Bloomer to Oliver O. Howard, 16 December 1870, "Bureau Records," letters received, January–December 1870; J. Miller McKim to J. E. Rhoads, 23 January 1866, McKim Papers.

56. Ira Pettibone to Samuel Hunt, 14 November 1866, AMA Archives.

57. J. Miller McKim to J. E. Rhoads, 23 January 1866, McKim Papers.

58. J. G. de Roulhac Hamilton, *Reconstruction in North Carolina*, Columbia University Studies in History, Economics and Public Law (New York: Columbia University, 1914), p. 625. Fisk P. Brewer was the brother of David J. Brewer, a United States Supreme Court Justice from 1889 to 1910.

59. J. Miller McKim to Arthur Albright, 1 February 1867, McKim Papers.

60. Obviously, a high level of education did not guarantee that all freedmen's teachers were cultured or academically talented. William Allen's description of a fellow teacher in Arkansas vividly illustrates this point: "Miss Fox is a pretty, black-haired young lady, straight and slender, naturally lady-like and with a good substantial education, but no special culture." William F. Allen Diary, entry for 16 October 1864, William F. Allen Papers, State Historical Society of Wisconsin, Madison, Wis.

61. Mortimer Warren to the chairman of the Educational Board of New Orleans, Louisiana, 5 May 1865, "Bureau Records, Education Division," Louisiana, letters received, 1864–1866.

62. Mortimer Warren to William de Loss Love, 12 January 1866, AMA Archives.

63. Holley, *A Life for Liberty*, pp. 51–52.

64. See Joseph Rayback, "The Liberty Party Leaders of Ohio: Exponents of Antislavery Coalition," *Ohio State Archaeological and Historical Quarterly* 18 (April 1948): 165–75; Gilbert H. Barnes, *The Antislavery Impulse, 1830–1844* (New York: American Historical Association, 1933; reprint ed., Gloucester, Mass.: Peter Smith, 1957), pp. 176–81.

65. Holley, *A Life for Liberty*, pp. 18–62.

66. Ibid., p. 191.

67. Ibid., pp. 203–4; James M. McPherson, *The Struggle for Equality: Abolitionists and the Negro in the Civil War and Reconstruction* (Princeton: Princeton University Press, 1964), p. 387.

68. Ralza Morse Manly to Orlando Brown, 27 April [1867], "Bureau Records, Education Division," Virginia, letters sent, 1866–1868; Haviland, *A Woman's Life Work*, p. 398.

69. Horace Greeley to Maria Weston Chapman, 15 July 1864, Weston Papers, Boston Public Library, Boston, Mass.

70. Mary Ames, *From a New England Woman's Diary in Dixie in 1865* (Springfield, Mass.: Plimpton Press, 1906), pp. 1–2.

71. See Hancock Manuscripts, Friends Historical Library, Swarthmore College, Swarthmore, Pa.; Cornelia Hancock, *South After Gettysburg: Letters of Cornelia Hancock from the Army of the Potomac, 1863–1865*, ed. Henrietta Stratton Jaquette (Philadelphia: University of Pennsylvania Press, 1937), pp. vii, 1–2.

72. Hancock, *South After Gettysburg*, pp. vii–viii, 275. Miss Hancock's assis-

tants at the Laing School in Pleasantville were two nieces (or cousins) of Bayard Taylor, the well-known author, lecturer, and correspondent for the *New York Times*. Hancock, *South After Gettysburg*, p. 221; Marie Hansen Taylor, *On Two Continents: Memories of Half a Century* (New York: Doubleday, Page & Co., 1905).

73. Elizabeth Cady Stanton, Susan B. Anthony, and M. J. Gage, *History of Woman Suffrage*, 6 vols. (New York: Fowler & Wells, 1881–[1922]), 2:26–39. The short biography of Josephine Griffing in this work was written by Catharine A. F. Stebbins.

74. Ibid., p. 39; Alma Lutz, *Created Equal: A Biography of Elizabeth Cady Stanton, 1815–1902* (New York: John Day Co., 1940), p. 168.

75. Josephine Griffing to Catharine A. F. Stebbins, 27 June 1870, quoted in Stanton, Anthony, and Gage, *History of Woman Suffrage*, 2:874–75.

76. Holley, *A Life for Liberty*, pp. 57, 148. For information on these teachers and their educational activities see Emily Howland Papers, Cornell University Library, Ithaca, N.Y.; Howland Family Papers, Friends Historical Library, Swarthmore College, Swarthmore, Pa.; Judith Colucci Breault, "The Odyssey of a Humanitarian: Emily Howland, 1827–1929. A Biographical Analysis" (Ph.D. diss., University of Pennsylvania, 1974).

77. Breault, "Odyssey," p. 51.

78. Ibid., pp. 218–19, 254.

79. J. Milton Hawks to Esther Hawks, 4 October 1864, J. Milton and Esther Hawks Papers. See also Charlotte L. Forten, *The Journal of Charlotte L. Forten, a Free Negro in the Slave Era*, ed. Ray Allen Billington (New York: Collier Books, 1961), pp. 173, 269.

80. Judging from the extensive correspondence in the Hawks Papers, J. Milton and Esther Hawks were often apart, and their marriage seems to have been a tempestuous one.

81. John Watson Alvord, *Eighth Semi-Annual Report*, p. 17.

82. See John O. Foster, *Our Standard Bearer: Life Sketches and Speeches of Gen. Clinton B. Fisk* (Chicago: Woman's Temperance Publication Association, 1888).

83. James Redpath, ed., *A Guide to Hayti* (Boston: Haytian Bureau of Emigration, 1861), pp. 9–11.

84. *Liberator*, 12 June 1863; Willis D. Boyd, "James Redpath and American Negro Colonization in Haiti, 1860–1862," *The Americas* 12 (October 1955): 169–82.

85. J. Milton Hawks to Rufus Saxton, 4 August 1862, Hawks Papers; *Liberator*, 25 October 1861.

86. *Liberator*, 12 June 1863.

87. Charles C. Arms to Charles W. Buckley, 22 June 1867, "Bureau Records, Education Division," Alabama, letters received, 1865–1867.

88. Edward Van Ness to the Freedmen's Bureau, 29 October 1867, "Bureau Records, Education Division," letters received, September 1866–May 1869.

89. *American Missionary* 10 (July 1866): 152–53.

90. See, for example, George L. German to Oliver O. Howard, 3 June 1867, "Bureau Records," letters received, September 1866–May 1869. German failed to gain appointment as a freedmen's teacher.

91. J. Willard Saxton to C. D. Wilcox and Otis Childs, 31 October 1867,

"Bureau Records, Education Division," letters sent, September 1867–July 1868; Will J. Deming to [name omitted], 20 September 1867, ibid., letters received, September 1866–May 1869.

92. Fragment of a letter written by F. A. Fiske, bureau school superintendent for North Carolina, ibid., North Carolina, letters sent, 1 April 1867–11 March 1868.

93. George W. Williams to J. C. Churchill, 2 September 1868, ibid., letters received, September 1866–May 1869.

94. J. H. Douglass to Marcus L. Ward, 26 May 1865, Marcus L. Ward Papers, New Jersey Historical Society, Newark, N.J.

95. *American Missionary* 14 (December 1870): 283; O. W. Dimick to [John] Ogden, 7 March 1866, AMA Archives.

96. *Charleston Mercury,* 24 February 1868; Joel Williamson, *After Slavery: The Negro in South Carolina during Reconstruction, 1861–1877* (Chapel Hill: University of North Carolina Press, 1965), pp. 205–6, 363–417.

97. *Freedmen's Record* 4 (May 1868): 1; John S. Reynolds, *Reconstruction in South Carolina* (Columbia, S.C.: State Co., 1905), pp. 60, 77, 87.

98. Joseph W. Clift to Edward P. Smith, 29 April 1867, AMA Archives.

99. *American Missionary* 12 (January 1868): 15–16.

100. Ibid. 11 (December 1867): 276–78; 12 (January 1868): 14–16.

101. *Christian Intelligencer* quoted in *American Missionary* 12 (April 1868): 85.

102. John W. Alvord to F. A. Seeley, 11 May 1867, "Bureau Records, Education Division," letters sent, January–September, 1867; Alvord to Oliver O. Howard, 14 January 1870, ibid., unentered letters received, January 1865–March 1871.

103. Charles C. Arms to Charles W. Buckley, 6 February 1867, ibid., Alabama, letters received, 1865–1867. The Southern white teacher was Miss Mary A. J. Ryan, a twenty-three-year-old graduate of a Tuscaloosa female institute. Perhaps Arms remembered his own financial difficulties as a medical student in Philadelphia.

104. Matthew O'Kean to Oliver O. Howard, 27 May 1867, ibid., letters received, September 1866–May 1869.

105. William Channing Gannett, "Steamer Atlantic" journal, entry for 7 March 1862, William Channing Gannett Papers, University of Rochester, Rochester, N.Y.

106. S. N. Clark to George Whipple, January 1870, AMA Archives.

107. Letter from W. L. Clark of Thomasville, Ga., 27 September 1869, published in *American Missionary* 14 (February 1870): 28.

108. Ibid. 14 (June 1870): 134–35.

109. Resolutions passed at a meeting of the Freedmen's Aid Union in 1865, quoted in *Freedmen's Record* 1 (June 1865): 91.

110. E. P. Hayes to [name omitted], [1869], AMA Archives (italics added).

111. The quotation is that of H. R. Pease, bureau superintendent of schools for Louisiana, in *American Missionary* 8 (June 1864): 150.

Chapter 3

1. John Watson Alvord, *Third Semi-Annual Report on Schools for Freedmen, January 1, 1867* (Washington, D.C.: Government Printing Office, 1868), p. 32.

2. Ibid., pp. 3–4.

3. Alvord, *First Semi-Annual Report on Schools and Finances of Freedmen, January 1, 1866* (Washington, D.C.: Government Printing Office, 1868), p. 10.

4. "The South As It Is," *Nation,* 21 December 1865, p. 779.

5. There is some question as to whether Cardozo's father was Jacob N. Cardozo, the economist and editor of the ardently anti-Nullification *Southern Patriot,* or Jacob's brother Isaac, who was employed at the Customs House in Charleston. Francis's mother was Lydia Williams. See Bertram W. Korn, "Jews and Negro Slavery in the Old South, 1789–1865," in Abraham J. Karp, ed., *The Jewish Experience in America: Selected Studies from the Publications of the American Jewish Historical Society,* vol. 3: *The Emerging Community* (New York: Ktav Publishing House, [1969]), pp. 203–4.

6. *American Missionary* 10 (April 1866): 79, 175, 271; *Freedmen's Record* 3 (January 1867): 10; William J. Simmons, *Men of Mark: Eminent, Progressive and Rising* (Cleveland: George M. Rewell & Co., 1887), pp. 428–31; Edward F. Sweat, "Francis L. Cardoza—Profile of Integrity in Reconstruction Politics," *Journal of Negro History* 46 (October 1916): 218; Francis Butler Simkins and Robert Hilliard Woody, *South Carolina during Reconstruction* (Chapel Hill: University of North Carolina Press, 1932), pp. 116–17; Edward P. Smith to George Whipple, 26 September 1866, AMA Archives, Amistad Research Center, New Orleans, La.; Robert A. Warner, *New Haven Negroes: A Social History* (New Haven: Yale University Press for the Institute of Human Relations, 1940), p. 149.

7. Thomas W. Cardozo to "My Dear Friends in the Rooms," 17 August 1865; Francis L. Cardozo to George Whipple and M. E. Strieby, 18 August 1865, both in AMA Archives.

8. Francis L. Cardozo to Samuel Hunt, 10 October 1865; Thomas W. Cardozo to M. E. Strieby, 16 June 1865, both in AMA Archives. For information on the Rollin sisters see *New York Times,* 3 April 1869; *Charleston Daily Republican,* 20 January 1871; *New York Herald,* 13 June 1871; Myrta Lockett Avary, *Dixie after the War* (New York: Doubleday, Page & Co., 1906), pp. 356–57.

9. Thomas W. Cardozo to M. E. Strieby, 16 June 1865, AMA Archives.

10. Ibid.

11. Ibid.; William Weston to Thomas Cardozo, 24 June 1865, AMA Archives. The ages given for the four teachers were as of June 1865.

12. Thomas W. Cardozo to M. E. Strieby, 18 June 1865, AMA Archives.

13. Francis L. Cardozo to Samuel Hunt, 13 January [1866], AMA Archives.

14. Francis L. Cardozo to Samuel Hunt, 2 December 1865, AMA Archives.

15. Francis L. Cardozo to George Whipple and M. E. Strieby, 2 December 1865, AMA Archives.

16. Amanda Wall to George Whipple, 14 December 1865 and 5 January 1866, Wall to Samuel Hunt, 19 January 1866, all three in AMA Archives; George Washington Williams, *A History of the Negro Troops in the War of the Rebellion, 1861–1865* (New York: Harper & Brothers, 1888), pp. 142–43.

17. Francis L. Cardozo to Samuel Hunt, 13 January [1866], AMA Archives.

18. The AMA listed sixteen teachers and missionaries serving under Cardozo from 1 September 1866 to 20 March 1867. Of this number, nine were from Charleston: Mrs. L. N. Lowe, Mrs. H. M. Chipperfield, William O. Weston, Mrs. Catharine Winslow, Richard S. Holloway, Mrs. Charlotte Holloway, Miss Har-

riet Holloway, Mrs. Rosabella Fields, and Amelia Shrewsbury. Those from the North were Mrs. M. H. Cardozo of New Haven, Misses M. W. Griffiths and Mary J. Lennon of New York City, Miss Jane Van Allen of Gloversville, N.Y., Miss S. J. Twitchel of Plantsville, Conn., Miss H. C. Bullard of Boston, and Rev. E. W. Merritt of North Madison, Conn. *American Missionary* 11 (April 1867): 74.

19. *American Missionary* 11 (March 1867): 58.

20. O. H. Howard to J. R. Lewis, 5 April 1868, "Bureau Records, Education Division," Georgia, letters received, 1868–1869.

21. C. Thurston Chase, "The Educational Situation," ca. 1868, ibid., unentered letters received, state superintendents, assistant commissioners, agents, 31 August 1865–21 May 1870.

22. Charles H. Foster to John W. Alvord, 18 July 1868, ibid., letters received, September 1866–May 1869.

23. G. L. Eberhart to [Ira] Pettibone, 19 October 1866, AMA Archives.

24. Erastus M. Cravath to D. Burt, 15 October 1866, J. Terrell to Burt, 9 November 1866, both in "Bureau Records, Education Division," Tennessee, letters received, 1866. See also Cravath to Burt, 14 November 1866, ibid.

25. Miss L. Crocker to H. C. Vogell, 8 September [1869], ibid., North Carolina, unentered letters received, 1866–1869.

26. American Freedmen's Union Commission, *The Results of Emancipation in the United States of America* (New York: American Freedmen's Union Commission, 1867), p. 33.

27. See, for example, S. S. Ashley to Samuel Hunt, 11 March 1867, AMA Archives.

28. George J. Elam to Joseph Welsh, 3 July 1869, "Bureau Records, Education Division," Texas, letters received, 1868–1870.

29. School report of T. K. Noble, enclosed in John W. Alvord to Oliver O. Howard, 1 July 1867, ibid., letters sent, 1 January 1866–10 October 1867.

30. N. J. Burton to J. Miller McKim, 25 February 1867, James Miller McKim Papers, Cornell University Library, Ithaca, N.Y.

31. Cope to McKim, 18 January 1867, McKim Papers. Marmaduke C. Cope was a member of the instruction committee of the Friends Freedmen's Association. See "Minutes of the Instruction Committee, 1864–1867," Friends Freedmen's Association Records, Friends Historical Library, Swarthmore College, Swarthmore, Pa.

32. Buckley to George Whipple, 13 March 1866, AMA Archives.

33. Roberts to Lewis, 7 December 1869, "Bureau Records, Education Division," Georgia, letters received, 1869–1870; Lewis to Roberts, 16 December 1869, ibid., letters sent, 27 July 1869–1 February 1870.

34. William R. Hooper, "The Freedmen's Bureau," *Lippincott's Magazine,* June 1871, p. 616.

35. Based on the statistics in Superintendent Alvord's semi-annual reports, the percentages for the end of each school year were: 38 percent in July 1867; 46 percent in 1868; and 53 percent in 1869 and 1870.

36. *American Missionary* 11 (April 1867): 78; ibid. 14 (June 1870): 128.

37. Presbyterian Church, General Assembly's Committee on Freedmen, *Second Annual Report* ... (Pittsburgh: published by the committee, 1867), pp. 11–12; idem, *Third Annual Report* ... (Pittsburgh: published by the committee, 1868), p. 7.

38. Statistics in Superintendent Alvord's semi-annual reports are not complete or precise enough to allow more detailed comparisons in this area.

39. *American Missionary* 11 (April 1867): 78; ibid. 14 (June 1870): 128.

40. These generalizations are based partly on a table entitled "Summary of Biographical Data for Negro Legislators, 1868–76" in Thomas Holt, *Black over White: Negro Political Leadership in South Carolina during Reconstruction* (Urbana: University of Illinois Press, 1977), pp. 229–41. In this table Holt lists thirty-three teachers and indicates the birthplaces of thirty-one of these— twenty-five from the Confederate States, five from the North, and one from the border state of Maryland. The number of Northern-born teachers is inaccurate, however, since the table lists Henry E. Hayne's birthplace as Massachusetts rather than South Carolina. As shown on page 131 of *Black over White,* Holt does not make this same mistake in the main body of his book. See also Emily Bellinger Reynolds and Joan Reynolds Faunt, comps., *Biographical Directory of the Senate of the State of South Carolina, 1776–1964* (Columbia: South Carolina Archives Department, 1964), p. 235. Moreover, Holt does not list legislator Benjamin F. Randolph as a teacher. For information on Randolph and his educational activities see *New York Times,* 4 March 1868, p. 8 and 28 October 1868, p. 5; Joel Williamson, *After Slavery: The Negro in South Carolina during Reconstruction, 1861– 1877* (Chapel Hill: University of North Carolina Press, 1965), pp. 205–6, 220, 260.

41. Albion W. Tourgée, *Bricks without Straw* (New York: Fords, Howard, & Hulbert, 1880), p. 165.

42. Ibid., p. 171.

43. Ibid., pp. 67–69.

44. Ibid., pp. 288–89.

45. Ibid., pp. 445–46.

46. For a transcript of Hill's testimony see U.S., Congress, *The Ku Klux Conspiracy: Report of the Joint Select Committee Appointed To Inquire into the Condition of Affairs in the Late Insurrectionary States, so far as Regards the Execution of the Laws, and the Safety of the Lives and Property of the Citizens of the United States and Testimony Taken,* 13 vols. (Washington, D.C.: Government Printing Office, 1872), 5:1406–15.

47. Ibid., p. 1410.

48. *Freedmen's Record* 5 (August 1869): 31.

49. Ibid. 2 (May 1866): 88.

50. W. T. Richardson to George Whipple, 10 January 1865, AMA Archives.

51. Susie King Taylor, *Reminiscences of My Life in Camp with the 33d United States Colored Troops.* . . . (Boston: by the author, 1902), pp. 5–6.

52. Ibid., pp. 6–55. Susie escaped from slavery with her uncle's family during the Union occupation of the sea islands. In the fall of 1862 she married Edward King, a freed slave, and taught the soldiers of his company in the First South Carolina (later re-named the Thirty-Third United States Colored Troops). Moving to Boston toward the end of Reconstruction, she married Russell Taylor in 1879.

53. Laura S. Haviland, *A Woman's Life Work: Labors and Experiences of Laura S. Haviland* (Cincinnati: Walden & Stowe, 1881), pp. 300–301.

54. John Watson Alvord, *Fifth Semi-Annual Report on Schools for Freedmen, January 1, 1868* (Washington, D.C.: Government Printing Office, 1868), pp. 29–30.

55. Lewis C. Lockwood, *Mary S. Peake: The Colored Teacher at Fortress*

Monroe (Boston: American Tract Society, [1863]), pp. 5–15; Augustus Field Beard, *A Crusade of Brotherhood: A History of the American Missionary Association* (Boston: Pilgrim Press, 1909), pp. 122–23.

56. Mary L. Chadwick to George Whipple, 31 January 1866, AMA Archives.

57. Letter from Anna Gardner, Charlottesville, Va., 24 October 1866, published in *Freedmen's Record* 2 (November 1866): 213.

58. See, for example, R. P. Clark to D. Burt, 1 November 1866, "Bureau Records, Education Division," Tennessee, letters received, 1866; Julia A. Marshall to Samuel Hunt, 1 May 1866, AMA Archives.

59. Henry R. Pease to John W. Alvord, 24 April 1868, "Bureau Records, Education Division," letters received, September 1866–May 1869. See also Pease to Alvord, 20 October 1868, ibid. For another instance of action against schools taught by "illiterate" Negroes see John E. Tucker to W. Willy, 15 November 1865, ibid., miscellaneous unentered letters received, 1865–1871.

60. Joseph B. Morris to Col. J. R. Lewis, 19 March 1870 and 2 April 1870, ibid., Georgia, letters received, 1869–1870; Lewis to Morris, 17 March 1870, ibid., letters sent, 1870. The petition and its signatures were obviously written by Morris. The summary on the wrapper enclosing this document describes it as a "poorly forged 'petition.' "

61. Solomon Derry to R. D. Harper, 20 April 1868 and 27 April 1868, ibid., Alabama, letters received, 1865–1868.

62. H. M. Bush to Solomon Derry, 1 May 1868, ibid., Alabama, letters sent, 1868.

63. Mary M. Reed to George Whipple, June 1865, AMA Archives.

64. James William D. Bland to George Whipple, 16 May 1865; H. C. Percy to Samuel Hunt, 28 September 1865; Notes accompanying financial accounts submitted to the American Missionary Association by Percy in April 1865, all in AMA Archives.

65. H. C. Percy to Samuel Hunt, 17 October 1865, Josephine E. Strong to Hunt, 26 November 1865, Robert Harris to Hunt, 1 December 1866, Lydia Auld to E. P. Smith, 20 February 1868, all in AMA Archives; Robert Harris to H. C. Vogell, 12 November 1868, "Bureau Records, Education Division," North Carolina, unentered letters received, 1866–1869; Harris to Vogell, 26 February 1869, ibid., letters received, vol. 38, 1865, 1868–1869.

66. J. W. Cromwell to Samuel Hunt, 12 September 1866, Cromwell to Hunt, 17 September 1866, H. C. Percy to Hunt, 12 September 1866, all in AMA Archives; Simmons, *Men of Mark*, pp. 899–900.

67. J. W. Cromwell to Samuel Hunt, 29 September 1866, Cromwell to Hunt, 1 December 1866, both in AMA Archives.

68. Simmons, *Men of Mark*, pp. 898–907; August Meier, *Negro Thought in America, 1890–1915: Racial Ideologies in the Age of Booker T. Washington* (Ann Arbor: University of Michigan Press, 1963), pp. 44, 213; John W. Cromwell, *The Negro in American History: Men and Women Eminent in the Evolution of the American of African Descent* (Washington, D.C.: American Negro Academy, 1914). In his Foreword, Cromwell wrote: "The rise to eminence of representative men and women . . . as educators, statesmen, artists, and men of affairs will be cited for the emulation of our youth, who are so liable from the scant mention of such men and women in the histories which they study and the books they read, to

conclude that only the lowest and most menial avenues of service are open to them."

69. John Watson Alvord, *Fourth Semi-Annual Report on Schools for Freedmen, July 1, 1867* (Washington, D.C.: Government Printing Office, 1868), p. 29.

70. John Watson Alvord, *Sixth Semi-Annual Report on Schools for Freedmen, July 1, 1868* (Washington, D.C.: Government Printing Office, 1868), p. 29; Charles H. Foster to John W. Alvord, 18 July 1868, "Bureau Records, Education Division," letters received, 1866–1869.

71. John Watson Alvord, *Seventh Semi-Annual Report on Schools for Freedmen, January 1, 1869* (Washington, D.C.: Government Printing Office, 1869), p. 24.

72. See C. W. Birnie, "Education of the Negro in Charleston, South Carolina, Prior to the Civil War," *Journal of Negro History* 12 (January 1927): 13–21; Carter G. Woodson, *The Education of the Negro Prior to 1861,* 2d ed. (Washington, D.C.: Associated Publishers, 1919), pp. 129–30; Daniel Alexander Payne, *Recollections of Seventy Years,* comp. and arr. Sarah C. Bierce Scarborough, ed. Rev. C. S. Smith (Nashville, Tenn.: Publishing House of the A.M.E. Sunday School Union, 1888), pp. 14–15, 19–26.

73. F. L. Cardozo to M. E. Strieby, 13 June 1866, AMA Archives.

74. Report of Reuben Tomlinson, Charleston, S.C., 15 February 1867 quoted in *Freedmen's Record* 3 (April 1867): 55–56.

75. Reynolds and Faunt, *Biographical Directory,* p. 235; Thomas Wentworth Higginson, *Army Life in a Black Regiment* (Boston: Fields, Osgood, & Co., 1870), p. 265.

76. *Freedmen's Record* 3 (April 1867): 58–59; Ednah Cheney to "Mary," 5 May 1869, Ednah Dow Cheney Papers, Boston Public Library, Boston, Mass.

77. *Freedmen's Record* 3 (April 1867): 55.

78. Payne, *Recollections of Seventy Years,* p. 15; James B. Browning, "The Beginnings of Insurance Enterprise among Negroes," *Journal of Negro History* 22 (October 1937): 424; Marina Wikramanayake, *A World in Shadow: The Free Black in Antebellum South Carolina* (Columbia: University of South Carolina Press, 1973), pp. 81–85, 91; George B. Tindall, *South Carolina Negroes, 1877–1900* (Columbia: University of South Carolina Press, 1952; reprint ed., Baton Rouge: Louisiana State University Press, 1966), p. 65. Daniel A. Payne, the educator and African Methodist Episcopal Church leader, spent four and a half years working in the Holloway carpenter's shop during his teens in the 1820s. The Holloways were related to Payne through marriage.

79. *Charleston Mercury,* 24 February 1868; Laura Josephine Webster, *The Operation of the Freedmen's Bureau in South Carolina,* Smith College Studies in History, vol. 1 (Northampton, Mass.: Smith College Department of History, 1916), p. 159; Holt, *Black over White,* pp. 46, 54, 70–71, 228–41; Joel Williamson, *After Slavery,* pp. 365–67. For a complete list of the delegates see *Proceedings of the Constitutional Convention of South Carolina, Held at Charleston, S.C., Beginning January 14th and Ending March 17th, 1868,* 2 vols. in 1 (Charleston: printed for the convention by Denny & Perry, 1868), 1: 6–8.

80. Holt, *Black over White,* pp. 37n, 46, 52–53, 141n, 164–65, [236]; Wikramanayake, *World in Shadow,* pp. 81–85; Browning, "Insurance Enterprise among Negroes," pp. 422–23, 426–27; Birnie, "Education of the Negro in

Charleston,'' p. 19. Benjamin Huger, Joseph Sasportas, and William McKinlay were trustees of the Coming Street school, where W. W. Wilburn was employed as the teacher.

81. *Charleston Mercury,* 24 February 1868; Reynolds and Faunt, *Biographical Directory,* p. 235; Williamson, *After Slavery,* pp. 366–67.

82. A minimum of thirty-eight black delegates had been slaves at some time before the war, but not all had remained in servitude throughout the ante-bellum period. Calvin Stubbs was perhaps the only teacher who did. *Charleston Mercury,* 24 February 1868; Williamson, *After Slavery,* pp. 367, 377.

83. *Charleston Mercury,* 24 February 1868.

84. Robert Hilliard Woody, ''Jonathan Jasper Wright, Associate Justice of the Supreme Court of South Carolina, 1870–77,'' *Journal of Negro History* 18 (April 1933): 114–31; Reynolds and Faunt, *Biographical Directory,* p. 339; *Proceedings of the Constitutional Convention of South Carolina,* p. 698; Williamson, *After Slavery,* p. 330. For Wright's description of his experience as a teacher for the 128th United States Colored Troops see Wright to M. E. Strieby, 27 July 1865, AMA Archives.

85. *New York Times,* 28 October 1868; *Proceedings of the Constitutional Convention of South Carolina,* p. 690; Holt, *Black over White,* pp. 74–76; Williamson, *After Slavery,* p. 206.

86. *Charleston Mercury,* 6 and 24 February 1868; *Charleston News,* 10 March 1870; *Charleston Courier,* 28 November 1872 and 10 January 1873; Luis F. Emilio, *History of the Fifty-Fourth Regiment of Massachusetts Volunteer Infantry, 1863–1865* (Boston: Boston Book Co., 1894), pp. 179, 268, 296, 336; Dudley Taylor Cornish, *The Sable Arm: Negro Troops in the Union Army, 1861–1865* (New York: Longmans, Green & Co., 1956), pp. 215, 268.

87. Emilio, *History of the Fifty-Fourth Regiment,* p. 347; Holt, *Black over White,* p. [235]. The designation Thirty-Third United States Colored Troops was the new name for the First South Carolina Volunteer Regiment.

88. *Proceedings of the Constitutional Convention of South Carolina,* p. 56. The remaining members of the committee were Dr. J. L. Neagle, F. F. Miller, Alexander Bryce, and David Harris, a Negro minister representing Edgefield.

89. Ibid., pp. 264–66, 685–92, 705–9, 747–49, 889, 899–902; *New York Times,* 3 July 1874; Williamson, *After Slavery,* pp. 219–22; Simkins and Woody, *South Carolina during Reconstruction,* pp. 434–43. It is worth noting that in the heat of the debate over the section of the committee report recommending ''compulsory'' education, Cardozo offered the amendment stipulating that ''no law to that effect shall be passed until a system of public schools has been thoroughly and completely organized, and facilities afforded to all the inhabitants of the state for the free education of their children.'' *Proceedings of the Constitutional Convention of South Carolina,* pp. 708–9.

90. Simmons, *Men of Mark,* pp. 429–31; Sweat, ''Francis L. Cardoza,'' p. 232; Korn, ''Jews and Negro Slavery,'' 3:204; Mary Gibson Hundley, *The Dunbar Story, 1870–1955* (New York: Vantage Press, 1965), pp. 17–19. Cardozo was principal of the M Street High School in Washington from 1884 to 1896. This school was founded in November 1870 as the Preparatory High School for Colored Youth.

91. Reynolds and Faunt, *Biographical Directory,* p. 318.

92. Ednah Cheney to ''Mary,'' 5 May 1869, Cheney Papers; H. J. Maxwell to

Reuben Tomlinson, 17 April 1868, "Bureau Records, Education Division," South Carolina, unentered letters received, 1865–1868; Reynolds and Faunt, *Biographical Directory*, p. 265; Holt, *Black over White*, pp. 74, 76n, [236].

93. Reynolds and Faunt, *Biographical Directory*, p. 339; Woody, "Jonathan Jasper Wright," pp. 127–29.

94. Thomas W. Cardozo to the National Union Commission, 31 May 1867, Marcus L. Ward Papers, New Jersey Historical Society, Newark, N.J.; Cardozo to M. E. Strieby, 16 June 1865, AMA Archives; William Wells Brown, *The Rising Son; or the Antecedents and Advancement of the Colored Race* (Boston: A. G. Brown & Co., 1874; reprint ed., Miami: Mnemosyne Publishing, 1969), pp. 495–96; Vernon Lane Wharton, *The Negro in Mississippi, 1865–1890* (Chapel Hill: University of North Carolina Press, 1947; reprint ed., New York: Harper & Row, 1965), p. 164. According to William Wells Brown's biographical sketch, Cardozo "finished his education at the Newbury Collegiate Institute."

95. Mungo M. Ponton, *Life and Times of Henry M. Turner* (Atlanta: A. B. Caldwell Pub. Co., 1917), pp. 33–35, 47, 51, 57; Simmons, *Men of Mark*, pp. 805–19. On pages 153–54 Ponton quotes Booker T. Washington as saying: "There are few, if any, individuals who, during reconstruction times and the period immediately following, did more than he to get the Negroes of the South to settle down and go to work." Washington explained that Turner helped establish churches that impressed on freedmen the importance of work, property, and education.

96. Ethel M. Christler, "Participation of Negroes in the Georgia Legislature, 1867–70" (M.A. thesis, Atlanta University, 1932), pp. 12–19; Edwin A. Cooley to G. L. Eberhart, 4 December 1865, "Bureau Records, Education Division," Georgia, letters received, 1869–1870.

97. *Raleigh Daily Standard*, 14 July 1868; William Harvey Quick, *Negro Stars in All Ages of the World*, 2d ed. (Richmond, Va.: S. B. Adkins & Co., 1898), pp. 119–26; *Freedmen's Record* 4 (September 1868): 147–48; Frenise A. Logan, *The Negro in North Carolina, 1876–1894* (Chapel Hill: University of North Carolina Press, 1964), p. 29; Howard N. Rabinowitz, *Race Relations in the Urban South, 1865–1890*, The Urban Life in America Series (New York: Oxford University Press, 1978), pp. 264–65, 277.

98. For a more detailed discussion of these leaders see my dissertation "Reading, 'Riting and Reconstruction: Freedmen's Education in the South, 1865–1870," (Ph.D. diss., University of Chicago, 1976), pp. 170–74.

99. Unidentified clipping enclosed in Edmonia G. Highgate to M. E. Strieby, 27 September 1867, AMA Archives.

100. John G. Mitchell to John W. Alvord, 12 October 1869, "Bureau Records, Education Division," letters received, 1869–1870; J. R. Lewis to John G. Mitchell, 13 November 1869, ibid., Georgia, letters sent, 27 July 1869–1 February 1870.

101. Joe M. Richardson, *The Negro in the Reconstruction of Florida, 1865–1877*, Florida State University Studies, no. 46 (Tallahassee: Florida State University, 1965), p. 103.

102. *American Freedman* 2 (April 1867): 205.

103. William Steward to Edward P. Smith, 24 June 1869, Steward to Smith, 21 May 1869, John A. Rockwell to Smith, 27 March 1869, AMA Archives.

104. Sidney Andrews, *The South since the War* (Boston: Ticknor & Fields, 1866), p. 123; *Wilmington Herald* (N.C.), 23 September 1865.

105. *Voice of the Negro* 3 (March 1906): 175–77; Meier, *Negro Thought in America,* pp. 156, 176, 221–22.

106. Robert Harris to H. C. Vogell, 12 November 1868, "Bureau Records, Education Division," North Carolina, unentered letters received, 1866–1869.

107. Robert G. Fitzgerald diary, entry for 27 July 1867, Robert G. Fitzgerald Papers (microfilm), Howard University Library, Washington, D.C.

108. Ibid., entry for 11 December 1868.

109. Ralza Morse Manly to Oliver O. Howard, 1 January 1870, "Bureau Records, Education Division," Virginia, letters sent, 1869–1870.

110. "Education of the Colored Population of Louisiana," *Harper's Magazine,* July 1866, p. 246; John W. Alvord to Oliver O. Howard, 1 January 1866, "Bureau Records, Education Division," letters sent, 1 January 1866–10 October 1867.

111. Mary J. R. Richards to the "superintendent of the Board of Education for Freedmen," 22 February 1867, "Bureau Records, Education Division," letters received, 1865–1867.

112. Thomas W. Cardozo to Samuel Hunt, 23 June 1865, AMA Archives.

113. *National Anti-Slavery Standard,* 6 and 20 November 1869; Lydia Maria Child to Elisa Scudder, 6 February 1870, Child to Lucy Osgood, 14 February 1870, Lydia Maria Child Papers, Cornell University Library, Ithaca, N.Y.; *Boston Commonwealth,* 6 August 1873; James M. McPherson, *The Struggle for Equality: Abolitionists and the Negro in the Civil War and Reconstruction* (Princeton: Princeton University Press, 1964), p. 413.

114. J. Miller McKim to A. E. Newton, 9 July 1867, McKim Papers.

115. *Freedmen's Record* 1 (March 1865): 34–38.

116. Harriet Jacobs [Linda Brent], *Incidents in the Life of a Slave Girl Written by Herself,* ed. Lydia Maria Child (Boston: published for the author, 1861), pp. 15–16, 174.

117. Ibid., pp. 266–67.

118. *Freedmen's Record* 1 (February 1865): 19; ibid. 1 (March 1865): 41; ibid. 2 (January 1866): 3. Harriet Jacobs's daughter also taught in Savannah, Ga.

119. Alumni file of Jonathan Clarkson Gibbs, Princeton Theological Seminary Alumni Office, Princeton, New Jersey; George T. Chapman, *Sketches of the Alumni of Dartmouth College, from the First Graduation to the Present Time, with a Brief History of the Institution* (Cambridge, Mass.: Riverside Press, 1867), p. 395; Dartmouth College, *General Catalogue of Dartmouth College and the Associated Schools, 1769–1925* (Hanover, N.H.: Dartmouth College, 1925), p. 188; Princeton Theological Seminary, *Biographical Catalogue . . . , 1815–1932,* comp. Edward Powell Roberts (Princeton: The Trustees of the Theological Seminary of the Presbyterian Church, 1933), p. 194; U. S., Office of Education, *Report of the Commissioner of Education for the Year 1874* (Washington, D.C.: Government Printing Office, 1875), p. 68; idem, *Report of the Commissioner of Education for the Year 1876* (Washington, D.C.: Government Printing Office, 1878), p. 64. Gibbs graduated from Dartmouth in 1852 and spent the 1853–54 academic year at Princeton Theological Seminary.

120. Dartmouth College, *General Catalogue,* p. 176; John Watson Alvord, *Ninth Semi-Annual Report on Schools for Freedmen, January 1, 1870* (Washington, D.C.: Government Printing Office, 1869), p. 40. Williams attended Dartmouth in the 1841–42 academic year but is listed as a "non-graduate." According to

college records, his home was in West Springfield, Mass. See also Warner, *New Haven Negroes,* pp. 73–74.

121. Forten, *Journal,* pp. 7–41.

122. Robert Samuel Fletcher, *A History of Oberlin College,* 2 vols. (Oberlin, Ohio: Oberlin College, 1943), 2: 534–35, 917; *New York Times,* 28 October 1868; Hundley, *The Dunbar Story,* pp. 18, 61; Thomas S. Staples, *Reconstruction in Arkansas, 1872–1874* (New York: Columbia University, 1923), p. 325; W. E. Burghardt DuBois, *Black Reconstruction in America: An Essay toward a History of the Part Which Black Folk Played in the Attempt to Reconstruct Democracy in America, 1860–1880* (Cleveland: World Publishing Co., Meridian Books, 1962), p. 659. A native of Raleigh, N.C., Mary Jane Patterson graduated from Oberlin in 1862 and for the next seven years taught at the Institute for Colored Youth in Philadelphia. She preceded Francis Cardozo as principal of the Preparatory High School for Colored Youth at Washington, D.C. (1871–72, 1873–84).

123. For biographical information on these men see Reginald H. Pitts, "A Study of the Ashmun Collegiate Institute for Colored Youth, 1854 to 1866," paper written at Lincoln University in 1976.

124. Fitzgerald diary, entries for 22 December 1867 and 24 October 1868, in Fitzgerald Papers; Pauli Murray, *Proud Shoes: The Story of an American Family* (New York: Harper & Bros., 1956), pp. 9–10, 64–67, 71–82, 92–94, 102–15.

125. Fitzgerald's diary on microfilm at Howard University covers the period from 1864 to 1871. Also included in Fitzgerald's papers are copies of his military records. In the diary he alludes to several Lincoln students teaching or doing missionary work in the South: William K. Price, J. I. Davis, Eustice Green and William P. Mabson. Price was Fitzgerald's assistant at the Amelia Court House school in the summer of 1867. See entries for 29 June 1867, 10 July 1867, and 28 May 1868. See also "Minutes of the Instruction Committee of the Friends Freedmen's Association, 1868–1875," minutes of 3 February 1868 meeting, Friends Freedmen's Association Records, Friends Historical Library, Swarthmore College, Swarthmore, Pa.

126. Lincoln University, Chester Co., Pa., *The Eleventh Annual Catalogue of Lincoln University, Oxford, Pa., June, 1868* (Oxford, Pa.: Lincoln University, 1868), p. 24; idem, *The Twelfth Annual Catalogue of Lincoln University, Oxford, Pa., June, 1869* (Oxford, Pa.: Lincoln University, 1869), p. 24; idem, *The Thirteenth Annual Catalogue of Lincoln University, Oxford, Pa., April, 1870* (Philadelphia: Lincoln University, 1870), p. 30. For the names of Lincoln students who taught in the Southern and border states see: Presbyterian Church, General Assembly's Committee on Freedmen, *Third Annual Report,* pp. 35–36; idem, *Fourth Annual Report . . .* (Pittsburgh: published by the committee, 1869), p. 60; idem, *Fifth Annual Report . . .* (Pittsburgh: published by the committee, 1870), pp. 12–16.

127. I. N. Rendall to R. M. Manly, 8 June 1868, and William F. Brooks to Samuel H. Jones, both in "Bureau Records, Education Division," Virginia, letters received, 1865–1868.

128. Carter G. Woodson, ed., *The Works of Francis James Grimké,* 4 vols. (Washington, D.C.: Associated Publishers, 1942), 1: vii–xxii; Catherine H. Birney, *The Grimké Sisters, Sarah and Angelina Grimké* (Boston: Lee & Sheperd, 1885), pp. 289–95; Lincoln University, Chester Co., Pa., *Lincoln University; Col-*

lege and Theological Seminary Biographical Catalogue (Lancaster, Pa.: Press of the New Era Printing Co., 1918), pp. 7–8.

129. Woodson, *Works of Francis James Grimké*, 1:viii–xxii; Lincoln University, *Biographical Catalogue*, pp. 7–8; Princeton Theological Seminary, *Biographical Catalogue*, p. 321; Simmons, *Men of Mark*, pp. 608–12.

130. Woodson, *Works of Francis James Grimké*, 1:212–18; Harvard University, *Harvard University Quinquennial Catalogue of Officers and Graduates, 1636–1930* (Cambridge, Mass.: Harvard University, 1930), p. 994; Lincoln University, *Biographical Catalogue*, pp. 7–8; Meier, *Negro Thought in America*, pp. 113–14, 171, 175, 178, 199, 223–24, 237, 242–44; Louis R. Harlan, *Booker T. Washington: The Making of a Black Leader, 1856–1901* (London: Oxford University Press, 1972), pp. 173–74; Stephen R. Fox, *The Guardian of Boston: William Monroe Trotter*, Studies in American Negro Life (New York: Atheneum, 1970), pp. 14, 26–28, 43, 55–57, 83, 86, 92–93, 105–6, 131–32.

131. See, for example, W. D. Harris to George Whipple, 2 July 1866 and Lumberd L. Nicken to the American Missionary Association, 13 October 1870, both in AMA Archives; Anna H. Wright to R. M. Manly, 29 September [1868], "Bureau Records, Education Division," Virginia, letters received, 1865–1868; John W. Alvord to Oliver O. Howard, 1 July 1867, ibid., letters sent, 1 January 1866–10 October 1867.

132. U.S. Education Office, *Special Report . . . on the Condition and Improvement of Public Schools in the District of Columbia*, part 2: *Legal Status of the Colored Population in Respect to Schools and Education in the Different States*, p. 380; Woodson, *Education of the Negro*, pp. 268–70; John Watson Alvord, *Eighth Semi-Annual Report on Schools for Freedmen, July 1, 1869* (Washington, D.C.: Government Printing Office, 1869), pp. 76–77.

133. H. C. Percy to Edward P. Smith, 1 March 1867, AMA Archives.

134. William D. Harris to George Whipple, 2 July 1866, AMA Archives; Anna H. Wright to R. M. Manly, 29 September [1868], "Bureau Records, Education Division," letters received, 1865–1868; folders for Emma L. Hagerman and Oscar Payne, both in the McKim Papers.

135. Alvord, *Eighth Semi-Annual Report*, pp. 75–80; idem, *Ninth Semi-Annual Report*, pp. 61–64; John Watson Alvord, *Tenth Semi-Annual Report on Schools for Freedmen, July 1, 1870* (Washington, D.C.: Government Printing Office, 1870), pp. 49–54.

136. Josiah Beardsley to Edwin Miller Wheelock, 24 January 1865, "Bureau Records, Education Division," Louisiana, letters received, 1864–1866.

137. See, for example, E. M. Kinney to D. Burt, 11 September 1867, ibid., Tennessee, letters received, 1867–1868.

138. See Amos G. Beman to S. S. Jocelyn, 7 March 1859, Beman to Lewis Tappan, 16 January 1860, Charles B. Ray to Jocelyn, 19 March 1848, all in AMA Archives; Clara Merritt De Boer, "The Role of Afro-Americans in the Origin and Work of the American Missionary Association: 1839–1877" (Ph.D. diss., Rutgers University, 1973), pp. 230–32, 337–53; Clifton H. Johnson, "The American Missionary Association, 1846–1861: A Study of Christian Abolitionism" (Ph.D. diss., University of North Carolina, 1959); Amos Beman Papers, Yale University Library, New Haven, Conn.; Robert A. Warner, "Amos Gerry Beman —1812–1874, a Memoir on a Forgotten Leader," *Journal of Negro History* 22 (April 1937): 200–21.

139. *National Freedman* 2 (15 February 1866): 49; H. M. Johnson to John W. Alvord, 15 April 1869, "Bureau Records, Education Division," letters received, September 1866–May 1869; Alvord, *Seventh Semi-Annual Report,* p. 54.

140. For a detailed study of the Negro convention movement see Howard H. Bell, "A Survey of the Negro Convention Movement" (Ph.D. diss., Northwestern University, 1953).

141. *Liberator,* 15 June 1840.

142. *Minutes of the State Convention of Colored Citizens, Held at Albany, on the 18th, 19th and 20th of August, 1840, for the Purpose of Considering Their Political Condition* (New York: Piercy & Reed, printers, 1840), pp. 3–4.

143. Ibid.

144. *Proceedings of the National Convention of Colored People, and Their Friends, Held in Troy, N.Y., on the 6th, 7th, 8th and 9th October, 1847* (Troy, N.Y.: J. C. Kneeland & Co., 1847); *Report of the Proceedings of the Colored National Convention, Held at Cleveland, Ohio on Wednesday, September 6, 1848* (Rochester, N.Y.: printed by John Dick, 1848); *Proceedings of the Colored National Convention, Held in Rochester, July 6th, 7th and 8th 1853* (Rochester, N.Y.: printed at the office of Frederick Douglass' Paper, 1853); *Proceedings of the Colored National Convention, Held in . . . Philadelphia, October 16th, 17th and 18th, 1855* (Salem, N.J.: printed at the National Standard Office, 1856); *Proceedings of the National Convention of Colored Men, Held in . . . Syracuse, N.Y., October 4, 5, 6, and 7, 1864* . . . (Boston: J. S. Rock & Geo. L. Ruffin, 1864).

145. For a list of the African Civilization Society officers and trustees see *Freedman's Torchlight,* December 1866.

146. *Colored National Convention, Held in Rochester, . . .* 1853, pp. 22–23.

147. Simmons, *Men of Mark,* pp. 805–19, 866–71, 1031–34, 1078–85; Josephus Roosevelt Coan, *Daniel Alexander Payne, Christian Educator* (Philadelphia: A.M.E. Book Concern, 1935); Daniel Alexander Payne, *A History of the African Methodist Episcopal Church* (Nashville, Tenn.: A.M.E. Sunday School Union, 1891); Carter G. Woodson, *The History of the Negro Church* (Washington, D.C.: Associated Publishers, 1921), pp. 211–12.

148. *Liberator,* 22 May and 5 June 1840; Benjamin Quarles, *Black Abolitionists* (London: Oxford University Press, 1969), pp. 45–46, 68.

149. Quarles, *Black Abolitionists,* pp. 184, 188.

150. Monroe N. Work, "The Life of Charles B. Ray," *Journal of Negro History* 4 (October 1919): 371.

151. Joseph A. Boromé, "The Vigilant Committee of Philadelphia," *Pennsylvania Magazine of History and Biography* 92 (July 1968): 320–31.

152. *National Freedman* 2 (15 February 1866): 49.

153. *Freedman's Torchlight,* December 1866; Alvord, *Seventh Semi-Annual Report,* p. 54.

154. DuBois, *Black Reconstruction,* p. 658.

155. North Carolina, *Public Laws of the State of North Carolina, Passed by the General Assembly at the Sessions of 1866, 67* (Raleigh: William E. Pell, state printer, 1867), pp. 294–95.

156. W. T. Richardson, report to Michael E. Strieby, 2 January 1865, AMA Archives; *National Freedman* 1 (1 February 1865): 11–12; ibid. 1 (1 April 1865): 98–99; ibid. 1 (15 July 1865): 197–98; *American Missionary* 9 (November 1865): 256–58; *Freedmen's Record* 2 (May 1866): 91.

157. *Freedmen's Record* 1 (June 1865): 92.

158. S. W. Magill to M. E. Strieby, 26 February 1865, AMA Archives.

159. Ibid.

160. Report of S. W. Magill to the American Missionary Association [1865], ibid.

161. Ibid.; S. W. Magill to M. E. Strieby, 26 February 1865; Magill to the American Missionary Association, 3 February 1865, ibid.

162. S. W. Magill to the American Missionary Association, 6 February 1865, W. T. Richardson to George Whipple, 21 January 1865, both in AMA Archives.

163. Edwin A. Cooley to Samuel Hunt, 20 December 1865, ibid. Cooley arrived from Sunderland, Mass. in March 1865.

164. A copy of Eberhart's plan is found in Edwin A. Cooley to Samuel Hunt, 2 January 1866, ibid.

165. Edwin A. Cooley to Samuel Hunt, 3 February 1866, ibid.

166. Edwin A. Cooley to Samuel Hunt, 20 March 1866, ibid. Louis B. Toomer had lived in Savannah all his life. He was active in Republican politics and from 1868 to 1890 worked in the Savannah post office, most of that time as superintendent of general delivery. See Robert E. Perdue, *The Negro in Savannah, 1865–1900* (New York: Exposition Press, 1973), pp. 56–57.

167. Cooley to G. L. Eberhart, 22 December [1866], "Bureau Records, Education Division," Georgia, letters received, 1865–1867.

168. G. L. Eberhart to Ira Pettibone, 19 October 1866, AMA Archives.

169. Edwin A. Cooley to Samuel Hunt, 11 May 1866, ibid.

170. Lucy Chase, "A Journey through the South," *Worcester* (Mass.) *Evening Gazette,* December 1865, reprinted in Lucy Chase and Sarah Chase, *Dear Ones at Home: Letters from Contraband Camps,* ed. Henry L. Swint (Nashville: Vanderbilt University Press, 1966), pp. 183–85. Lucy and Sarah Chase were Quaker teachers from Worcester.

171. *National Freedman* 1 (April 1865): 99; DuBois, *Black Reconstruction,* p. 507.

172. Edward P. Smith to Gen. C. H. Howard, 2 April 1870, AMA Archives.

173. Edmund A. Ware to E. M. Cravath, 25 [October] [1870], AMA Archives.

174. J. E. Bryant, "The Georgia Educational Movement," 31 January 1867, manuscript submitted for publication in the *American Missionary,* AMA Archives.

175. Alvord, *Fifth Semi-Annual Report,* p. 29.

176. J. E. Bryant to Edward P. Smith, 9 July 1867, AMA Archives.

177. John Watson Alvord's semi-annual reports on bureau schools provide the following statistics:

Freedmen's Teachers in Georgia

	Negro	White		Negro	White
Jan. 1867	68	70	Jan. 1869	31	113
July 1867	91	148	July 1869	71*	134*
Jan. 1868	36	101	Jan. 1870	87*	143*
July 1868	47*	127*	July 1870	73*	158*

*Figures only for "schools regularly reported."

178. John G. Fee, *Autobiography of John G. Fee* (Chicago: National Christian Association, 1891), pp. 180–81.

179. Samuel Chapman Armstrong to Edward P. Smith, 15 May 1865, AMA Archives.

180. H. C. Percy to Edward P. Smith, 6 October 1868, AMA Archives.

181. Fannie Gleason to Edward P. Smith, 6 November 1868; Thomas Henson to Smith, 6 October 1868; D. White to Gen. __, 8 December 1868; Phebe E. Henson to Smith, 1 May 1869, all in AMA Archives. Phebe Henson ended up teaching at Onancock, Va. She was in her mid-thirties and a Methodist.

182. S. S. Ashley to Samuel Hunt, 22 January 1866, ibid.

183. Martha L. Kellogg to George Whipple, 17 December 1866, ibid.

184. J. P. Bardwell to Samuel Hunt, 22 June 1866, Asa Severance Fiske to John Eaton, 13 March 1863, both in AMA Archives; Fletcher, *History of Oberlin College,* 1:218, 2:754. Wright began as a domestic missionary to the Indians of the Northwest in 1843. His sponsor was the Western Evangelical Missionary Society, an organization largely controlled by Oberlin College. During the Civil War, he was a chaplain with the Seventieth United States Colored Troops.

185. J. P. Bardwell to George Whipple, 20 March 1866, S. G. Wright to Whipple, 26 April 1866, both in AMA Archives. For a partial defense of Wright by a fellow educator from Oberlin, Ohio see Palmer Litts to Whipple, 27 April 1866, ibid. Litts himself was accused of racial discrimination.

186. Blanche V. Harris to George Whipple, 10 March 1866, ibid.

187. Ibid.

188. S. G. Wright to George Whipple, 12 March 1866, ibid.

189. S. G. Wright to George Whipple, 28 March 1865, AMA Archives.

190. J. P. Bardwell to George Whipple, 21 May 1866, ibid.

191. For examples of conservative black teachers see Charles W. Robbins to G. L. Eberhart, 6 June 1867, "Bureau Records, Education Division," Georgia, letters received, 1867–1868; N. Whiting to Edwin Miller Wheelock, 31 March 1866, ibid., Texas, letters received, 1866–1867; John M. Brown to "My Dear Brother," 1 September 1865, and Marie A. Magnos to George Whipple, 28 August 1866, both in AMA Archives.

Chapter 4

1. *Freedmen's Record* 1 (July 1865): 112. See also ibid. 1 (April 1865): 61–64; ibid. 1 (May 1865): 73; Elizabeth G. Rice, "A Yankee Teacher in the South. An Experience in the Early Days of Reconstruction," *Century Magazine,* May 1901, pp. 151–52.

2. John W. Alvord, Report to Oliver O. Howard, 1 January 1866, "Bureau Records, Education Division," letters sent, 1 January 1866—10 October 1867; John Watson Alvord, *First Semi-Annual Report on Schools and Finances of Freedmen, January 1, 1866* (Washington, D.C.: Government Printing Office, 1868), pp. 3, 6.

3. John Watson Alvord, *Eighth Semi-Annual Report on Schools for Freedmen, July 1, 1869* (Washington, D.C.: Government Printing Office, 1869), p. 23.

4. Charles W. Buckley to Wager Swayne, 9 February 1867, R. D. Harper to Oliver O. Howard, 4 May 1868, both in "Bureau Records, Education Division,"

Alabama, letters received, 1865–1868; E. B. Duncan to Oliver O. Howard, 8 November 1866, ibid., letters received, September 1866–May 1869; *American Freedman* 1 (August 1866): 74.

5. Edmund A. Ware to Dr. Barnas Sears, 13 August 1868, "Bureau Records, Education Division," Georgia, letters sent, 29 February 1868–24 March 1869.

6. *American Freedman* 1 (August 1866): 75; ibid. 3 (April 1868): 397.

7. W. L. Clark to J. R. Lewis, 4 February 1869, "Bureau Records, Education Division," Georgia, letters received, 1868–1869.

8. William Birnie to Andrew Geddes, 13 June 1868, ibid., North Carolina, letters received, 1868.

9. James Burke to John W. Alvord, 12 March 1870, ibid., letters received, January 1865–March 1871.

10. Burke seems to have been preoccupied with the subjects of Negro immorality and interracial sexual activity. In a representative letter to Oliver O. Howard he glibly asserted: "Want of Chastity is the great sin among the [Negro] race." In a letter to John W. Alvord he claimed that 90 percent of the Negro ministers in Texas were "whoremasters." Burke to Howard, 13 May 1869, "Bureau Records," letters received, September 1866–May 1869; Burke to Alvord, 12 March 1870, "Bureau Records, Education Division," unentered letters received, January 1865–March 1871.

11. Edwin Easton to Joseph Welch, 28 August 1869, "Bureau Records, Education Division," Texas, letters received, 1868–1870; Joseph Welch to Josce Stell, 31 August 1869, ibid., Texas, letters sent, 1869–1870.

12. Charles W. Buckley to Wager Swayne, 24 October 1866, ibid., Alabama, miscellaneous reports, 1866–1870. See also William Seawell to Buckley, May 1866, ibid., Alabama, letters received, 1865–1867. Believing that many Alabama churchmen were genuinely interested in educating freedmen, Buckley favored the use of Southern white teachers.

13. See W. Harrison Daniel, "Southern Protestantism and the Negro, 1860–1865," *North Carolina Historical Review* 41 (summer 1964): 338–59; idem, "Virginia Baptists and the Negro, 1865–1902," *Virginia Magazine of History and Biography* 76 (July 1968): 340–63; John L. Bell, Jr., "The Presbyterian Church and the Negro in North Carolina during Reconstruction," *North Carolina Historical Review* 40 (January 1963): 15–36; idem, "Baptists and the Negro in North Carolina during Reconstruction," ibid. 42 (October 1965): 391–409.

14. E. C. Wilmot quoted in an undated report entitled "Progress of Education in Different Schools," "Bureau Records, Education Division," letters received, January 1865–March 1871.

15. M. W. McGill to William Colby, 11 June 1867, ibid., Arkansas, letters received, 1866–1868.

16. E. M. Cravath to D. Burt, 19 September 1866, ibid., Tennessee, letters received, 1866.

17. Ednah D. Cheney to G. L. Eberhart, 6 December 1865, ibid., Georgia, letters received, 1865–1867.

18. Lyman Abbott, *Reminiscences* (Boston: Houghton Mifflin Co., 1915), pp. 265–66. See also *American Freedman* 1 (November 1866): 114–15.

19. John Watson Alvord, *Sixth Semi-Annual Report on Schools for Freedmen, July 1, 1868* (Washington, D.C.: Government Printing Office, 1868), pp. 6–7, 38.

20. John Watson Alvord, *Third Semi-Annual Report on Schools for Freedmen,*

January 1, 1867 (Washington, D. C.: Government Printing Office, 1868), p. 32.

21. *American Freedman* 1 (September 1866): 91; *National Freedman* 2 (15 February 1866): 55; *Freedmen's Record* 3 (May 1867): 74. It should be noted that the bureau state superintendent Reuben Tomlinson questioned the qualifications of many prospective instructors, writing to J. Miller McKim in the summer of 1867: "The truth is the white South Carolinians who are fit to teach are rare indeed." Tomlinson to McKim, 2 August 1867, James Miller McKim Papers, Cornell University Library, Ithaca, N. Y.

22. Alvord, *Eighth Semi-Annual Report,* pp. 23–24.

23. Jacqueline Jones, " 'The Great Opportunity': Northern Teachers and the Georgia Freedman, 1865–73" (Ph.D. diss., University of Wisconsin, 1976), p. 88.

24. Joe M. Richardson, *The Negro in the Reconstruction of Florida, 1865–1877,* Florida State University Studies, no. 46 (Tallahassee: Florida State University, 1965), p. 108.

25. Alvord, *Eighth Semi-Annual Report,* p. 60.

26. Frank R. Chase to George Whipple, 18 September 1866, AMA Archives, Amistad Research Center, New Orleans, La.

27. Ibid.; Alvord, *Third Semi-Annual Report,* pp. 19–21.

28. J. H. Caldwell to G. L. Eberhart, 3 April 1867, "Bureau Records, Education Division," Georgia, letters received, 1865–1867.

29. David Mahoney to J. R. Lewis, 19 February 1869, ibid., Georgia, letters received, 1868–1869.

30. P. L. Walker to H. Neide, 1 July 1869, ibid., South Carolina, unentered letters received, 1869.

31. William B. Thompson to G. L. Eberhart, 2 March 1867, ibid., Georgia, letters received, 1865–1867.

32. Ralza Morse Manly to J. E. Yoder, 7 October 1869, ibid., Virginia, letters sent, 12 June–1 November 1869.

33. D. W. Rosson to D. Burt, 29 February 1868, Rosson to Burt, 27 March 1868, William S. Holley to Burt, 22 April 1868, all in "Bureau Records, Education Division," Tennessee, letters received, 1867–1868.

34. Frederick Ayer to the Reverend William Hunt, 30 June 1866, AMA Archives.

35. John J. Judge to H. C. Vogell, 27 February 1869, "Bureau Records, Education Division," North Carolina, unentered letters received, 1869–1870.

36. *Freedmen's Record* 4 (December 1868): 193.

37. Mrs. H. G. Cadwallader to Orlando Brown, 10 September 1867, "Bureau Records, Education Division," Virginia, letters received, 1865–1868.

38. *Freedmen's Record* 3 (April 1867): 54.

39. *American Missionary* 10 (May 1866): 111.

40. E. B. Bingham to J. R. Lewis, 1 February 1869, "Bureau Records, Education Division," Georgia, letters received, 1868–1869. For another example of an ex-Confederate teacher see Isaac A. Rosekrans to H. C. Vogell, 21 November 1868, ibid., North Carolina, letters received, 1866–1869.

41. James McMaster to Louis Stevenson, 13 May 1870, ibid., Texas, letters received, 1868–1870.

42. Letter from J. C. Lyman, Fort Smith, Arkansas, 15 May 1869, quoted in *American Missionary* 13 (September 1869): 199.

43. E. L. Benton to Edward P. Smith, 26 August 1867, AMA Archives.

44. Anthony Toomer Porter, *Led On! Step by Step: Scenes from Clerical, Military, Educational and Plantation Life in the South, 1828–1898* (New York: G. P. Putnam's Sons, 1898), pp. 2–24, 82.

45. Ibid., p. 66.

46. Ibid., pp. 70–71.

47. Ibid., p. 71.

48. Ibid.

49. Ibid., pp. 115, 121, 128, 133, 199, 224–25.

50. Ibid., pp. 199, 224–25.

51. Ibid., pp. 210–22; Francis Butler Simkins and Robert Hilliard Woody, *South Carolina during Reconstruction* (Chapel Hill: University of North Carolina Press, 1932), pp. 380–81.

52. Porter, *Led On!*, p. 214; *Public Ceremonies in Connection with the War Memorials of the Washington Light Infantry* (Charleston: Edward Perry & Co., 1894), pp. 46–53.

53. Porter, *Led On!*, p. 223; Anthony Toomer Porter, *The History of a Work of Faith and Love in Charleston, South Carolina* (New York: D. Appleton & Co., 1881). For further information on Porter's involvement in freedmen's education see *American Missionary* 10 (April 1866): 79; *Freedmen's Record* 2 (May 1866): 85; ibid., 4 (April 1868): 63; Porter to John W. Alvord, 22 September 1870, "Bureau Records, Education Division," letters received, January–December 1870.

54. James R. Smith to G. L. Eberhart, 4 June 1866, "Bureau Records, Education Division," Georgia, letters received, 1865–1867; Smith to Oliver O. Howard, 22 August 1869, "Bureau Records," letters received, September 1866–May 1869.

55. James R. Smith to G. L. Eberhart, 4 June 1866, "Bureau Records, Education Division," Georgia, letters received, 1865–1867.

56. Ibid.

57. James R. Smith to G. L. Eberhart, 6 March 1867, ibid.

58. Laura M. Towne, *Letters and Diary of Laura M. Towne, Written from the Sea Islands of South Carolina, 1862–1863*, ed. Rupert S. Holland (Cambridge, Mass.: Riverside Press, 1912), p. 178.

59. S. H. Brown to Joseph Welch, 19 September 1868, "Bureau Records, Education Division," Texas, letters received, 1868–1870.

60. Lorinzo Lea to [D. Burt], 12 May 1867, ibid., Tennessee, letters received, 1867–1868; D. Burt to Lorinzo Lea, 18 May 1868, Burt to Lea, 24 May 1867, ibid., Tennessee, letters sent, 26 February 1866–26 August 1868.

61. George I. Ruby to J. T. Kirkman, 1 July 1867, ibid., Texas, letters received, 1867.

62. Dr. Brown to Oliver O. Howard, n.d., "Bureau Records," letters received, September 1866–May 1869.

63. Dr. Brown to Ralza Morse Manly, 14 March 1867, "Bureau Records, Education Division," Virginia, letters received, 1865–1868; John W. Alvord to Dr. Brown, 11 March 1867, ibid., letters sent, January–September 1867. It should be noted that Dr. Brown and her husband were in financial trouble and needed a source of income.

64. Valie Meriwether to Edmund A. Ware, 9 June 1868, ibid., Georgia, letters received, 1867–1868.

65. Edmund A. Ware to Mrs. R. C. Meriwether, 27 October 1868, ibid., Georgia, letters sent, 29 February 1868–24 March 1869.

66. Mrs. R. C. Meriwether to Edmund A. Ware, 30 October 1868, ibid., Georgia, letters received, 1867–1868.
67. See, for example, J. N. Murdock to Ralza Morse Manly, 14 January 1867, ibid., Virginia, letters received, 1865–1868.
68. Matthew W. Jackson to Orlando Brown, 26 October 1867, ibid., Virginia, letters received, 1865–1868.
69. J. H. Caldwell to J. R. Lewis, 5 October 1867, ibid., Georgia, letters received, 1867–1868.
70. William H. Howard to Joseph Welch, 26 August 1868, ibid., Texas, letters received, 1868–1870.
71. E. T. Lamberton to H. C. Vogell, 31 August 1868, ibid., North Carolina, letters received, 1868.
72. Henry Ayres to [name omitted], 28 October 1868, copy in AMA Archives of a letter at Hampton Institute, Hampton, Va.
73. A. P. Abell to Ralza Morse Manly, 10 February 1870, "Bureau Records, Education Division," Virginia, letters received, 1869–1870.
74. John A. Rockwell to G. L. Eberhart, 26 February 1867, ibid., Georgia, letters received, 1865–1867.
75. Daniel, "Virginia Baptists and the Negro," p. 347.
76. J. N. Murdock to Ralza Morse Manly, 14 October 1867, "Bureau Records, Education Division," Virginia, letters received, 1865–1868.
77. J. N. Murdock to Ralza Morse Manly, 13 December 1867, Murdock to Manly, 14 October 1867, ibid., Virginia, letters received, 1865–1868.
78. Fragment of letter from Julia A. Shearman to [name omitted], n.d. (filed under October 1867), AMA Archives.
79. Lewis W. Stevenson, semi-annual school report to John W. Alvord, 30 June 1870, Stevenson to Oliver O. Howard, 10 May 1870, both in "Bureau Records, Education Division," Texas, letters sent, 1869–1870.
80. Lewis W. Stevenson, semi-annual school report to John W. Alvord, 30 June 1870, ibid., Texas, letters sent, 1869–1870.
81. W. L. Clark to J. R. Lewis, 4 February 1869, ibid., Georgia, letters received, 1868–1869.
82. C. P. Wheeler to Edward P. Smith, 22 August 1869, Wheeler to Smith, 4 September 1869, AMA Archives.
83. Alfred J. Rose to Henry R. Pease, 25 October 1865, "Bureau Records, Education Division," Louisiana, letters received, 1864–1866.
84. *American Freedman* 1 (September 1866): 88.
85. Isaac W. West to F. A. Fiske, 1 December 1865, "Bureau Records, Education Division," North Carolina, unentered letters received, 1865.

Chapter 5

1. S. S. Ashley to N. A. McLean, 7 February 1866, AMA Archives, Amistad Research Center, New Orleans, La.
2. N. A. McLean to S. S. Ashley, 20 February 1866, ibid.
3. S. S. Ashley to N. A. McLean, 7 February 1866, ibid.
4. John W. Alvord to J. Miller McKim, 21 October 1867, "Bureau Records, Education Division," letters sent, September 1867–July 1868.
5. John Watson Alvord, *First Semi-Annual Report on Schools and Finances of*

Freedmen, January 1, 1866 (Washington, D.C.: Government Printing Office, 1868), p. 12.

6. *American Missionary* 9 (August 1865): 180.

7. J. Miller McKim to William Lloyd Garrison, 19 January [1866], James Miller McKim Papers, Cornell University Library, Ithaca, N.Y.

8. William Hauser to Caleb C. Sibley, 23 May 1867, "Bureau Records, Education Division," Georgia, letters received, 1865–1867.

9. *Freedmen's Record* 1 (November 1865): 178.

10. Oliver O. Howard quoted in *The American Freedmen's Union Commission* (n.p., n.d.), p. 3.

11. Ira Pettibone to George Whipple and M. E. Strieby, 1 December 1865, AMA Archives; *American Missionary* 1 (January 1866): 8.

12. *Freedmen's Record* 1 (July 1865): 116.

13. Ibid. 1 (March 1865): 44. The writer also emphasized that those who heard Garnet seemed to agree "that his discourse was sensible and timely, and, though on slavery, moderate in its tone, and free from all bitterness."

14. Ibid. 4 (September 1868): 140.

15. Alvord, *First Semi-Annual Report,* pp. 12–13.

16. R. M. Manly to Lyman Abbott, 25 September 1866, "Bureau Records, Education Division," Virginia, letters sent, 1866–1868.

17. Benjamin Franklin Whittemore to George Whipple, 25 August 1866, AMA Archives. Whittemore had been a minister in Mauldin, Mass. He was active in the South Carolina constitutional convention of 1868 and later that year was elected to Congress. In the wake of a scandal he resigned and returned to South Carolina in 1870. Between 1870 and 1877 he served as state senator from Darlington. Joel Williamson, *After Slavery: The Negro in South Carolina during Reconstruction, 1861–1877* (Chapel Hill: University of North Carolina Press, 1965), p. 206.

18. Benjamin Franklin Whittemore to George Whipple, 25 February 1867, AMA Archives.

19. Samuel Chapman Armstrong to "General," 7 July 1866, copy in AMA Archives of a letter at Hampton Institute.

20. Letter from Samuel Chapman Armstrong, published in *American Missionary* 12 (March 1868): 49–50.

21. Ibid.

22. Ibid. 13 (June 1869): 123–25. Negro teacher A. J. Montgomery allowed his students to return after they cried at being removed. A. J. Montgomery to Edward P. Smith, 31 May 1869, AMA Archives.

23. Samuel C. Armstrong, "The Founding of the Hampton Institute," *Old South Leaflets,* General Series, vol. 6, no. 149 (Boston: directors of the Old South Work, 1904), p. 526. This essay was first published in 1890.

24. Editorial in *Southern Workman,* February 1877, p. 10.

25. Orlando Brown quoted in R. M. Manly to J. Miller McKim, 11 September [1867], "Bureau Records, Education Division," Virginia, letters sent, 1866–1868. In this letter Manly and Brown suggest that the American Freedmen's Union Commission establish a training school for teachers in which students would work on a farm connected with the school to help support the institution and at the same time contribute to their overall education.

26. R. M. Manly to Barnas Sears, 23 March 1869, ibid., Virginia, letters sent, 1868–1869.

27. *Minutes and Proceedings of the First Annual Convention of the People of Colour* (Philadelphia: published by order of the Committee of Arrangements, 1831), pp. 5–6; Carter G. Woodson, *The Education of the Negro Prior to 1861*, 2d ed. (Washington, D.C.: Associated Publishers, 1919), pp. 260, 268–70, 292–96; Linda Marie Perkins, "Quaker Beneficence and Black Control: The Institute for Colored Youth, 1852–1903," in *New Perspectives on Black Educational History*, ed. Vincent P. Franklin and James D. Anderson (Boston: G. K. Hall & Co., 1978), pp. 19–43.

28. Western Freedmen's Aid Commission, *Second Annual Report . . . , 1865* (Cincinnati: Western Freedmen's Aid Commission, 1865), p. 16.

29. John Watson Alvord, *Fourth Semi-Annual Report on Schools for Freedmen, July 1, 1867* (Washington, D.C.: Government Printing Office, 1868), p. 3.

30. John W. Alvord to the Cashiers of all Freedmen's Banks, 1 October 1866, "Bureau Records, Education Division," letters sent, July 1866–January 1867.

31. John Watson Alvord, *Third Semi-Annual Report on Schools for Freedmen, January 1, 1867* (Washington, D.C.: Government Printing Office, 1868), p. 33.

32. Alvord, *Fourth Semi-Annual Report*, p. 72.

33. Ibid., p. 73.

34. *American Missionary* 13 (June 1869): 126–27.

35. John Watson Alvord, *Sixth Semi-Annual Report on Schools for Freedmen, July 1, 1868* (Washington, D.C.: Government Printing Office, 1868), pp. 75–76.

36. See "Home Influence Among the Freedmen," *American Missionary* 11 (March 1867): 58–59.

37. William R. Hooper, "The Freedmen's Bureau," *Lippincott's Magazine*, June 1871, p. 616; *American Missionary* 13 (October 1869): 218.

38. See Louis R. Harlan, *Booker T. Washington: The Making of a Black Leader, 1856–1901* (London: Oxford University Press, 1972), pp. 62–63.

39. *American Missionary* 13 (March 1869): 62.

40. Armstrong, "Founding of the Hampton Institute," pp. 521–36; Harlan, *Booker T. Washington*, pp. 58–59, 61, 64–65; Luther P. Jackson, "The Origin of Hampton Institute," *Journal of Negro History* 10 (April 1925): 148.

41. Henry M. Turner, "The Hampton Institute," *Richmond Virginia Star*, 11 May 1878; idem, "Wayside Dots and Jots," *Christian Recorder*, 2 May 1878.

42. William A. Sinclair, *The Aftermath of Slavery: A Study of the Condition and Environment of the American Negro* (Boston: Small, Maynard & Co., 1905), pp. 264–65.

43. Oliver O. Howard to H. Mariel, 4 December 1865, "Bureau Records," letters sent.

44. John Watson Alvord, *Eighth Semi-Annual Report on Schools for Freedmen, July 1, 1869* (Washington, D.C.: Government Printing Office, 1869), p. 50.

45. Edward P. Smith to M. E. Strieby, 28 April 1866, AMA Archives; *American Missionary* 13 (July 1869): 162.

46. J. Miller McKim to Salmon P. Chase, 15 October 1866, James Miller McKim Papers, Cornell University Library, Ithaca, N.Y.

47. *American Missionary* 11 (January 1867): 7–8.

48. Ibid. 9 (March 1865): 175; *American Freedman* 1 (July 1866): 51.

49. For a frank and concise statement of this position see *Freedmen's Record* 1 (June 1865): 90–91.

50. *American Missionary* 11 (October 1867): 228–34.

51. See John Mercer Langston to Oliver O. Howard, 3 August 1867, "Bureau Records," letters received, September 1866–May 1869; Caroline F. Putnam to Ralza Morse Manly, 26 September 1869, "Bureau Records, Education Division," Virginia, letters received, 1868–1869; *American Missionary* 12 (August 1868): 183.

52. See, for example, Fisk P. Brewer to George Whipple, 20 March 1867, AMA Archives.

53. John Watson Alvord, *Eighth Semi-Annual Report on Schools for Freedmen, July 1, 1869* (Washington, D.C.: Government Printing Office, 1869), pp. 17, 50; Robert G. Fitzgerald diary, entry for 27 February 1868, Robert G. Fitzgerald Papers (microfilm), Howard University Library, Washington, D.C.; W. H. Butler to F. A. Fiske, 23 October 1867, "Bureau Records, Education Division," North Carolina, letters received, 1867; John Scott to Edward P. Smith, 30 April 1868, Alva A. Hurd to Smith, 2 March 1868, both in AMA Archives.

54. John W. Alvord, Report to Oliver O. Howard, 1 July 1867, "Bureau Records, Education Division," letters sent, 1 January 1866–10 October 1867. For detailed information on these racial theories see William S. Jenkins, *Pro-Slavery Thought in the Old South* (Chapel Hill: University of North Carolina Press, 1935), pp. 242–84.

55. Thomas Carlyle, "Occasional Discourse on the Negro Question," *Fraser's Magazine,* December 1849, pp. 670–79.

56. See Josiah Nott, *Types of Mankind, or, Ethnological Researches Based upon the Ancient Monuments, Paintings, Sculptures, and Crania of Races, and upon Their Natural, Geographical, Philological, and Biblical History . . .* (Philadelphia: Lippincott, Grambo & Co., 1854).

57. *De Bow's Review,* after the war ser. 2 (September 1866): 313.

58. J. Stuart Hanckel, *Report on the Colored People and Freedmen of South Carolina* (Charleston: n.p., 1866).

59. John W. Alvord to Oliver O. Howard, 1 July 1867, "Bureau Records, Education Division," letters sent, 1 January 1866–10 October 1867.

60. Ibid.

61. Alvord, *Third Semi-Annual Report,* p. 22.

62. John Watson Alvord, *Tenth Semi-Annual Report on Schools for Freedmen, July 1, 1870* (Washington, D.C.: Government Printing Office, 1870), pp. 6–7.

63. John Watson Alvord, *Fifth Semi-Annual Report on Schools for Freedmen, January 1, 1868* (Washington, D.C.: Government Printing Office, 1868), p. 22.

64. American Tract Society, New York, *Fortieth Annual Report . . . , 1865* (New York: American Tract Society, 1865), pp. 66–67.

65. *American Missionary* 7 (July 1863): 160. J. N. Murdock, a native white bureau instructor, was convinced that his students were equal to whites in learning capacity. Likewise, after observing a freedmen's school run by a black teacher for a period of over six months, a white resident of Saint Mary, Louisiana declared that he discerned "as great, if not greater progress" than he ever saw in a white elementary school. In a letter to Oliver O. Howard he emphasized that the progress in this school "can not be written down by all the Dr. Notts or Carlyles in the world." J. N. Murdock to Ralza Morse Manly, 23 December 1868, "Bureau Records, Education Division," Virginia, letters received, 1868–1869; Dr. Shakespeare Allen to Oliver O. Howard, 28 December 1866, "Bureau Records," letters received, September 1866–May 1869.

66. Alvord, *First Semi-Annual Report,* p. 10.

67. *Freedmen's Record* 1 (April 1865): 50.

68. Ibid. 1 (August 1865): 121.

69. Ibid. 1 (April 1865): 52. It is noteworthy that in this article the editors also labelled as inferior "the Asiatic, the Polynesian, [and] the Esquimaux races."

70. Ibid. 1 (November 1865): 170–71.

71. Ibid. 4 (November 1868): 170–71.

72. John William DeForest, "The Man and Brother," *Atlantic Monthly*, October 1868, pp. 414–25. The quotation is from page 416.

73. *Freedmen's Record* 4 (November 1868): 170–73.

74. Ibid. 4 (September 1868): 139.

75. Freedmen's Aid Society of the Methodist Episcopal Church, *Third Annual Report* (Cincinnati: Western Methodist Book Concern, 1869), pp. 13–19.

76. *American Freedman* 1 (April 1866): 2–3.

77. Lyman Abbott quoted in Augustus Field Beard, *A Crusade of Brotherhood: A History of the American Missionary Association* (Boston: Pilgrim Press, 1909), pp. 265–66.

78. Francis L. Cardozo to M. E. Strieby, 12 September 1866, Reuben Tomlinson to Maj. O. D. Kinsman, 15 March 1866, Cardozo to Strieby, 13 June 1866, all in AMA Archives; *American Missionary* 10 (May 1866): 110.

79. *American Missionary* 14 (January 1870): 7.

80. Rev. C. L. Woodworth, "Encouragements and Discouragements," ibid. 14 (June 1870): 133.

81. Report by John Mercer Langston, quoted in Eliphalet Whittlesey, "Negro Preachers," ibid. 16 (July 1872): 154.

82. See Richard B. Drake, "The American Missionary Association and the Southern Negro, 1861–1888" (Ph.D. diss., Emory University, 1957).

83. Dwight Oliver Wendell Holmes, *The Evolution of the Negro College* (New York: Teachers College, Columbia University, 1934), pp. 99–109.

Chapter 6

1. The following description of a day in a freedmen's school is a composite. The exercises are direct quotations from nineteenth-century accounts. The source for each quotation is listed in the notes. Sources for the above paragraph include: Edward L. Pierce, "The Freedmen at Port Royal," *Atlantic Monthly*, September 1863, pp. 291–315; *Freedmen's Record* 5 (August 1869): 34; ibid. 2 (July 1866): 137.

2. Stephen W. Clark, *First Lessons of English Grammar* (New York: A. S. Barnes & Co., 1868), p. 10.

3. Pierce, "The Freedmen at Port Royal," p. 304.

4. *Pennsylvania Freedmen's Bulletin* 1 (December 1865): 65–66. This exercise was used by Laura Towne and is quoted directly except for the substitution of "the pursuit of happiness" for "etc." in line 6.

5. David Macrae, *The Americans at Home: Pen-and-Ink Sketches of American Men, Manners and Institutions*, 2 vols. (Edinburgh: Edmonston & Douglas, 1870), 1:98.

6. [Israel P. Warren], *The Freedman's Third Reader* (Boston: American Tract Society, 1866), pp. 81–84.

7. *American Missionary* 13 (October 1869): 222.

8. *Liberator*, 12 December 1862; Pierce, "The Freedmen at Port Royal," p. 304.

9. Warren, *The Freedman's Third Reader*, p. 226.

10. Ibid., p. 261.

11. *Freedmen's Record* 3 (April 1867): 54.

12. *Sumter Watchman* (S.C.), 18 July 1866.

13. Hope R. Daggett to George Whipple, April 1865, AMA Archives, Amistad Research Center, New Orleans, La.

14. Francis L. Cardozo to George Whipple, 27 January 1866, ibid.

15. Edgar W. Knight, *The Influence of Reconstruction on Education in the South* (New York: Teachers College, Columbia University, 1913), p. 25.

16. Miss L. D. Burnett to George Whipple, 30 May 1865, AMA Archives.

17. Lucy Chase and Sarah Chase, *Dear Ones at Home: Letters from Contraband Camps*, ed. Henry L. Swint (Nashville, Tenn.: Vanderbilt University Press, 1966), p. 253. This work contains letters of the Chase sisters through June 1868. Presumably the poem was written between 1866 and 1868.

18. John Watson Alvord, *Fourth Semi-Annual Report on Schools for Freedmen, July 1, 1867* (Washington, D.C.: Government Printing Office, 1868), p. 23.

19. John Watson Alvord, *Sixth Semi-Annual Report on Schools for Freedmen, July 1, 1868* (Washington, D.C.: Government Printing Office, 1868), p. 24.

20. Broadside entitled "High School of Tarboro [N.C.] Commencement Exercises, June 1, 1870," and James H. M. Jackson to Oliver O. Howard, 28 August 1867, both in "Bureau Records," letters received, September 1866–May 1869; David Todd to George Whipple, 1 November 1866, and W. D. Harris to Whipple, 17 February 1866, both in AMA Archives.

21. *American Missionary* 13 (July 1869): 147.

22. *Freedmen's Record* 3 (July 1867): 122.

23. J. N. Murdock to Ralza Morse Manly, 23 December 1868, "Bureau Records, Education Division," Virginia, letters received, 1868–1869.

24. Lydia Maria Child, ed., *The Freedmen's Book* (Boston: Ticknor & Fields, 1865), pp. 260–61. Mrs. Child wrote many of the selections in this textbook herself.

25. Ibid., pp. 262–63.

26. U.S., Congress, *The Ku Klux Conspiracy: Report of the Joint Select Committee Appointed To Inquire into the Condition of Affairs in the Late Insurrectionary States, so far as Regards the Execution of the Laws, and the Safety of the Lives and Property of the Citizens of the United States and Testimony Taken*, 13 vols. (Washington, D.C.: Government Printing Office, 1872), 8:236. It is interesting to note that Henry L. Swint failed to identify Clanton as a Klan leader when discussing his testimony in his book *The Northern Teacher in the South, 1862–1870* (Nashville: Vanderbilt University Press, 1941), pp. 103–4.

27. Joseph Warren to George Kitchen, 22 March 1866, "Bureau Records, Education Division," Mississippi, letters sent, 2 January–14 June 1866.

28. Joseph Warren to J. D. Moore, 18 May 1866, ibid., Mississippi, letters sent, 2 January–14 June 1866.

29. Joseph Warren to the editor of *The Sunny South*, 27 February 1866, ibid., Mississippi, letters sent, 2 January–14 June 1866.

30. S. G. Wright to George Whipple, 28 March 1865, AMA Archives.

31. W. H. Robert to G. L. Eberhart, 25 October 1865, "Bureau Records, Education Division," Georgia, letters received, 1865–1867.

32. Charles Raushenberg to Edmund A. Ware, 5 October 1868, ibid., Georgia, letters received, 1867–1868.

33. Ibid.

34. *Atlanta Daily Opinion* quoted in *American Missionary* 11 (October 1867): 225.

35. *Atlanta Daily New Era,* 9 December 1866.

36. E. A. Ware to E. M. Cravath, 4, 17 November, 2, 5, 12 December 1871, 11 February 1874, AMA Archives; *Independent,* 23 April 1874; James M. McPherson, *The Abolitionist Legacy, from Reconstruction to the NAACP* (Princeton: Princeton University Press, 1975), pp. 177, 181–82.

37. David Todd to George Whipple, 1 November 1866, AMA Archives.

38. *Norfolk Virginian,* 2 July 1866, quoted in *American Missionary* 10 (August 1866): 174.

39. *Memphis Avalanche* quoted in *American Missionary* 10 (August 1866): 174. For similar quotations from other Southern newspapers see ibid., p. 175; ibid. 10 (October 1866): 235.

40. *New Englander* (New Haven, Conn.) 23 (1864): 701, quoted in Ira V. Brown, "Lyman Abbott and Freedmen's Aid, 1865–1867," *Journal of Southern History* 15 (February 1949): 23.

41. Daniel Alexander Payne, *Recollections of Seventy Years,* comp. Sarah C. Bierce Scarborough, ed. Rev. C. S. Smith (Nashville, Tenn.: Publishing House of the A.M.E. Sunday School Union, 1888), pp. 162–63.

42. *Freedmen's Record* 1 (June 1865): 95, 100; ibid. 1 (July 1865): 113–14.

43. "Reformed Text Books," *DeBow's Review,* after the war ser., 5 (December 1868): 1108.

44. *DeBow's Review,* after the war ser., 2 (August 1866): 222–23.

45. *The Tables Turned: A Letter to the Congregational Association of New York, Reviewing the Report of Their Committee on "The Relation of the American Tract Society to the Subject of Slavery"* (Boston: Crocker & Brewster, New York: Edward P. Rudd, [1855]), pp. 19, 21.

46. Ibid., p. 21.

47. William Jay, *Letter to the American Tract Society . . . February 14, 1853* (n.p. [1853]), pp. 2–5; *The Tables Turned,* pp. 12, 40.

48. American Tract Society, Boston, *Forty-Fifth Annual Report . . . , 1859* (Boston: American Tract Society, 1859), pp. 3–11; American Tract Society, New York, *Thirty-Fifth Annual Report . . . , 1860* (New York: American Tract Society, 1860), pp. 37, 64–69, 351–55.

49. American Tract Society, New York, *Thirty-Eighth Annual Report . . . , 1863* (New York: American Tract Society, 1863), p. 8.

50. American Tract Society, New England Branch, *Fifth Annual Report . . . , 1864* (Boston: American Tract Society, New England Branch, 1864), pp. 18–20. The American Missionary Association had suggested as early as 1861 that "liberty loving Tract Societies get up spelling books, with striking illustrations of the remarkable change of chattels into freemen." *American Missionary* 5 (June 1861): 163.

51. *Chicago Tribune* quoted in American Tract Society, Boston, *Forty-Eighth*

Annual Report..., *1862* (Boston: American Tract Society, 1862), p. 35. See also p. 149.

52. Titles and prices of texts may be found, for example, in the Boston society's newspaper-textbook the *Freedman,* February 1867, p. 8 and in American Tract Society, New England Branch, *Eighth Annual Report...*, *1867* (Boston: American Tract Society, New England Branch, 1867), verso of front cover. For information on the use of freedmen's texts see American Tract Society, Boston, *Forty-Ninth Annual Report...*, *1863* (Boston: American Tract Society, 1863), pp. 81–82, *Fifty-Fourth Annual Report...*, *1868* (Boston: American Tract Society, 1868), pp. 77, 80–85, 99; American Tract Society, New York, *Forty-Third Annual Report...*, *1868* (New York: American Tract Society, 1868), p. 103; Alvord, *Fourth Semi-Annual Report,* p. 13; Lydia B. Chace to Miss Greene, 30 April 1866, Lydia B. Chace Letters, Boston Public Library, Boston, Mass. The Savannah Educational Association formally adopted the Boston society's series of schoolbooks. Since John W. Alvord was a secretary of the society and played a part in founding the SEA, this was not surprising. American Tract Society, Boston, *Fifty-First Annual Report...*, *1865* (Boston: American Tract Society, 1865), p. 74.

53. John Celivergos Zachos, *The Phonic Primer and Reader: A Rational Method of Teaching Reading by the Sounds of the Letters without Altering the Orthography* (Boston: John Wilson & Son, 1864).

54. Jared Bell Waterbury, *Friendly Counsels for Freedmen* (New York: American Tract Society, [186–]), pp. 3–5.

55. Helen E. Brown, *John Freeman and His Family,* The Freedman's Library (Boston: American Tract Society, 1864), pp. 10–11.

56. Ibid., pp. 5, 91.

57. Ibid., p. 64.

58. Clinton B. Fisk, *Plain Counsels for Freedmen: In Sixteen Brief Lectures* (Boston: American Tract Society, 1866), p. 8.

59. Ibid., pp. 10–12.

60. Ibid., pp. 13–14.

61. Ibid., p. 14.

62. Ibid., p. 23.

63. Ibid., pp. 41–42.

64. Ibid., pp. 17–18.

65. Alphonso A. Hopkins, *The Life of Clinton Bowen Fisk* (New York: Funk and Wagnalls, 1888), p. 8.

66. Isaac W. Brinckerhoff, "Autobiographical Links in a Life of Fourscore Years," Isaac W. Brinckerhoff Papers, Rutgers University; idem, *A Warning to Freedmen against Intoxicating Drinks* (New York: American Tract Society, [1865]); idem, *The Freedman's Book of Christian Doctrine* (Philadelphia: American Baptist Publication Society, [1864]). The author's note is found in a copy of this book at the American Baptist Historical Society, Rochester, N.Y.

67. Isaac W. Brinckerhoff, *Advice to Freedmen* (New York: American Tract Society, 1864).

68. Ibid., p. 4.

69. Isaac W. Brinckerhoff, *Advice to Freedmen,* 2d ed. rev. (New York: American Tract Society, [186–]), p. 4.

70. Brinckerhoff, *Advice to Freedmen* (1864), pp. 5–6.

71. Brinckerhoff, *Advice to Freedmen,* 2d ed. rev., pp. 5–7.

72. *Christian Index and South-Western Baptist,* 6 August 1868, p. 122.

73. *Freedman,* August 1864, p. 30. For another selection likely to antagonize Southerners just after the Civil War see "The First and Last Gun of the Rebellion. Suicide by Edmund Ruffin," ibid., September 1865, p. 36.

74. *Freedman,* December 1866, p. 48. See also ibid., July 1865, p. 28.

75. Ibid., July 1868, p. 28.

76. *DAB,* s.v. "Warren, Israel Perkins"; American Tract Society, Boston, *Forty-Ninth Annual Report . . . , 1863,* pp. 4, 97–98.

77. See Israel P. Warren to John W. Alvord, 17 February 1866, "Bureau Records, Education Division," miscellaneous unentered letters received, January 1865–March 1871.

78. American Tract Society, Boston, *Fifty-First Annual Report . . . , 1865,* pp. 10–17; *Freedman,* February 1867, p. 8.

79. [Israel P. Warren] *The Freedman's Spelling-Book* (Boston: American Tract Society [1866]), pp. 22, 78, 80, 85, 89, 157.

80. Warren, *The Freedman's Third Reader,* note on copyright page.

81. Ibid., p. 47.

82. Ibid., p. 32.

83. Ibid., p. 53. On 10 April 1866 Warren wrote to Superintendent Alvord: "How grandly Congress has done its duty by the Civil Rights Bill. Let Andy [Johnson] now say he will execute it—if he dare." Israel P. Warren to John W. Alvord, 10 April 1866, "Bureau Records, Education Division," miscellaneous unentered letters received, January 1865–March 1871.

84. Warren, *The Freedman's Third Reader,* pp. 49–50.

85. Ralza Morse Manly to William C. Child, 25 June 1866, "Bureau Records, Education Division," Virginia, letter sent, 1866–1868.

86. *American Freedman* 1 (May 1866): 32. This kind of criticism and advice may have had an effect, for, although the society continued to stock the original textbooks, it also issued a series which substituted the name "Lincoln" for the word "Freedman's" in the individual titles.

87. See A. B. Corliss to Edward P. Smith, 31 March 1868, AMA Archives.

88. *American Freedman* 1 (May 1866): 32.

89. M. A. Burnett to David Ripley, 7 January 1868, AMA Archives.

90. E. S. Grover to C. W. Buckley, 20 August 1867, "Bureau Records, Education Division," Alabama, letters received, 1865–1868.

91. Child, ed., *The Freedmen's Book,* pp. 28, 39, 163, 181; *Freedman's Torchlight,* December 1866.

92. Child, ed., *The Freedmen's Book,* p. 181.

93. Lydia Maria Child, *An Appeal in Favor of That Class of Americans Called Africans* (New York: John S. Taylor, 1836), p. 84.

94. Child, *An Appeal,* pp. 95–96.

95. Ibid., pp. 88–89.

96. Child, ed., *The Freedmen's Book,* p. 141.

97. Ibid., pp. 273–74.

98. Ibid., pp. 269–76.

99. Ibid., p. 89.

100. Ibid., p. 89.
101. Ibid., p. 274.
102. Ibid., p. 275.
103. Lydia Maria Child to [Lucy Osgood], 19 June 1864, Lydia Maria Child Papers, Cornell University Library, Ithaca, N.Y.
104. Child to Sarah B. Shaw, 1865, Child Papers.
105. Child to [Lucy Osgood], 14 February 1870; [Lydia Maria Child] to Sarah B. Shaw, 1864, both in Child Papers.
106. Child to Lucy Osgood, 28 March 1869; Child to [Lucy Osgood], 14 February 1870, both in Child Papers. These letters show that Mrs. Child had donated $20 a year to the American Missionary Association since emancipation to help the organization support "a teacher among the freedmen who is true blue orthodox." The 1870 letter to Miss Osgood also indicates that Child by that time had spent $1,200 in getting the textbook distributed. In 1865 she had convinced Ticknor and Fields to publish the book by agreeing to invest $600 of her own money to purchase copies at the outset. See Child to Sarah B. Shaw, 1865, ibid.
107. *Freedman's Torchlight,* December 1866.
108. Ibid.
109. Ibid.
110. See *Freedmen's Record* 2 (April 1866): 68–71.
111. *Independent,* 5 April 1866. See also *Freedmen's Record* 4 (March 1868): 41.
112. Chase and Chase, *Dear Ones at Home,* p. 236.
113. *Freedmen's Record* 6 (February 1870): 61–62.
114. Chase and Chase, *Dear Ones at Home,* p. 119.
115. *American Missionary* 12 (August 1868): 177.
116. Asa B. Whitfield to the American Missionary Association, 17 April 1867, AMA Archives. Whitfield was born in Richmond County, Georgia in 1830. According to his teacher, he was very observing, and his ideas were "for the most part original." Sarah M. Bent to Edward P. Smith, 10 May 1867, ibid.
117. *Freedmen's Record* 3 (May 1867): 80.
118. John Scott to Samuel Hunt, 28 February 1866, AMA Archives.
119. J. H. Caldwell to J. R. Lewis, 5 October 1867, "Bureau Records, Education Division," Georgia, letters received, 1867–1868.

Chapter 7

1. S. W. Magill to the American Missionary Association, 8 May 1865, AMA Archives, Amistad Research Center, New Orleans, La.
2. Unidentified newspaper account of a speech by Langston apparently delivered in Missouri on 27 November 1865, contained in a scrapbook, John Mercer Langston Papers, Fisk University Library, Nashville, Tenn.
3. J. Miller McKim to Samuel J. May, 7 November 1865, James Miller McKim Papers, Cornell University Library, Ithaca, N.Y.
4. See Lydia Maria Child to Elisa Scudder, 22 October 1865, Lydia Maria Child Papers, Cornell University Library, Ithaca, N.Y.
5. Francis L. Cardozo to George Whipple, 21 October 1865, AMA Archives.
6. *Proceedings of the Colored People's Convention of the State of South Carolina, Held in Zion Church, Charleston, November, 1865. Together with the*

Declaration of Rights and Wrongs, an Address to the People, a Petition to the Legislature, and a Memorial to Congress (Charleston: n.p., 1865), pp. 24–31.

7. *New Berne Daily Times* (N.C.), 24 August 1865.

8. *New York Daily Tribune,* 7 October 1865.

9. J. Miller McKim to Joseph Simpson, 23 February 1866, McKim to Simpson, 28 February 1866, both in McKim Papers. For a teacher's reaction to the veto see Edward Barker to Ralza Morse Manly, 20 February 1866, "Bureau Records, Education Division," Virginia, letters received, 1865–1868.

10. *Freedmen's Record* 2 (April 1866): 62–63.

11. Letter from E. H. Leland, Raleigh, N.C., 18 May 1866, published in *Freedmen's Record* 2 (June 1866): 120; Joseph Warren to S. C. Logan, 19 October 1865, "Bureau Records, Education Division," Mississippi, letters sent, 8 July–30 December 1865; W. L. Coan to William E. Whiting, 31 October 1865, Elizabeth James to George Whipple, 29 November 1865, S. G. Wright to Whipple, 11 November 1865, Seymour Straight to Whipple, 3 March 1866, H. S. Beals to Whipple, 21 April 1866, all in AMA Archives; Reuben Tomlinson to John W. Alvord, 5 November 1866, "Bureau Records, Education Division," letters received, September 1866–May 1869.

12. Hugh Kennedy to Andrew Johnson, 21 July 1865, J. Madison Wells to Johnson, 29 July, 23 September 1865, J. S. Fullerton to Johnson, 28 October, 1, 9 November 1865, all in Andrew Johnson Papers, Library of Congress, Washington, D.C.; Fullerton to O. O. Howard, 20 July, 18 August 1865, Howard to J. Miller McKim, 29 December 1865, Oliver Otis Howard Papers, Bowdoin College Library, Brunswick, Maine; Howard to Edwin M. Stanton, 13 September 1865, "Bureau Records," letters sent, 1: 276; Thomas Conway quoted in *Freedmen's Record* 2 (April 1866): 71–72; Henry R. Pease to John W. Alvord, 1 April 1867, "Bureau Records, Education Division," unentered letters received, state superintendents, assistant commissioners, agents, 31 August 1865–21 May 1870; C. Peter Ripley, *Slaves and Freedmen in Civil War Louisiana* (Baton Rouge: Louisiana State University Press, [1970]), pp. 185–89.

13. Francis L. Cardozo to Edward P. Smith, 11 September 1867, AMA Archives.

14. Joel Williamson, *After Slavery: The Negro in South Carolina during Reconstruction, 1861–1877* (Chapel Hill: University of North Carolina Press, 1965), p. 217.

15. J. Silsby to Edward P. Smith, 11 September 1867, AMA Archives.

16. *American Missionary* 9 (July 1865): 147.

17. Ibid. 9 (December 1865): 273.

18. See, for example, *Proceedings of the Constitutional Convention of South Carolina Held at Charleston, S.C., Beginning January 14th and Ending March 17th, 1868,* 2 vols. in 1 (Charleston: printed for the convention by Denny & Perry, 1868), pp. 352, 713, 723, 725–32, 826–28, 832–35; Sallie Holley, *A Life for Liberty: Anti-Slavery and Other Letters of Sallie Holley,* ed. John White Chadwick (New York: G. P. Putnam's Sons, 1899), p. 199; "Universal Suffrage," an article from an unidentified newspaper, John Mercer Langston scrapbook, Langston Papers.

19. Anthony Toomer Porter, *Led On! Step by Step: Scenes from Clerical, Military, Educational, and Plantation Life in the South, 1828–1898* (New York: G. P. Putnam's Sons, 1898), pp. 224–25.

20. *Freedmen's Record* 1 (November 1865): 184. In an editorial in the *American*

Freedman written one year later, Lyman Abbott declared: "We do not . . . demand universal suffrage. We can see that there may be reasons for appending qualifications of intelligence and morality." *American Freedman* 1 (July 1866): 51.

21. *Freedmen's Record* 1 (April 1865): 54.

22. *American Missionary* 9 (March 1865): 61.

23. Ibid. 9 (July 1865): 153.

24. Ibid., p. 162.

25. *Freedmen's Record* 1 (June 1865): 90–91.

26. See, for example, *American Freedman* 1 (April 1866): 3; *American Missionary* 11 (February 1867): 35.

27. *American Freedman* 1 (May 1866): 30.

28. *Freedmen's Record* 1 (December 1865): 145; *American Freedman* 1 (May 1866): 30. For an example of a Southern white teacher explaining to freedmen that they were entitled to equal rights see J. N. Murdock to Ralza Morse Manly, 23 December 1868, "Bureau Records, Education Division," Virginia, letters received, 1868–1869.

29. For examples of conservative black teachers see Charles W. Robbins to G. L. Eberhart, 6 June 1867, "Bureau Records, Education Division," Georgia, letters received, 1867–1868; N. Whiting to Edwin Miller Wheelock, 31 March 1866, ibid., Texas, letters received, 1866–1867; John M. Brown to "My Dear Brother," 1 September 1865, Marie A. Magnos to George Whipple, 28 August 1866, both in AMA Archives.

30. S. G. Wright to George Whipple, 12 March 1866, AMA Archives. For a more accurate indication of Wright's attitude toward Southern whites see Wright to Whipple, 4 April 1866, ibid.

31. Howard's speech quoted in *Freedmen's Bulletin* (Chicago) 1 (October 1865): 181, 183. See also *Freedmen's Record* 1 (November 1865): 178.

32. Reuben Tomlinson to [name omitted], 23 September 1865, "Bureau Records, Education Division," miscellaneous unentered letters received, January 1865–March 1871.

33. James A. Hawley, Report on a tour of inspection in the area of Jackson, Canton, and Yazoo City, Miss., 28 October 1865, "Bureau Records," Mississippi assistant commissioner, letters received, 1865.

34. C. B. Wilder to "Dear Brethren," [October 1865], AMA Archives. For other examples of criticism see H. S. Beals to Samuel Hunt, 30 December 1865, W. L. Coan to William E. Whiting, 31 October 1865, all ibid.

35. C. W. Buckley to Thomas W. Conway, 18 June 1865, quoted in *Philadelphia Inquirer*, 17 July 1865.

36. Emily Stuart to George Whipple, 27 July 1865, AMA Archives. This letter was published in *American Missionary* 9 (September 1865): 197.

37. *American Missionary* 9 (August 1865): 174.

38. John Scott to Edward P. Smith, 6 March 1867, AMA Archives.

39. Robert Harris, letter dated 20 January 1866, published in *American Missionary* 10 (March 1866): 51–52.

40. S. S. Ashley to C. L. Woodworth, 21 December 1868, AMA Archives. Parts of this letter were published in *American Missionary* 13 (February 1869): 37.

41. S. S. Ashley to C. L. Woodworth, 1 January 1868, AMA Archives.

42. *American Missionary* 13 (February 1869): 35.

43. *Proceedings of the Constitutional Convention of South Carolina,* pp. 460, 685, 747.

44. Ibid., pp. 379–81.

45. *American Missionary* 12 (June 1868): 135–36; ibid. 12 (July 1868): 155–56; ibid. 12 (September 1868): 206–7; ibid. 13 (February 1869): 35; ibid. 13 (May 1869): 107–11; Carrie M. Blood to Edward P. Smith, 14 December 1869, G. Greely to George Whipple, 4 January 1866, both in AMA Archives.

46. J. Miller McKim to Oliver O. Howard, 27 November 1866, Howard to McKim, 1 December 1866, McKim Papers.

47. Oliver O. Howard to John M. Schofield, 5 November 1868, "Bureau Records," letters sent, 5: 161. Statistics on the number of white students are found in John W. Alvord's semi-annual reports.

48. Ednah D. Cheney to Misses Buttrick, Hosmer, and Parker, 6 February 1866, quoted in *Freedmen's Record* 2 (March 1866): 38. Prior to the merger the American Freedmen's Aid Commission was flexible on the issue of integrated schools. According to a *Freedmen's Record* article, the committee on teachers did not approve of "the principle of separating the negroes entirely from the whites," but if the federal government and blacks themselves wished "to try the experiment," the committee would do all in its power "to give them a fair chance." Ibid. 1 (April 1865): 55.

49. *American Freedman* 1 (May 1866): 30.

50. Ibid. 2 (March 1866): 38.

51. Letter from Jane Hosmer, 5 March 1866, quoted in *Freedmen's Record* 2 (April 1866): 67–68.

52. *American Freedman* 1 (August 1866): 76. Adams also visited an integrated school maintained by Gen. James Beecher and his wife at Waterbury, S.C. For information on the integrated AFUC school taught by Esther H. Hawks see *Freedmen's Record* 3 (December 1867): 190. Located at Port Orange, Fla., the school had fifteen "full blacks," two mulattoes, and eight whites on its rolls.

53. *American Freedman* 1 (August 1866): 79.

54. Ibid. 1 (April 1866): 5, 6, 43; ibid. 1 (June 1866): 43.

55. Ibid. 1 (April 1866): 6. Later in the year Brewer established a school under the auspices of the American Missionary Association. He and his sister tried to operate the school on an integrated basis in the beginning but after one month divided blacks and whites into separate classes in the same building. When Fisk and Adele Brewer returned to an integrated system, the white students left. Fisk P. Brewer to George Whipple, 8 November 1866, Adele Brewer to the American Missionary Association, 3 December 1866, Fisk P. Brewer to Whipple, 6 February 1867, AMA Archives.

56. *American Freedman* 1 (August 1866): 70–76.

57. Lyman Abbott, *Reminiscences* (Boston: Houghton Mifflin Co., 1915), p. 270.

58. "Brief History of the New England Branch of the American Freedmen's Union Commission," manuscript in "Bureau Records, Education Division," unentered letters received, January 1865–March 1871. See also J. Miller McKim to S. Quackenbush, 19 June 1866, McKim Papers.

59. "Romanism in the South," *American Missionary* 12 (July 1868): 162.

60. "Rome among the Freedmen," *American Missionary* 13 (March 1869):

60–61. See also "Romanist Schools among the Freedmen," ibid. 13 (November 1869): 250.

61. The AMA Archives contain a number of letters pertaining to an unsuccessful attempt by S. J. Whiton to convince Association officials to force H. S. Beals to admit Negroes to his school for poor whites at Beaufort, N.C. See also H. M. Richardson to George Whipple, 31 January 1865, AMA Archives.

62. Ralph E. Morrow, *Northern Methodism and Reconstruction* (East Lansing: Michigan State University Press, 1956), pp. 197–99.

63. Ibid.; Richard S. Rust, ed., *Isaac W. Wiley, Late Bishop of the M.E. Church* (Cincinnati: Cranston & Stowe, New York: Phillips & Hunt, 1885), p. 140.

64. See William Preston Vaughn, *Schools for All: The Blacks & Public Education in the South, 1865–1877* (Lexington: University Press of Kentucky, 1974), pp. 50–102.

65. *Proceedings of the Constitutional Convention of South Carolina*, pp. 691–93, 706, 724, 901.

66. Richard T. Williams, "History of Public Education and Charitable Institutions in South Carolina during the Reconstruction Period" (M.A. thesis, Atlanta University, 1933), pp. 60–61, 114; John S. Reynolds, *Reconstruction in South Carolina, 1865–1877* (Columbia: State Co., 1905), pp. 237–38; Williamson, *After Slavery*, p. 222; Vaughn, *Schools for All*, pp. 68–69.

67. Edward King, *The Great South* (Hartford, Conn.: American Publishing Co., 1875), p. 316; Stuart G. Noble, *Forty Years of the Public Schools in Mississippi* (New York: Teachers College, Columbia University, 1918), pp. 29–30; Vaughn, *Schools for All*, pp. 61–62.

68. John Watson Alvord, *Ninth Semi-Annual Report on Schools for Freedmen, January 1, 1870* (Washington, D.C.: Government Printing Office, 1869), p. 39; idem, *Tenth Semi-Annual Report on Schools for Freedmen, July 1, 1870* (Washington, D.C.: Government Printing Office, 1870), p. 31; Thomas W. Conway to John W. Alvord, 19 September 1870, "Bureau Records, Education Division," letters received, 1870; Vaughn, *Schools for All*, pp. 78–102.

69. Vaughn, *Schools for All*, p. 88. See also Louis R. Harlan, "Desegregation in New Orleans Public Schools during Reconstruction," *American Historical Review* 67 (April 1962): 663–75; John W. Blassingame, *Black New Orleans, 1860–1880* (Chicago: University of Chicago Press, 1973), pp. 120–22. Harlan concluded that between 500 and 1,000 Negroes and several thousand whites attended mixed schools at the height of desegregation.

70. U.S., Congress, House, *Message from the President of the United States, Transmitting Report of the Commissioner of the Bureau of Refugees, Freedmen, and Abandoned Lands*, 39th Cong., 1st sess., 1865–66, H. Exec. Doc. 11, p. 13.

71. See, for example, G. L. Eberhart to Samuel Hunt, 23 May, 4 June 1866, AMA Archives; John Watson Alvord, *Seventh Semi-Annual Report on Schools for Freedmen, January 1, 1869* (Washington, D.C.: Government Printing Office, 1869), p. 44.

72. This exchange, including the quotation from the *Raleigh Biblical Recorder*, is found in *Freedmen's Record* 3 (November 1867): 171.

73. Esther W. Douglass diary, entry for 8 May 1867, Esther W. Douglass Papers, University of Michigan Historical Collections, Ann Arbor, Michigan.

74. *American Missionary* 11 (December 1867): 268; Julia Shearman to [name omitted], 14 April 1866, AMA Archives.

75. R. F. Campbell to Colonel [Samuel] Thomas, 5 April 1866, Charles Moynhoff to Thomas, 2 April 1866, "Bureau Records," Mississippi assistant commissioner, letters received, 1865–1866.

76. Miss S. W. Stansbury to Edward P. Smith, 21 May 1867, AMA Archives. Miss Stansbury was a teacher from Rahway, N.J.

77. Sara G. Stanley to J. R. Shipherd, 6 April 1868, Stanley to Shipherd, 2 May 1868, Shipherd to George L. Putnam, 7 May 1868, all ibid.

78. *Charleston Daily Courier,* 23 June 1866.

79. *Denton Monitor,* as quoted in an unidentified newspaper clipping in a wrapper labelled "Tarrant Co. July 1869," "Bureau Records, Education Division," Texas, letters received, 1868–1870.

80. Unidentified newspaper clipping in wrapper labelled "Tarrant Co. July 1869," "Bureau Records, Education Division," Texas, letters received, 1868–1870. Joseph Warren, Bureau School Superintendent for Mississippi, reported in 1865 that at a public meeting in Jackson a prominent man claimed over sixty of the seventy female teachers sent to General Rufus Saxton's district in 1864 had illegitimate Negro children. Warren labelled this charge a "foul slander." Joseph Warren to Stuart Eldridge, 15 November 1865, "Bureau Records, Education Division," Mississippi, letters sent, 8 July–30 December 1865.

81. Robert Hilliard Woody, "Jonathan Jasper Wright, Associate Justice of the Supreme Court of South Carolina, 1870–77," *Journal of Negro History* 18 (April 1933): 114–31; Ira V. Brown, "Pennsylvania and the Rights of the Negro, 1865–1887," *Pennsylvania History* 28 (January 1961): 45–63.

82. Francis L. Cardozo to William E. Whiting, 4 July 1866, AMA Archives.

83. *Freedmen's Record* 2 (October 1866): 55.

84. W. T. Richardson to Mrs. E. A. Lane, 29 April 1865, J. C. Haskell to Edward P. Smith, 28 October 1867, both in AMA Archives; H. A. Miller to William Colby, 28 December 1869, "Bureau Records, Education Division," Arkansas, letters received, 1868–1870.

85. Melville C. Keith to Louis W. Stevenson, 18 June 1870, "Bureau Records, Education Division," Texas, letters received, 1868–1870.

86. Hugh Ames to Joseph Welch, 9 August 1868, Ames to Welch, 10 August 1869, Ames to Welch, 4 November 1869, M. P. Hunnicutt to C. E. Morse, 30 August 1869, all ibid., Texas, letters received, 1868–1870; Welch to Oliver O. Howard, 28 August 1869, Welch to Ames, 30 August 1869, ibid., Texas, letters sent, 1869–1870.

87. Isaac Myers to John W. Alvord, 15 November 1869, with broadside enclosed entitled *National Labor Convention of the Colored Men of the United States,* Baltimore, 1 September 1869, "Bureau Records, Education Division," letters received, 1869–1870; *Proceedings of the Colored National Labor Convention Held in Washington, D.C., on December 6th, 7th, 8th, 9th, and 10th, 1869* (Washington, D.C.: printed at the office of the New Era, 1870); W. E. Burghardt Du Bois, *Black Reconstruction in America: An Essay toward a History of the Part Which Black Folk Played in the Attempt to Reconstruct Democracy in America, 1860–1880* (New York: Harcourt, Brace & Co., 1935), p. 362.

88. See *Proceedings of the Colored National Labor Convention . . . 1869.*

89. For a discussion of the early phases of the movement see Sterling D. Spero and Abram L. Harris, *The Black Worker: The Negro and the Labor Movement,* Studies in American Negro Life (New York: Atheneum, 1968), pp. 16–35.

90. See chapter 3.

91. In addition, Bureau Assistant Commissioner Thomas Conway served as Louisiana's public school superintendent, 1868–1872.

92. In the period after Reconstruction, John Mercer Langston was a congressman from Virginia (1890–91).

93. See John Mercer Langston to Oliver O. Howard, 3 August 1867, "Bureau Records," letters received, September 1866–May 1869; Caroline F. Putnam to Ralza Morse Manly, 26 September 1869, "Bureau Records, Education Division," Virginia, letters received, 1868–1869; *American Missionary* 12 (August 1868): 183; John Watson Alvord, *Eighth Semi-Annual Report on Schools for Freedmen, July 1, 1869* (Washington, D.C.: Government Printing Office, 1869), pp. 17, 50; Robert G. Fitzgerald diary, entry for 27 February 1868, Robert G. Fitzgerald Papers (microfilm), Howard University Library, Washington, D.C.; W. H. Butler to F. A. Fiske, 23 October 1867, "Bureau Records, Education Division," North Carolina, letters received, 1867; John Scott to Edward P. Smith, 30 April 1868, Alva A. Hurd to Smith, 2 March 1868, both in AMA Archives.

94. Henry R. Pease, to John W. Alvord, 22 October 1867, with Alvan C. Gillem's Order No. 47 enclosed, quoted in George R. Bentley, *A History of the Freedmen's Bureau* (Philadelphia: University of Pennsylvania Press, 1955), p. 199.

95. John W. Alvord to Henry R. Pease, 2 November 1867, "Bureau Records, Education Division," letters sent, September 1867–July 1868.

96. Henry R. Pease to John W. Alvord, 1 June 1869, with postscript dated 26 June 1869, ibid., letters received, 1869–1870.

97. James Lynch to Oliver O. Howard, 2 October 1869, ibid., letters received, 1869.

98. R. C. Powers to Oliver O. Howard, 2 October 1869, ibid., letters received, 1869.

99. James Lynch to Oliver O. Howard, 2 October 1869, with endorsement by Adelbert Ames, "Bureau Records, Education Division," letters received, 1869; Adelbert Ames to Howard, 28 May 1869, Howard Papers.

100. Oliver O. Howard to Henry R. Pease, 29 July 1869, "Bureau Records," letters sent, 5:454.

101. For a discussion of Virginia politics during Reconstruction see Alrutheus Ambush Taylor, *The Negro in the Reconstruction of Virginia* (Washington, D.C.: Association for the Study of Negro Life and History, 1926), pp. 208–86.

102. *Richmond Whig* (Va.), 28 May 1869. Among the leaders of this convention was J. W. D. Bland, who had taught in a freedmen's school at Norfolk. J. W. D. Bland to George Whipple, 16 May 1865, Bland to Whipple, 29 June 1865, both in AMA Archives.

103. AMA Archives 17 and 21 July 1869. For information on the relationship between education and politics in the election of 1869 see letters of Manly, Richmond Robinson, and George Stephens in "Bureau Records, Education Division," Virginia, letters sent, 1869–1870, and letters received, 1869–1870. For Manly's activities in the 1868 election see Watson R. Wentworth to Manly, 15 September 1868, ibid., Virginia, letters received, 1868–1869; Thomas P. Jackson to Manly, 23 May 1868, J. M. Stradling to Manly, 22 April 1868, T. J. Rice to Manly, 27 August 1868, all ibid., Virginia, letters received, 1865–1868.

104. *Atlanta Daily New Era*, 5 March 1869; Alan Conway, *The Reconstruction of Georgia* (Minneapolis: University of Minnesota Press, 1966), p. 188.

105. J. R. Lewis to W. L. Clark, 12 March 1870, Lewis to Clark, 28 April 1870, "Bureau Records, Education Division," Georgia, letters sent, 8 February–18 June 1870.

106. For a more detailed description of this election see Williamson, *After Slavery*, pp. 353, 360–61, 396–97; Francis Butler Simkins and Robert Hilliard Woody, *South Carolina during Reconstruction* (Chapel Hill: University of North Carolina Press, 1932), pp. 466–67.

107. John W. Alvord to Henry R. Pease, 27 October 1868, "Bureau Records, Education Division, " letters sent, July 1868–May 1869. For similar sentiments expressed by a teacher see Susan Gilbert to J. D. Pike, 29 October 1868, AMA Archives.

108. R. G. Patten to Edward P. Smith, 25 May 1868, AMA Archives. Smith's reply is written on the back of this letter.

109. S. S. Ashley to William E. Whiting, 3 July 1868, AMA Archives.

110. Robert G. Fitzgerald diary, entry for 5 November 1868, Fitzgerald Papers.

111. *American Missionary* 13 (March 1869): 62–63.

112. *American Freedman* 2 (April 1867): 195.

113. Philip C. Garrett to George Dixon, 19 October 1867, Friends Freedmen's Association, letters sent, 1867–1868, Friends Freedmen's Association Records.

114. U.S., *Statutes at Large*, 15:193.

115. Alvord, *Tenth Semi-Annual Report*, p. 3.

116. Ibid., p. 38.

117. Conway to Alvord, 19 September 1870, "Bureau Records, Education Division," letters received, 1870. Other responses to Alvord's letter can also be found in this section of his records.

118. Alvord, *Tenth Semi-Annual Report*, pp. 31–32.

119. Ibid., p. 48.

120. Ibid., pp. 4–7.

121. Julius H. Parmelee, "Freedmen's Aid Societies, 1861–1871," in Thomas Jesse Jones, ed., *Negro Education: A Study of the Private and Higher Schools for Colored People in the United States*, United States Department of the Interior, Office of Education, Bulletin, 1916, no. 38. 2 vols. (Washington, D.C.: Government Printing Office, 1917), 1:274–75, 286, 296–98.

122. *American Missionary* 14 (October 1870): 234–35.

123. "The Freedman As a Legislator," ibid. 18 (April 1874): 85.

124. Ibid. 20 (September 1876): 204–6. Redpath's contention notwithstanding, Negroes never controlled state government in Mississippi.

125. Ibid. 18 (September 1874): 211.

126. Ibid. 22 (January 1878): 15–16.

127. Ibid., pp. 16–17.

Bibliography

Primary Sources
Manuscripts

Ann Arbor, Mich. University of Michigan Historical Collections.
Esther W. Douglass Papers.

Boston, Mass. Boston Public Library. Ednah Dow Cheney
Papers.

———. Weston Papers.

———. William Lloyd Garrison Papers.

Boston, Mass. Massachusetts Historical Society. Edward Atkinson Papers.

Brunswick, Maine. Bowdoin College Library. Oliver Otis Howard Papers.

Cambridge, Mass. Houghton Library. Harvard University.
Thomas Wentworth Higginson Papers.

Chapel Hill, N.C. Southern Historical Collection, University of
North Carolina. Arthur Sumner Papers.

———. Martha Schofield Diary (typescript).

Ithaca, N.Y. Cornell University Library. American Freedmen's
Aid Commission Minute Book.

———. American Freedmen's Union Commission. Executive
Committee Minute Book, 31 January 1866–29 March 1869.

———. Emily Howland Papers.

———. Jacob R. Shipherd Letterbook, 13 February 1866–14 June
1866.

———. James Miller McKim Papers.

———. Lydia Maria Child Papers.

Madison, Wis. State Historical Society of Wisconsin. William F.
Allen Papers.

Nashville, Tenn. Fisk University Library. John Mercer Langston
Papers.

New Brunswick, N.J. Rutgers University Library. Isaac W.
Brinckerhoff Papers.

New Haven, Conn. Yale University Library. Amos Beman
Papers.
———. Rufus and S. Willard Saxton Papers.
New Orleans, La. Amistad Research Center. American Mis-
sionary Association Archives.
Newark, N.J. New Jersey Historical Society. Marcus L. Ward
Papers.
Rochester, N.Y. University of Rochester. William Channing
Gannett Papers.
Swarthmore, Pa. Friends Historical Library. Swarthmore Col-
lege. Friends Freedmen's Association Records.
———. Hancock Manuscripts.
———. Howland Family Papers.
Washington, D.C. Howard University Library. Robert G.
Fitzgerald Papers (microfilm).
Washington, D.C. Library of Congress. Andrew Johnson Papers.
———. George A. Trenholm Papers.
———. J. Milton and Esther Hawks Papers.
———. Nathaniel P. Banks Papers.
———. Salmon P. Chase Papers.
Washington, D.C. National Archives. Navy and Old Army Rec-
ords Division. Record Group 105. "Records of the Bureau of
Refugees, Freedmen, and Abandoned Lands."

Bureau records are divided into several series. In the notes,
"Bureau Records" not followed by the name of a division or
office refers to records kept for Commissioner O. O. Howard in
the Office of the Assistant Adjutant General of the Freedmen's
Bureau. Records of assistant commissioners for the states are
designated as such. "Bureau Records, Education Division" not
followed by the name of a state refers to the files in the office of
General Superintendent John W. Alvord. When followed by the
name of a state, this designates the files of individual assistant
superintendents of education.

Printed Records, Reports, and Minutes

Alvord, John Watson. *Letters from the South Relating to the
Condition of the Freedmen. Addressed to Major General O. O.
Howard, Commissioner, Bureau R., F., and A.L.* . . . Washing-
ton, D.C.: Howard University Press, 1870.
———. *Semi-Annual Reports on Schools for Freedmen, 1866–*

1870. Washington, D.C.: Government Printing Office, 1868–1870.

American Anti-Slavery Society. *Fourth Annual Report*... New York: American Anti-Slavery Society, 1837.

American Baptist Home Mission Society. *Thirty-Fifth Annual Report*... New York: American Baptist Home Mission Rooms, 1867.

American Tract Society (Boston). *Annual Reports, 1860–1870*. Boston: American Tract Society, 1860–1870.

——— (New England Branch). *Annual Reports, 1860–1869*. Boston: American Tract Society, New England Branch, 1860–1869.

——— (New York). *Annual Reports, 1860–1870*. New York: American Tract Society, 1860–1870.

Bell, Howard Holman, ed. *Minutes of the Proceedings of the National Negro Conventions, 1830–1864*. New York: Arno Press and the New York Times, 1969.

Boston Educational Commission for Freedmen. *First Annual Report..., 1863*. Boston: Boston Educational Commission for Freedmen, 1863.

Colyer, Vincent. *Brief Report of the Services Rendered by the Freed People to the United States Army in North Carolina in the Spring of 1862, after the Battle of Newbern*. New York: by the author, 1864.

Eaton, John. *Extracts from Documents, Office of the General Superintendent of Refugees and Freedmen*. Memphis: Freedmen's Press, 1865.

———. *Report of the General Superintendent of Freedmen Department of the Tennessee and the State of Arkansas*. Memphis: published by permission of the U.S. Army, 1865.

Freedmen's Aid Society of the Methodist Episcopal Church. *Third Annual Report*. Cincinnati: Western Methodist Book Concern, 1869.

Friends' Association of Philadelphia and Its Vicinity for the Relief of Colored Freedmen. *Statistics of the Operations of the Executive Board..., as Presented to a Public Meeting of Friends...1st Month 19, 1864, Together with the Report of Samuel R. Shipley, President of the Board, of His Visit to the Camps of the Freedmen on the Mississippi River*. Philadelphia: Inquirer Printing Office, [1864].

Hanckel, J. Stuart. *Report on the Colored People and Freedmen of South Carolina*. Charleston: n.p., 1866.

James, Horace. *Annual Report of the Superintendent of Negro Affairs in North Carolina, 1864*. Boston: W. F. Brown & Co., [1865].

Journal of the Proceedings of the Constitutional Convention of the People of Georgia, Held in the City of Atlanta in the Months of December, 1867, and January, February and March 1868. Augusta, Ga.: published by order of the convention, 1868.

Louisiana, Constitutional Convention, 1864. *Official Journal of the Convention for the Revision and Amendment of the Constitution of the State of Louisiana*. New Orleans: W. R. Fish, printer to the convention, 1864.

Minutes and Proceedings of the First Annual Convention of the People of Colour. Philadelphia: published by order of the Committee of Arrangements, 1831.

Minutes of the Convention of Freedmen's Commissions, Held at Indianapolis, Indiana, July 19 and 20, 1864. Cincinnati: Methodist Book Concern, 1864.

Minutes of the National Convention of Colored Citizens: Held at Buffalo . . . August, 1843 . . . New York: Piercy & Reed, Printers, 1843.

Minutes of the Proceedings of the Third Convention of Delegates from the Abolition Societies Established in Different Parts of the United States, Assembled at Philadelphia, on the First Day of January, One Thousand Seven Hundred and Ninety Six, and Continued, by Adjournments, until the Seventh Day of the Same Month, Inclusive. Philadelphia: printed by Zachariah Poulson, Jr., 1796.

Minutes of the State Convention of Colored Citizens, Held at Albany, on the 18th, 19th, and 20th of August, 1840, for the Purpose of Considering Their Political Condition. New York: Piercy & Reed, Printers, 1840.

New England Freedmen's Aid Society. *Second Annual Report . . .* Boston: published by the society, 1864.

North Carolina. *Public Laws of the State of North Carolina, Passed by the General Assembly at the Sessions of 1866, 67*. Raleigh: William E. Pell, state printer, 1867.

Presbyterian Church. *The Report of the Eastern Committee for the Education of the Freedmen* ... Philadelphia: published by the committee, 1865.

Presbyterian Church. General Assembly's Committee on Freedmen. *Annual Reports,* 1866–70. Pittsburgh: published by the committee, 1866–70.

Proceedings of the Colored National Convention, Held in ... *Philadelphia October 16th, 17th and 18th, 1855.* Salem, N.J.: printed at the National Standard Office, 1856.

Proceedings of the Colored National Convention, Held in Rochester, July 6th, 7th and 8th, 1853. Rochester, N.Y.: printed at the office of Frederick Douglass' Paper, 1853.

Proceedings of the Colored National Labor Convention Held in Washington, D.C., on December 6th, 7th, 8th, 9th, and 10th, 1869. Washington, D.C.: printed at the office of the New Era, 1870.

Proceedings of the Colored People's Convention of the State of South Carolina, Held in Zion Church, Charleston, November, 1865. Together with the Declaration of Rights and Wrongs, an Address to the People, a Petition to the Legislature, and a Memorial to Congress. Charleston: n.p., 1865.

Proceedings of the Conference for Education in the South. The Sixth Session. New York: Committee on Publication, 1903.

Proceedings of the Conference for Education in the South. The Seventh Session. New York: issued by the Committee on Publication, 1904.

Proceedings of the Constitutional Convention of South Carolina, Held at Charleston, S.C., Beginning January 14th and Ending March 17th, 1868. 2 vols. in 1. Charleston: printed for the convention by Denny & Perry, 1868.

Proceedings of the National Convention of Colored Men, Held in ... *Syracuse, N.Y., October 4, 5, 6, and 7, 1864* ... Boston: J. S. Rock & Geo. L. Ruffin, 1864.

Proceedings of the National Convention of Colored People, and Their Friends, Held in Troy, N.Y., on the 6th, 7th, 8th and 9th October, 1847. Troy, N.Y.: J. C. Kneeland & Co., 1847.

Report of the Proceedings of a Meeting Held at Concert Hall, Philadelphia, on Tuesday Evening, November 3,·1863 To Take into Consideration the Condition of the Freed People of the South. Philadelphia: Merrihew & Thompson, Printers, 1863.

Report of the Proceedings of the Colored National Convention,

Held at Cleveland, Ohio on Wednesday, September 6, 1848. Rochester, N.Y.: printed by John Dick, 1848.

U.S., Army, Department of the Gulf, Board of Education for Freedmen. *Report...for the Year 1864.* New Orleans: U.S. Army, 1865.

U.S., Congress. *The Ku Klux Conspiracy: Report of the Joint Select Committee Appointed to Inquire into the Condition of Affairs in the Late Insurrectionary States, so far as Regards the Execution of the Laws, and the Safety of the Lives and Property of the Citizens of the United States and Testimony Taken.* 13 vols. Washington, D.C.: Government Printing Office, 1872.

U.S., Congress. *Report of the Joint Committee on Reconstruction.* 39th Cong., 1st sess., 1866.

U.S. Education Office. *Special Report of the Commissioner of Education on the Condition and Improvement of Public Schools in the District of Columbia.* Washington, D.C.: Government Printing Office, 1871.

War of the Rebellion: A Compilation of the Official Records of the Union and Confederate Armies. 130 vols. Washington, D.C.: Government Printing Office, 1880–1901.

Western Freedmen's Aid Commission. *Second Annual Report...1865.* Cincinnati: Western Freedmen's Aid Commission, 1865.

Yeatman, James E. *A Report on the Condition of the Freedmen of the Mississippi...* St. Louis: Western Sanitary Commission, 1864.

Books and Pamphlets

Abbott, Lyman. *Reminiscences.* Boston: Houghton Mifflin Co., 1915.

American Freedmen's Union Commission. *The Results of Emancipation in the United States of America.* New York: American Freedmen's Union Commission, 1867.

American Union Commission. *The American Union Commission: Its Origin, Operations and Purposes.* New York: Sanford, Harroun & Co., 1865.

Ames, Mary. *From a New England Woman's Diary in Dixie in 1865.* Springfield, Mass.: Plimpton Press, 1906.

Andrews, Sidney. *The South since the War.* Boston: Ticknor & Fields, 1866.

Avary, Myrta Lockett. *Dixie after the War.* New York: Doubleday, Page & Co., 1906.

Barnes, Gilbert H., and Dumond, Dwight L., eds. *Letters of Theodore Dwight Weld, Angelina Grimké Weld, and Sarah Grimké, 1822–1844.* 2 vols. New York: D. Appleton-Century Co., 1934.

Birch, Thomas E. *Virginian Orator.* Lexington, Ky.: William Gibbes Hunt, 1823.

Boynton, Charles B. *The Duty Which the Colored People Owe to Themselves: A Sermon Delivered at Metzerott Hall, Washington, D.C., November 17, 1867.* Washington, D.C.: printed at the office of the Great Republic, n.d.

Brinckerhoff, Isaac W. *Advice to Freedmen.* New York: American Tract Society, [186–].

————. *Advice to Freedmen.* 2d ed. rev. New York: American Tract Society, [186–].

Brown, Helen E. *John Freeman and His Family.* The Freedman's Library, no. 1. Boston: American Tract Society [1864].

Brown, William Wells. *The Rising Son; or the Antecedents and Advancement of the Colored Race.* Boston: A. G. Brown & Co., 1874. Reprint ed. Miami: Mnemosyne Publishing, 1969.

Chase, Lucy and Chase, Sarah. *Dear Ones at Home: Letters from Contraband Camps.* Edited by Henry L. Swint. Nashville: Vanderbilt University Press, 1966.

Child, Lydia Maria. *An Appeal in Favor of That Class of Americans Called Africans.* New York: John S. Taylor, 1836.

————. *The Right Way the Safe Way.* New York: by the author, 1862.

Child, Lydia Maria, ed. *The Freedmen's Book.* Boston: Ticknor & Fields, 1865.

Clark, Stephen W. *First Lessons of English Grammar.* New York: A. S. Barnes & Co., 1868.

Coffin, Levi. *Reminiscences of Levi Coffin, the Reputed President of the Underground Railroad . . .* Cincinnnati: Western Tract Society, 1876.

Cromwell, John W. *Address on the Difficulties of the Colored Youth in Obtaining an Education in the Virginias, before the*

Colored Educational Convention Held at Richmond, Va. August 23d, 1875. Philadelphia: G. T. Stockdale, Printer, [187–].

————. *The Negro in American History: Men and Women Eminent in the Evolution of the American of African Descent.* Washington, D.C.: American Negro Academy, 1914.

Delany, Martin R. *The Condition, Elevation, Emigration, and Destiny of the Colored People of the United States.* Philadelphia: printed by King & Baird, 1852.

Eaton, John. *Grant, Lincoln and the Freedmen: Reminiscences of the Civil War with Special Reference to the Work for the Contrabands and Freedmen of the Mississippi Valley.* New York: Longmans, Green, & Co., 1907.

Emancipation League, The. *Facts Concerning the Freedmen: Their Capacity and Destiny.* Boston: by the league, 1863.

Fee, John G. *Autobiography of John G. Fee.* Chicago: National Christian Association, 1891.

Finney, Charles Grandison. *Memoirs of Charles G. Finney Written by Himself.* New York: A. S. Barnes & Co., 1876.

Fisk, Clinton B. *Plain Counsels for Freedmen: In Sixteen Brief Lectures.* Boston: American Tract Society, 1866.

Forten, Charlotte L. *The Journal of Charlotte L. Forten, A Free Negro in the Slave Era.* Edited by Ray Allen Billington. New York: Collier Books, 1961.

Foster, John O. *Our Standard Bearer: Life Sketches and Speeches of Gen. Clinton B. Fisk.* Chicago: Woman's Temperance Publication Association, 1888.

Gibbs, Mifflin W. *Shadow and Light: An Autobiography with Reminiscences of the Last and Present Century.* Washington, D.C.: n.p., 1902.

Goodrich, Samuel Griswold. *A Pictorial History of the United States.* New York: F. J. Huntington & Macon & Law, 1852.

Grant, Ulysses S. *Personal Memoirs of U. S. Grant.* 2 vols. New York: C. L. Webster & Co., 1885.

Hancock, Cornelia. *South after Gettysburg: Letters of Cornelia Hancock from the Army of the Potomac, 1863–1865.* Edited by Henrietta Stratton Jaquette. Philadelphia: University of Pennsylvania Press, 1937.

Harris, James H. *Speech of Hon. James H. Harris on the Military Bill, Delivered Monday, January 17, 1870.* n.p.: by the author, n.d.

Haviland, Laura S. *A Woman's Life Work: Labors and Experi ences of Laura S. Haviland.* Cincinnati: Walden & Stowe, 1881.

Hepworth, George H. *The Whip, Hoe, and Sword; or, the Gulf-Department in '63.* Boston: Walker, Wise, & Co., 1864.

Higginson, Thomas Wentworth. *Army Life in a Black Regiment.* Boston: Fields, Osgood, & Co., 1870.

History of the American Missionary Association: Its Churches and Educational Institutions among the Freedmen, Indians, and Chinese. With Illustrative Facts and Anecdotes. New York: S. W. Green, printer, 1874.

Hitchcock, Henry. *Marching with Sherman: Passages from the Letters and Diaries of Henry Hitchcock; Major and Assistant Adjutant General of Volunteers, November 1864–May 1865.* Edited by M. A. DeWolfe Howe. New Haven: Yale University Press, 1927.

Holley, Sallie. *A Life for Liberty: Anti-Slavery and Other Letters of Sallie Holley.* Edited by John White Chadwick. New York: G. P. Putnam's Sons, 1899.

Holloway, Laura C. *Howard: The Christian Hero.* New York: Funk & Wagnalls, 1885.

Hopkins, Alphonso A. *The Life of Clinton Bowen Fisk.* New York: Funk & Wagnalls, 1888.

Howard, Oliver Otis. *Autobiography of Oliver Otis Howard, Major General United States Army.* 2 vols. New York: Baker & Taylor, 1907.

Ingraham, Joseph H. *The Sunny South.* Philadelphia: G. G. Evans, 1860.

Jacobs, Harriet [Linda Brent]. *Incidents in the Life of a Slave Girl Written by Herself.* Edited by Lydia Maria Child. Boston: published for the author, 1861.

Jay, William. *Letter to the American Tract Society . . . February 14, 1853.* n.p., [1853].

King, Edward. *The Great South.* Hartford: American Publishing Co., 1875.

Langston, John Mercer. *Freedom and Citizenship.* Washington, D.C.: Rufus H. Darby, 1883.

———. *From a Virginia Plantation to the National Capital.* Hartford: American Publishing Co., 1894.

Lincoln, Abraham. *The Collected Works of Abraham Lincoln.*

Edited by Roy P. Basler. 9 vols. New Brunswick, N.J.: Rutgers University Press, 1953–55.

Lockwood, Lewis C. *Mary S. Peake: The Colored Teacher at Fortress Monroe*. Boston: American Tract Society, [1863].

Lynch, John R. *The Facts of Reconstruction*. New York: Neale Publishing Co., 1913.

McKim, James Miller. *The Freedmen of South Carolina: An Address Delivered by J. Miller McKim in Sansom Hall, July 9th, 1862*. Philadelphia: Ellis P. Hazard, 1862.

Macrae, David. *The Americans at Home: Pen-and-Ink Sketches of American Men, Manners and Institutions*. 2 vols. Edinburgh: Edmonston & Douglas, 1870.

Memorial Services: Tribute to the Hon. Charles Sumner, Held in St. Phillip's A.M.E. Church, Savannah, Georgia March 18th 1874. Savannah: D. G. Patton, 1874.

The Nation Still in Danger; or, Ten Years after the War: A Plea by the American Missionary Association with Confirmatory Articles by Rev. T. D. Woolsey, D.D., LL.D., Hon. Frederick Douglass, Rev. Washington Gladden, Gov. D. H. Chamberlain, and Hon. J. P. Hawley. [New York]: American Missionary Association, 1875.

National Freedmen's Relief Association Organized in the City of New York on 22nd of February 1862. New York: National Freedmen's Relief Association, 1862.

New England Freedmen's Aid Society. *Extracts from Letters of Teachers and Superintendents of the New England Educational Commission for Freedmen*. 4th ser., 1 January 1864. Boston: David Clapp, printer, 1864.

Payne, Daniel Alexander. *A History of the African Methodist Episcopal Church*. Nashville, Tenn.: A.M.E. Sunday School Union, 1891.

———. *Recollections of Seventy Years*. Compiled and arranged by Sarah C. Bierce Scarborough, edited by Rev. C. S. Smith. Nashville: Publishing House of the A.M.E. Sunday School Union, 1888.

———. *The Semi-Centenary and the Retrospection of the African Meth. Episcopal Church in the United States of America*. Baltimore: Sherwood & Co., 1866.

Pearson, Elizabeth Ware, ed. *Letters from Port Royal, Written at the Time of the Civil War*. Boston: W. B. Clarke Co., 1906.

Perry, Rufus L. *The Cushite, or the Descendants of Ham.* Springfield, Mass.: Willey & Co., 1893.

Porter, Anthony Toomer. *The History of a Work of Faith and Love in Charleston, South Carolina.* New York: D. Appleton & Co., 1881.

———. *Led On ! Step by Step: Scenes from Clerical, Military, Educational and Plantation Life in the South, 1828–1898.* New York: G. P. Putnam's Sons, 1898.

Public Ceremonies in Connection with the War Memorials of the Washington Light Infantry. Charleston: Edward Perry & Co., 1894.

Redpath, James, ed. *A Guide to Hayti.* Boston: Haytian Bureau of Emigration, 1861.

Reid, Whitelaw. *After the War: A Southern Tour, May 1, 1865 to May 1, 1866.* Cincinnati: Moore, Wilstach & Baldwin, 1866.

Simms, William Gilmore. *The History of South Carolina from Its First European Discovery to Its Erection into a Republic; with a Supplementary Book, Bringing the Narrative down to the Present Time.* New and rev. ed. New York: Redfield, 1860.

Sinclair, William A. *The Aftermath of Slavery: A Study of the Condition and Environment of the American Negro.* Boston: Small, Maynard & Co., 1905.

Slaughter, Linda Warfel. *The Freedmen of the South.* Cincinnati: Elm Street Printing Co., 1869.

Smith, James L. *Autobiography of James L. Smith.* Norwich, Conn.: Press of the Bulletin Co., 1882.

The Southern Reader and Speaker. Charleston: W. R. Babcock Co., 1850.

Stanly, Edward. *A Military Governor among Abolitionists: A Letter from Edward Stanly to Charles Sumner.* New York: n.p., 1865.

Stanton, Elizabeth Cady. *Elizabeth Cady Stanton, as Revealed in Her Letters, Diary and Reminiscences.* Edited by Theodore Stanton and Harriott Stanton Blatch. 2 vols. New York: Harper & Bros., [1922].

The Tables Turned: A Letter to the Congregational Association of New York, Reviewing the Report of Their Committee on "The Relation of the American Tract Society to the Subject of Slavery." Boston: Crocker & Brewster, New York: Edward P. Rudd, [1855].

Taylor, Susie King. *Reminiscences of My Life in Camp with the 33rd United States Colored Troops....* Boston: by the author, 1902.

Tourgée, Albion W. *Bricks without Straw.* New York: Fords, Howard & Hulbert, 1880.

Towne, Laura M. *Letters and Diary of Laura M. Towne, Written from the Sea Islands of South Carolina, 1862–1884.* Edited by Rupert S. Holland. Cambridge, Mass.: Riverside Press, 1912.

Wallace, John. *Carpet-Bag Rule in Florida.* Jacksonville: Da Casta Printing & Publishing House, 1888.

[Warren, Israel P.] *The Freedman's Spelling-Book.* Boston: American Tract Society, [1866].

————. *The Freedman's Third Reader.* Boston: American Tract Society, 1866.

Waterbury, Jared Bell. *Friendly Counsels for Freedmen.* New York: American Tract Society, [186–].

————. *Southern Planters and the Freedmen.* New York: American Tract Society, [186–].

Wheelock, Edwin Miller. *Harper's Ferry and Its Lesson: A Sermon for the Times.* Boston: by the fraternity, 1859.

Wiley, Calvin H. *The North Carolina Reader: Containing a History and Description of North Carolina, Selections in Prose and Verse, Historical and Chronological Tables and a Variety of Miscellaneous Information and Statistics.* Philadelphia: Lippincott, Grambo & Co., 1851.

Willson, Marcius. *History of the United States.* New Haven: Durie & Peck, 1832.

Woman's Work for the Lowly, As Illustrated in the Work of the American Missionary Association among the Freedmen. Boston: South Boston Inquirer Press, 1873.

Woolson, Constance Fenimore. *Rodman the Keeper: Southern Sketches.* New York: D. Appleton & Co., 1880.

Zachos, John Celivergos. *The Phonic Primer and Reader: A Rational Method of Teaching Reading by the Sounds of the Letters without Altering the Orthography.* Boston: John Wilson & Son, 1864.

Articles

Abbott, Lyman. "The South and Education." *Outlook,* 27 July 1907, pp. 634–39.

Armstrong, Samuel C. "The Founding of the Hampton Institute." *Old South Leaflets*, General Series, vol. 6, no. 149. Boston: Directors of the Old South Work, 1904.

Atkinson, Edward. "The Reign of King Cotton." *Atlantic Monthly*, April 1861, pp. 451–65.

Carlyle, Thomas. "Occasional Discourse on the Negro Question." *Fraser's Magazine*, December 1849, pp. 670–79.

Chesnutt, Charles W. "The March of Progress." *Century Magazine*, January 1901, pp. 422–28.

DeForest, John W. "The Man and Brother." *Atlantic Monthly*, October 1868, pp. 414–25.

"Education of the Colored Population of Louisiana." *Harper's Magazine*, July 1866, p. 246.

[Forten, Charlotte]. "Life on the Sea Islands." *Atlantic Monthly*, May 1864, pp. 587–96, and June 1864, pp. 666–76.

[Gannett, William Channing, and Hale, Edward Everett]. "The Education of the Freedmen." *North American Review*, October 1865, pp. 528–49.

———. "The Freedmen at Port Royal." *North American Review*, July 1865, pp. 1–28.

Hooper, William R. "The Freedmen's Bureau." *Lippincott's Magazine*, June 1871, pp. 609–16.

Pierce, Edward L. "The Contrabands at Fortress Monroe." *Atlantic Monthly*, November 1861, pp. 626–40.

———. "The Freedmen at Port Royal." *Atlantic Monthly*, September 1863, pp. 291–315.

Rice, Elizabeth G. "A Yankee Teacher in the South. An Experience in the Early Days of Reconstruction." *Century Magazine*, May 1901, pp. 151–52.

"The South As It Is." *Nation*, December 1865, pp. 779–80.

Stowe, Harriet Beecher. "The Education of the Freedmen." *North American Review*, June 1879, pp. 605–15.

Thorpe, Margaret Newbold. "Life in Virginia: By a 'Yankee Teacher,' Margaret Newbold Thorpe." Edited by Richard L. Morton. *Virginia Magazine of History and Biography* 65 (April 1956): 180–207.

———. "A 'Yankee Teacher' in North Carolina." Edited by Richard L. Morton. *North Carolina Historical Review* 30 (October 1953): 564–82.

Walker, Susan. "The Journal of Miss Susan Walker, March 3rd

to June 6th, 1862." Edited by Henry Noble Sherwood. *Quarterly Publication of the Historical and Philosophical Society of Ohio* 7 (January–March 1912): 1–48.

Wheelock, Edwin Miller. "The Psyche—A Study in Evolution." *Open Court*, September 1920, pp. 570–76.

Newspapers and Periodicals

American Freedman, 1866–1869. Monthly organ of the American Freedmen's Union Commission.

American Missionary, 1846–1900. Monthly organ of the American Missionary Association.

Boston Commonwealth, 1864–1865.

Boston Recorder, 1866.

Boston Transcript, 1862.

Christian Recorder, 1864.

DeBow's Review, 1846–1864, 1866–1870, 1879–1880.

Freedman's Torchlight, December 1866.

Freedmen's Record, 1865–1873.

Home Evangelist, 1863–66.

Liberator, *1831*–1865.

National Anti-Slavery Standard, 1862–1865.

National Freedman, 1865–1866. Monthly organ of the National Freedmen's Relief Association.

New York Times, 1862–1870.

Pennsylvania Freedman's Bulletin, 1865–1867.

Secondary Sources
Books and Pamphlets

Abbott, Martin. *The Freedmen's Bureau in South Carolina, 1865–1872.* Chapel Hill: University of North Carolina Press, 1967.

Adams, Myron W. *A History of Atlanta University, 1865–1929.* Atlanta: Atlanta University Press, 1930.

Bacote, Clarence A. *The Story of Atlanta University.* Atlanta: Atlanta University Press, 1969.

Barnes, Gilbert H. *The Antislavery Impulse, 1830–1844.* New York: American Historical Association, 1933. Reprint ed. Gloucester, Mass.: Peter Smith, 1957.

Beard, Augustus Field. *A Crusade of Brotherhood: A History of the American Missionary Association*. Boston: Pilgrim Press, 1909.

Bentley, George R. *A History of the Freedmen's Bureau*. Philadelphia: University of Pennsylvania Press, 1955.

Blassingame, John W. *Black New Orleans, 1860–1880*. Chicago: University of Chicago Press, 1973.

Brown, Hugh Victor. *A History of the Education of Negroes in North Carolina*. Goldsboro, N.C.: Irving Swain Press, 1961.

Brown, Ira V. *Lyman Abbott, Christian Evolutionist: A Study in Religious Liberalism*. Cambridge: Harvard University Press, 1967.

Bullock, Henry Allen. *A History of Negro Education in the South from 1619 to the Present*. Cambridge: Harvard University Press, 1967.

Carpenter, John A. *Sword and Olive Branch: Oliver Otis Howard*. Pittsburgh: University of Pittsburgh Press, 1964.

Cash, Wilbur J. *The Mind of the South*. New York: Alfred A. Knopf, 1941. Random House, Vintage Books, 1960.

Coan, Josephus Roosevelt. *Daniel Alexander Payne, Christian Educator*. Philadelphia: A.M.E. Book Concern, 1935.

Conway, Alan. *The Reconstruction of Georgia*. Minneapolis: University of Minnesota Press, 1966.

Cornish, Dudley Taylor. *The Sable Arm: Negro Troops in the Union Army, 1861–1865*. New York: Longmans, Green & Co., 1956.

Coulter, E. Merton. *The South during Reconstruction, 1865–1877*. A History of the South, vol. 8. Baton Rouge: Louisiana State University Press, 1947.

Dabney, Lillian G. *The History of Schools for Negroes in the District of Columbia, 1807–1947*. Washington, D.C.: Catholic University of America Press, 1949.

Davis, William Watson. *The Civil War and Reconstruction in Florida*. Gainesville: University of Florida, 1964.

Du Bois, W. E. Burghardt. *Black Reconstruction in America: An Essay toward a History of the Part Which Black Folk Played in the Attempt to Reconstruct Democracy in America, 1860–1880*. New York: Harcourt, Brace & Co., 1935. Cleveland: World Publishing Co., Meridian Books, 1962.

Emilio, Luis F. *History of the Fifty-Fourth Regiment of Mas-*

sachusetts Volunteer Infantry, 1863–1865. Boston: Boston Book Co., 1894.

Fehrenbacher, Don E., ed. *The Leadership of Abraham Lincoln.* Wiley Problems in American History Series. New York: John Wiley & Sons, 1970.

Fletcher, Robert Samuel. *A History of Oberlin College.* 2 vols. Oberlin, Ohio: Oberlin College, 1943.

Fox, Stephen R. *The Guardian of Boston: William Monroe Trotter.* Studies in American Negro Life. New York: Atheneum, 1970.

Franklin, John Hope. *From Slavery to Freedom: A History of Negro Americans.* 3d ed., rev. and enlarged. New York: Alfred A. Knopf, 1967.

———. *Reconstruction: After the Civil War.* Chicago History of American Civilization. Chicago: University of Chicago Press, [1961].

Hamilton, J. G. de Roulhac. *Reconstruction in North Carolina.* Columbia University Studies in History, Economics and Public Law. New York: Columbia University, 1914.

Harlan, Louis R. *Booker T. Washington: The Making of a Black Leader, 1856–1901.* London: Oxford University Press, 1972.

———. *Separate and Unequal: Public School Campaigns and Racism in the Southern Seaboard States, 1901–1915.* Chapel Hill: University of North Carolina Press, 1958.

Harrington, Fred H. *Fighting Politician: Major General N. P. Banks.* Philadelphia: University of Pennsylvania Press, 1948.

Holmes, Dwight Oliver Wendell. *The Evolution of the Negro College.* New York: Teachers College, Columbia University, 1934.

Holt, Thomas. *Black over White: Negro Political Leadership in South Carolina during Reconstruction.* Urbana: University of Illinois Press, 1977.

Hundley, Mary Gibson. *The Dunbar Story, 1870–1955.* New York: Vantage Press, 1965.

Hyman, Harold M., ed. *The Radical Republicans and Reconstruction, 1861–1870.* Indianapolis: Bobbs-Merrill Co., 1967.

Jenkins, William S. *Pro-Slavery Thought in the Old South.* Chapel Hill: University of North Carolina Press, 1935.

Jordan, Winthrop D. *White over Black: American Attitudes toward the Negro, 1550–1812.* Chapel Hill: University of North

Carolina Press, 1968. Baltimore: Penguin Books, 1969.

Knight, Edgar W. *The Influence of Reconstruction on Education in the South*. New York: Teachers College, Columbia University, 1913.

Litwack, Leon F. *Been in the Storm So Long: The Aftermath of Slavery*. New York: Alfred A. Knopf, 1979.

————. *North of Slavery: The Negro in the Free States, 1790–1860*. Chicago: University of Chicago Press, 1961, Phoenix Books, 1965.

Logan, Frenise A. *The Negro in North Carolina, 1876–1894*. Chapel Hill: University of North Carolina Press, 1964.

Logan, Rayford W. *Howard University, 1867–1967*. New York: New York University Press, 1969.

Lutz, Alma. *Created Equal: A Biography of Elizabeth Cady Stanton, 1815–1902*. New York: John Day Co., 1940.

McFeely, William S. *Yankee Stepfather: General O. O. Howard and the Freedmen*. New Haven: Yale University Press, 1968.

McPherson, James M. *The Abolitionist Legacy, from Reconstruction to the NAACP*. Princeton: Princeton University Press, 1975.

————. *The Struggle for Equality: Abolitionists and the Negro in the Civil War and Reconstruction*. Princeton: Princeton University Press, 1964.

Mandel, Bernard. *Labor, Free and Slave: Workingmen and the Anti-Slavery Movement in the United States*. New York: Associated Authors, 1955.

Meier, August. *Negro Thought in America, 1880–1915: Racial Ideologies in the Age of Booker T. Washington*. Ann Arbor: University of Michigan Press, 1963.

Meier, August, and Rudwick, Elliott. *From Plantation to Ghetto: An Interpretive History of American Negroes*. American Century Series. New York: Hill & Wang, 1966.

Montgomery, David. *Beyond Equality: Labor and the Radical Republicans, 1862–1872*. New York: Alfred A. Knopf, 1967.

Morrow, Ralph E. *Northern Methodism and Reconstruction*. East Lansing: Michigan State University Press, 1956.

Murray, Pauli. *Proud Shoes: The Story of an American Family*. New York: Harper & Bros., 1956.

Noble, Stuart G. *Forty Years of the Public Schools in Mississippi*. New York: Teachers College, Columbia University, 1918.

Olsen, Otto H. *Carpetbagger's Crusade: The Life of Albion*

Winegar Tourgée. Baltimore: The Johns Hopkins Press, 1965.

Owen, Thomas McAdory. *History of Alabama and Dictionary of Alabama Biography.* 4 vols. Chicago: S. J. Clarke Publishing Co., 1921.

Peirce, Paul S. *The Freedmen's Bureau, A Chapter in the History of Reconstruction.* State University of Iowa Studies in Sociology, Economics, Politics, and History, vol. 3, no. 1. Iowa City: University of Iowa, 1904.

Perdue, Robert E. *The Negro in Savannah, 1865–1900.* New York: Exposition Press, 1973.

Ponton, Mungo M. *Life and Times of Henry M. Turner.* Atlanta: A. B. Caldwell Pub. Co., 1917.

Quarles, Benjamin. *Black Abolitionists.* London: Oxford University Press, 1969.

Quick, William Harvey. *Negro Stars in All Ages of the World.* 2d ed. Richmond, Va.: S. B. Adkins & Co., 1898.

Rabinowitz, Howard N. *Race Relations in the Urban South, 1865–1890.* The Urban Life in America Series. New York: Oxford University Press, 1978.

Reynolds, John S. *Reconstruction in South Carolina.* Columbia, S.C.: State Co., 1905.

Richardson, Joe M. *The Negro in the Reconstruction of Florida, 1865–1877.* Florida State University Studies, no. 46. Tallahassee: Florida State University, 1965.

Ripley, C. Peter. *Slaves and Freedmen in Civil War Louisiana.* Baton Rouge: Louisiana State University Press, [1976].

Rose, Willie Lee. *Rehearsal for Reconstruction: The Port Royal Experiment.* Indianapolis: Bobbs-Merrill Co., 1964. New York: Random House, Vintage Books, 1967.

Rust, Richard S., ed. *Isaac W. Wiley, Late Bishop of the M.E. Church.* Cincinnati: Cranston & Stowe. New York: Phillips & Hunt, 1885.

Schukers, Jacob W. *The Life and Public Services of Salmon Portland Chase.* New York: D. Appleton & Co., 1874.

Simkins, Francis Butler, and Woody, Robert Hilliard. *South Carolina during Reconstruction.* Chapel Hill: University of North Carolina Press, 1932.

Simmons, William J. *Men of Mark: Eminent, Progressive and Rising.* Cleveland: Geo. M. Rewell & Co., 1887.

Spero, Sterling D., and Harris, Abram L. *The Black Worker: The*

Negro and the Labor Movement. Studies in American Negro Life. New York: Columbia University Press, 1931. Atheneum, 1968.

Stanton, Elizabeth Cady; Anthony, Susan B.; and Gage, M. J., eds. *History of Woman Suffrage*. 6 vols. New York: Fowler & Wells, 1881–[1922].

Stanton, William R. *The Leopard's Spots: Scientific Attitudes toward Race in America, 1815–1859*. Chicago: University of Chicago Press, 1960.

Staples, Thomas S. *Reconstruction in Arkansas, 1872–1874*. New York: Columbia University, 1923.

Still, William. *The Underground Railroad*. Philadelphia: Porter & Coates, 1872.

Swint, Henry L. *The Northern Teacher in the South, 1862–1870*. Nashville: Vanderbilt University Press, 1941.

Taylor, Alrutheus Ambush. *The Negro in the Reconstruction of Virginia*. Washington, D.C.: Association for the Study of Negro Life and History, 1926.

Thomas, Benjamin P., and Hyman, Harold M. *Stanton: The Life and Times of Lincoln's Secretary of War*. New York: Alfred A. Knopf, 1962.

Tindall, George B. *South Carolina Negroes, 1877–1900*. Columbia: University of South Carolina Press, 1952. Reprint ed., Baton Rouge: Louisiana State University Press, 1966.

Trefousse, Hans L. *The Radical Republicans: Lincoln's Vanguard for Racial Justice*. New York: Alfred A. Knopf, 1969.

Vaughn, William Preston. *Schools for All: The Blacks and Public Education in the South, 1865–1877*. Lexington, Ky.: University Press of Kentucky, 1974.

Voegeli, V. Jacque. *Free but Not Equal: The Midwest and the Negro during the Civil War*. Chicago: University of Chicago Press, 1967.

Warner, Robert A. *New Haven Negroes: A Social History*. New Haven: Yale University Press for the Institute of Human Relations, 1940.

Webster, Laura Josephine. *The Operation of the Freedmen's Bureau in South Carolina*. Smith College Studies in History, vol. 1. Northamton, Mass.: Smith College Department of History, 1916.

Wesley, Charles H. *Negro Labor in the United States, 1850–*

1925; A Study in American Economic History. New York: Russell & Russell, 1927.

Wharton, Vernon Lane. *The Negro in Mississippi, 1865–1890.* Chapel Hill: University of North Carolina, 1947. Reprint ed. New York: Harper & Row, 1965.

White, Howard A. *The Freedmen's Bureau in Louisiana.* Baton Rouge: Louisiana State University Press, [1970].

Wikramanayake, Marina. *A World in Shadow: The Free Black in Antebellum South Carolina.* Columbia: University of South Carolina Press, 1973.

Williams, George Washington. *A History of the Negro Troops in the War of the Rebellion, 1861–1865.* New York: Harper & Brothers, 1888.

Williamson, Harold F. *Edward Atkinson: The Biography of an American Liberal, 1827–1905.* Boston: Old Corner Book Store, 1934.

Williamson, Joel. *After Slavery: The Negro in South Carolina during Reconstruction, 1861–1877.* Chapel Hill: University of North Carolina Press, 1965.

Woodson, Carter G. *The Education of the Negro Prior to 1861.* 2d ed. Washington, D.C.: Associated Publishers, 1919.

————. *The History of the Negro Church.* Washington, D.C.: Associated Publishers, 1921.

Wynes, Charles E. *Race Relations in Virginia, 1870–1902.* Charlottesville: University of Virginia Press, 1961.

Articles

Alderson, William T. "The Freedmen's Bureau and Negro Education in Virginia." *North Carolina Historical Review* 29 (January 1952): 64–90.

Alexander, Roberta Sue. "Hostility and Hope: Black Education in North Carolina during Presidential Reconstruction, 1865–1867." *North Carolina Historical Review* 53 (April 1976): 113–32.

Aptheker, Herbert. "South Carolina Negro Conventions, 1865." *Journal of Negro History* 31 (January 1946): 91–97.

Armstrong, Warren B. "Union Chaplains and the Education of the Freedmen." *Journal of Negro History* 52 (April 1967): 108–15.

Bell, John L., Jr. "Baptists and the Negro in North Carolina during Reconstruction." *North Carolina Historical Review* 42 (October 1965): 391–409.

————. "The Presbyterian Church and the Negro in North Carolina during Reconstruction." *North Carolina Historical Review* 40 (January 1963): 15–36.

Bethel, Elizabeth. "The Freedmen's Bureau in Alabama." *Journal of Southern History* 14 (February 1948): 49–92.

Birnie, C. W. "Education of the Negro in Charleston, South Carolina, Prior to the Civil War." *Journal of Negro History* 12 (January 1927): 13–21.

Blassingame, John. "The Union Army as an Educational Institution for Negroes, 1862–1865." *Journal of Negro Education* 34 (1965): 152–59.

Boromé, Joseph A. "The Vigilant Committee of Philadelphia." *Pennsylvania Magazine of History and Biography* 92 (July 1968): 320–31.

Boyd, Willis D. "James Redpath and American Negro Colonization in Haiti, 1860–1862." *The Americas* 12 (October 1955): 169–82.

Brown, Ira V. "Lyman Abbott and Freedmen's Aid, 1865–1867." *Journal of Southern History* 15 (February 1949): 22–38.

————. "Pennsylvania and the Rights of the Negro, 1865–1887." *Pennsylvania History* 28 (January 1961): 45–63.

Browning, James B. "The Beginnings of Insurance Enterprise among Negroes." *Journal of Negro History* 22 (October 1937): 417–32.

Cheek, William F. "John Mercer Langston: Black Protest Leader and Abolitionist." *Civil War History* 16 (June 1970): 101–20.

Coulter, E. Merton. "Henry M. Turner: Georgia Negro Preacher-Politician during the Reconstruction Era." *Georgia Historical Quarterly* 48 (December 1964): 371–410.

Cox, La Wanda. "The Promise of Land for the Freedmen." *Mississippi Valley Historical Review* 45 (December 1958): 413–40.

Daniel, W. Harrison. "Southern Protestantism and the Negro, 1860–1865." *North Carolina Historical Review* 41 (summer 1964): 338–59.

————. "Virginia Baptists and the Negro, 1865–1902." *Virginia Magazine of History and Biography* 87 (July 1868): 340–63.

Dodd, Dorothy. " 'Bishop' Pearce and the Reconstruction of Leon County." *Apalachee* (1946), pp. 5–12.

Doyle, Elizabeth J. "Nurseries of Treason: Schools in Occupied New Orleans." *Journal of Southern History* 26 (May 1960): 161–79.

Drake, Richard B. "Freedmen's Aid Societies and Sectional Compromise." *Journal of Southern History* 29 (May 1963): 175–86.

Fishel, Leslie H., Jr. "Northern Prejudice and Negro Suffrage, 1865–1870." *Journal of Negro History* 39 (January 1954): 175–86.

Franklin, John Hope. "Jim Crow Goes to School: The Genesis of Legal Segregation in Southern Schools." *South Atlantic Quarterly* 58 (spring 1959): 225–35.

Fuke, Richard Paul. "The Baltimore Association for the Moral and Educational Improvement of the Colored People, 1865–1870." *Maryland Historical Magazine* 66 (winter 1971): 369–404.

Harlan, Louis R. "Desegregation in New Orleans Public Schools during Reconstruction." *American Historical Review* 67 (April 1962): 663–75.

Hirsch, Leo H., Jr. "The Negro and New York, 1783 to 1865." *Journal of Negro History* 16 (October 1931): 423–73.

Hornsby, Alton, Jr. "The Freedmen's Bureau Schools in Texas, 1865–1870." *Southwestern Historical Quarterly* 76 (April 1973): 397–417.

Jackson, Luther P. "The Educational Efforts of the Freedmen's Bureau and Freedmen's Aid Societies in South Carolina, 1862–1872." *Journal of Negro History* 8 (January 1923): 1–40.

———. "The Origin of Hampton Institute." *Journal of Negro History* 10 (April 1925): 131–49.

Jaquette, Henrietta Stratton. "Friends' Association of Philadelphia for the Aid and Elevation of the Freedmen." *Bulletin of Friends Historical Association* 46 (autumn 1957): 67–83.

Johnson, Clifton H. "The American Missionary Association: A Short History," in *Our American Missionary Association Heritage*. New York: American Missionary Association, 1966.

Jones, Lewis W. "The Agent as a Factor in the Education of Negroes in the South." *Journal of Negro Education* 19 (winter 1950): 28–37.

Kassel, Charles. "Educating the Slave—A Forgotten Chapter of Civil War History." *Open Court*, April 1927, pp. 239–56.

————. "Edwin Miller Wheelock." *Open Court*, September 1920, pp. 564–69.

————. "Edwin Miller Wheelock: A Prophet of Civil War Times." *Open Court*, February 1922, pp. 116–24.

————. "Edwin Miller Wheelock and the Abolition Movement." *Open Court*, March 1923, pp. 167–75.

————. "The Herald of Emancipation: A Memory of Edwin Miller Wheelock." *Open Court*, April 1925, pp. 230–42.

————. "An Interpreter of Destiny: Edwin Miller Wheelock and the War between the States." *Open Court*, July 1924, pp. 406–18.

————. "A Knight-Errant in the Department of the Gulf: Episode in the Life of Edwin Miller Wheelock." *Open Court*, September 1925, pp. 563–76.

————. "The Labor System of General Banks—A Lost Episode in Civil War History." *Open Court*, January 1929, pp. 35–50.

Kelley, Alfred H. "The Congressional Controversy over School Segregation, 1867–1875." *American Historical Review* 64 (April 1959): 537–63.

Knight, Edgar W. "Reconstruction and Education in South Carolina." *South Atlantic Quarterly* 18 (October 1919): 350–64.

McPherson, James. "A Brief for Equality: The Abolitionist Reply to the Racist Myth, 1860–1865," in *The Antislavery Vanguard*, edited by Martin Duberman. Princeton: Princeton University Press, 1965.

Messner, William F. "Black Education in Louisiana, 1863–1865." *Civil War History* 22 (March 1976): 41–59.

Parmelee, Julius H. "Freedmen's Aid Societies, 1861–1871," in Thomas Jesse Jones, ed., *Negro Education: A Study of the Private and Higher Schools for Colored People in the United States.* United States Department of the Interior, Office of Education, Bulletin, 1916, no. 38. 2 vols. Washington, D.C.: Government Printing Office, 1917.

Pearce, Larry Wesley. "The American Missionary Association and the Freedmen in Arkansas, 1863–1878." *Arkansas Historical Quarterly* 30 (summer 1971): 123–44.

————. "The American Missionary Association and the Freedmen's Bureau in Arkansas, 1866–1868." *Arkansas Historical Quarterly* 30 (autumn 1971): 241–59.

————. "Enoch K. Miller and the Freedmen's Schools." *Arkansas Historical Quarterly* 31 (winter 1972): 305–27.

Pease, William H. "Three Years among the Freedmen: William C. Gannett and the Port Royal Experiment." *Journal of Negro History* 42 (April 1957): 98–117.

Pease, William H., and Pease, Jane H. "Antislavery Ambivalence: Immediatism, Expediency, Race." *American Quarterly* 17 (winter 1965): 682–95.

Perkins, Linda Marie. "Quaker Beneficence and Black Control: The Institute for Colored Youth, 1852–1903," in *New Perspectives in Black Educational History*. Edited by Vincent Franklin and James D. Anderson. Boston: G. K. Hall & Co., 1978.

Qualls, Youra, " 'Successors of Woolman and Benezet': The Beginnings of the Philadelphia Friends Freedmen's Association." *Bulletin of Friends Historical Association* 45 (1956): 82–104.

Riegel, Robert E. "The Split of the Feminist Movement in 1869." *Mississippi Valley Historical Review* 49 (December 1962): 485–96.

Sheeler, J. Reuben. "The Struggle of the Negro in Ohio for Freedom." *Journal of Negro History* 31 (April 1946): 208–26.

Sweat, Edward F. "Francis L. Cardoza—Profile of Integrity in Reconstruction Politics." *Journal of Negro History* 46 (October 1961): 217–32.

Swint, Henry Lee. "Northern Interest in the Shoeless Southerner." *Journal of Southern History* 16 (November 1950): 457–71.

Turnbull, L. Minerva. "The Southern Educational Revolt." *William and Mary Quarterly* 14 (January 1934): 60–75.

Vance, Joseph C. "Freedmen's Schools in Albemarle County during Reconstruction." *Virginia Magazine of History and Biography* 61 (October 1953): 430–38.

Warner, Robert A. "Amos Gerry Beman—1812–1874, A Memoir on a Forgotten Leader." *Journal of Negro History* 22 (April 1937): 200–21.

Wesley, Charles H. "The Participation of Negroes in Anti-Slavery Political Parties." *Journal of Negro History* 29 (January 1944): 32–74.

Woody, Robert Hilliard. "Jonathan Jasper Wright, Associate Justice of the Supreme Court of South Carolina, 1870–77." *Journal of Negro History* 18 (April 1933): 114–31.

Work, Monroe N. "The Life of Charles B. Ray." *Journal of Negro History* 4 (October 1919): 361–71.

Papers, Theses, and Dissertations

Alexander, Philip Wade. "John Eaton, Jr., Preacher, Soldier, and Educator." Ph.D. diss., George Peabody College for Teachers, 1940.

Bahney, Robert Stanley. "Generals and Negroes: Education of Negroes by the Union Army, 1861–1865." Ph.D. diss., University of Michigan, 1965.

Bell, Howard H. "A Survey of the Negro Convention Movement." Ph.D. diss., Northwestern University, 1953.

Breault, Judith Colucci. "The Odyssey of a Humanitarian: Emily Howland, 1827–1929. A Biographical Analysis." Ph.D. diss., University of Pennsylvania, 1974.

Butchart, Ronald Eugene. "Educating for Freedom: Northern Whites and the Origins of Black Education in the South, 1862–1875." Ph.D. diss., State University of New York at Binghamton, 1976.

Christler, Ethel M. "Participation of Negroes in the Georgia Legislature, 1867–70." M.A. thesis, Atlanta University, 1932.

Cohen, William. "James Miller McKim, Pennsylvania Abolitionist." Ph.D. diss., New York University, 1968.

De Boer, Clara Merritt. "The Role of Afro-Americans in the Origin and Work of the American Missionary Association: 1839–1877." Ph.D. diss., Rutgers University, 1973.

Drake, Richard B. "The American Missionary Association and the Southern Negro, 1861–1888." Ph.D. diss., Emory University, 1957.

Johnson, Clifton H. "The American Missionary Association, 1846–1861: A Study of Christian Abolitionism." Ph.D. diss., University of North Carolina, 1959.

Jones, Jacqueline. "The 'Great Opportunity': Northern Teachers and the Georgia Freedmen, 1865–73." Ph.D. diss., University of Wisconsin, 1976.

Morton, Richard L. "The Negro in Virginia Politics, 1865–1902." Ph.D. diss., University of Virginia, 1918.

Parker, Marjorie H. "The Educational Activities of the Freedmen's Bureau." Ph.D. diss., University of Chicago, 1951.

Patrick, Thomas Love. "Southern Criticism of Northern Educational Influence, 1820–1860." Ph.D. diss., University of North Carolina, 1950.

St. Clair, Sadie Daniel. "The National Career of Blanche Kelso Bruce." Ph.D. diss., New York University, 1947.

Smedley, Katherine. "The Northern Teacher on the South Carolina Sea Islands." M.A. thesis, University of North Carolina, 1932.

Twaddell, Elizabeth. "The American Tract Society, 1814–1860: A Study of Institutional Development." Term paper, University of Wisconsin, 1945. A copy of this paper is found in the library of the American Tract Society, Oradell, N.J.

White, Howard Ashley. "The Freedmen's Bureau in Louisiana." Ph.D. diss., Tulane University, 1955.

Index

Abbott, Lyman: American Freedman's Union Commission general secretary, 45–46; and American Freedmen's Union Commission policies on school integration, 225–26; and American Freedmen's Union Commission policy on use of Southern white teachers, 134–35; and issue of religion in freedmen's education, 59–63; on Negro inferiority issue, 170; and suffrage question, 297–98 n.20

Abell, A. P., 146

Abolitionism, 3, 14, 46

Abolitionists: and freedmen's aid approach, 47; in freedmen's aid society leadership, 45–49; in freedmen's education, 4, 8–9, 24, 36–37, 39–40, 47, 68, 70, 72, 110–11, 128–29

Adams, E. B., 225

Advice to Freedmen (Brinckerhoff), 190, 194–97

African Civilization Society, 13–14, 116–19, 190

African Methodist Episcopal Church, 13, 118

Agassiz, Louis, 165

Alabama, 43, 92, 135, 228

Alcorn, James L., 124–25

Alcorn College, 125

Alexander, Louisa, 88

Alexandria, Virginia, 111, 251 n.1

Allen, William F., 10, 15–17, 131

Alvord, John W., 115, 198, 236–37; abolitionist background, 36–37; and black teachers, 85; and Catholic schools for freedmen, 80; and economic argument for freedmen's education, 153–54; Freedmen's Bureau general superintendent of schools, 37; and moral education, 159; on Negro inferiority issue, 165–67; on purposes of freedmen's education, 150; and Savannah Educational Association, 37, 120–22; and Southern white teachers, 131, 144; supports U. S. Grant for President, 241; surveys Freedmen's Bureau schools, 42–43; on teacher education and qualifications, 52–53; and temperance organizations for freedmen, 74–75; and termination of Bureau educational operations, 243–45

American Baptist Home Mission Society, 13, 64, 183, 246

American Freedmen's Aid Commission, 12–13, 44, 299 n.48. *See also* American Freedmen's Union Commission (AFUC)

American Freedmen's Inquiry Commission, 32–33

American Freedmen's Union Commission (AFUC), 43, 90; defection of Cincinnati, Cleveland, and Chicago branches to American Missionary Association, 45; dissolution of, 243; *Handbook for American Citizens,* 220; and integration of schools, 224–26; and land for freedmen, 224; officers, 45; opposition to inclusion of American Union Commission, 44; and religion in freedmen's education, 59–63; and Southern white teachers, 134–35

331

American Missionary Association (AMA), 246; begins involvement in freedmen's education, 1–2; and black teachers, 92; conflict with Board of Education for Freedmen, Department of the Gulf, 26–27; in Department of the Gulf, 23, 26–27; in Department of the Tennessee, 16; dispute with American Freedmen's Union Commission over religious instruction, 61–63; evangelical orientation of, 3, 13; and industrial education, 162–63; and integration of schools, 227; and land for freedmen, 223–24; and Lydia Maria Child, 207; officers, 48–49; and political involvement, 164; promotes freedmen's work as a suitable employment for women, 58–59; on purposes of education, 151; racial discrimination and segregation among AMA educators, 126–29; and Savannah Educational Association, 120–23; on South Carolina Sea Islands, 7
American Negro Academy, 101, 114
American Tract Society, 5, 188–202
American Tract Society, Boston, 37, 198
American Tract Society, New York, 189–91, 194–97, 201–2
American Union Commission, 44. See also American Freedmen's Union Commission (AFUC)
Ames, Adelbert, 238
Ames, Hugh, 234
Ames, Mary, 72
Andrew, John A., 3
Anti-Catholic biases, 79–82, 227
Arkansas, 43, 228, 244
Arms, Charles C., 76, 80
Armstrong, Samuel Chapman, 126–27, 154–57, 160–61
Army Appropriations Act of 1866, 49
Ashley, Samuel S., 78, 127–28, 149–50, 222, 235, 241
Ashmun Institute, 112
Atkinson, Edward, 3, 6. See also Free labor programs
Atlanta University, 66, 115, 172, 185

Augusta Baptist Institute, 109
Avery Normal Institute, 102
Ayer, Frederick, 65–66

Baldwin, Matthias W., 4
Baltimore Association for the Moral and Educational Improvement of the Colored People, 44
Banks, Nathaniel P., 22–25, 27–28
Bardwell, John P., 128, 159
Barre, John A., 102–3
Baumfree, Isabella. See Truth, Sojourner
Beecher, Henry Ward, 35
Beecher, James, 299 n.52
Beman, Amos G., 116–19
Berea College, 126
Biases in teacher selection, 79–83
Bishop, Nathan, 60
Black codes, 214
Bland, J. W. D., 99, 302 n.102
Blevens, John, 71
Bliss, Emily, 72
Board of Education for Freedmen, Department of the Gulf, 23–32. See also Enrollment Commission, Department of the Gulf
Boston Educational Commission, 3, 6–7. See also New England Freedmen's Aid Society
Botume, Elizabeth, 35
Bowditch, Henry Ingersoll, 3
Bowen, James, 26
Bradley, Aaron Alpeoria, 107–8
Brewer, Fisk P., 69, 225–26; 299 n.55
Brinckerhoff, Isaac W., 5, 190, 194, 253 n.17
Brooks, William F., 113–14
Brown, Helen E., 190–92, 198
Brown, Orlando, 137, 256 n.64; district superintendent of Negro affairs in Department of Virginia and North Carolina, 20; political involvement, 239–40; on practical education, 156–57; on progress of Negro students, 167
Brown Fellowship Society, 103
Bryant, J. E., 125–26, 240
Buckley, Charles W., 133–34; assistant

district school superintendent in the Department of the Tennessee, 14; and black teachers in Alabama, 91; Congressman, 78, 236; Freedmen's Bureau assistant superintendent of schools for Alabama, 38; and land for freedmen, 222; and Southern white teachers, 132, 284 n.12
Bureau of Refugees, Freedmen and Abandoned Lands, 32–34, 36–42, 164
Burke, James, 133
Burt, D., 143
Bush, H. M., 98–99
Butler, Benjamin F., 20

Cabot, Samuel, 3
Cadwallader, Mrs. H. G., 137
Cain, Richard Harvey, 117–18, 214, 223, 234
Caldwell, J. H., 136, 145–46, 211
Campbell, Jabez P., 117–18
Campbell, R. F., 231
Canfield, E. H., 59–60
Cardozo, Francis L., 86, 105–6, 217; and advanced subjects in Negro schools, 170–71; and black teachers, 87–89, 102; freedmen's school principal, 86–89; and integration of public schools, 228–29, 276 n.89; and land for freedmen, 223; and racial discrimination, 232; on Reconstruction policies, 214; secretary of state in South Carolina, 235; in South Carolina constitutional convention, 103, 105–6; and South Carolina state election of 1872, 240
Cardozo, Thomas W., 86–88, 106–8, 110, 229
Carlin, William P., 228
Carlyle, Thomas, 165
Carr, Mary E., 136
Cash, Wilbur J., 54
Chadwick, Mary, 97
Charleston, South Carolina, 86–89, 102–7
Chase, C. Thurston, 41, 89, 101
Chase, Frank R., 136
Chase, Lucy, 209

Cheney, Ednah Dow, 224–25
Chesnutt, Charles W., 55–56
Child, Henry T., 72
Child, Lydia Maria, 111, 190, 202–7, 214, 296 n.106; *The Freedmen's Book*, 181–82, 190, 202, 204–7
Claflin University, 172
Clanton, James H., 182
Clark, Margaret S., 133
Clark, S. N., 81–82
Clark, W. L., 132
Clark College, 172
Clarke, James Freeman, 247
Clayton, Powell, 244
Clift, Joseph W., 78
Cobb, L. H., 15, 17–18
Coffin, Levi, 45–47
Colby, William, 39, 135
Collier, Fred J., 138
Colored Educational Association of North Carolina, 107
Colored National Labor Convention, 234
Colored National Labor Union, 235
Colwell, Stephen, 4
Colyer, Vincent, 18–20
Conway, Thomas, 216–17, 229, 244–45, 302 n.91
Cooley, Edwin A., 121–23
Cope, Francis R., 60
Cope, Marmaduke, 91
Corbin, J. C., 112
Craft, Ellen, 110
Craft, William, 110
Cravath, Erastus M., 49, 134, 263 n.157
Crocker, L., 90
Cromwell, John Wesley, 100–101, 129, 274–75 n.68
Crossman, C. S., 15
Curriculum, 7; advanced subjects, 166, 170–71; antislavery lessons, 8; civics and politics, 180, 185–86, 220; industrial education, 9; oral exercises, 7–9, 174–79; religious instruction, 1, 61–63, 80; sectional bias in instruction, 186; songs, 176–79, 184–85

Danforth, Samuel J., 138
Daniels, Grandison B., 66

DeForest, J. W., 169
Delany, Martin R., 117
Denison, George S., 28, 258 n.86
Derry, Solomon, 98
Dillard University, 172
Dimick, O. W., 77
Discrimination. *See* Racial discrimination
Douglass, Esther W., 230
Douglass, Frederick, 47
Dudley, T. V., 165
Duncan, E. B., 40–41, 132, 135

East Tennessee Wesleyan University, 227–28
Eaton, John, 14–18
Eberhart, G. L., 40–41, 141–42; and black teachers, 89; Freedmen's Bureau assistant superintendent of schools for Georgia, 40; and Georgia Educational Association, 126; on integration of schools, 226; and Savannah Educational Association, 122–23
Educational statistics: black teachers, 92, 282 n.177; at close of Bureau operations, 245–46; for Department of the Tennessee, 18; for Department of the Gulf, 30, 32; for Department of Virginia and North Carolina, 20–22; industrial schools, 157–58; institutions of higher learning, 160; John W. Alvord's initial survey of Bureau schools, 43; Northern white teachers, 57–58; Southern white teachers, 135; students in advanced subjects, 166; white students, 224, 229; for South Carolina Sea Islands in 1863, 7
Eliot, Thomas D., 33
Emerson, George B., 3
Enrollment Commission, Department of the Gulf, 22–23
Ethnic biases, 79–83
Evans, Joseph S., 68

Faris, J. C. R., 17–18
Fee, John G., 126
Finney, Charles Grandison, 36–37

First Lessons, 189
Fisk, Clinton B., 71; *Plain Counsels for Freedmen*, 187–88, 190, 192–94, 198; prohibitionist leader, 75; on school integration, 226
Fisk University, 115, 160, 172
Fitzgerald, Robert G., 109, 112–13, 241–42
Florida, 43, 89, 101–2, 135, 228
Forten, Charlotte L., 8–10, 112
Fortress Monroe, 1
Foster, Charles H., 89, 101
Foster, John G., 20
Freedman, 197
Freedman's Primer; or First Reader, 198
Freedman's Second Reader, 198
Freedman's Spelling-Book, 198–99
Freedman's Third Reader, 175–76, 198–201
Freedman's Torchlight, 190, 207–9
Freedmen's aid societies: beginning of involvement in freedmen's education, 1; declining resources of, 246; denominational, 64; factionalism among, 3, 13, 59–63, 79–80; increase in number of, 12–14
Freedmen's Aid Society of the Methodist Episcopal Church, 13, 64, 170, 172, 246
Freedmen's Bank. *See* Freedmen's Savings and Trust Company
Freedmen's Book (Child), 181–82, 190, 202, 204–7, 209
Freedmen's Bureau acts, 34, 49–50
Freedmen's Bureau bills, 33–34, 49–50
Freedmen's educators: antislavery advocates, 70–72; charges of immorality against individual teachers, 66–67; Confederate Army veterans, 138–40; educational backgrounds of Northern white teachers, 70–71; feminists, 72–74; image of Northern white teacher, 54–57; missionary backgrounds of, 63–67; Negro, 1–2, 6–7, 16, 23, 38–39, 43, 58, 85–130; Negro teachers from the North, 87–88, 99–100, 104–5, 107–14; Negro

teachers from the South, 86–89, 92, 94–95, 97, 99–114, 123–24, 127, 282 n.166; Northern white, 2, 4–5, 8–12, 16, 20, 24, 43, 54–130; number of teachers, 57, 92, 126, 135, 282 n.177; qualifications of, 51–52, 59–64, 85, 88–91, 97–103; role of women teachers, 58–59; former slaveholders, 136–40, 143–44; former slaves, 89, 95–97, 100, 104, 110–11, 113–14; Southern free Negroes, 86–89, 102–14, 123–24, 127; Southern white, 21–24, 26–27, 43, 131–48; teaching experience of, 67–69, 146–47; Union Army veterans, 77–78, 136–37

Freedmen's Savings and Trust Company, 158

Free labor programs, 5–6, 24–25

Freeman, Amos N., 116–18

French, Mansfield, 4, 120

Friendly Counsels for Freedmen (Waterbury), 190–91, 202

Friendly Moralist Association, 104

Friends' Association for the Aid and Elevation of the Freedmen, 13, 246

Friends' Association of Philadelphia and its Vicinity for the Relief of Colored Freedmen, 13, 64, 114, 246

Friends' Freedmen's Association. *See* Friends' Association of Philadelphia and its Vicinity for the Relief of Colored Freedmen

Frisbie, Henry N., 24

Frothingham, Octavius B., 60–61

Fullerton, J. S., 216

Galloway, A. H., 215

Gannett, Ezra Stiles, 4

Gannett, William Channing, 4, 11–12, 81, 120

Gardner, Anna, 97

Garrett, Philip C., 243

Garrison, William Lloyd, 30, 44–45, 157

Georgia: African Civilization Society schools in, 14; freedmen's education in, 14, 43, 89, 92, 120–26, 135–36,

211; segregated public schools in, 228

Georgia Educational Association, 125–26

Georgia Equal Rights Association, 125

Gibbons, Isabella, 97

Gibbs, Jonathan C., 108, 111, 232, 234–35

Gillem, Alvan C., 236

Gleason, Fannie, 127

Granson, Milla, 96–97

Grant, Joel, 15, 17–18

Grant, Ulysses S., 14, 241, 255 n.47

Griffing, Josephine S., 71, 73

Grimké, Angelina. *See* Weld, Angelina Grimké

Grimké, Archibald H., 113–14, 129

Grimké, Francis J., 113, 129

Grimké, Sarah Moore, 113

Hale, Edward Everett, 3, 11–12

Hampton Institute, 155–57, 160–61

Hanckel, J. Stuart, 165

Hancock, Cornelia, 72

Handbook for American Citizens, 220

Harper, R. D., 38, 98–99, 132

Harris, James H., 107–9, 119–20, 215, 234–35

Harris, Robert, 99, 222

Hart, Mrs. H. A., 67

Haskell, J. C., 233

Hauser, William, 151

Haviland, Laura, 68–69, 71

Hawks, Esther H. (Mrs. J. Milton), 74, 299 n.52

Hawks, J. Milton, 74–75

Hawley, James A., 15, 17–18, 221

Hayne, Charles D., 103–4

Hayne, Henry E., 102–3, 105, 240

Hayne, James N., 103–4

Hedges, Peter Plato, 112

Henley, Thomas P., 137

Henry, C. S., 21

Henson, Phebe, 127, 283 n.181

Hettie (Negro teacher), 6–7

Hickman, John, 19

Higher education: black colleges and universities, 114–15, 124–25, 159–

62, 172–73; Freedmen's Bureau support for, 91–92, 114; training of black ministers, 171–72
Hill, Elias, 94–95
Holley, Myron, 70
Holley, Sallie, 70–71, 73–74
Holley, William S., 136
Holloway, James H., 103
Hood, James Walker, 108, 235
Hosmer, Jane, 224–25
Hovey, Horace, 71–72
Howard, O. H., 89
Howard, Oliver Otis, 34–36, 141, 227–28; advice to freedmen, 151; in danger of losing Bureau post, 217; and industrial education, 162; and land for freedmen, 220–21; and political involvement by educators, 236–37; on "social equality," 230; views on freedmen's education, 34–35
Howard University, 114–15
Howe, Samuel Gridley, 32
Howland, Emily, 68, 71, 73–74
Hubbs, Isaac, 24, 26–27
Hunn, Hannah, 8, 253 n.29
Hunt, Samuel, 48, 263 n.155
Hunter, William H., 112

Industrial education, 156–58, 160–61; criticized, 161–62, 170; in Department of the Tennessee, 16; at Hampton Institute, 156–57, 160–61; praised, 162; on South Carolina Sea Islands, 9
Institute for Colored Youth, 87, 91, 100, 112, 114
Integration: American Freedmen's Union Commission policies on, 224–26, 299; American Missionary Association policies on, 227, 300 n.61; of Charleston, South Carolina public schools, 42; and education in South Carolina, 42, 105; and public schools, 228–29, 300 n.69; statistics, 224. See also Segregation

Jackson, Matthew W., 145

Jacobs, Harriet, 110–11, 233
Jacobs, Louisa, 111, 233
James, Horace, 20, 22, 222
Jillson, Justus K., 78, 105, 228–29, 235
Jocelyn, Simeon S., 48, 157
"John Brown's Body," 9, 178–79
John Freeman and His Family (Brown), 190–92, 198
Johnson, Andrew, 213–16, 242
Joiner, W. Nelson, 104
Jones, Singleton T., 117
Judge, John J., 137

Kansas, 43
Keith, Melville, C., 234
Kellogg, Martha, 66, 127–28
Kelly, H. A., 81–82
Kennedy, Crammond, 80
Kennedy, Hugh, 216
Kentucky, 43, 126
Kinsman, J. Burnham, 20
Ku Klux Klan, 93–95, 182

Labor programs. See Free labor programs
Land for freedmen, 220–24
Lane, Mrs. E. A., 233
Langley, L. S., 104–5, 228
Langston, John Mercer, 53, 88, 125; on Andrew Johnson, 213; educated at Oberlin College, 112; Freedmen's Bureau general inspector of schools, 38–39; on need for educating black ministers, 171–72; in Negro labor movement, 234–35; and termination of Bureau educational operations, 245; United States Congressman, 302 n.92
Lawton, Virginia, 111
Lea, Lorinzo, 143
Lewis, John R., 91, 98, 240
Lincoln National Temperance Association, 74
Lincoln University, 112–14
Louisiana: African Civilization Society schools in, 14; freedmen's education in, 14, 22–32, 43, 85–86, 92, 110,

135–36, 162, 244–45; issue of public school integration, 229
Low, Abiel A., 140
Lynch, James D., 108, 120, 123, 234–35, 237–39
Lyons, Judson, 109

McClelland, B. F., 233
McGill, M. W., 134
McKaye, James, 32
McKim, James Miller: on Andrew Johnson, 213–15; argues for merger establishing American Freedmen's Union Commission, 44–45; civil rights activity, 232; corresponding secretary of American Freedmen's Union Commission, 45; and Port Royal Relief Committee, 4; on purposes of education, 151; on relationship of education and suffrage, 163
McKinlay, William J., 103
McKinney, C. C., 88
McKinney, Mrs. C. C., 88
McLean, N. A., 149–50
McMaster, James, 138
Maddox, George, 91
Magill, S. W., 120–21, 213
Mahoney, David, 136
Manly, Ralza Morse, 154; Freedmen's Bureau assistant superintendent of schools for Virginia, 38; on freedmen's textbooks, 201; and Hampton plan, 157; on integration of schools, 226; political involvement, 239–40; and Southern white teachers, 132
Manning, Jacob, 2–3
Martin, John Sella, 116–17
Mason, E. W., 162, 245
Massachusetts Anti-Slavery Society, 32
Maxwell, Henry J., 106
May, Samuel, J., 47
May, Samuel, Jr., 47
Means, James, 20
Meriwether, Mrs. R. C., 144–45
Meriwether, Vallie, 144–45
Methodist Church, 227–28
Methodist Freedmen's Aid Society.

See Freedmen's Aid Society of the Methodist Episcopal Church
Miscegenation. *See* Racial intermarriage
Mississippi, 14, 43, 124–25, 128–29
Missouri, 43
Mitchell, John G., 69, 107–8
Mitchell, William F., 69
Moore, H. H., 38
Morehouse College, 109, 172
Morel, Junius C., 117
Morris, Joseph, 98
Murdock, J. N., 146–47, 180, 298 n.28

National Freedmen's Relief Association, 3–4, 7, 33, 35, 44. *See also* American Freedmen's Union Commission (AFUC)
Negro Convention movement, 116–18
Negro educational organizations, 116–26
Negro inferiority issue: addressed by freedmen's educators, 164–71; Anthony Toomer Porter and, 139; John W. Alvord's statements on, 51; observations of educators in the Department of the Gulf, 31; observations of educators in the Department of the Tennessee, 17–18; racial theories, 165–67; views of educators on South Carolina Sea Islands, 9–12
Negro labor movement, 234–35
Negro suffrage, 31, 163, 218–20, 297–98 n.20
New England Educational Commission for the Freedmen, 47
New England Freedmen's Aid Society, 44, 58, 246; and appointment of O. O. Howard as Freedmen's Bureau commissioner, 35; and black teachers, 90, 95; calls for creation of a bureau of emancipation, 33; and formation of American Freedmen's Aid Commission, 12–13; and Negro inferiority issue, 167–70; and Savannah Educational Association, 120; and Southern white teachers, 134; teacher qualifications, 59. *See also*

American Freedmen's Union Commission (AFUC); Boston Educational Commission
New Orleans Tribune, 28
New Orleans University, 172
New Reform Society, 159
Normal schools, 160
North Carolina: African Civilization Society schools in, 14; freedmen's education in, 14, 18–22, 43, 92, 127–28; segregated public schools, 228
Northwestern Freedmen's Aid Commission, 13, 44. *See also* American Freedmen's Union Commission (AFUC)
Nott, Josiah, 165–66

Oberlin College, 90–91; attended by freedmen's educators, 36, 38–39, 70–71, 104, 107, 112; freedmen's educators associated with, 48–49
Ogden, John F., 38, 77
O'Hara, James E., 108
Owen, Robert Dale, 32

Parker, Joseph W., 47
Patterson, Mary Jane, 112, 279 n.122
Patton, William, 247–48
Payne, Daniel A., 118–19, 275 n.78
Peake, Mary S., 1–2, 96–97
Pearce, Charles H., 108
Pease, Henry R., 78; Freedmen's Bureau assistant superintendent of schools in Louisiana and in Mississippi, 38; North Carolina state public school superintendent, 235; political involvement, 236–39; on qualifications of black teachers, 98; on suspension of the school tax in Louisiana, 216; United States Senator, 236
Peck, Solomon, 2
Pennsylvania Freedmen's Relief Association, 4, 7, 13, 33, 44. *See also* American Freedmen's Union Commission (AFUC); Port Royal Relief Committee

Pennsylvania State Equal Rights League, 232
Percy, H. C., 99, 126–27
Perry, Rufus L., 118–19
Pettibone, Ira, 69, 89, 152
Philbrick, Edward, 6
Phillips, Samuel, 6
Phillips, Wendell, 4, 28–30, 47
Picture Lesson Book, 189–90
Pierce, E. R., 66–67
Pierce, Edward L., 7, 9; on effects of freedmen's education, 210–11; and Port Royal Experiment, 2, 4–5
Plain Counsels for Freedmen (Fisk), 187–88, 190, 192–94
Plumly, B. Rush, 24–31
Politics: American Missionary Association policies on, 164; and freedmen's aid program, 163–64; Freedmen's Bureau policies regarding, 39, 236–40; freedmen's educators in, 78, 87, 94, 104–8, 125–26, 235–40; and school lessons, 180, 185–86
Porter, Anthony Toomer, 139–41, 218
Porter, James D., 108, 123–24
Port Royal Experiment, 2–12
Port Royal Relief Committee, 4. *See also* Pennsylvania Freedmen's Relief Association
Potter, William J., 32
Potts, Joseph, 64
Powers, R. C., 238
Presbyterian Church, General Assembly's Committee on Freedmen, 13, 64, 92, 113, 246
Price, Mary, 68
Prince, Charles H., 78, 235–36
Princeton Theological Seminary, 111, 113
Protestant Episcopal Church, 140–41
Protestant Episcopal Freedmen's Commission, 64, 141
Public schools, 228–29, 244–45
Putnam, Caroline, 70–71, 73–74
Putnam, George L., 231

Racial discrimination: by freedmen's educators, 126–29, 144–45, 233;

against Negro educators, 232–33; legal status of Negroes, 217–20
Racial intermarriage, 231–32
Randolph, Benjamin Franklin, 104, 112, 228
Randolph, John, 214
Raushenberg, Charles, 184
Ray, Charles B., 116–19
Redpath, James, 131; expresses disillusionment with Reconstruction, 247; and integration of schools, 42; on literacy requirement for suffrage, 219; passed over for Bureau school superintendency of South Carolina, 39; promotes black emigration to Haiti, 75–76; superintendent of public instruction for Charleston, South Carolina, 42
Reed, Mary M., 99
Reform societies, 74–75, 158–59
Religion and freedmen's education, 59–67
Rendall, I. N., 113
Richards, Mary J. R., 108, 110
Richardson, W. T., 95
Robert, W. H., 184
Roberts, J. L., 15
Roberts, T. C., 91
Rollin, Frances, 87
Rose, Alfred J., 148
Ruby, George I., 143
Ryland, Robert, 146

Sampson, J. P., 108–9
Sasportas, Thaddeus K., 103
Savannah Educational Association (SEA), 37. 120–24
Savannah, Georgia, 95
Saxton, Rufus, 35, 39, 121
Saxton, S. Willard, 264 n.162
Schermack, Gottfried, 233–34
School taxes, 26
Scott, John, 211
Sectional bias in freedmen's education, 186–87
Segregation: in American Freedmen's Union Commission schools, 226; in Charleston, South Carolina public

schools, 42; in housing freedmen's teachers, 126–29; in labor movement, 234–35; percentage of white students in Freedmen's Bureau schools, 224, 229; and public schools, 228–29. *See also* Integration
Shaw, Francis George, 45
Shaw University, 172
Shearman, Julia A., 147, 230–31
Shield, H. C., 146
Shipherd, Jacob R., 49, 53, 231
Shrewsbury, Amelia, 87
Shrewsbury, Henry L., 87, 102–3, 105–6
Simmons, H. E., 167
Sinclair, William A., 161–62
Sloan, Richard, 66
Smith, Edward P., 162; American Missionary Association officer, 48–49; comments on Talladega Normal School, 160; opposes idea of Negro control of Tougaloo College, 125; and Presidential election of 1868, 241–42; and racial intermarriage, 231
Smith, Gerrit, 30
Smith, James R., 141–42
Social equality, 41–42, 126–29, 230–32
Society for Propagating the Faith, 79–80
South Carolina: African Civilization Society schools in, 14; black educators in, 86–89, 92, 102–6; Constitutional Convention of 1868, 103–5, 228–29; educational statistics, 43; freedmen's education on the Sea Islands, 2–12; segregated public schools, 228–29; Southern white teachers in, 135
Southern Industrial School and Labor Enterprise, 110
Southern white reaction to freedmen's education, 177, 184–85; charges of sectional bias, 186–87; objections to instruction in civil and political rights, 180; opposition in Department of the Gulf, 25, 31–32; response to Isaac Brinckerhoff's *Advice to Freedmen*, 196–97; review of Clin-

ton Fisk's *Plain Counsels for Freedmen*, 187–88
Sprague, John T., 102
Stanley, Sara G., 231
Stanly, Edward, 18–20
Stansbury, S. S., 231
Stanton, Edwin M., 35
Stanton, Elizabeth Cady, 30
Statistics. *See* Educational statistics
Stebbins, Mrs. L. W., 68
Stell, Josce, 133
Stevenson, Hannah E., 44
Steward, William, 108
Stickney, William B., 23–24
Still, Mary, 108
Straight University, 112, 115, 172
Strieby, Michael E., 49, 263 n.157
Stubbs, Calvin, 104
Students, reaction to freedmen's textbooks, 202, 209; response to instruction, 178–79, 209–10; Southern white, 21
Sumner, Charles, 19
Supplementary Freedmen's Bureau Act. *See* Freedmen's Bureau acts
Swails, Stephen A., 104–6, 240
Swayne, Wager, 217
Syracuse Freedmen's Aid Society, 47

Tade, Mrs. A. L., 162–63
Talladega College, 160, 172
Tamblyn, John, 180
Tanner, Benjamin T., 234
Tappan, Arthur, 157
Tappan, Lewis, 3–4, 48
Tate, James, 66
Taxes, 26
Taylor, R. P., 146
Taylor, Susie King, 95–96, 273 n.52
Temperance movement, 74–75, 158–59
Tennessee, 43, 228
Texas, 43, 228, 233–34
Textbooks, 7, 174; specifically for freedmen, 175, 184, 187–209
Thompson, J. P., 247–48
Thompson, William B., 136
Tillson, Davis, 132
Todd, David, 185–86

Tomlinson, Reuben, 179–80, 221, 240, 285 n.21; Freedmen's Bureau assistant superintendent of schools for South Carolina, 39; and land for freedmen, 221; on political instruction, 179–80; political involvement, 78
Toomer, Louis B., 123, 282 n.166
Tougaloo College, 124–25, 172
Tourgée, Albion W., 56–57, 92–95, 265 n.17
Towne, Laura M., 9, 132, 142–43
Truth, Sojourner, 110
Tubman, Harriet, 110–11
Tucker, John C., 27
Tuition fees, 16, 155–56
Turner, Henry McNeal, 107–8, 118, 161, 277 n.95

Union League, 94, 107, 236
Unionists: American Union Commission schools for, 44; employed as teachers in Department of the Gulf, 22–24, 26–27; schools for, in Department of Virginia and Tennessee, 21; schools for, in the South, 43; as teachers during Reconstruction, 135–37, 148
United Presbyterian Church, 16
United States Army: chaplains and freedmen's education, 14, 15, 16, 38, 49, 66, 104, 107; Department of the Gulf educational program, 22–32; Department of the Tennessee educational program, 14–18; Department of Virginia and North Carolina educational program, 20–22; educational role during Civil War, 12–32; freedmen's education in Department of North Carolina, 18–20; provost marshals reluctant to aid teachers in Department of the Gulf, 25–26
University of South Carolina, 106, 229

Vanguard of Freedom, 74–75, 158
Van Ness, Edward, 76
Virginia: first freedmen's schools established in, 1–2, 251 n.1; freedmen's

education in, 1–2, 20–22, 43, 126–27, 135, 211; segregated public schools, 228

Virginia Union University, 172

Walker, P. L., 136
Wall, Amanda, 88
Wall, Orindatus S. B., 88
Ward, George Cabot, 45
Ware, Edmund Asa, 38, 125, 132, 144–45, 184
Warren, Israel P., 197–201, 295 n.83
Warren, Joseph, 16–18, 38, 41–42, 182–83
Warren, Mortimer A., 70
Washington, Booker T., 101, 109, 114, 129
Washington, D. C., 43
Waterbury, Jared Bell, 190–91, 202
Waterman, Susan L., 108
Welch, Joseph, 143
Weld, Angelina Grimké, 113
Weld, Theodore Dwight, 113
Wells, J. Madison, 216
Western Freedmen's Aid Committee, 33
Western Freedmen's Aid Commission, 13, 16, 44
Weston, Jacob, 65, 87
Weston, Mary F., 87
Weston, William O., 87

Wheelock, Edwin Miller, 26–31, 38–40
Whipper, William J., 117
Whipple, George, 4, 48, 263 n.154
White, William Jefferson, 109, 129
White students, 21, 43–44, 51, 264 n.164
Whitfield, Asa B., 210, 296 n.116
Whittemore, Benjamin Franklin, 78, 154, 236, 240, 288 n.17
Wilder, Charles B., 2, 20, 221, 256 n.64
Wilkes, Charles, 77
Wilkes, Mrs. Charles, 77
Williams, George W., 77
Williams, Pelleman M., 23, 107, 111–12, 278–79 n.120
Wilson, Henry M., 117
Wilson, William J., 117
Winsor, Ellen, 5, 8
Woodworth, C. L., 171
Woolfolk, Peter H., 95
Woolson, Constance Fenimore, 54–55
Wright, Jonathan Jasper, 104, 106, 214, 228–29, 232, 235
Wright, Sela G., 17–18, 128–29, 183, 220, 283 n.184

Young Men's Enterprising Society, 154

Zachos, John C., 5, 191
Zealy, J. T., 147